WITHDRAWN

WITHDRAWN

Planning for Freedom

PLANNING FOR FREEDOM

The Public Law of American Capitalism

By EUGENE V. ROSTOW

New Haven and London

YALE UNIVERSITY PRESS

CARL A. RUDISILL LIBRARY
LENOIR RHYNE COLLEGE

338.973
R 73 p
56004
Nov. 1966

Copyright © 1959 by Yale University Press, Inc.
Fourth printing, October 1963
Printed in the United States of America
by The Murray Printing Co., Forge Village, Mass.
All rights reserved. This book may not be
reproduced, in whole or in part, in any form
(except by reviewers for the public press),
without written permission from the publishers.
Library of Congress catalog card number: 59-12701

FOR D.

Contents

Contents

Preface

THE SUBSTANCE of this book was offered as William W. Cook Lectures at the University of Michigan during March 1958. That lecture series is devoted "to the study and preservation of American institutions." It honors the career of a distinguished patron of higher education, whose acts of philanthropy contributed more than one rich man's tithe to strengthen the tradition of freedom in this country. I am grateful to the authorities of the University for their invitation. It is a compliment to be in the company of the earlier Cook Lecturers. And it was a pleasure for my wife and me, as guests of the University, to have enjoyed the generous hospitality of Dean and Mrs. E. Blythe Stason, and of other friends and colleagues on the faculty.

In revising the text of the lectures for publication, I have sought to keep the lecture form. Although the temptation to expand has been considerable, and has not been consistently resisted, the privileges of the lecture are not to be lightly exchanged for the burdens of the treatise. The lecturer, after all, has invaluable prerogatives. He is permitted to generalize without data; and he is allowed, even encouraged, to call on others to write books and make studies obviously beyond the limits of his Hour.

In one particular, however, I have departed from the lecture plan. The subject matter of these talks is the legal control of the economy. Dealing with issues in different areas of specialized study—law and economics, in this instance—invariably raises the question of fixing an appropriate level of discourse. I have long been engaged in trying to expound economic problems to lawyers, and legal problems to economists—a task yielding unexpected comfort, since some members of each group tend to accept my credentials in the other without the usual tests. In this effort I have not yet come upon a book that explains the operation of the economy in terms which meet the needs of the lawyer or the law student, nor have I found one about the legal setting of economic life which answers the kind of questions businessmen and economists habitually ask. The Intelligent Common Reader's guides to economics never quite reach the complicated problems of public policy which are of acute daily concern to lawyers and law students. And the advanced books on economics take for granted a working knowledge of basic ideas, techniques of analysis, and institutions, knowledge which is not yet part of the intellectual universe of that mythical creature, the liberally educated man. The literature about law presents the same difficulty for economists and other laymen. Most elementary books about law are too elementary to be interesting; the interesting work presupposes a framework of reference usually available only within the guild. Conscious of this barrier to the possibility of intercourse, I have added several passages of exposition to the text: Chapter 5 and a good deal of Chapter 6 for the special benefit of noneconomists; most of Chapters 7, 8, and 11, for nonlawyers. And, in keeping with the tenor and policy of the Cook lectures, I have sought to speak to a general audience.

While various obligations and detours have interrupted my work on this manuscript, its subject matter represents continuing professional interests. Inevitably, therefore, some of the material here echoes passages from articles and speeches which have appeared at intervals over several years. I am particularly conscious of touching on themes also treated in the law reviews of the Universities of Illinois, Chicago, Notre Dame, and Louisiana, and in the *Virginia Quarterly Review*. A few paragraphs are borrowed from "The Professions of Social Action," given at the convocation of the University of Pittsburgh on May 9, 1957, and printed in *New Dimensions of Learning in a Free Society* (Pittsburgh,

1958). An earlier version of parts of this book was presented in lectures before the Faculty of Law, the Institute of Comparative Law, and the Institute of Higher Political Studies of the University of Paris in November and December 1949—a stimulating and agreeable academic adventure, for the pleasures of which I am greatly indebted to Professor Henri Peyre, Dean Julliot de la Morandière, and Professor J. H. Chapsal. The lectures given at Paris were published in *Économie contemporaine*, Oct.–Nov. 1949; in *La Documentation française*, a French official publication, as No. 1,816, "L'Économie dirigée aux États-Unis" (March 27, 1950), and in *Lo Spettatore italiano*, of Rome, during 1950. Several lectures use parts of my chapter in *Income Stabilization for a Developing Democracy*, edited by Max F. Millikan and published by the Yale University Press in 1953. I acknowledge the kind permission of these several editors and publishers to draw at will on their respective copyrights.

Friends have read and helpfully criticized various versions of some of these chapters. For this devoted aid, I wish here to thank Ward S. Bowman, Jr., Ralph S. Brown, Jr., William J. Fellner, Kent T. Healy, Carroll Kilpatrick, John P. Miller, Max F. Millikan, Leo Raskind, Kenneth Roose, Harold Stein, Robert Triffin, H. H. Villard, Henry Wallich, and my brother Walt. Winfield W. Riefler, Guy E. Noyes, and Ralph Young of the Federal Reserve Board most usefully reviewed Chapter 9. Three law students, Neale M. Albert, Victor E. Ferrall, and William R. Greiner, have helped check the text and prepare footnotes and charts. Allen R. Malone labored on several charts and Robert L. Williams skillfully drew them. And in this round of drafts, my secretary, Mrs. Isabel F. Malone, has, as always, been indefatigable and imperturbable.

Basically, this work has grown out of my teaching in the Law School and Graduate School of Yale University, and especially from my introductory Law School course on the Public Control of Business. It measures my deep obligation to the students and colleagues who have been my collaborators in the development of that course, and to the Ford

Foundation, which through a grant helped finance the preparation of a revision of the teaching materials used in it.

E.V.R.

Geneva, Switzerland
New Haven, Connecticut
Peru, Vermont
1949–1958

Preface to the Paperbound Edition

ALTHOUGH it is two and a half years since the manuscript of this book was finished, it has not been thought necessary to revise it fundamentally for publication as a paperbound. It is lucky for the venture that the decision took this form. Present obligations would have made extended revision a prolonged affair. Still, if interest in the book warrants such a course, I should like some day to prepare a basically new edition, with chapters on the labor market, the regulation of utilities, speculation, agriculture, and other features of the economy not treated here in detail.

During a sabbatical year at Cambridge in 1959–60, I was able to do some further work on the neglected subject of Chapter 10—the relationship between market structure and industrial fluctuations. That enquiry, and the lectures to which it gave rise at Cambridge, Oxford, and Glasgow, did not alter the conclusion of the original text: that a good deal of competitiveness in markets is a desirable goal of public policy, which should improve both the resilience of the economy, in its responses to fluctuations in the total of spendings, and its progressiveness, in taking advantage of technological and managerial opportunities for cost reduction. In due course, those studies should lead to another and, hopefully, more complete version of the chapter, addressed both to classical capital theory and its modern variants, and to recent experience. After all, Marx viewed monopoly as the Achilles' heel of capitalism, condemning it to inescapable crises of unemployment and stagnation. And considerable competitive flexibility is regarded as an indispensable term or condition in contemporary macroeconomic models and theories, although its importance as a condition is more often assumed than demonstrated, either logically or empirically.

Some reviews, notably that of Professor Wolfgang Friedmann in the *Modern Law Review* (March 1961), have properly raised the question whether the American system of legal and economic organization should be regarded as an export which other countries—and particularly the so-called underdeveloped (or nonindustrialized) countries—could usefully adopt or adapt. A chapter on this difficult and important subject was scrapped during the writing of the book.

In general, I should start an answer to this question with the proposition that while ideas can and do migrate from one social environment to another, no social institutions can ever be transplanted as such. They always exist in a matrix of customs, habits, and ideas which make them almost as local as wines.

This being said, however, it by no means follows that countries can learn nothing from the successes and failures of others. After all, each society wishes its economic organizations to carry out certain common functions and to accomplish its economic goals in ways which serve larger political and social purposes. One country may put great stress on rapid increases in the production of food or steel, even at the cost of abandoning or suspending the procedures of democracy; another may be more concerned with organizing economic activities through scattered groups which can never accumulate enough power to threaten the political foundations of group life. What is sauce for the goose in one society may be poison in another. Private business organizations in the United States, for example, are kept in tolerable balance by the rivalry of business competition; by labor unions of independent power; by the tax system; by the character of the country's federal and fragmented political life. A society which lacked some or all of these countervailing influences could readily be dominated by business institutions as strong as those of the United States.

One should always be cautious, therefore, in contemplating the transfer of institutions wholesale from one country to another. On alien soil, they may not produce the same results they accomplish at home. Quite different arrangements may be needed to assure rapid economic growth or the possibility of democracy in Ghana, for example, than in the United States.

Another criticism directed to the book has been that of confusing the well-intentioned democratic "Socialism" of Western progressive socialist parties with the monolithic "Socialism" of the totalitarian states. This charge has come with some heat from readers who especially appreciate, as I do, the contribution which the democratic socialist parties of the West have made to the humaneness of modern society. I have attempted to be entirely explicit (as on pp. 32–37) that the socialism I was talking about as a menace to the possibility of democracy is that system in which the state owns or controls all the instruments of production, "save for a fragmentary private sector devoted to the manufacture and sale of handicrafts and the like." Such arrangements, I persist in believing, are incompatible with political and social democracy. It does not follow, of course, that their absence guarantees democracy.

The last few years have witnessed a wide-range discussion of planning methods, both in Western and in Communist countries. Several Communist countries, including the Soviet Union, have sought to put greater reliance on decentralized procedures of market decision than on those of bureaucracy, and these techniques have been extended in considerable part to the allocation of capital as well. While no Communist country has yet organized a stock exchange through which its industrial managers can bid for available supplies of investment capital, some of their banking habits are beginning to show a close family resemblance to such practices. In the West, and especially in France, planning has effectively used methods of persuasion to guide investment into preferred channels, as well as the more orthodox stimuli of taxes, tariffs, competition, and the pressure of rising incomes. And the technique of planning by publishing information, so typical in the work of the American Council of Economic Advisers, has continued to spread, especially in Western

Europe, Latin America, and India. These developments, thus far, are variants of the practices described in this book, and do not as yet require a basic revision of its text or of its conclusions.

Unfortunately, the course of events in the international sphere since 1959 has not made the gloomy analysis of Chapter 4 obsolete. On the contrary, the increasing pressure of Communist foreign policy, and the further disintegration of the free world as a community, has made its somber outlook an understatement.

I should like to add to the acknowledgments of the Preface my thanks to my friends and colleagues on the faculty of the Law School of the University of Chicago, whose invitation in 1941 helped stir me to begin there the series of experiments in law teaching which led to this book.

E.V.R.

New Haven, Conn.
January 2, 1962

Preliminary Observations on Ends
and Means

1. The Economic Order as a
Problem of Law

THE AIM OF THIS BOOK is to sketch a forest, not to fill in
the detail of every leaf on every tree. Its concern is public
policy toward economic affairs—that is, the dispositions of
the law for directing, stimulating, releasing, encouraging,
repressing, or regulating the economic proclivities of Americans. It will attempt to survey and to appraise the legal
mechanisms intended to control the chief working parts of
the economy. They will be portrayed in the light of their
functions, and of the public policies they should serve. The
stress here will be on the character of these arrangements
as a system, whose segments complement each other, sometimes advancing, sometimes frustrating the ends of the economic order as a whole.

To view the economic institutions of American society as
institutions of law requires that they be weighed in large part
by noneconomic standards. Economic activity, after all,
is a means as well as an end in the hierarchy of democratic
ambitions. An economy should be judged by what it adds
to the wealth of a nation, and to the wealth of nations.
Beyond that goal, judgment should measure its effect on men,
on politics, and on the values and culture of the society. The
purpose of this effort, therefore, will be to examine the
economic element among the essences of the American
being: to consider the workability and creativeness of the
American economy as an instrument of the public law for
advancing what Carl Becker called the historic cause of
"freedom and responsibility in the American way of life." [1]

1. *Freedom and Responsibility in the American Way of Life*, New York,
Knopf, 1945.

Until recently, crucial parts of American economic life —most of the field of labor relations, for example—were outside the domain of positive law. Within a generation, political and social action has achieved the acceptance as law of the principle that government has ultimate responsibility for the level of employment, and for the basic welfare of the individual citizen. The emergence of this idea marks one of the Great Divides of modern social history. It is expressed in a variety of new statutes, and new policies, which have radically altered the older law of economic regulation. The old and the new are being fused. They are emerging as a new entity, responding throughout the whole of its reach to the impact of the new policies—most particularly, to the policy and reality of full employment.

When I urge that these patterns of action are taking form as a system of law, I do not mean to imply that they are stiff with symmetry. Any living law contains anomalies. It reflects the compromise of conflicts, and the accommodation of rival ideas. If the presence of paradox is a badge of vitality, the American law of economic policy is fully alive. It is rich in inconsistencies, special deals, exceptions, and subsidies. Where the Sherman Act is king, for example, the law is as stern as Adam Smith in the faith of the free market. Yet the law is eighteenth-century mercantilism at its worst in the methods which have been developed to control sugar, oil, railroads, and certain other industries.

For all its variety, however, the law of the economy is, in the long view, a coherent whole. It is not a jumble of unrelated and incompatible laws and practices. Today, as was not the case twenty-five years ago, we have a viable economic system, organized by an equally viable body of law. Together, they constitute an appropriate economic foundation for the public life of a capitalist democracy. These establishments seek to express and to realize in the economic field a series of ideas and values, both about economic policy, and, more generally, about the right ordering of power and opportunity in a free society. Thus they mirror, and in turn they shape, the Spirit of the Law, in Montesquieu's sense of that term, as the dominant influence guiding the development of American institutions, and one of the important forces forming the character of Americans.

A large canvas is always a risk. The result can easily be an outline so broad and so general as to be obvious. But there are advantages in trying to achieve perspective from time to time, even at the expense of detail. Super-obvious ideas are never the easiest ones to express, or to accept. And a view of the whole is indispensable to the study of society, both in promoting insight into the causes of social change, and in developing just policies for controlling its course.

The social sciences, which might better be called the professions of social action, can never escape the necessity for reaching conclusions about values. Their work is not properly identified if we say that they are concerned only with increasing knowledge about society. For them, neutrality is not an available option. They should of course be detached and academic in their methods of study. But their problems inevitably have an ethical dimension. The professions of social action are dedicated to improving human and social welfare, just as the health professions are dedicated to improving human health. The good lawyer cannot be a cynic, whose skill is available to any client, on the client's own terms. The lawyer is an officer of the court, and his work takes on meaning, even in the pettiest case, as part of the process by which society seeks justice. The economist's ultimate concern is not the aesthetic charm of his theories, but the contribution they could well make to progress against poverty. As Pigou once remarked, no matter how intimately an astronomer knew the ways of the stars, it did not occur to him that his studies could influence their orbits. In the age of sputniks, the analogy may have lost some of its pertinence, but not its point. The student of society, on the other hand, should never be quite free of the thought that his work, however theoretical, might well in the end provide some more rational basis for private or public policy.

The daily work of the professions of social action depends upon and derives from sets of ideas and values which are normally unstated and incomplete. Every study of a particular problem in law, in economics, in social relations, or in politics presupposes a concept of society as a living organism—some sense of its shape, an idea as to the connections among its separate parts, and a choice among its values, its ends, and its modes of change.

For better or worse, each student, working in his corner of the garden, is possessed by his own private vision of the social order as a whole. That vision may be articulate or inarticulate, fully considered or blindly accepted. It may be, as Keynes once suggested, the residue in his mind of half-forgotten lectures heard in a remote youth. It may be the vision of Adam Smith, or Karl Marx, or Pareto, or Montesquieu, or that of some other great artist or system-maker of the past. Whatever its quality, this particular bee in each student's bonnet is of crucial importance to his work. For the propositions he accepts at this level of generality shape what he thinks and writes about taxes, or prices, or corporations, or whatever it may be that concerns him at a given moment.

The postulates in the back of our minds necessarily form a myth—what Kenneth Boulding has suggestively called an image.[2] The question always is, "Which myth?" Is policy being formed in the image of a relevant and appropriate model? Is it closely linked both to the pattern of the past, and to our hearts' desire, or is it one which could only be related to the historical flow of events by coercive or revolutionary action? Is the model "true," as Ortega y Gasset uses the word, in the ultimate sense that it serves to advance the social and political goals of the culture, or purposes valid in more absolute terms?[3] Or is society adapting its institutions to a Pied Piper's myth which could lead into a jungle or a prison, or over the precipice?

Too often the model of society which constitutes the effective image in a student's mind is outmoded or worse. He may view the world as full of Robber Barons, and yearn nostalgically for the golden age of agrarian innocence. His mind may still be echoing to the thundering tones of Theo-

2. *The Image,* Ann Arbor, University of Michigan Press, 1956.
3. *Man and People* (New York, Norton, 1957), chap. 1.

dore Roosevelt or Woodrow Wilson, of Brandeis or William Jennings Bryan, of Ricardo or Malthus, or of a follower of Marx or Hitler. One of America's handicaps in the ideological war of the times is that many American students of society are still rather apologetically defending the capitalism of William McKinley.

Our social sciences lack the influence of a contemporary image. They will be relatively confused, fragmented, and ineffective until they can be polarized, once more, within the field of force of a compelling vision of society and its goals—a vision as appropriate to our day as that of Adam Smith was to his. Some scholar or group of scholars should seek to draw our knowledge about society into a philosophical view of the human condition. Such a view should be a mature product of this generation. It should take a fresh look at the past, without rancor. And it should use the best of modern learning in all the behavioral and social sciences, from anthropology to econometrics. Above all, it should be animated by a theory of human freedom specifically addressed to the circumstances of contemporary life.

I have no formula to prescribe how such a job could be done, save to be rather skeptical of encyclopedias. The great social philosophers of previous generations lived in easier times, when a cultivated man might well know every book worth reading in two or three languages. Montesquieu took twenty years to write *The Spirit of the Laws*. The task almost killed him, although he had no committees, classes, budgets or learned conferences to contend with. Even so, he was a historian, a judge, a man of letters, a dabbler in natural science. He traveled, conducted a wine business, and had time, we are told, for a moderate amount of love. It would, I suppose, be inconceivable for one man to write a comparable book today.

Yet the need is acute. American society has been in a phase of creative change. Recently, it has made progress in carrying out some of the promises of its creed, and in developing their meaning. In certain areas, such as education and family life, it may have lost ground. But the society is not static. The process of social change is continuous, sustained by new and old demands which the law must mediate, compromise, satisfy, or refuse. The flow of change can go well or ill. Emerging conflicts can be dealt with in ways which deepen the sense of unity among the people, and of their confidence in the legal order, or in ways which weaken or even destroy the accepted foundation of community life.

All studies of society, however remote, are colored by this fact. They will be sterile unless they are addressed to the world as it is, and to the free community we wish it to become.

For the contribution of a general view of society and its purposes—the contribution of Adam Smith, for example, in his time, or of Karl Marx, among the millions for whom *Das Kapital* is still gospel—is that of relevance.

No meaningful conclusion can be reached about the adequacy of any given branch of the law save in such a matrix. The study of law becomes a game of words if it is isolated from the flow of social experience, and the moral code, which give it life. Considered as an intellectual game, law doesn't compare with chess or bridge. It is more tedious, and not nearly so complicated. But the law has more to offer than a set of puzzles. In Holmes' words:

> How can the laborious study of a dry and technical system, the greedy watch for clients and practice of shopkeepers' arts, the mannerless conflicts over often sordid interests, make out a life? . . . They are the same questions you meet in any form of practical life. If a man has the soul of Sancho Panza, the world to him will be Sancho Panza's world; but if he has the soul of an idealist, he will make—I do not say find—his world ideal. Of course, the law is not the place for the artist or the poet. The law is the calling of thinkers. But to those who believe with me that not the least godlike of man's activities is the large survey of causes, that to know is not less than to feel, I say—and I say no longer with any doubt—that a man may live greatly in the law as well as elsewhere; that there as well as elsewhere his thought may find its unity in an infinite perspective;

that there as well as elsewhere he may wreak himself upon life, may drink the bitter cup of heroism, may wear his heart out after the unattainable. . . . If your subject is law, the roads are plain to anthropology, the science of man, to political economy, the theory of legislation, ethics, and thus by several paths to your final view of life. . . . To be master of any branch of knowledge, you must master those which lie next to it; and thus to know anything you must know all.[4]

Like other social studies, the law will run dry unless the lawyers listen occasionally to old Triton's wreathed horn, and catch liberating glimpses of their own work as a meaningful part, however small, of a hope and vision they share with their fellows.

4. O. W. Holmes, Jr., "The Profession of the Law" (1886), in *Speeches* (Boston, Little, Brown, 1913), pp. 22–23.

2. The Economic Order as a System of Law

THE FIRST PRINCIPLE of the law for the control of the economy is that the government is responsible for the general level of employment. Twenty-five years ago even the idea was not taken seriously. Politicians, it is true, regularly claimed the credit if dinner pails were full during their terms of office. Prosperity or its absence had consequences at the polls. But this political ritual was largely irrational. Neither public nor professional opinion had agreed about what government could do to control the level of employment. Both lawyers and economists wrote about the public control of business as if its chief problems were utility rate-making, unfair competition, and the antitrust laws, with an occasional nod of recognition to the importance of patents.

In 1933, President Roosevelt asked an able economist what he would recommend to help end the depression. The economist excused himself. He couldn't answer the question, he said, because knowledge had not yet advanced far enough to permit him to give a scientific reply with conviction. Many years of research would be necessary, he added, before he could offer the President any advice at all. President Roosevelt turned to others, whose scruples were less sensitive.

The same economist would not give the same answer today. The minds of economists have been altered by the experience and thought of the last twenty-five years. The realm of economics is a new world, full of unsolved problems, and of old problems which have taken on a new aspect. It acknowledges dangers unknown during the thirties, save as ghosts: creeping inflation; an apparently perpetual shortage of trained labor and of savings; the threats to productivity implicit in the structure of taxation, industry, and labor relations. It is also a world of new promise—the promise of sustained growth without long depressions, and of economic progress through the more competitive use of research, resources, and opportunities.

If the intellectual atmosphere among economists has changed in twenty-five years, there has been change, too, in the state of public opinion. One does not have to be a seer or a conductor of depth interviews to conclude that there will never be another prolonged depression in this country like the twelve years which began in 1929. President Roosevelt was elected four times on a record which unmistakably demonstrated his willingness to use inflation in order to fight unemployment. It is hard to imagine that any American statesman or politician of either party, however backward or stubborn, has failed to grasp the lesson. It is now the first principle of political economy that during depression periods, cheap money or government deficits, or both, can create jobs and win elections.

At the turn of the century, Sir William Harcourt remarked, "We are all Socialists now." In 1958, both Socialists and non-Socialists in Western Europe and the United States would have to amend Sir William's quip. They have all graduated from Socialism to Keynesism, at least in the vulgar sense of believing that most of the economic dislocations which lead to unemployment can be cured or offset by sufficient doses of inflation. The Republican party at home and the Conservative party in Great Britain can be expected, if anything, to outdo the political heirs of President Roosevelt in the promptness of their counterattacks on developing depressions. The charge of responsibility for the Great Depression has been hurled at them in every election since 1930. They could hardly afford to allow events to revive the identification of their parties with depression—an identification with a good deal of residual political power in both countries. Thus the Eisenhower Administration initiated corrective action at least as promptly in the history of its two recessions—those of 1953–54 and of 1957–58— as President Truman did in 1949–50.

The public at large is not fully convinced that depressions

and inflations can be controlled by governmental action. People devoutly wish it to be so, but fear the task is impossible. The spokesmen for such a view are met with the rather tolerant incredulity reserved for cranks like Daedalus and the Wright brothers. The conviction that good times alternate with bad goes back at least to the parable of the seven lean years. Very probably it projects the farmer's eternal nightmare about the weather and his crops into the whole range of economic activity. It is an image with tenacious roots in man's notion of the natural order of things.

On the other hand, opposing forces are strong. Bitter experience with the Great Depression of the 1930's and with postwar inflation has had its impact. And the content of everyman's expectations was greatly influenced by the thought that the full employment incident to war should not be beyond the wit of government in times of peace. For better or for worse, the idea has disappeared that the state can be a passive spectator while booms alternate unpredictably with busts. Depressions are not only tragic and costly, but politically intolerable. Confronting rival systems of social organization, American law, like the law of other capitalist democracies, has accepted the view that prolonged depressions and inflations threaten the fabric of society far too gravely to be tolerated. It was this conviction, more than any other, which sustained the passage of one of the most important statutes of this generation, the Employment Act of 1946.[1]

1. For an account of the passage of the Act see Stephen K. Bailey, *Congress Makes a Law*, New York, Columbia University Press, 1950; on its administrative aspects, Edwin Nourse, *Economics in the Public Service*, New York, Harcourt, Brace, 1953; Arthur F. Burns, *Prosperity without Inflation*, New York, Fordham University Press, 1957. For other material see R. E. Flanders, "Administering the Employment Act—the First Year," *Public Administration Review*, 7 (1942), 221–27; Charles I. Grogg and Stanley F. Teele, "The Proposed Full Employment Act," *Harvard Business Review*, 23, No. 3 (1945), 323–37; Stanley Lebergott, "Shall We Guarantee Full Employment?" *Harper's Magazine*, 190 (1945), 193–202; Emerson P. Schmidt, *Can Government Guarantee Full Employment?* U.S. Chamber of Commerce, Postwar Readjustment Bulletin 13 (1945); Gerhard Colm, ed., *The Employment Act, Past and Future*, Washington, D.C., National Planning Association, 1956.

The Act declares it to be the obligation of the national government to use all its powers in order to create and maintain "conditions under which there will be afforded useful employment opportunities, including self-employment, for those able, willing and seeking to work, and to promote maximum employment, production and purchasing power." This goal is to be sought, the Act commands, in ways which "foster and promote free competitive enterprise."

In their most general form, the questions with which this book deals are whether the hypothesis of the Employment Act is realistic, and whether its twin purposes are compatible. Can the American government effectively achieve the conditions necessary for high levels of employment? Can it foster free competitive enterprise at the same time? Does government planning for full employment necessarily doom the institutions of private business and private labor? If this approach to planning is feasible at all, under what conditions, and according to what criteria should the planning powers of the government be exercised?

The Employment Act is an unusual statute. It creates no bureaus with powers to issue licenses or fix prices. It authorizes no credits, nor does it require or forbid any particular course of conduct. The sanction upon which the Act relies for the achievement of its goal is analysis and persuasion. It rests on the realization that statistics and ideas are among the most important tools of government. The theory of the statute is that if the President, the executive departments, and the Congress are required to confront up-to-date analytical reports on the crucial elements of the economic situation, the necessary action will be taken in time.

The Act sets up a Council of Economic Advisers in the President's Office. The Council is charged with keeping the state of the national economy under continuous review, and with making recommendations for action. At the same time, the statute establishes a special Joint Committee of both Houses of Congress, to work with the Council and to serve in effect as professors of political economy for their colleagues in the Congress. The work of this Joint Committee

has been unusually constructive. Backed by a strong professional staff and often led by Senator Douglas of Illinois,
an able economist, formerly professor at the University of
Chicago, the Committee has developed into an important
part of the process of decision.

The Council of Economic Advisers has been consistently
useful within the government as an agency of research. Its
effectiveness as an agency of action has varied with the
personalities of its members, their relations with the President, and their somewhat different conceptions of the Council's duties. Some have put stress on the provision of the Act
requiring the Council

> (3) to appraise the various programs and activities
> of the Federal Government in the light of the policy
> declared in section 2 for the purpose of determining
> the extent to which such programs and activities are
> contributing, and the extent to which they are not
> contributing, to the achievement of such policy, and to
> make recommendations to the President with respect
> thereto; and
>
> (4) to develop and recommend to the President na-
> tional economic policies to foster and promote free
> competitive enterprise, to avoid economic fluctuations
> or to diminish the effects thereof, and to maintain
> employment, production, and purchasing power.

They interpret these provisions of the statute as authority
to coordinate all the economic programs of the government
in the President's behalf, and to press vigorously, both within
and without the government, for action they deem important.
Others have taken a more academic view. They have regarded
the Council's function as entirely advisory, and feel their duty
is done when their reports are printed and filed. It is still early
in the development of the Council as an instrument of
government for a clearcut resolution of these issues. Given
the inherent strength of the Treasury, the Bureau of the
Budget, and the Federal Reserve Board, however, it seems
reasonable to suppose that the Council and its reports will
be ignored in the long run unless it comes forward strongly

as an arm of the presidency, both in recommending programs of action, and in seeing to it that they are carried out. In the competitive world of Washington bureaucracy, shy theorists have never prevailed unaided.

The voters' demand for high levels of employment at home is not the only force which has helped make the American government accept a direct responsibility for the state of trade. The international position and obligations of the United States create strong pressures on domestic economic policy. Articles 55 and 56 of the United Nations' Charter require each signatory government, in accordance with its own constitutional procedures, to take joint and separate action in the interest of promoting "full employment and conditions of economic and social progress and development." This undertaking is repeated with some variation of language and emphasis in the Articles of Agreement of the International Monetary Fund. The same theme appears in the mutual assistance provisions of the North Atlantic Treaty, and in the agreements establishing the Organization of American States.

These commitments measure more than the appeal of a pious wish. About half the economic transactions of the free world are made in the United States. Fluctuations in economic activity within the United States immediately alter American imports of basic raw materials, and many other products, thereby influencing the level of economic activity throughout the free world. They may interrupt the international movements of capital, on which international economic equilibrium has always depended. In that way, they disturb the precarious foreign exchange balance of the postwar period, narrowly held against deep-rooted difficulties which were intensified by two disastrous wars. The mild American recession of 1949, for example, helped throw all the other Western countries into a devaluation crisis. The American inflation which raged for eight or nine months after the outbreak of hostilities in Korea, in June 1950, created a new cycle of disturbance for Britain, for France, and for almost every other member of the Atlantic community. The recession which began here during the summer of 1957 has likewise had a wide ranging impact abroad, especially in Latin America and Asia. Its effect in Europe was masked for some time by the level of our military purchases there, and by the improvements which have recently been achieved in the economies of that region.

Carrying out the responsibilities of the Employment Act involves three sets of legal and economic arrangements. The first are those of fiscal and monetary policy, which should be characterized as primary instruments for carrying out the purposes of the Act. Secondly, there are the competitive and regulated markets for goods and services—the institutions through which the impulses of fiscal and monetary policy are translated into actual employment, production, and prices. Third, the system of planning involves the economically similar but socially distinct problem of the organized and unorganized labor markets. All three sets of institutions and bodies of law have different histories, reflecting the influence of different forces and needs. They all developed long before the policies of the Employment Act were known or accepted, and they are oriented historically to altogether different ideas and purposes. In all, older rules are being subordinated, recast, or subdued. One of the important tasks of research, as it is of policy, is to review and reconsider the law in each of these three areas as a means for accomplishing both the purposes of the Employment Act and other accepted goals of economic policy.

This section attempts to outline the architectural shape of the system of law, consisting of these three essential structural elements. Later chapters deal with them separately and in detail, seeking finally to view their impact on each other during the course of recent industrial fluctuations.

Together, fiscal and monetary policy now constitute the first and decisive tool of the law of economic planning. Its basic thesis is that the government and the Federal Reserve system should see to it that money is being spent for goods and services of various kinds in a volume sufficient to assure high levels of useful employment, without precipitating the pressures of general inflation. Drawing upon the improved modern analysis of national income, this policy relies on the hydraulic pressure of an adequate level of spending to elicit the most valuable possible combination of outputs from the economy at full employment.

Fiscal and monetary action to govern the federal budget, the banking system, and the securities market are remote controls, but within their limits they are vitally effective. By using them, the state can influence the environment in which business makes its decisions. Recourse to such indirect controls alters the range of possibilities the businessman faces, and makes certain courses of action feasible or not, as the case may be. But such methods of control do not make government a direct participant in business decisions nor require any change in the extent to which the ordinary conduct of business or labor is directly licensed or subjected to other administrative regulation. So far as the businessman or the labor leader is concerned, controls of this kind determine the opportunities before him. They color the vistas of the future he keeps in his mind's eye. But they do not change the degree of his freedom in the conduct of his business or require him to ask anybody's permission before doing what he wants to do.

The second principal set of institutions we have inherited and developed for governing the economy are those of the market. The assumption of the system of planning is that over-all government control of the level of spendings would bring forth an appropriate level of employment and output from thousands of businessmen, large and small, who would react to the prospect of profit by producing and offering their wares. In a society which possesses a considerable class of entrepreneurs, capable of organizing production in response to consumer demand, or in anticipation of it, this premise is a sensible one. Where it is an available rule, the principle of market competition, policed by antitrust laws, is the most satisfactory of known methods for directing business activity within the private sector of the economy.

A functioning market determines the allocation of resources to various competing uses—that is, the production, pricing, and distribution of most goods and services. The allocations of a competitive market have an ethical justification at least as strong as that of any alternative rule for distribution. The competitive market directs production in the private sector of the economy in ways which roughly correspond to the comparative intensity of consumer preferences for different goods and services.

The attractive vision of Consumer Sovereignty ordering the output it values most urgently should be qualified in several ways.

In the first place, the growth of modern taxation fundamentally limits the principle of Consumer Sovereignty. Taxation allocates a share of possible output to governmental use, both for defense purposes and for those services which we have decided are best performed by public authority— the building of roads and airports, the conduct of social welfare programs, education, conservation, and the like. And the tax system finances this public requisition upon output in ways which accomplish a radical if not altogether planned redistribution of income, so that the effective income of individuals no longer corresponds at all closely to their productivity.

Secondly, the presence of monopoly introduces distortions, dividing income in ways which do not correspond to differences in productivity. Here, however, the income tax is a great leveler.

Thirdly, many expenditures for advertising go far beyond the economic function of broadening the market by informing consumers what is available for sale. Much advertising seeks to divert trade from one well-known seller to another —from the social point of view, an almost unmitigated waste of resources. Some aim to create wants and needs the consumer hardly knew he had. This response of demand to selling costs has traditionally been called the plasticity of demand. Kenneth Galbraith has vividly described it as the Dependence Effect of wants on advertising and output—the push for emulation in a society where conspicuous consumption has always carried prestige.[2] While no persuader, how-

2. *The Affluent Society* (Boston, Houghton Mifflin, 1958), chap. 11.

ever hidden and subtle, can create effective demand where there is no income, advertising of this kind can divert income from saving to consumption, or from one form of consumption to another. And the pressure of such wants may induce people to resist socially desirable projects of public expenditure in order to keep enlarging their programs of private consumption.

With these qualifications, however, the case for a competitive allocation of resources has much strength. The most striking tribute I ever heard paid to the market system was given during a dinner conversation in Warsaw, early in 1950. I happened to sit next to an official of the Polish Planning Ministry. Answering my questions about the planning methods they had found most useful, he commented that the Polish government had abolished rationing and price controls for food, clothing, and other consumers' goods as quickly as possible after the war. Workers, he said, were altogether too satisfied with their rations. Without the price system, the Planning Ministry felt it was losing the incentive power of wages. Rationing was abolished in order to help induce people to work harder. I remarked that this view had been strongly supported as an argument for ending the OPA in the United States, particularly by spokesmen for business groups. Money seemed to be a socially neutral instrument, equally useful in capitalist and in communist economies. "Yes," he answered solemnly, "that is correct doctrine. Marshal Stalin has said so."

The conversation turned quickly to other topics.

It does not require Marshal Stalin's faith in the beauties of the Invisible Hand and its work to appreciate both the economic and the political advantages of the market system. Requiring no cumbersome bureaucracy to control it, the competitive market can accomplish miracles in an atmosphere of considerable flexibility and freedom. The experienced businessmen of a commercial and industrial society may not be so single-minded and efficient as ants or bees in carrying on cooperative social activity without specific orders. Their instincts and conditioned reflexes go a long way, however, toward accomplishing a comparable result. And, of course, businessmen are superior to the bees and ants at least in one regard. They do change techniques from time to time, if they are under sufficient pressure to do so.

In those areas of the economy where competition does not exist or cannot readily be required, the market is often supervised by permanent regulation, usually by governmental or other public bodies. This kind of control is normally accomplished by administrative agencies with jurisdiction over prices, or quotas of output, or both; sometimes jurisdiction is also given over the entry of new firms, and the merger, combination, or withdrawal of existing firms. Somewhat different public mechanisms for the partial control of markets have been developed for some of the agricultural industries, and for regulating oil production. In certain cases, these devices are international in character, and rest on public or private international agreements.

Administrative controls of this kind used to be viewed with high hope as important means both for "planning," and for protecting the public against the abuses of monopoly. Latterly, it has become fashionable to deplore their rigidity, their comparative ineffectiveness, their slowness, and the static atmosphere they seem to develop. It is hard, perhaps impossible, for an agency regulating an industry to avoid taking on that industry's outlook. In some cases, the economic value of the permissions such agencies have to give—franchises, the exclusion of competitors, rate increases, and so on—generates an immense pressure, and has led to corruption of direct and indirect kinds. Opinion has been troubled by the discovery of some bribery in government, whether in the form of the occasional mink coat, deep-freeze, or vacation, or the even more important expectation of jobs, retainers, or commissions to come. There is a good deal, too, of political pressure, and the pressure of public opinion, skillfully mobilized to debauch the administrative process. Perhaps, however, the swing of the pendulum in the state of thought about administrative controls has gone too far. While such controls can never be ideal, and undoubtedly require reform, they are a necessary counterweight to private power in certain areas where competition is in fact unavailable.

In a considerable number of large industries, where a few firms produce most of the supply, existing markets can hardly be called competitive in any practical sense, but direct administrative control by governmental agencies has not yet been deemed necessary or desirable. This kind of situation— the economists call it oligopoly—presents important problems of policy, notably during periods when the economy is working under the forced draft of high levels of demand.

The third major element in the planning system is the set of rules which is being developed to govern the negotiations between business and organized labor, and otherwise to fix certain key aspects of the structure of the labor market. The revolution in labor law and in labor relations during the last thirty years has been one of the most constructive achievements of American society in this century. It has helped to give the working man new forms of protection, and a less precarious role in society. The factory and the factory town have been transformed as social organisms. At the same time, of course, the increasing strength and wealth of trade unions have precipitated a whole series of new problems, both for their members and for society. The law-making process has barely begun to respond to these developments in wage levels, in internal trade-union organization, and in the handling of union funds.

These three sets of institutions constitute a single entity, a whole which is more than the sum of its parts. The unifying force in this system derives from the changes which have been accomplished during recent years in thinking about monetary and fiscal policy, and in the practice of these governmental arts. What combines these three disparate bodies of law and custom into a dynamic whole is the proposition, implied in the Employment Act, that the government can and should achieve a considerable degree of stability in spending and employment through the judicious use of fiscal and monetary policy. Reliance on fiscal and monetary policy as the government's chief positive weapon of stabilization has vital implications for the rest of the economy. By occasional action in this limited sphere, the government could keep prospects for profit generally favorable, without allowing the feverishly high profits of inflation to appear. Thus, in the main, government could safely rely on the decisions of business and labor to determine the actual course of production in the private sector of the economy.

What is novel in this conception of planning is the idea that employment stabilization is the decisive purpose of monetary and fiscal policy. This conclusion rests on the proposition, more fully discussed in Part III, that the free enterprise system does not of itself invariably achieve equilibrium at full employment. No degree of competition can protect a free-enterprise and free-labor society against booms and slumps. Such deviations are not errors, to be blamed on excessive monopoly in labor or product markets, or other forms of "sin," but are inherent in the process by which cumulative opinion can lead to excessive or inadequate levels of total spending. The free markets of a capitalist economy lack a balance wheel. This only the government can provide, through fiscal and monetary action. There are no alternative means in a free economy to smooth otherwise inevitable fluctuations in the volume of private and public spendings, and therefore in employment and production.

Part II will consider some of the reasons of theory and of experience which support the view that monetary and fiscal action of this kind can in fact considerably influence the level of spending, and thus of employment. The United States and the governments of other capitalist societies have had considerable success in carrying out programs for preventing prolonged depressions. They have been less successful, on the whole, in preventing persistent price inflation. While the nature of the problem is not obscure, the sensible remedies are far less popular and are more seriously resisted.

In perspective, the developing American law of fiscal and monetary policy, of market organization, and of labor fit together reasonably well as a workable plan for planning, to use one of the most ambiguous and misleading words in the vocabulary of our times. "Planning" has been used to characterize many forms of state action in the economic sphere. At one end of the spectrum it identifies zoning and city planning; at the other, the wartime control procedures through which the government allocated resources, fixed prices, and production quotas, and sometimes designated customers for industry. The word "planning" is even used occasionally to characterize a "welfare" state which has highly developed systems of social insurance, and other methods for providing the citizen with basic social services.

From much that is written and said, one would think the American people faced an impossible choice between two equally unattractive alternatives. On the one hand, they could vote for complete laissez-faire, implying booms, slumps, great inequalities of wealth and income, and total insecurity. Or they could opt for a program of complete totalitarianism, in which the state took over the ownership and direction of all economic institutions, became the sole employer of labor, and engulfed the people in a regime of sanitary, well-fed serfdom.

This black-and-white stereotype of the planning question is utterly false. That the Communists and Socialists use the word "planning" is no reason to give them a monopoly of it. After all, as Myrdal has recalled, Marx used neither the word nor the idea of "planning." Marx thought that the state would "wither away" under Socialism, after a brief period of proletarian dictatorship.

The problem of planning, as it will be presented here, is inescapable for a modern government, especially in a democracy, which seeks to use the energies of capitalists in organizing a good deal of the daily economic work of the society it governs. It is inescapable because a capitalist economy doesn't keep itself at high levels of employment, nor can it accomplish unaided certain other economic goals of the community. And there are no institutions, apart from those of government, to carry out the essential preliminary function of planning—that of seeing to it that the aggregate of all spendings in the economy is high enough to ensure full employment, and not so high as to produce inflation. This kind of planning—to balance demand and production at full employment—can be done well or badly, in ways which further democracy or in ways which would weaken it. The issue is not whether to plan, but what to plan and how to plan.

The conclusion of the argument which will be developed in this essay is that the legal machinery for controlling the American economy can and should be used effectively to keep economic activity in high gear. Its structure is an indigenous mixture of public and private elements, equally dependent on government and on the market. Some of the legal control methods now being used are unnecessary and wasteful. A few are even dangerous. Their existence does not, however, seriously reduce the capacity of the legal system as a whole to fulfill its basic task of eliminating extensive depressions and inflations, and facilitating a steady increase in standards of life. That task is not easy; but neither should it be impossibly difficult.

The system whose essential structure has been sketched here in preliminary form is one of offsets. In a capitalist economy, the decision-making process is diffuse. It is influenced by cumulative, wavelike movements of opinion, responding to certain economic signals. Economic forecasting of trends in the private and in the governmental sectors of the economy is too weak a reed to permit precise advance planning. The best we can expect—and it is an altogether adequate and practical goal—is that the government use its powers to counterbalance trends toward inflation or deflation which are bound to develop from time to time in a free economy. As people gradually become used to the effectiveness of such interventions, the need for them should be reduced. Business calculations, especially in inventory purchases and other forms of investment, would come to rest on the expectation that the government will effectively prevent the level of spending from dropping for long below that sufficient to produce full employment. The spread of that conviction as the starting point for private business decisions will of itself help to stabilize the volume of private investment spending. When business comes to believe that quick recoveries like those of 1938, 1949, and 1954 are normal, the cost of the government intervention required to bring them about should be reduced. The government deficit in all these cases was small; in 1949 it became a surplus, under the pressure of rising income, in less than six months.

Stabilizing the economy by the judicious use of fiscal and monetary policy is hardly a magic solution for the economic problems of society. It should permit the permanent elimination of big depressions. But it leaves other problems untouched, or moderately altered, and it creates a host of new and unfamiliar ones.

The economists have only begun to consider the pressures and the risks of a regime of nearly perpetual full employment. In every phase of economics—wages, prices, savings, taxation, the problems of monopoly, of farm prices, and of resource conservation—the assumption of full employment changes not only the appearance, but the fundamental character of many issues of policy. By restoring the case of full employment, which was the problem most fully discussed by the classical economists, it also restores many of their conclusions. Old-fashioned economic virtues, like thrift and hard work, have become virtues again. The economy puts a high premium on production, the main long-run force working against the pressure of inflation seemingly inherent in sustained periods of full employment. The social cost of monopolistic arrangements becomes more obvious as the plausible depression arguments for monopoly are stripped away. Wages forced beyond the margin of productivity are seen once more to involve huge and cumulative costs, without raising the standard of living of the workers nominally benefited. The international limits of freedom in domestic price policy become apparent, after having been largely forgotten for more than twenty years. The age of expansion, sustained by the full-employment policies of government, has its headaches. If uncontrolled, it could threaten the structure of society as gravely as a prolonged depression. But it has much to offer, if policy can walk the narrow path between stability and inflation.

For "full" employment, or "reasonably full" employment,

or "high levels" of employment—however the goal should properly be defined—is not the only end to be served by the legal system for directing the economy. An adequate program for the public control of business requires the government to formulate a series of economic policy objectives, and not merely to achieve full employment.

Such a program should include at least these elements, in addition to employment stabilization:

1. The rate of growth. Should the government use its monetary policy, and the complex network of incentives and deterrents embodied in its tax system, to favor more or less savings and capital formation? Should it be neutral in accepting the rate and direction of capital formation which emerges as the result of private decisions, against the background of the existing system of taxation? Should it try to match the rate of growth in the Soviet Union, Norway, France, or other countries going through periods of unusually rapid increases in output? Should taxation and price policy be tilted to favor more consumption, the present rate of growth, or a higher one?

2. Efficiency and economy in the short-run and the long-run use of resources. To what extent can the forces of competition or administrative regulation be relied upon to elicit socially acceptable production from the economy, at socially justifiable prices? What criteria should be employed to determine when the state should supplement or supersede the market as a regulatory mechanism, or undertake the direct provision of goods or services itself? Should the government provide more or less education, more or less atomic energy, more or less social insurance, more or less money for slum clearance, resource conservation and health services? Should it continue to regulate the price of trucking, or undertake to regulate the price of steel?

3. Equity in the distribution and redistribution of wealth and income. All taxation involves a redistribution of income. Taking into account its other social and economic goals, how egalitarian should economic policy be? If it be deemed sensible to favor savings and to reduce consumption, in

order to increase the rate of growth, does it follow that the income tax should be less progressive? In view of the importance of union welfare programs, do people in the middle- and lower-income brackets now save a higher fraction of their income than those in the higher-income brackets?

4. The level of prices. One of the persistent problems of the first decade or so of the full employment economy has been a tendency for prices to rise, a movement with far-reaching effects on the social system, and the pattern of economic incentives. This trend was perhaps caused, and at the least exaggerated, by the effects of the World War, and of Korean and post-Korean military and political tensions.

The price level is a vital element in judging the social performance of the economy. Stable prices over long periods of time can accomplish more than any other one economic policy to transform a population into a people. A community of stable prices is a community of stable, understood, and accepted patterns of status, respect, and reward. It does not cheat the saver of the object of his thrift. Nor does it radically alter the pattern of payments for different kinds of work, drastically affecting the social position of groups and classes within the community, and the flow of talent into different kinds of work. It is no accident that societies which endured great inflations have produced powerful political parties dedicated to the proposition that the whole social order is a fraud. Inflation ruins those who own bonds, while those who own property flourish. The process is manifestly haphazard and unjust, and it provokes a bitter resentment which permanently alienates many victims and observers from the existing social order.

The general level of prices is more than an acute social question. It is a fundamental factor also in determining the economic relationship between the country and the international economy. Indeed, it has a vital bearing on the question whether a regime of stable international exchange rates will be at all possible.

Beyond these four permanent and familiar aspects of any economic program, there looms a novel fifth—the claim of foreign policy on the economy. It is so ominous and so burdensome that it requires separate treatment.[3]

If a label is necessary for the concept of planning outlined here, it might be identified as Planning for Freedom, or Capitalist Planning, to distinguish it from many forms of planning which would require a far greater degree of detailed control over economic activities by the state. Perhaps the best name for this set of ideas would be "Liberal Planning," using the word "liberal" in its old sense, still valid, to recall the liberalism of those utilitarian radicals, the English Classical Economists, with their faith in free trade, competition, and progress; their sympathy for practical and humanitarian reforms; their complete dedication to human freedom as an end in itself.

It should be apparent that the goals of policy implicit in the public law are of equal advantage to all classes of the community. It may be worth repeating the obvious fact that no important group profits from depressions, and that no one ever deliberately organizes one. Prosperity is universally popular. General stabilization should strengthen free enterprise in business and free trade unions in the labor market—the main economic pillars of social and political freedom. The ideas which now dominate the law about economic planning should unite the American people, not divide them on issues of principle.

There is, however, a paradox in the reception these views have had in American public opinion. They have been accepted, in variant forms, by some businessmen and business groups—most notably, perhaps, by the Committee for Economic Development. Nonetheless, they are still vehemently attacked as "collectivism," "creeping socialism," and worse. Even the editors of *Fortune*, in expounding opinions of this general orientation, usually preface their conclusions with a few critical remarks about the late Lord Keynes, who has become a favorite symbol of modern error among the more fervent guardians of an uncontaminated faith.

Keynes was a powerful contributor to the literature of

3. See below, Chap. 4.

modern economics, although in retrospect his contribution was by no means so fundamental as some of his followers thought. Possessed of a brilliant gift for epigram, and a literate style, he was the best-known economist of his generation among the general public, and his name is often used to identify the school of economists to which he belonged—a school which includes many other strong men, notably Wicksell, Robertson, Myrdal, Pigou, Hicks, and Viner.

It is hard to see how the policy recommendations that were derived from the work of this school can be attacked as "Socialist" in any meaningful sense of that word. The ideas of Liberal Planning give capitalism every reason to expect even more spectacular progress in the future than in the past, without disturbing the basic conditions of property ownership and control. There is much in J. K. Galbraith's acute comment that

> the Keynesian System, though it implied a decidedly non-revolutionary change in the relation of the government to the economy, implied nonetheless, an important one. For a doctrine that excluded government it substituted one that made government indispensable. Keynes was sufficiently unpalatable when he made depression and inflation, not adventitious or war-induced misfortunes, but normal occurrences. He went on to make government the indispensable partner of business. In failing to recognize the prestige that goes with power and decision-making in American life, American liberals fail to recognize that, for some businessmen, the Keynesian remedy was at least as damaging as the depression it presumed to eliminate. . . . To share the prestige of decision-making is to lose prestige.[4]

4. *American Capitalism* (Boston, Houghton Mifflin, 1952), pp. 84–85. Perhaps I should add that I don't share Galbraith's seeming attribution of all the ideas in what he calls the "Keynesian system" to Keynes.

3. Capitalism as a Condition of Freedom: The Major Premise

BY WAY OF anticipating the argument of the book, the first two chapters advanced the view that the recent development of law in its relation to the economic order permits us to count on a reasonably firm footing for economic policy, at least at home. This view assumes that diplomacy can accommodate our national interests to the pressures of revolutionary political change in the external world. If so optimistic an assumption is permissible, it should be altogether possible for capitalist democracy in the United States to carry out enlightened economic programs, in pretty much its present posture of legal and social organization, and without giving up either capitalism or democracy.

The obverse of this proposition has equal force: neither political nor social freedom for the individual, as ultimate goals of American life, can be imagined without the working reality of American capitalism. In this perspective, capitalism is not merely one among many alternative methods for organizing commerce and industry: it is a system of power which accomplishes a reasonably wide dispersal of economic authority and of economic opportunity within the society. American capitalism divides influence into independent focal points which are relatively unprotected against the impact of competition and technological change, although some are linked by relations of reciprocity as well as of conflict. This quality of pluralism is an essential condition of American liberty.

Astute practitioners of the art of semantics urge that a new word be substituted for "capitalism" in this connection.

Its connotations are unfavorable, they say, especially in Europe and Asia. It evokes disastrous memories of imperialism and unemployment, exploitation and brutality, of opulent bankers and starving hordes of barefoot workmen. Jacques Maritain proposes that the mild and protective economic environment of the present era in the West be called one of Economic Humanism, and others have suggested less felicitious and more defensive substitutes for "capitalism."

There are advantages, however, in confronting the fact that it is capitalism we are talking about, after all, capitalism and its rivalry with socialism as competing principles of economic order.

Capitalism is not a static concept of unalterable meaning. Its present legal position is one of steady change, under evolving rules of law which define rights of property in terms of overriding public interests. The ballot has long since proved mightier than the safe deposit box. Taxes, welfare programs, and programs to mitigate the trade cycle have revolutionized the atmosphere of ordinary living in the Western world.

Capitalism today hardly resembles its ancestors, the capitalist regimes of the late middle ages or the early industrial period. We have come a long way from the slums and sweatshops which are the popular image of nineteenth-century capitalism. Some of the economic historians contend that Dickens, Engels, and Disraeli were lurid and inaccurate, and that the popular image is a myth. Whether or not the older pictures were overdrawn, there can be no doubt of the advance that has taken place in the conditions of life among the working people of Western communities during the last century.

But for all its development, capitalism is still recognizably a system that permits and protects the private ownership of property, and the making of private decisions about its use. There is still a difference between the rights of property in the Soviet Union and in the United States. And that difference, even if it is called a difference of degree, is crucial to the possibility of personal and political freedom.

It should by now be apparent, both in theory and in practice, that Democratic Socialism is a contradiction in terms. Neither personal nor political freedom could survive a monopolization of power by the state, nor indeed its monopolization by any other group of institutions under unified control within a society. Socialist societies can have good, bad, or indifferent economies, educational systems, armies or churches. There is no inherent reason why the state cannot conduct the steel industry or the railways as well or as badly as it conducts an atomic energy program, the traffic controls at air fields, or the weather service. Indeed, it would be hard to demonstrate that government administration of the railroads would necessarily be worse than the railroad administration now prevailing in the United States. The American preference for capitalism represents more than inertia, inherited loyalties, and a belief in its superior efficiency. It rests ultimately on a recognition of its role in the strategy of freedom. Unless the members of an opposition can make a living without the permission of the government; unless they can function as a political party, obtain newsprint and presses, hire meeting halls, publish freely; unless they can have access to television without complete dependence on the good will and sporting instincts of the government in power, their opposition is bound to be a feeble, meaningless force, existing only by sufferance. Capitalism is a vital part of the price of liberty.

The point has never been more sharply put than by Harold Laski. Laski was acutely conscious of the shortcomings of capitalism, and quite unaware of its economic processes. He considered himself a Socialist, though not a Communist. But he was also, perhaps even more emphatically, a democrat and a libertarian. In his writing on the conditions of freedom, he was one of the fervent modern spokesmen for pluralism —the dispersal and federalization of authority among the people and institutions of society—as the indispensable basis of liberty. He urged that great inequality in economic power was incompatible with freedom. It was his prediction, denied by what has happened since both in Britain and in the United States, that universal suffrage would never succeed in mitigating the political power of wealth. But he saw the other side of the coin with clarity: "If in any state," he wrote, "there is a body of men who possess unlimited political power, those over whom they rule can never be free. For the one assured result of historical investigation is the lesson that uncontrolled power is invariably poisonous to those who possess it. They are always tempted to impose their canon of good upon others, and, in the end, they assume that the good of the community depends upon the continuance of their power." [1] "There will never be liberty," he continued, "in any state where there is an execessive concentration of power at the centre." [2]

Many of the theorists of Socialism, including Laski himself, have experimented with the notion of decentralized Socialism. They have considered cooperatives, syndical groups, guilds and other forms of industrial organization which would have the advantages of dispersed power, without the supposed disadvantages of private property. In their systems of Socialism, the managers of state-owned enterprises would be given great discretion, although they would be ultimately answerable to the state.

The status of management in such decentralized socialist enterprises has sometimes been analogized to that of the men who direct great American corporations. By and large, the managers of these vast enterprises have achieved extraordinary freedom from the influence of stockholders, and an extraordinary capacity for self-perpetuation. The stockholders are the legal source of the managers' power, as the nominal owners of their companies' property. But in many publicly held companies the stockholders obey the managers, not the management the stockholders. The managers "own" their companies, for all practical purposes, although their investment is usually small. The stockholders accept the managers' advice, and re-elect them regularly, voting them also the generous option and pension plans which have become so popular.

Corporations of this kind present American law with

1. *Liberty in the Modern State* (New York, Harper, 1930), pp. 2–3.
2. Ibid., p. 64.

difficult questions of responsibility. The stockholders of many publicly held companies discharge their duties in the most perfunctory manner, and allow the corporate management, for long periods of time, almost complete freedom, tempered only by the managers' own standards of behavior, and their concern for the possibility of an accounting.[3]

The question is occasionally put, whether the situation in the United States would be very different if all or a good deal of the stock of the United States Steel Corporation, and of other like corporations, were owned by the government, and voted at annual meetings by the Secretary of Commerce. Could not such a preservation of the forms of capitalism preserve also its desirable flexibility, and its relative freedom from governmental control? Would not such a solution establish active and intelligent procedures of review for the stewardship of the managers, who are at law trustees of other people's money? Experiments along this line have been proposed as a general policy by some leaders of the Labour party in England. "Decentralization" has become a popular slogan also in the Soviet Union, and in other countries which suffer from traffic jams in the machinery for making decisions.

Public ownership of the stock of great companies would provide adequate oversight for the internal affairs of American corporations. But the remedy would be far worse than the disease. For Socialism via stock ownership would involve as complete a monopolization of power as any other form of Socialism. If applied to any considerable segment of American commerce or industry, the effects of such an approach would be ruinous.

The government would of course be a most vigilant stockholder. In the nature of things, the government as stockholder would necessarily assert effective control over the policy of the corporations involved. Government officials are conscientious and diligent, by and large, and no civil

3. Discussed at some length in "To Whom and for What Ends Is Corporate Management Responsible?" a chapter of Edward S. Mason, ed., *The Corporation in Modern Society*, Cambridge, Harvard University Press (1960), p. 46.

servant charged with responsibility for the government's shares in a corporation would be as casual and as careless as many private investors are in voting their own shares. Such has been American experience with government-owned corporations, from the Panama Canal Company to the various banks, barge lines, and other incidental enterprises which belong to the United States Government. And experience with government-owned companies in Britain, France, and Italy is not notably different. Some are imaginative and active, others relatively routine. The head of the Italian government-owned oil company is a man of great influence and power, as is the Director of Électricité de France. But all these companies, the good and the bad alike, are in the end subject to sustained control by the state.

There is no possible objection to this fact so long as the state-owned sector is a relatively small share of the whole economy. Indeed it would be most objectionable if the pattern were otherwise, and the state passively allowed its funds to be spent without effective supervision.

The objection arises only if a program of genuine Socialism is put into effect, and the state becomes the sole employer of labor, or the sole significant employer, save for a fragmentary private sector devoted to the manufacture and sale of handicrafts and the like. Consider the position of Mr. Molotov, who was recently removed as Foreign Minister of the Soviet Union, after forty years of considerable experience, for the offense of having caucused with some friends before a meeting of the Politburo. He could not return to private law practice or run for the Senate. He was not made president of a Moscow bank, or head of a great can or typewriter company, or rector of a university, or chief of the Russian Red Cross. His future was at the mercy of the government, the monopolist of respectable employment at his level. No manager ultimately dependent on the smiles and frowns of the government, however decentralized the system of Socialism might become, would dare give a man in Molotov's position a reasonable job. For a small man, discharged from the government service as "disloyal," or "a security risk," or an opponent of the regime in any other guise, the problem would be even more hopeless. Men of stature sometimes defy a tyrant and survive, because they are too conspicuous to be punished. So it was with Croce under Mussolini's rule. But a defenseless minor official in disfavor with a socialist regime would be lucky to find work in the mines, as the malcontents have done in Czechoslovakia.

The problem is not uniquely a political one. During the war a minor official was fired from a government post on the day a Congressional committee revealed that he had once written an innocent and enthusiastic book in praise of nudism, illustrated in part with topical photographs of himself. His boss discharged him when the news arrived, without a hearing, and indeed without pausing for breath. It is hard to be altogether unsympathetic to the director of the agency. He had troubles enough in Congress without taking on the defense of nudism. The implications of the episode, however, are not such as to encourage making the government the ultimate employer of labor in the United States. Starvation is hardly an appropriate penalty for nonconformity—even when nonconformity includes a period of nudism.

The problem is not exclusively governmental; it exists wherever concentrated power exists. In the early thirties, it wasn't easy for a union organizer to stay in many company towns of Pennsylvania or West Virginia. It isn't easy for a union organizer, or for a representative of the NAACP, to remain in many parts of the South today. And there have been times when life was not a bed of roses for a member of the Progressive Mine Workers of America who happened to live in United Mine Workers' territory.

Under such circumstances, there can be no reality in the idea of personal or political freedom.

Even if the case for the possibility of Democratic Socialism were more convincing, the risks of tyranny would surely be greater in a socialist state than in one of dispersed authority. Why should such risks be accepted, if Capitalist Democracy can reasonably meet the universal demand for employment stabilization and social security; the achievement of a widely shared, rising standard of living; and the opening of ed-

ucational and social opportunities to the whole population?
As Morris R. Cohen once said:

> A government of limited powers, which cannot indoc-
> trinate all its citizens with its dogmas and does not make
> all of its citizens directly dependent on it for their
> daily bread, cannot possibly be so dangerous to free
> thought and to all the achievements of art and science
> which depend on free thought. In view of the inherent
> uncertainty of all human arrangements, can we afford
> the risk of putting all our eggs into one basket and
> depending on one central government to exercise un-
> limited power? History does not show any example of
> genuine intellectual progress under a regime of absolute
> power. We must allow for variation and research, so
> that the existing good may not prevent the better from
> coming into being.[4]

The force of this conclusion is strongly and often emo-
tionally resisted in many quarters. The socialist tradition is
of great political influence abroad, and has a more pervasive
place in this country than is sometimes realized. Many men
who function politically as Socialists are patently democrats
in their working faith, and that fact, so evident in the
politics of Western Europe and of Asia, has tended to
obscure the inevitable consequences of genuinely socialist
action—that is, the abolition of private property and the
public ownership of all means of production. Both the
historical role of Socialists in the process of reform and
their identification with widely accepted ideals of progress
have given to Socialism a quite general position of acceptance,
indeed of authority, not often challenged in the intellectual
world of the West.

For the democratic socialist movements of Western countries took the initiative, during the last hundred years, in
giving leadership and impetus to many nonsocialist programs of humanitarian advance. They helped to establish
new attitudes of respect toward manual work and manual

4. *Faith of a Liberal* (New York, Holt, 1946), p. 106.

workers within the factory system. Through the growth of trade unions, which were often led by Socialists, they helped achieve a status of dignity and security for the working man, and an opportunity for him to participate in the life of society on terms which everywhere begin to approach those of equality. The socialist movement and the development of unions were among the forces serving to mitigate the dominance of the middle classes in Western society, and, for better or for worse, to change its style. The efforts of Socialists and other reformers were important in promoting the acceptance by all modern societies, however bourgeois, of the principle that the state has fundamental responsibilities for the economic welfare of citizens.

Socialist influences were not alone in persuading Western democracies to accept this view. In one sense, its acceptance became inevitable once universal suffrage was achieved, through the long political battles of the nineteenth century, vindicating the ideals of the American and the French revolutions. Agrarian protest made its contribution, notably in the United States, and so did religious and humanitarian movements of many kinds. Two universal wars, which demanded the solidarity of the entire population, gave great impetus to the feeling that a community which sends men to the front should protect them in times of peace against unemployment, the accident of disease, and the unproductiveness of old age.

In recent years, of course, the manifest success of Western capitalist communities in raising standards of living, and in meeting the demand for other forms of social progress, has somewhat weakened the economic if not the political appeal of socialist programs, at least in the industrialized countries of the West. In a society visibly accomplishing rapid advances in its standard of living and social services, it is not so plausible as it used to be to contend that the nationalization of the means of production was the one sure road to social Utopia.

Despite the obsolescence of its economic platform, the socialist movement has immense political momentum in many Western countries. It is gaining rapidly throughout Asia and Africa. In part, the gain of the socialist idea in Asia and Africa reflects the prestige and political power of China and the Soviet Union; in part, it is a reaction to the mixed and often disastrous economic record of most of the countries recently liberated from imperial control. In 1957, for the first time, the world bought more copies of *Das Kapital* than of the Bible.

It is therefore of some importance to emphasize at the outset that if the analysis presented here should be correct, the economics of Socialism is not only erroneous, but irrelevant. The central rallying cry of Socialism—public ownership of the means of production—is one of the least pertinent of all the issues of modern economic policy. Public ownership of industry would not assure full employment under conditions of stability, nor much change the problem of achieving it. It would not guarantee the highest possible rate of economic progress, nor make it easier to secure the cost advantages of improved technique and more efficient management. Nor would Socialism as such necessarily lead to more equality in the distribution of incomes than prevails in many capitalist communities which use modern death and income taxes. Neither economic theory nor economic history suggests that the public ownership of productive property is a significant part of any plans realistically addressed to the elimination of unemployment and social insecurity, and the achievement of steady increases in the standards of living. Public ownership may sometimes be an easy escape from otherwise insoluble dilemmas of private monopoly, or of widespread bankruptcy in a declining industry, such as the British coal industry, or the railroads of many countries. But it has nothing to do with the general problem of keeping the resources of a modern economy fully and usefully employed, either in the United States or in the Soviet Union.

It is one of the gayer paradoxes of political controversy that "Keynesism" is a recognized heresy in the demonology of Communism, ranking with Bukharinism and Bebelism, and just below Trotskyism and Titoism, as offenses against the faith. It was one of the damaging charges leading to Earl Browder's expulsion from the Communist party, even though the unfortunate Browder denied having read the British economist.

The Communists have good reason to treat the work of Keynes and other modern Western economists as a threat to their orthodoxy. For Keynes' writings, and the wide literature of which they are a part, rest on a core of generally agreed ideas about how to manage a capitalist economy. If the economists are right, the premises of Marxism are wrong. In their universe, as Galbraith sums it up, "instead of revolution there would be a budget deficit." [5] This challenges head on the familiar Marxist argument, widely accepted during the last few generations, that the capitalist system suffers from "inherent contradictions," galloping monopoly, and progressive impoverishment of the working classes; that it cannot be reformed in a socially acceptable way; that it has so far managed to survive only by promoting wars; and that unless it is replaced by a form of Socialism, it will end by destroying civilization in an orgy of unemployment, Fascism and war.

If this series of propositions is denied, the Marxist cause loses the appeal of its intellectual conviction. It abandons even the pretense of being what it claims so often to be— the only "scientifically" correct interpretation of history. It becomes a naked call to class warfare. Without its theory of economics and of history, Marxism breaks contact with the tradition of rational humanism, from which Western life has drawn so much of its moral force, and its impulse for self-improvement. The somber and dedicated fanatics who man the world-communist movement say, and in all probability believe, that the existing order must be overturned because it can produce only suffering, exploitation, and tragedy. No attack on their position can hope for success without confronting this premise.

In dealing with modern problems of economic planning and control, Marxism is a sterile literature, offering nothing —a body of dogma, not a useful technique of analysis. Yet its influence is strongly felt among men of all classes. It has spread erroneous ideas, especially about the relation of gov-

5. *The Affluent Society*, p. 67.

ernment to industry and of wages to profits, which often militate against effective action in dealing with the problems of managing modern societies. And in Europe and Asia the incubus of socialist ideas has been one of the most important causes for the relative failure of socialist governments during the postwar period.

That failure is one of the melancholy events of the century. Socialists took office in many countries at the end of the war. Generally humane and well-intentioned men of the democratic tradition, they had long since ceased to be revolutionary ogres and had become symbols of progressive aspiration. Despite some remarkable achievements in advancing welfare, however, their administrations have not been notably successful, especially in stimulating growth. Quite often, they were prisoners of their own doctrine and therefore unable to rally working class support for more promising programs of liberal progress. The rank and file of the socialist parties are historically suspicious of their leaders, who more than once have followed the example of Pierre Laval and Ramsay MacDonald. For this reason, socialist leaders have had to devote time and attention to proving their loyalty to party principles, and especially to the cause of nationalization. Too often these doctrines have impaired their view both of domestic and of foreign policy, committing them to high wages and excessive inflation at home, and occasionally to pacificism or myopia abroad. The relative failure of socialist governments heightens the risks of even more extreme political divisions in many countries of Europe and Asia.

For the economic theories of Karl Marx are by no means the only, or even the most important, sources of strength of Socialism as a political movement. In many countries, but luckily not in the United States, political parties committed to the program of Socialism have been successfully identified in peoples' minds with the yearning for equality. The protest against inequality is a smoldering political emotion. From time to time it becomes a call to arms, which may erupt as Jacobinism or worse. Americans have been spared, in large part, the divisive influence of a party system which splits the country into Disraeli's two nations of the rich and the poor. The illogical American party system, which requires most issues to be compromised within the parties, and not between them, is a strong force for unity within American society. But other countries have not been so fortunate.

It is a curious fact that capitalism is an idea which does not stir much passionate feeling among the mass of the people. The general opinion, as Tocqueville observed, seems rather soberly and passively acquiescent in capitalism, not affirmatively enthusiastic about it. "Wall Street" is not an expression of love and affection in the ordinary vocabulary of the American people. Even the official priests tend to be rather apologetic.

Yet the capitalist principle in economic organization has been and is a remarkable success. In the material realm it has accomplished a rate of economic growth and an enlargement of social and economic opportunity totally unmatched in any previous stage of history. As a force affecting the conditions of human life, it has been an integral part of a great explosion, which has swept away old forms and permitted a release of creative energy, a degree of freedom for the human imagination, rarely equaled.

These improvements have been achieved at considerable costs. The great migrations of men and classes, both within societies and among the continents, have had their victims. Aristocracies of wealth have not proved obviously superior, save in energy, to those of family or caste. The supremacy of the market as a measure of values has threatened to weaken the power of the ideal in Western cultures. Prolonged depressions exacted their cruel toll. Old age is still too often a period of waste and decay. The incidence of illness falls at random on society, frequently bringing economic and social disaster in its wake.

But, on balance, the record of capitalism is one of extraordinary and general advance. And through its historical alliance with political democracy, capitalism has submitted to its own extensive and far-reaching reform. It took many years of struggle—often of violent, bitter struggle—before the battle was won. But it seems to be safely won today. That fact, so shocking to the logic of the early socialist prophets, is one of the most important features of Western political and economic life. For all their influence, the great chieftains of industry and finance are now docile and co-operative, by and large, in accepting the consequences of universal suffrage.

These comments on capitalism are not intended to suggest that the status quo is ideal, or that American society no longer requires the devoted zeal of its strong reforming conscience. For all the progress which has been made, our situation offers the Puritan spirit plenty of work for the indefinite future. Further advances in solving social and economic problems may well require further extensions of government authority, without establishing a threatening concentration of power in the state. The openness of Western society is a flexible quality. It could survive as many changes in the next thirty years as it did during the last thirty, without ceasing in any sense to be a guarantee of freedom. What freedom could not survive is a genuinely socialist program of massive nationalization, or the development of governmental regulations having an equivalent effect.

In this sense, competitive capitalism is a characteristic expression of the American culture. In all its arrangements, American society manifests a preoccupation with the problem of power. Persistently, almost instinctively, its policy is always to avoid concentrations of authority as a threat to the possibility of freedom. Capitalism stands with federalism, the separation of powers, the disestablishment of religion, the antitrust tradition, the autonomy of educational bodies, and the other major articles of the American creed, in expressing a deep suspicion of authority. Americans are committed pluralists, if not quite anarchists, in their social attitudes, willing to concede to Caesar only as much power as circumstance may require.

The law for the government of capitalism now in process of development has much to recommend it, however, beyond the important but rather negative advantage of not constituting a menace to the possibility of liberty. It should permit something far more exhilarating than a routine and stabilized performance by the economy, grinding out full employment and ample leisure, without much effort, or pride of craft.

The American standard of living is not nearly so high as our national penchant for self-congratulation makes it out to be. If certain components of the standard of living not usually included in the indices are taken into account, it may not even be the highest in the world. Education is a matter of vital concern to every family. Neither the cost nor the quality of public education is reflected in statistics of per capita expenditure for consumption, or most other measures of the standard of living. The American people are beginning to realize that their public education is provided on a mass scale, but that its average quality is below that offered in many other countries. Similarly, if, in measuring standards of living, one counted the low quality of much American housing, the chaos of most American cities, the quality and organization of American health services, and the spotty character of our social insurance, the result might be a wholesome shock to American pride. We do not, of course, measure economic performance in such sensible ways. As Kenneth Galbraith has recently pointed out, fulfilling his duty as our most useful iconoclast since Thorstein Veblen, the statistics solemnly assume that consumer expenditures on tobacco, liquor, and patent medicines have the same social utility, dollar for dollar, as expenditures for essential housing, food, education, or health.[6] They make no distinction between money spent for good or bad housing, for shoddy merchandise, or for overpriced or even harmful commodities or services. Yet even these statistics show an increase of only 60 per cent, or less than 2 per cent a year, in per capita personal consumption expenditures between 1929 and 1957, in constant prices. And in 1957, the average amount spent for consumption by each person in the United States was $1,638, which hardly represents affluence by any standard.

6. *The Affluent Society*, chap. 9.

With a reasonable measure of foresight, energy and luck, however, the next fifty years should permit a substantial real improvement in American and Western standards of living, and a start toward significant improvement in most of the countries of Asia, Africa, and South America. For the Western countries the improvement could well be so conspicuous, in terms even of Galbraith's dour criteria, as to justify calling it the end of poverty as our most important economic problem. For the world as a whole, that target is more remote and far less certain. The difficulty of mitigating the burden of poverty in many parts of Asia, Africa, and South America—indeed, the risk of further declines in standards of living there—is one of the crucial elements of American foreign policy, defining a major future claim against American output.

4. The Economic Claim of Foreign Policy

IN 1944 the chief concern of American public opinion was whether the Depression of the thirties would be resumed at the end of the war. Today, the dominant factors fixing the task of the American economy in the years ahead are the communist assault upon the balance of power and the far-reaching consequences of the end of empire.

It is true that in 1944 a few government officials were already drafting the first precursors of the Marshall Plan and the Point Four program. But the magnitude and extent of the nation's burdens abroad were hardly visible even to experts of good judgment, and certainly not to the public at large.

At this point, problems of preventing domestic depression and inflation, real as they are, are relatively minor aspects of the economic responsibility of the United States. Full employment, price stability, continued social progress, equality of opportunity—these phrases represent ambitions widely supported among the American people. But they should be viewed as subordinate to the imperatives of the continuing crisis in international affairs.

It is difficult to say anything about national security without falling back on words which repetition has already drained of meaning: the "menace," the "challenge," the "threat" of Communism, and of the so-called underdeveloped countries, to the security of the nation. The tale has been told many times, and with rising intensity, because people have been relatively unwilling, during these last few years, to listen at all seriously to the facts about developments in the communist world and in Southeast Asia, in the Middle East, and in Africa. It was so before the shock of the sputnik, and it seems to be so once again, as I now write, less than a year after that severe blow to our *amour-propre*.

Every generation, it seems, has to re-enact the legend of Cassandra. The last few years painfully recall the atmosphere of the thirties, when men tried to arouse the West to the reality of Hitler's purpose. They discovered then what has been so evident recently—that the human mind has an infinite capacity for resisting and ignoring the disagreeable.

The consequence of accepting the most reliable evidence we have about the Soviet world, and about the underdeveloped countries, would be to embark at once upon programs of action more energetic and expensive than any which have been planned or carried out in recent years. Such programs would take many Americans a long way from Main Street and its familiar joys, to spend years of hard work in Africa and Southeast Asia. As a people, we do not seem to have a genius for duty of this sort. Hence we do our best to dismiss or discount the evidence, and to continue in our comfortable course. On the whole, we prefer to stay at home, building our own roads and cars, extending our suburbs, and complaining about taxes.

Nonetheless, our instinct for self-preservation is being stirred by events. Responding to the earnest croakings of several angry prophets, we seem finally to be overcoming the national yearning for ease and "normalcy." For the international position of the United States is most unmistakably serious. The *New Yorker* put the matter very well in a recent cartoon. Two sandwich men met in the street, wearing sandals, white robes and beards, and carrying placards announcing the end of the world. "Have you noticed," one asked the other, "that people don't smile at us any more?"

There are two central focal points of danger: the strength and the purposes of Communism; and the weakness, which in some cases already amounts to decay, of many of the countries which have recently achieved self-government.

More than one-third of the world's population—a group, too, whose rate of reproduction is rapid—is now living under the discipline of Communism. They are working within the shaping patterns of Communism, and being educated by its schools and social order. Gifted peoples, they are being intensively trained to high levels of skill and productivity. Their rate of capital formation is higher than our own. And the capital they are forming is largely military in character or potential. In important areas, the output of the Soviet Union alone already surpasses that of the United States. Within recent years their military establishments have outstripped ours in many categories of strength, and probably in over-all strength. The organization of these hardy, resilient peoples into the hostile phalanxes of Communism constitutes a menace to the balance of world power upon which the primitive safety of the Republic depends. It calls into question every aspect of our future. The communist leaders, having elicited Western rearmament by their mistake in Korea, are now pursuing an infinitely more dangerous foreign policy of slow penetration in the Middle East and Asia, while they chant hymns to peace. Their first goal is to reduce our military forces, and drive them out of Europe, North Africa, and the Far East. Their program has made significant progress in recent years.

Almost another third of the people of the world reside in countries recently freed from the control and guidance of great empires. They, too, are growing rapidly in number. During the last forty years, all the empires, save only the Russian, have been destroyed or weakened, one after another, in consequence of war and the rise of nationalist sentiments. Influenced by our historic attitude toward imperialism, we enthusiastically cheered these developments while they were taking place. In the spirit of 1776, Americans scorn every aspect of imperialism. The American government tends to sympathize with any rebel who wraps himself in the mantle of George Washington, and demands freedom for his people. Our Civil War, almost one hundred years ago, decisively rejected the plausible idea of self-determination for our own states. But we believe in it as a natural right for others. Now, however, some of the costs of epidemic nationalism, both for ourselves and for the world community, are becoming all too apparent.

The two world wars of this century released forces which destroyed the old order of things. The Austrian, Turkish, and German Empires were broken up first, and the Russian Empire lost a few of its peripheral provinces. The succession states created in the name of national self-determination were often weak and unstable, and have proved consistently tempting to aggressors. In the case of Russia and Germany, the old empires were also succeeded by powerful and ambitious home governments, harboring the bitter desire to avenge defeat. Now, in a cycle speeded up by the second World War, the British, French, and Dutch Empires are dissolving, together with the related system of protectorates, mandates, and special spheres of influence which served as the cement of the old structure.

Whatever else may be said of the fading system of empire, it must be conceded in retrospect that it drew many isolated and autonomous cultures into a single world and, all things considered, into a more coherent world than the one which has succeeded it. This is not to apologize for the sins of Empire nor to mourn its passing, but simply to recall that the old Empires performed many functions of great moment to the world community. For all its faults, the old regime permitted us to emerge as a nation in 1783. Between that time and the recent past it permitted us the luxury of breathing, within the context of a world balance of power favorable to our freedom—a balance of power, be it said, which on the whole required relatively small and intermittent military exertions on our part. For long periods of time, imperialism preserved a semblance of order and stability in international affairs. It established an international economy, which encouraged the nations of the earth to profit from the division of labor, and the comparatively free movement of funds, of skills, and of people. That world economy was far more effectively integrated than those which have come since. The Empires brought the powerful ideas and techniques of Western life to every corner of the globe. Ancient cultures like those of Islam, India, and the Orient were set on a new course, and primitive cultures were equally exposed to European life.

The response of the non-European world to the promise and the power of Western science, education, methods of organization, and social outlook has not, of course, been uniform. For all the non-European cultures, contact with the West has been the process of action and reaction, of attraction and repulsion, so vividly described in *Anna Karenina*. As Christopher Dawson recently remarked, the revolt of the colonial peoples against empire cannot be considered merely one of revolt against the influence of an alien, European civilization; rather, it is a more complex cultural movement, involving the extension of Western civilization and of Western international society into the extra-European world.[1] If wisely conducted, this movement could lead to a consensus among all peoples on certain values which in fact they share, despite their cultural diversity. Alternatively, it could produce deeper and more destructive commitments to revolt.

The new states, and the civilizations which nurture them, are living through organic changes of the utmost importance, both to their own peoples and to ourselves. These nations are seeking to add the techniques and ideas of modern industrial life to their own cultures. They are trying to establish institutions capable of accomplishing extremely difficult tasks, outside the patterns of their experience. New classes must be trained, competent to direct ambitious programs of economic and social progress. Capital must be saved or borrowed—hardly an easy job in countries which do not produce much more than the subsistence needs of their rising populations, and countries, too, which often lack adequate banks, securities markets, and financial traditions. All this must be done in the setting of the Cold War, and in an atmosphere complicated by the presence of strong emotional factors—exuberant pride, and surviving hostility to the nations which formerly exercised imperial authority.

These countries have not so far succeeded in raising their pitifully low standards of living very much. Some are going backward in this vital sense—Morocco and Indonesia, for

1. Christopher Dawson, "The Relevance of European History," *History Today*, 6 (1956), 606, 612.

example. Others are progressing, but at rates of growth far lower than those of the West or of the communist bloc. By and large, it is fair to say that the poor people of the non-Soviet world, who are largely colored peoples, are getting poorer, while the rich, in the industrialized countries, are getting richer. The standard of living of the average human being in the world is probably lower now than it was thirty years ago, and perhaps lower than it was in 1900. In a large part, two reasons account for this phenomenon: the spread of cheap and easy public health procedures, and the slackening flow of international investment. It is not difficult to learn how to use clean water, penicillin, DDT, and silver nitrate, although birth control is another matter. And medical knowledge of this kind is being widely applied, reducing mortality, both of infants and of adults. Meanwhile, the flow of capital from the former imperial powers has been cut off, or abruptly reduced; and the other mechanisms of international economic integration are weaker today than they were in 1914.

The combination of these factors defines an ominous problem. It does not take a great deal of imagination to visualize the implications of this trend for world politics in the years ahead.

The realities about imperialism have been more stubbornly and more universally obscured than those of almost any other modern issue of public policy. It is difficult to decide which side in the debate harbored more illusions. And it is hard to imagine a more dramatic illustration of how unimportant economic interest can be, compared with other factors, in determining the course of history.

The countries exercising imperial authority refused to believe what Norman Angell's *Great Illusion* demonstrated in 1908—that empire is expensive and not profitable, and inevitably constitutes a growing drain on the economy and standard of living of the imperial country. The imperial powers clung to their overseas possessions despite the clamor of nationalist ambition and the logic of Sir Norman's argument. Their response to the rising tide of nationalism was to offer the "native" more and more expensive programs of roads, schools, hospitals, power stations, and public housing.

Imperial motivation was mixed, and often mysterious. Pride, romanticism, and a sense of mission and adventure played a part. In this country we brushed the spirit of the movement in Theodore Roosevelt and in the mood of Manifest Destiny. Dreams of military power and doctrines of military policy had an important influence. There were often the vested interests of small but effective pressure groups, and the inertia of long-standing habit. When the imperial countries were pushed out of their colonies at last, their sense of grandeur suffered a shock. But they discovered that they were better off economically than before as a consequence of their withdrawal. The Dutch, the British, and the French are beginning to see what the Swedes and the Swiss have long known, and the Germans have most unwillingly learned —that economically, at least, it is a relief not to have colonies. The standard of living in Britain and the Netherlands has forged ahead dramatically since the war. One of the reasons for their progress is that they have ceased sharing their capital with the people of India, Ceylon, and Indonesia. As an Italian minister recently remarked, "We lost the war, it is true; but in compensation, we lost our Empire."

The economics of imperialism are nowhere more dramatically evident than in the dilemma of Algeria, the most difficult of all such problems the world has yet witnessed, because of the large percentage of Frenchmen in the Algerian population. Even if the Moslems of Algeria were prepared to accept prosperity in lieu of freedom—a most doubtful proposition, since Morocco, Tunisia, and Libya are free countries—it is now becoming clear to people in Metropolitan France how much it would cost them to raise the Arab population of Algeria to the European level. André Philip calculates that while an equalization of living standards between France and Algeria is virtually impossible even to imagine, it would require astronomic French investments in Algeria, risking universal inflation at home, to initiate long-range programs for slowly increasing the productivity of Algerian workers.

The great Bentham summed up the problem in terms which are being debated in France today:

I say, give up your colonies—because you have no right to govern them, because they had rather not be governed by you, because it is against their interest to be governed by you, because you get nothing by governing them, because you cannot keep them, because the expense of trying to keep them would be ruinous, because your constitution would suffer by your keeping them, because your principles forbid you to keep them, and because you would do good to all the world by parting with them.[2]

The peoples who lived under imperial control shielded themselves from the unpalatable truth with equal zeal. They were, and are, convinced that imperialism was largely a device to exploit them economically. With the end of empire they have found it hard to realize how heavily their development had in fact been subsidized. They read Lenin or Hobson on the economics of imperialism, rather than Norman Angell. In their minds it was certain that freedom would automatically make available to them a vast surplus of their own wealth which had been borne across the seas by the rapacious imperialists.

The end of Empire has weakened these illusions, although they are so tenaciously held that the facts may never really dispel them. The peoples newly liberated from imperial control are now, however, confronting for themselves the inherent difficulty of organizing effective programs of economic growth. This process, which derives from and reflects the whole fabric of a peoples' social development, education, and capacity for self-discipline, is hardly an easy one, even under favorable circumstances, as the history of South America abundantly demonstrates. But it must be undertaken. For a great deal of the future depends upon the success of these ventures in accelerated economic development.[3]

2. J. Bentham, "Emancipate Your Colonies!" Address to the National Convention of France (1793), in *Works*, ed. John Bowring (Edinburgh and London, 1843), pp. 407, 417.

3. Of a voluminous literature, note W. W. Rostow, *The Process of Economic Growth*, New York, Norton, 1952; Albert O. Hirschman, *The Strategy of Economic Development*, New Haven, Yale University Press, 1958.

The dissolution of the non-Russian empires destroyed the old political order. We have not as yet been able to replace that order, through the United Nations or otherwise, with anything nearly so cheap, pacific, or stable. The weak and uncertain countries which have recently gained their freedom constitute one of the main theaters for the rivalry of the United States, China, and the Soviet Union. And they are among the principal goals of that rivalry. For the adherence of the newly freed countries of Asia or Africa to the communist group could decisively alter the balance of world power. That possibility will become more menacing when Chinese industrialization gains momentum, as it surely will during the decades ahead. In those countries, at the moment, China and not the Soviet Union has a position of special glamour and prestige because of its relative success, as a fellow member of the non-European world, in launching a program of development under adverse conditions.

In this setting the demand of the nonindustrialized nations for help in their programs of economic development is peculiarly urgent. Peoples of the world who do not yet fully share the methods and skills of Western culture now aspire to its standard of life. They cannot begin to earn that level of subsistence, in any sense, without first forming the institutions, finding the capital, and absorbing the techniques and habits which are essential parts of the procedure for using the secret of modern wealth. Those nations which have not yet gained command of Western technology will not stand passively aloof from the Cold War if their standards of living rise very slowly, or even continue to decline. Their demand for progress is therefore a dynamic—indeed, an explosive—reality in the equation of peace and war. If the West does not help them solve these difficulties through regimes of freedom, their demand to gain ground at least as rapidly as the Chinese will push them strongly toward the alternative of Communism.

Thus far the United States has undertaken to provide some of the subsidies to economic growth formerly paid by the imperial countries. And various efforts have been initiated to revive the pre-1914 flow of capital and of technique through procedures of international cooperation—the Colombo Plan; several United Nations projects; and the proposal that Western Europe take on comparable responsibilities for North and Central Africa collectively. Not surprisingly, the United States has moved slowly and rather sadly in accepting this unforeseen consequence of the end of Empire. Foreign aid programs have had rough going in Congress, despite the pressures of the Cold War. It is fair to say that we have hardly begun to face this expensive prospect in anything like a realistic way.

Opinion polls indicate that the public has grasped the issue more affirmatively than the Congress. The idea of such programs is hardly alien to a people for whom few church services are complete without a collection for the victims of an earthquake, a famine, or a massacre in some remote corner of the world.

To be effective, development programs will require much more than money alone. They will be wasted unless local people and local institutions are capable of using money effectively. And there is little point in exporting capital for development unless we adopt for ourselves a trade policy that could permit development loans to be repaid. The effects of loans can be lost unless they are accompanied by assistance in technical development, including assistance in the arts of governmental administration. Programs of education and of educational exchange are indispensable. Many countries will require all that used to be implied in the idea of sympathetic and active diplomatic support. Others, culturally unprepared for the responsibilities of freedom, or aggressively committed to breaking the normal rules of international comity, may require international receivership, in the form of some politically acceptable modern substitute for the old protectorate or mandate. The Cromers and Lyauteys may in the future wear the uniform of the United Nations. But their day is not done.

This is not, however, the occasion to consider the substance and the most appropriate forms of technical assistance programs, or to discuss the conditions essential to their success. It suffices for present purposes to conclude that the

climactic changes in political organization which have resulted from two world wars make it certain that such efforts
will have to be made on a sustained basis, and will necessarily
involve the United States on a large scale.

Ideally, the task of training and of aid should be conducted
by the family of nations. Those who have already mastered
the techniques of wealth owe obligations of humanity as
well as of self-interest to assist others in gaining these
essential skills. That training should be part of the flow of
influence through which the world community fulfills at
least certain minimal obligations toward the peoples of the
world. These obligations should include far more than the
privilege of having a flag of their own, the trappings of
sovereignty, and a seat in the General Assembly. Freedom
for local autocracy, corruption, and stagnation is not "freedom" within the broad meaning of the United Nations
Charter.

The peoples of many non-European cultures wish to
undergo the experience of adding the techniques and outlook of the West to their conscious and unconscious lives.
There should be international procedures for helping them
through this adventure, without requiring them to give up
their own dignity, autonomy, or integrity. The responsibility
for leadership in what is essentially an educational process
should not depend upon the accidents of discovery or
conquest, centuries ago. Nor should the imperial powers
alone, or the United States alone, bear the staggering costs
involved.

It is most unlikely, however, that the process of development will be carried out through anything like the paths of
international cooperation. It is more probable that the bulk
of the effort will be done in the setting of the Cold War,
through competitive bids of the Eastern and Western rivals,
acting individually or in groups.

This part of the struggle to protect the safety of the nation
against the spread of communist power will be far more
expensive than the existing level of spending for foreign aid.
The communist attack on the old order of international
politics and international law has made great progress in

recent years. It will take an effort of renewed energy, imagination, and boldness merely to recoup the losses which the Communists have inflicted on us in Indochina and the Middle East, in Indonesia and in Hungary. Even more will be required in order to achieve the kind of equilibrium of force, of custom, and of accepted rules which could assure our security in these parts of a most dangerous world.

It is sometimes urged that it is not really necessary for the United States to undertake costly long-run programs of foreign aid. Our foreign policy, it is contended, could safely rely on processes of development within communist societies to transform their aims, and lead them to beat their swords into plowshares. Several American observers conclude that the spread of education in the communist world, and the inherent force of Russian and Chinese cultural traditions, will in the end produce a society of law with which we could easily live at peace.

There are two answers to this contention. In the first place, the cost and magnitude of the problem of economic and social development in the countries newly liberated from imperial rule would not be substantially changed even if the Czar were restored to the throne of Russia. Such an event, or its political equivalent, might reduce the crushing cost of the arms race, but could not exorcise the difficulties faced by the peoples of India, Morocco, or Ghana. And in the second place, the replacement of terror by legality in the communist world could well make their competition more formidable for us, not less, in the so-called "uncommitted" areas of the world.

Both Russian and Chinese history show irregular patterns of alternation between the forms of law in the Western sense and those of oriental despotism. The Russians have never resolved the debate in their national life between the Westerners and the Old Believers, between Peter the Great and Ivan the Terrible, between Dostoevsky and Turgenev. There is a comparable counterpoint in Chinese life, although the "Western" theme is weaker there than in Russia.

After the death of Stalin, the yearning for a more settled, a freer, and a more orderly public life found passionate expression in communist Europe and Asia. Government officials were among those most directly threatened by the practice of Stalinist tyranny. They led the way in denouncing his regime, and looked for security by seeking to restore respect for the guarantees of the formal law. Their initiative encouraged writers and ordinary people to start along the dangerous path of open talk. Even the prudent, cynical caution of those accustomed to living with tyranny yielded somewhat to the intoxication of the moment, especially in Poland and in Hungary. The spirit of freedom spoke up, sometimes with power.

"Destalinization" didn't last long. It led to the revolt in Hungary, and its repression. The pendulum swung back to the side of the despots. Controls over intellectual life were strengthened again; the political police became more active; and a new method of political terrorism, operating outside the machinery of ordinary law, has emerged: the procedure which permits a public assembly of a man's neighbors to condemn him to deportation and forced labor as a "social parasite," for the "malicious evasion of socially useful work" or for living on unearned income. As Leon Lipson observes, the political basis of communist life "necessarily prevents socialist legality, Soviet-style, from meeting the standards of legality upheld by other countries." There can be no sure guarantees against the revival of purge and terror "as long as the party, and the elements of Soviet society striving for supremacy through or against the party, remain unwilling to grant effective autonomy to the legal system, keeping it above the political struggle as a safeguard of general order and liberty." [4]

The pendulum will doubtless swing again, in the direction of a milder and more open dictatorship. But it would be wrong to mistake such a development, however desirable in itself, as a step toward peace or freedom.

The requirements of peace go beyond the achievement of partial or minimal legality in the Soviet Union, China, and

---

4. Leon S. Lipson, "The New Face of 'Socialist Legality,'" *Problems of Communism*, 7, No. 4 (July–Aug. 1958), 22, 29.

their satellites. The Germany of the kaisers, the Russia of the czars, and Imperial Japan before World War II were all countries in which the relationship of citizens to each other and to the state was governed by established rules and procedures of law. These governments did not imprison people without trials, nor punish them save for violating published laws. Yet the rule of law in this sense did not keep them from engaging in acts of international aggression.

An orderly and "legal" new model Communism would be a far more difficult foe in Asia and Africa than the brutal regime of Stalin. Such a communist movement could promise those continents economic progress without the gross forms of tyranny and deceit which now characterize the atmosphere of communist politics.

The missionary dynamism of the communist movement would not end if communist governments learned how to rule without terror. The world will not be safe, and the United States will not be safe, until the growth of law within the communist world includes freedom as well as order alone. The existing monopoly of power within the communist states could be gradually ended in various peaceful ways, if freedom were really to become an aim of government there. Perhaps the simplest would be to invoke the model of the TVA in communist countries: to set up "yardstick" ventures in private business, which would function alongside existing state-owned firms. Such experiments in capitalism could be conducted by foreign or by domestic companies. If a considerable fraction of the nation's economic growth were carried out by enterprises of this kind, the country would soon possess a mixed economy, offering the citizen a variety of alternatives in employment. At that point it could begin to hope for the reality of personal and political freedom. Then, perhaps, there would be some chance that the drive of the communist movement for power would lose its point, and its momentum.

Meanwhile, American foreign policy must continue to rest on a recognition of the fact that the communist movement is strong, aggressive, hostile, and determined, and that it does not lack opportunities for gain, from Formosa to Morocco, and indeed to Latin America.

Thus far this discussion has not referred to the kind of purely military establishment the nation will require, nor indicated the order of magnitude of its costs. Two things in the military realm are now clear. The stalemate in atomic arms imposes upon us the necessity to reverse the trend of recent years. The United States should resume the costly process of maintaining large conventional military forces, in addition to the deterrent power of the Strategic Air Command, or its equivalent in naval or missile power. The second principal aspect of the military horizon is that the pace of science is opening all sorts of vistas—whole new systems of weapons, whose comparative military values are almost impossible to chart. The only prudent course, confronting this proliferation of ideas about the military art, is to try to recover the lead in thought, and in strength, which the West has so recklessly and needlessly given up.

Careful students of the problem put the cost of an adequate military program, in terms of presently foreseeable procedures, at about $80 billions a year, in 1957 dollars—about twice our current rate of purely military expenditure.

Taking the problem of world economic development and the cost of a conservative military program together, it is apparent that protecting our stake in the contest with Communism will take a greatly increased share of the national output. Given that fact, we can hardly expect a relaxed future in governing the domestic economy. There is little chance that our efforts in this field can be limited to perfecting and coordinating the control devices developed during the last generation, so that the nation could enjoy steady and rather effortless increments to its standard of living. It will not be enough to congratulate ourselves on the progress we have made in our domestic affairs since the Great Depression. Nor will it suffice to explain the dynamics of our economy to those at home and abroad who regard it still as the unjust, cruel, and moribund system so vividly protrayed by Karl Marx, Bernard Shaw, Upton Sinclair, and other widely read writers of the last hundred years. To hold its own, and to prevail, the government must have the extremely expensive economic ammunition of modern diplomacy. In order to provide this ammunition, and at the same time preserve anything close to present standards of living, the rate of growth of the American economy will have to be radically increased.

The Primary Tools of Control:
Fiscal and Monetary Policy

THE *chapters grouped in Part II examine the thesis that the first task of fiscal and monetary policy is to regulate the level of spending in the economy, and thus the level of employment. And they seek to describe and assess the chief legal institutions through which that policy can be carried out. With the problems of noneconomists in mind, Chapter 5 will briefly summarize the basis for the view that fiscal and monetary policy can in fact be conducted in ways which help to control the level of employment, and identify the conditions of success or failure in such ventures.*

In general terms, that idea is now accepted orthodoxy among the economists, although it has not yet strongly colored public opinion. Even some businessmen and lawyers close to economic affairs do not fully understand the argument, although they are often aware of its existence and general drift. Yet this approach to employment policy has now conquered the slogans which were long accepted as the basic principles, or at least the rules of thumb, both of banking policy and of public finance. "Full employment" has become more important as a standard of banking policy than liquidity, "meeting the legitimate needs of trade," controlling the price level, or even exchange stability. And it has correspondingly weakened the older maxims of balanced budgets, neutrality in taxation, and the like, which once held the field without challenge in public finance.

The balance of Part II will consider the governmental machinery for the preparation and control of the federal budget, and the present structure of the banking system, as instruments of employment stabilization policy.

5. The Flow of Spending and the Level of Employment [1]

THE CONTENTION that the government and the banking authorities, by turning a few spigots and valves, can govern the volume of aggregate demand, and therefore the level of output and employment, presupposes two key relationships in the working of the economy. It assumes, in the first place, that the Treasury and the banks not only can provide people with the right volume of funds but can effectively influence them to spend those funds. And secondly, it assumes a relatively predictable relationship between the flow of spending, on the one hand, and the flow of goods and services, on the other. The first of these assumptions will be taken up in Part II and the second in Part III, while Part IV will review the propriety of both premises in the light of recent experience.

Assumptions of this order are comforting but dangerous. It is easy to understand why harried students of society, and even more harried practitioners of government and banking, turn to mechanical analogies for aid in visualizing their tasks. A. P. Lerner and other ingenious economists have built machines, full of glass tubes and colored fluids, to demonstrate with apparent precision just how monetary and fiscal agencies can maintain enough demand at all times to assure full employment. And some of the clarifying mathematical models used in economic analysis give an impression of comparable exactitude.

But the social sciences, as Shackle has recently remarked,

1. A chapter primarily of exposition intended for noneconomists. See p. viii, above.

are inherently more difficult than the physical sciences. It is helpful, and probably inevitable, to approach problems by breaking them down into mathematical stages, based on progressively less drastic simplifying assumptions. In the social sciences such simplified versions of reality can never be even an approximate substitute for directly confronting the full range of the evidence. Every theorem in social studies is a function of numerous and complex variables, many of which have the disconcerting quality of changing through time, according to different and often unknown formulae. For the habits and institutions of the economy are by no means passive, stable, and predictable in their response to fiscal and monetary policy. The pressures of high levels of money demand can alter wages and prices in irregular and cumulative patterns, altering in turn the problem confronting the fiscal and monetary managers. Changes of this kind in the response of people and markets to variations in the level of demand may frustrate the intended impact of what the banks and the Treasury have done, or create situations —like several during the last decade—where ineffectual policy must choose between unemployment and inflation as the penalty for its earlier failures.

With this qualification in mind it is permissible to talk about the relationship between goods and money, spending and production, outlays and output—that is, between the aggregate flow of demand and the aggregate supply of goods and services constituting the stock in trade for sale by the business agencies of society. At a given moment of time one can visualize the supply of money being spent both for the current output of the economy and for the output of earlier periods still on hand to be sold—new cars and old ones, new furniture and antiques, Rembrandts or Buffets, land or houses or stamp collections, as the case may be. The larger part of the money available for this purpose is the current income of people, defined as what they have received as wages or profits or rents for the services they have rendered in the production of current output. Part, however, represents accumulated savings, or the realization of capital gains, or the receipt of pensions, social security benefits, and interest on the national debt.[2] Part may be the proceeds of loans, which, if they are bank loans, may in fact be new money, created by the act of lending, and thus a net addition to the flow of funds being spent. The total amount available for spending—current earnings plus all other funds—is the source of market value for what the economy produces. When money is spent for currently produced goods or services, it becomes part of the new national income, whether it originated as wages, a veteran's bonus, or the contents of a safe deposit box.

From the point of view of national policy the most important part of this process of exchanging money for goods and services is that which involves the current output of the economy, as distinguished from transactions concerned with output produced in earlier periods. This is the subject matter of the familiar "gross national product" and "national income" statistics—the flow of economic goods and services being currently produced, and of the incomes earned in producing them.

Every year people work—with their hands, with the soil, with machinery, trucks, and tools. They work alone or in groups, as corporations, as partnerships, or as individuals. Every year they produce an infinite variety of things—food and transportation, shoes and locomotives, books and songs, gadgets and widgets. What they produce may be sold for final consumption, as food is sold to the housewife. It may be sold to be used in making something else, as iron ore is sold to a steel mill. It may be sold to be added to inventories —the stock of goods held by business for later sale—or it may not be sold, but remain on manufacturers' shelves as part of their inventory.

The market value of what is currently produced for final use by business or by individuals is the "gross national product." "Market value" is used in a practical sense. It means only the total of the prices actually paid for all the things and services provided every year by the factories

2. The latter four items are not counted statistically as part of the national income because they are not payments for a contribution to current production. See below, pp. 75, 77, and 81.

and farms, the theaters and the doctors' offices, the railroads and grocery stores of the economic system. In addition, it includes the market value of goods added to inventory in the period being measured. Adam Smith called this total or aggregate the nation's economic "dividend," and it is technically defined as "the national product."

The identification of current production within the larger mass of property being bought and sold is desirable for several reasons. First, it distinguishes capital, or wealth, from income, and permits a sense of reality and perspective about the availability of resources over longer periods of time. Part of current production is added each year to the nation's stock of wealth, in the form of buildings, machines, and inventories of goods to be sold later. It is useful for many reasons not to confuse what the economy can produce, in the form of new output to be consumed or used in capital formation, from the capital it has on hand from earlier periods of production. Secondly, producing the national income is the chief economic function of people in their current employment. The policy of maintaining high levels of employment therefore implies a policy of seeking to make the current output of the economy a maximum—that is, to obtain as valuable a yield as possible from the intelligent current use of the nation's natural resources, and its inheritance of capital, organization, skill, and habit. This goal is the first economic problem of any responsible government. Thirdly, the development of the statistical series which provide rough tools of accounting for the current economic performance of the economy has improved our opportunities for studying the behavior of the economy, and for making both private and public policy decisions more rational and effective.

The idea of the national income has two sides—the national income as money earnings, and the national income as money spending. The total amount spent for current production fixes its market value, the gross national product. That volume of spending therefore simultaneously determines the income earned in producing current output—counting profits actually accrued, as well as wages and salaries, as current earnings. From the point of view of the economy as a whole, what is taken in as revenue from the sale of current output is also a total of the costs incurred in its production, if profit be counted as a cost attributable to capital and management as one of the factors of production. Hence the familiar accounting identity of the market value of current output as the total of earnings and costs attributable to its being produced. This identity is the basis for the national income statistics which permit a reasonably concrete view of the economy as a whole, and therefore constitute the starting point for stabilization policy.

These two ways of measuring national income—as a total of spendings and as a total of earnings—may at first conceal the events and decisions which lead to changes in the level of national income, and thus determine whether times are good or bad. Whatever is spent for currently produced output becomes somebody's income, obviously enough. But all that is earned as part of the national income is not necessarily spent in turn, either for current output or for anything else. Nor is there any good reason to assume that the total shift of money to and from hoards, savings, and other liquid balances will always keep the total of spending for current output equal to the prior level of incomes earned in producing it. Such a balance could come about only if the forces of speculative uncertainty and of monetary management, in combination, succeeded in establishing an interest rate which, confronting the real marginal efficiency of capital, produced just the right amount of investment—a most unlikely feat.[3]

That people may spend more or less than their current incomes for current production is the crucial mechanism of business fluctuation.

If spendings for current output fall below the previous level of income, there is not enough purchasing to clear the market at the previous level of prices. Receipts will not cover the costs incurred in producing the output. Profits drop, prices sometimes fall, and less will be produced. Employment, of course, falls off also.

3. See below, pp. 87–89, 188–90.

If, however, the total of spending for current production exceeds the prior level of incomes, an excess of purchasing pushes prices and profits up. So long as unemployed resources are available—or equally, so long as there are resources less profitably employed—the prospect of high profits can draw them into use. The pressure of purchasing which is "excessive" in this sense can result in higher and more productive levels of employment.

If spending for current production equals the prior level of incomes, the economy as a whole should be in equilibrium, at least while wages and other direct costs remain unchanged. The amount of buying clears the market at the prior level of prices and, in the short run, at the prior level of profits as well.

When the economy is so fully employed that increases in output are difficult to obtain, even though prospects for profit are high, spendings in excess of the prior level of incomes will merely generate erratic rises in prices and in profits, and then in wages too. The situation is that described in the popular cliché as "too much money chasing too few goods." Under such circumstances, the volume of spending represents an attempt to live beyond the real means of the economy. People bid for more than can be produced and offered for sale. Big construction projects may have to be postponed or even abandoned before they are finished, because component parts cease to be available, or become prohibitively expensive. Wages are pulled up all over the economy, as business searches for manpower, and draws it from less to more productive employment; they may be pushed up, too, since a boom is a favorable time for labor negotiation. Society confronts the classic case of general inflation beyond the limits of full employment.

Many factors can result in a level of spending different from the prior level of incomes. In one sense, the flow of money spending is independent of the flow of production and of earnings. Most of the money people have to spend for current production accrues to them as part of the national income, for their participation in the process of producing the gross national product. Most, but not all.

The government, for example, may pay its bills with money it has printed, or created in more subtle and conventional ways. If it follows this course—and in financing deficits it usually does—the volume of spending for currently produced goods and services rises automatically. The banking system, whose structure is described in Chapter 8, can accomplish the same miracle in financing the deficit spending of private borrowers. Within wide limits fixed by law it may lend them more than it has received as customer's deposits, thus enlarging the flow of spending. On the other hand, the government may take in as taxes more than it pays out as salaries, wages, social security payments, or the cost of purchasing supplies. If its surplus is kept idle, the flow of spending drops. Similarly, banks, insurance companies, and other financial institutions may lend customers less than they have taken in from depositors. Thus they would in effect "hoard" some of the funds entrusted to them as savings, and reduce in turn the flow of expenditure and of income-receipt.

There are other forces which may alter the level of spending, without regard to the course of production. People may change the rate at which they spend their liquid balances, or sell bonds, stocks, or other capital balances in order to finance spending for current output. If they expect prices to fall, they may stop using current income to finance the purchase of current output, and sell securities in order to hold cash or government bonds. Contrariwise, if they expect prices to rise, the public may rush to buy goods and securities, using idle balances, and borrowing more, to finance their purchases. In this way, changes in public opinion about the future course of the economy may result in far-reaching changes in the level of spending and of security prices (and thus of interest rates), without the benefit of any prior decision on the part of the government or the banking system.

The flow of newly produced goods and services—the "real" income of the country—on the other hand, can only be increased by more work, or by improvements in methods of work. People can work longer hours. Their skill can be improved by additional training. The labor force may be enlarged by immigration, by attracting the unemployed or schoolboys or women or old people to the factories, or by shifting people from less to more productive occupations. The extra waiters at the Waldorf, whose attentions behind the tables give diners an agreeable sense of luxury, can be drawn into some other employment. Or the army of advertising experts whose ingenuity persuades people to buy one brand of toothpaste rather than another might be cut down to enlarge the actual production of toothpaste, or of other things. Finally, and most important of all, actual production may be slowly increased by more and more intensive use of machinery, and more and more effective organization and management. There are clear limits to the possible expansion of the real national income, set by the size and talents of the population, the proportion of the population of working age, the availability of resources, and the willingness of people to work rather than to keep house, study, enjoy leisure, and so on.

While the physical and social limits of total possible production are evident, it is sometimes forgotten in discussing them that work is done for money. When people and resources are unemployed, increases in the flow of money income may bring about quick increases in the flow of goods and services. Money added to the flow of incomes, if spent, may make it profitable for businessmen to hire more workers, and to produce and sell more goods. When the economy is fully employed, increases in the flow of money cannot elicit increases in the flow of goods, and therefore they cause price rises throughout the economy. Whether or not the economy is fully employed, contractions in the flow of money spending may lead to price falls, or contractions in the flow of goods, which may be desirable or undesirable, depending on circumstances. In these ways, the national income in money and the national income in goods, while influenced by separate forces, deeply influence each other.

One way of attempting to portray the relation between the national income in money and in goods is through the

use of index numbers. The money value of current production in current prices rose from $104.4 billions in 1929
to $440.3 billions in 1957, or almost 321 per cent. While the
actual physical output of the cars and food, the clothes, and
the new houses which compose the national product rose
less than 321 per cent, the task of measuring changes in real
output is not altogether simple. A good deal more than half
the apparent increase consisted of the illusion of higher
prices. If one could compare the price of things in 1929
and in 1957, it would be possible to estimate the increase
in physical output. Such comparisons, however, are difficult
to make. Many new products have appeared since 1929,
and even where products remain the same, their quality
alters. On what terms can the Model T or the Model A
Fords be compared with a 1957 car? And the proportionate
weight of different commodities in the total of expenditures
has changed. Ingenious attempts have been made to present
national income statistics in terms of the price levels which
prevailed in any given year, so as to permit a close measure
of changes in physical production and in real welfare associated with changes in the level of money income. Table 1
and Chart 1 present the results of one such calculation.

Although the general notion of a national income or
dividend measured both as the total of current earnings
and of spending for current output is a simple one, there
are formidable problems in trying to calculate it statistically.
National income statistics are usually given on an annual
basis. In the United States they are an official responsibility
of the Department of Commerce. Private and governmental
economists work together on the task of measuring national
income, and important efforts are being made to clarify
national income accounts and to put them on a uniform
basis, both through the United Nations and through the
efforts of the Western nations cooperating in the Organization for European Economic Cooperation.

The official statistics of the United States define "national
income" as "the aggregate earnings of labor and property
which arise from the current production of goods and
services by the nation's economy." National income esti-

TABLE 1. GROSS NATIONAL PRODUCT OR EXPENDITURE IN
CURRENT AND CONSTANT PRICES, 1929–1958
(*billions of dollars*)

Period	Total Gross National Product in Current Prices	Total Gross National Product in 1958 Prices
1929	104.4	201.0
1930	91.1	182.0
1931	76.3	168.3
1932	58.5	143.1
1933	56.0	139.5
1934	65.0	152.9
1935	72.5	168.3
1936	82.7	191.7
1937	90.8	202.5
1938	85.2	192.8
1939	91.1	208.8
1940	100.6	227.0
1941	125.8	264.1
1942	159.1	299.4
1943	192.5	335.7
1944	211.4	360.0
1945	213.6	354.1
1946	210.7	312.2
1947	234.3	311.8
1948	259.4	323.7
1949	258.1	324.0
1950	284.6	351.6
1951	329.0	379.6
1952	347.0	393.3
1953	365.4	411.1
1954	363.1	403.2
1955	397.5	435.4
1956	419.2	446.1
1957	440.3	451.1
1958	436.7	436.7

Source: *Economic Report of the President* (1959), pp. 139–40.

mates count the payments made to residents of the United States for labor or property they supply to the process of current production. This sum includes wages and salaries, profits, dividends, rents, and interest—the earnings of farmers and coupon clippers, of workers, civil servants, and professional people. In current usage, it does not include payments by the government of social security benefits or of

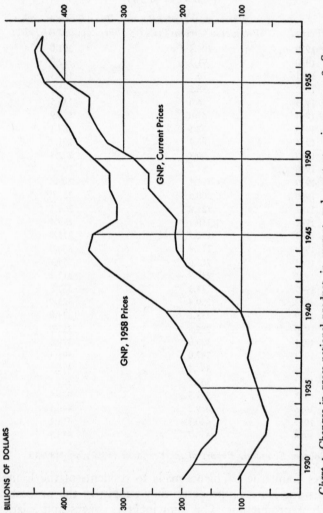

Chart 1. Changes in gross national product, in current and constant prices, 1929–58. Source: *Economic Report of the President,* 1959.

benefits or retirement payments to veterans, for these are not payments for a contribution to current production. On the other hand, employer contributions for social insurance or for private pension or welfare funds, or for workmen's compensation, are counted as compensation received by employees, in addition to their wages or salaries, for their contribution to current production. The fees paid to directors are included in national income on similar grounds. Interest payments on government debt have been excluded from the national income (and product) series, on the ground that since most of the debt was created to finance wars and current expenditures rather than durable capital of permanent usefulness, interest payments on the debt are not made for "the current use of economic resources."

The other side of the national income balance sheet measures the total value of goods and services currently produced, officially the national product. It is given both in gross and in net form. The gross national product is defined as "the market value of the output of goods and services produced by the nation's economy, before deduction of depreciation charges and other allowances for business and institutional consumption of durable capital goods." Net national product reduces this sum both by the amount of capital destroyed and not replaced during the year and by the value of output required to maintain existing capital. There are deductions for the estimated value of the goods and services destroyed by fire, collision, and other accidents. Equally, the Department of Commerce deducts the estimated amount needed to maintain existing capital and to offset its depreciation, and the value of capital outlays charged by business as current expense. The measure of depreciation and capital consumption is no more than an approximation at best. For many purposes the gross national product will be a more significant figure than the estimate of net national product. In trying to calculate how much output is available for transfer to war purposes, for example, the gross national product is more relevant that the net, since one may use for war a good deal of the output which normally would have gone into the maintenance of existing capital. One can allow houses, cars, schools, and office buildings to run down, if need be, in order to enlarge a war effort.

One basic step required in the calculation of the national product is the elimination of double counting. Coal is produced, and is used in making coke, which is used in making pig iron, which is used in making steel ingots, which are used in making steel sheets, which are used in making cars. The price ultimately paid for the car includes the prices paid for coal, coke, iron, steel ingots, and sheets previously produced, and used in the course of the manufacturing process. If the values of each component were counted separately, many items would be counted repeatedly, and the final figure for gross national product would not represent the value of production in the period being measured. Therefore the figure of gross national product excludes the value of products used up by business in the accounting period. It includes the market value added to the products used at each stage of production by the labor, management, and organization of the producing business at that stage. It measures the dollar value of the "final" goods and services produced—that is, the goods and services purchased for ultimate use, not for direct consumption in the production of other goods.

There are a good many activities which are not part of the market process of exchange for money. Most of these activities are therefore not counted as part of the nation's economy in the national income and product statistics. The value of the unpaid labor of housewives, for example, is not included in the national product figures, although the statistics do include the value of housework done by paid servants and the rental value of homes occupied by their owners. And no attempt is made to estimate the amounts paid for the illegal pleasures of gambling or prostitution, or the profits of crime, although money earned in providing or performing these services is subject to the income tax, when it can be discovered by the Treasury.

A large part of the difficulty in measuring the national income arises from the fact that national income accounts distinguish income from capital. The national income statistics exist to measure the value of current production and the total of earnings arising from current production. They must, therefore, separate transactions which affect current production from those which represent transfers or changes in the form or value of existing wealth. The growth and sale of crops, for example, are clearly part of the process of creating current income; the sale of antique furniture, of real estate, or of stocks and bonds issued in the past are not. But the fertility of the soil may be used up if farmers do a poor job of growing crops. Part of the price paid for the crops may thus represent a destruction of the permanent productive capacity of the soil. And antiques, real estate, or securities may be sold at prices well above the prices originally paid for them. Therefore part of the sales price of the antiques, the real estate, or the securities currently sold may represent an increase in capital values, which is treated as a special form of income for tax purposes in the year it is converted into money by a sale. In measuring national income, however, such changes in value are excluded, since they do not represent current production. On the other hand, the earnings of those in the antique business, the securities business, or the real estate business are payments for currently produced services in making such property available for sale. To take another series of puzzles, the mining of coal or ore, the production of oil or natural gas, or the cutting of timber are all transactions which in one sense represent a use of capital rather than the production of current income. Except for timber, resources of this kind are irreplaceable once they are absorbed in current production, and timber can be grown again only over a long period of time. National income figures must also take into account the fact that every year part of the national wealth is destroyed by accident—by flood, fire, or hurricane, for example, or by accidents on the roads, railways, or airlines. During the war the sinking of ships was for this reason reflected in measuring annual production.

Profit measurement for national income purposes requires some arbitrary decisions. Profit for tax purposes is not necessarily profit in calculating national income. The national income figures include an inventory valuation adjustment, which records the difference between ordinary business accounting for inventory profits, and the standards of the national income accounts. Ordinary business (and tax) accounting treats changes in the book value of inventories as part of profit and loss, usually according to some acceptable rule of accounting practice. For the purposes of national income calculation, the figure for profits is corrected by eliminating the difference between the change in the book value of inventories [4] and the change in their value at average prices during the period. In this way only the average current market value of the physical change in inventories is counted as part of the national income. Similarly, the Department of Commerce does not treat other changes in capital values, even when realized, as part of the income of the firm. For this reason, "Corporate Profits before Tax," shown in the National Income Table, are corporate earnings accruing to residents of the nation, exclusive of capital gains or losses. The national income statistics do not, however, count the depletion charges made in mining, lumbering, or other extractive industries as corporate costs, to be deducted before profits, as the Bureau of Internal Revenue does. The reason for this practice is that the value of newly discovered natural resources is not treated as "profit" in the year of their discovery. It would therefore be inappropriate, for national income purposes, to deduct the amount by which the capital value of exhaustible resources is reduced by extraction, when no entry is made for changes in the size of that stock of capital, accruing during the year as a result of new discoveries, or as the result of the growth of forests. While this decision is a common-sense way of coping with the problems presented by the oil and gas industries particularly, it introduces a substantial distortion into the measure of income over long periods of time, for it tends to conceal the fact that some current income in fact represents a consumption of capital, and will in the future reduce capacity to produce.

Indirect taxes, such as the excise tax on cigarettes or liquor,

4. Nonfarm only.

are included in the price of goods sold. Unlike income taxes, they are part of the value of current output, and are included in calculating both gross and net national product. On the other hand, they are not considered to be direct payments, like wages or dividend payments, for a service used in the process of current production. The total of indirect taxes is therefore included in the national product figures, but excluded from the computation of national income. Similarly, because transfer payments, like social security benefits or interest on the national debt, are not viewed as payments for contributions to current production, they do not appear in the national income column, as income paid to individuals, but do appear in the separate calculation of personal income, which also excludes corporate profits and taxes.

Government purchases of currently produced goods and services are counted as part of the gross national product at the prices actually paid.

It would be remarkable if national income measured by adding up earnings turned out to be exactly the same as national income measured as the total value of goods and services sold, at market prices. Different statistics are used, of imperfect coverage at best. And many of the adjustments required necessarily permit wide margins of error. Nonetheless, the statistical discrepancies between the two measures are not great. And for all their imperfections, the calculations accurately reflect both trends and the approximate relations among the different sectors of the economy. So long as they are computed in a uniform way year after year, they permit an approximate measure of changes and of the pace at which they occur.

For policy purposes, theoretical problems in establishing and refining national income statistics are less important than the factors which cause these series to change through time. After all, these columns of numbers chart employment and unemployment, stagnation and progress. They provide the most direct available means of identifying the forces which

TABLE 2. PERCENTAGE DISTRIBUTIONS OF GROSS NATIONAL PRODUCT, 1929–1957

	1929	1930	1931	1932	1933	1934	1935	1936	1937	1938	1939	1940	1941	1942	1943
Gross Nat. Prod.	104.4	91.1	76.3	58.5	56.0	65.0	72.5	82.7	90.8	85.2	91.1	100.6	125.8	159.1	192.5
Personal consumption expenditures	79.0	71.0	61.3	49.3	46.4	51.9	56.3	62.6	67.3	64.6	67.8	71.9	81.9	89.7	100.5
% of GNP	75.7	77.9	80.3	84.3	82.9	79.8	77.7	75.7	74.1	75.8	74.4	71.5	65.1	56.4	52.2
Gross private domestic investment	16.2	10.3	5.5	.9	1.4	2.9	6.3	8.4	11.7	6.7	9.3	13.2	18.1	9.9	5.6
% of GNP	15.5	11.3	7.2	1.5	2.5	4.4	8.7	10.2	12.9	7.9	10.2	13.1	14.4	6.2	2.9
Net foreign investment	.8	.7	.2	.2	.2	.4	−.1	−.1	.6	1.1	.9	1.5	1.1	−.2	−2.2
% of GNP	.8	.8	.3	.3	.4	.6	−.1	−.1	.7	1.3	1.0	1.5	.9	−.1	−1.1
Gov't purchases of goods and services	8.5	9.2	9.2	8.1	8.0	9.8	10.0	11.8	11.7	12.8	13.3	14.1	24.8	59.7	88.6
% of GNP	8.1	10.1	12.1	13.8	14.3	15.1	13.8	14.3	12.9	15.0	14.6	14.0	19.7	37.5	46.0

Source: Department of Commerce, National Income Supplement, *Survey of Current Business*, July 1958.

TABLE 2. PERCENTAGE DISTRIBUTIONS OF GROSS NATIONAL PRODUCT, 1929-1957 (Continued)

	1944	1945	1946	1947	1948	1949	1950	1951	1952	1953	1954	1955	1956	1957
Gross Nat. Product	211.4	213.6	210.7	234.3	259.4	258.1	284.6	329.0	347.0	365.4	363.1	397.5	419.2	440.3
% of GNP	100.0	100.0	100.0	100.0	100.0	100.0	100.0	100.0	100.0	100.0	100.0	100.0	100.0	100.0
Personal consumption expenditures	109.8	121.7	147.1	165.4	178.3	181.2	195.0	209.8	219.8	232.6	238.0	256.9	269.4	284.4
% of GNP	52.0	57.0	69.8	70.6	68.7	70.2	68.5	63.8	63.3	63.6	65.5	64.6	64.3	64.6
Gross private domestic investment	7.1	10.4	28.1	31.5	43.1	33.0	50.0	56.3	49.9	50.3	48.9	63.8	68.2	65.3
% of GNP	3.3	4.9	13.3	13.4	16.6	12.8	17.6	17.1	14.4	13.8	13.2	16.1	16.3	14.8
Net foreign investment	−2.1	−1.4	4.6	8.9	2.0	.5	−2.2	−.2	−.2	−2.0	−.4	−.4	1.4	3.4
% of GNP	−1.0	−.7	2.1	3.8	.8	.2	−.8	−.1	−.1	−.5	−.1	−.1	.3	.8
Gov't purchases of goods and services	96.5	82.9	30.8	28.5	36.1	43.4	41.8	62.6	77.5	84.4	76.6	77.1	80.3	87.1
% of GNP	45.6	38.8	14.6	12.2	13.9	16.8	14.7	19.0	22.3	23.1	21.1	19.4	19.2	19.9

(small errors due to rounding off)

Source: Department of Commerce, National Income Supplement, Survey of Current Business, July 1958.

alter the volume of spending, and therefore of employment and production.

At any time, people have money to spend—money they have received as income; their liquid savings; money they can borrow from friends or from the banks; money they can raise by selling assets. Some of their money they spend directly, with some they pay taxes, and the rest they hold, or entrust to banks or insurance companies, or use to buy securities or real estate or other assets. By tracing the way in which people dispose of their money, one can isolate the elements which cause variations in the level of spending, and hence in the flow of income.

The statistical presentation of the national product divides all spending into four chief categories: these are consumption, purchases of goods and services by government, private domestic investment, and net foreign investment. Table 2, above, indicates the percentage divisions of the national product among these categories during the last two decades.

The largest part of spending is devoted to personal domestic consumption—the purchase of food and clothing, recreation, and refrigerators, the services of doctors and fortune tellers, and other goods and services directly put to their final use by consumers. A considerable and latterly an increasing share of current output has been bought by government, both state and local. Government required 8.2 per cent of current production in 1929, 46.0 per cent in 1943, 12.2 per cent in 1947, 14.7 per cent in 1950, 19.0 per cent in 1951, and 19.9 per cent in 1957. Net foreign investment—the balancing item reflecting the impact of foreign economic transactions on the American economy—accounts for a small but by no means a steady part of current output. And finally, private domestic investment—the sum of private spending for new houses, machinery, factories, office buildings, and inventories—constitutes the most acutely variable class of outlays and the most important private source of general fluctuations in the level of employment and output.

The first broad category of spending to which income and other funds are devoted is that of spending for the services of the government. People pay taxes of all kinds in steadily increasing amounts. Total tax collections of the national, state, and local governments of the United States were over $60 billion in 1950, $79.2 billion in 1951, and $115.2 billion in 1957. Of course, they are rising. Quite apart from the problem of military spending, the long-term political trend is increasing the number of functions of government. Social security, education, research, and welfare services keep growing. The passage of time will greatly increase the costs of social insurance. For several vital community services, most notably for education and health, it is apparent that public expenditure has fallen short of meeting urgent needs and is failing by an ever greater margin to meet desirable community standards. And in many fields —the construction and management of highways and air fields, for example—government has taken over activities of a type which once were the province of private business. Currently produced goods and services costing $41.8 billion were purchased by all units of government in 1950, absorbing slightly less than 15 per cent of the gross national product; in 1951, the total rose to $62.6 billion, 19 per cent of output; and in 1957, to $87.1 billion, or almost 20 per cent of output. This figure includes purchases of goods and service for transfer under foreign aid programs.

If government expenses are met from current taxes, there is of course no surplus or deficit to initiate considerable changes in the flow of over-all spending. But the effect of even a balanced budget on the national income can be significant. If, for example, there is unemployment because the amount of saving is greater than the value of investment, at previous prices,[5] taxation which converted such savings into government expenditures could raise the level of total spending and help end unemployment. On the other hand, the tax system can make even a balanced budget deflationary if it reduces private spending by more than the amount of government spending. And a balanced budget to finance *increases* in government spending can raise the gross national product even when it is entirely neutral in

5. Henry C. Wallich, "Income-Generating Effects of a Balanced Budget," *Quarterly Journal of Economics,* 59 (1944), 78.

its effects on private spending—that is, when those who pay the additional taxes have about the same habits in spending and saving as those who receive additional income as a result of government spending, if it comes about quickly enough. There are secondary factors to consider: the effect of taxes on costs and incentives, for example, and of government spending procedures on the rate of turnover of funds. But in the first instance the arithmetic of government finance in relation to national income is a matter of balancing the amount taken from the flow of income as taxes against the amount returned to that flow in cash payments as the salaries of diplomats and mailmen, the checks received by farmers, and the amounts paid for mimeograph machines, carbon paper, atomic bombs and the other essential tools of modern government. The actual budget figures of government do not immediately show the relation of its financial activities to the cash flow of income. Many items of government expenditure—interest paid by the Treasury on bonds held by the social security system, for example—do not represent a return of funds to the stream of income. And some taxes, like the estates tax, may be paid with funds that might not otherwise have been spent. The Bureau of the Budget and the Treasury therefore publish figures which attempt to present the effect at least of the federal government's taxing and spending activities on the cash position of the public. And other estimates have sought in greater detail to determine the impact of governmental finance on the flow of incomes.

As has been pointed out, it is comparatively easy for the government, by calling on the banking system for new money, to add to the stream of income more than it has withdrawn as taxes, or as the purchase price of the bonds it has sold to the public. In relation to the actual flow of cash expenditures governments, and especially the federal government, can withdraw from the stream of income either more or less than they put back as expenditures. Federal tax practice is such, for example, that the federal government almost invariably operates at a large cash surplus in the first quarter of the year, so that some slackening of business in the second quarter seems normal.

The second circuit of expenditures, the savings-investment circuit, is by all odds the most sensitive, complicated, and important of the four. The terms "savings" and "investment" are commonly used in various ways, often as equivalents. They will be employed here to distinguish two aspects or phases of the process of capital formation. Current "saving" is defined as the amount of the national income not spent for consumption or paid as taxes. "Investment," on the other hand, is defined as expenditure for that part of current production reserved for use in producing future production—new machinery, construction, and the value of additions to inventory. People often say they "invest" their funds when they buy securities or real estate. Such acts are usually forms of "saving," as that word is defined here, but not of investment, since they do not involve spending for the purchase of currently produced capital goods.

It is apparent that "saving" and "investing" in these two senses are different kinds of acts, which may be carried on by different people and are influenced by different motives. Saving is the sum of all the decisions of people and corporations to abstain from spending current income after taxes for consumption—the amount put into banks or insurance companies, into the securities market, or into a box under the mattress. Sometimes savings are spent directly for permanent equipment to be used over a period of time. A man may buy a new house, or a company new machinery. Despite the importance in recent years of investment spending financed with corporate profits, corporations go to the banks, to the securities market, or to insurance companies for a large and variable part of the funds they need for capital purposes. Individuals borrow from their relatives, from banks, or from pawnbrokers. There are three principal categories of private domestic investment expenditure in the national product statistics: spending for construction, which includes houses, factories, stores, barns, and other buildings; spending for producers' durable equipment—machinery, trucks, railway cars and locomotives, and the like; and net changes in the value of inventories. When money is actually spent for investment purposes, it reappears, like other spending, as income in the hands or bank accounts of those who work in steel, construction, machine tools, and the other capital goods sectors of the economy. The effect of saving and of investment expenditures on the flow of incomes therefore requires a comparison of the amounts withdrawn from income as savings with the amounts returned to it as investment spending in all forms.

The most striking characteristic of the saving-investment circuit is that it is never in balance. To a considerable extent, decisions about saving and investment are made by different people and for different reasons. Even when saved income is spent directly for investment goods, motivation is different for the two parts of the process. High profits may accrue to a corporation, for any one of a number of reasons, resulting in high savings. But the corporation may leave its profits idle.

In dollar volume the amount spent for investment purposes is rarely if ever the same as the amount in dollars accumulated as savings out of income in the preceding period. The amounts of money returned to the income stream through investment spending may be greater or less than the dollar amount previously withdrawn from it as individual savings, or as corporate retained profits and depreciation reserves. Consumers and private business may be operating, like the government, at a "deficit" or a "surplus" in their relation to the flow of income. Thus variations in the level of spending for the investment goods part of the gross national product drive the value of the gross national product above or below the previous level of incomes.

The quantities involved in private domestic investment transactions are large and extraordinarily variable. Gross private domestic investment in the United States has varied from 1.5 per cent of the gross national product, in 1932, to 16.6 per cent in 1948, 12.8 per cent in 1949, 17.6 per cent in 1950, and about 14.8 per cent in 1951. In 1954, it was 13.2 per cent, then rose by 14.9 billion in 1955 to 16.1 per cent. Changes of $10 billion or more a year in the amount spent for such purposes have been not uncommon from year to year in the postwar period.

The relationship between the dollar volume of savings

and the dollar volume of investment spending in successive periods of economic activity is the most powerful single business force determining the level of national income and the state of trade. When for any reason, or for no particular reason, businessmen anticipate a drop in profits, their spending for inventory will fall, and then their spending for equipment and for plant. The amount of investment spending may be less than the number of dollars originally set aside out of previous income as savings. New issues of securities fall off. Bank loans are repaid. Balances remain idle, inventories build up, and unemployment spreads from the capital goods industries to the whole economy. National income drops, and goods cannot be sold at their previous prices. Unless the banking system or the government intervenes to offset the fall in national income, or business expectations change for other reasons, a downward movement may begin, and spread. Most of the economic literature about trade cycles consists of speculation about how and why investment spending sometimes outstrips and sometimes falls behind the available volume of current saving.[6]

The spending of money for consumption purposes presents fewer short-run problems of policy than the other three circuits of expenditure. People rarely fail to spend the bulk of their incomes for consumption purposes. In fact, a considerable part of the population manages to spend more than its income for consumption. Consumption has recently absorbed 65 per cent or less of the gross national product, as compared with 75.7 per cent in 1929 and 84.3 per cent in 1932, when investment had fallen off drastically, and only 52.0 per cent in 1944, when the war engulfed a large fraction of output. These variations, however, were largely, although not entirely, the result of changes elsewhere in the economy —in the last few years, the share of output requisitioned by government for defense purposes. They do not represent major shifts in the pattern of people's disposition to consume.

Studies of the relation between peoples' consumption habits and desires and their incomes show a tantalizing ambiguity. Enough is known to throw doubt on the hypothesis that

6. See below, pp. 112–26.

people insist on consuming a fixed or a rising fraction of their incomes, as they move up the income scale; or, alternatively, that they make such decisions in terms of "real" consumption rather than consumption at current prices. Consumers are not equipped with slide rules, and tables of price deflators. They react slowly even to gross changes in the price level. Still, variations do occur, although their scope and motivation are still obscure. It is fair to say that while the flow of money toward consumption is by no means a fixed fraction of current income, variations in its size are far less significant, at least in peacetime, than variations in government or in investment spending.

The share of their incomes and other funds people spend for consumption roughly represents the way in which they divide their resources between consumption and savings. That choice has a profound effect on a society's possible rate of economic development. Poor societies, existing close to the margin of subsistence, cannot afford to postpone much consumption to the future. Richer countries may find the share of income spent on consumers' goods increased, at the expense of progress, by taxation, the fear of inflation, or other social forces affecting the motives for saving. If taxes rise, people may prefer to cling to their standard of living rather than to the pace at which they prepare for illness, old age, and death.

The proportion of output which is directly consumed is affected by the level of private investment activity. If less is spent for investment purposes than has been saved, the gross national product will fall, but the share of it given over to consumption may rise, since the absolute amount consumed is likely to fall less than the drop in the national product. On the other hand, investment may be so high as to outstrip the volume of previous savings. Financially, this excess of investment spending, the private investment "deficit," may be met by bank loans or by a more active use of cash holdings. In "real" terms, however, the investment can be carried out only if goods and labor are made available. A bank may create some new money for building a house, but the house will not be built unless the borrower can find lumber, nails, and carpenters. When carpenters are unemployed and industry has unused capacity for making nails, investment may increase without cutting down the absolute amount of consumption, in the first instance. When, however, there is little possibility of increasing supply immediately, high levels of spending for investment purposes often bid resources away from consumers by driving prices up. Domestic servants leave home to work in factories. Steel and lumber is bought for factory or office building construction at prices which discourage home building. Throughout the economy the boom in capital goods may absorb goods which consumers might have bought at lower prices. Some economists like to identify this effect of investment spending in excess of previous savings as the "forced saving" of higher prices. The effect of the process is like that of voluntary saving, in that an inflation of the money supply for investment purposes permits labor and other resources which would have gone to consumption to be transferred to investment activities. The early postwar years saw the share of output devoted to consumption drop below 70 per cent of the gross national product, while the rate of private domestic investment for the first time outstripped the record pace of the period before 1914. This extraordinary rate of growth was achieved by a considerable degree of "forced savings." The same phenomenon of "forced saving" can be imposed by the government, if it chooses to finance its programs by outbidding the public for resources, rather than by reducing personal incomes through taxation.

The flow of expenditure for consumption is a function of peoples' attitudes toward saving. Saving habits represent a variety of sociological and economic forces. Certainly habits of thrift, responsibility, family size, and emulation play their parts. Some studies show immigrant families to be more tenacious savers than native-born Americans. Fears of the future are important. The availability of social and private welfare programs seems to have an influence, as do the general level and stability of interest rates, and other returns for saving. The volume of saving is affected by the level of incomes. It is often assumed that people will save a larger fraction of their incomes as they go up in the income scale. Although this fact is not statistically established, a rise in incomes produces a rise in the volume of savings, even if the ratio of saving to income remains the same. Many economists feel that this phenomenon is a basic cause of instability, in that savings increase during a period of boom just as investment needs may be abating, so that savings may outrun investment and lead to a fall in spending and income. On the other hand, the limits within which people will tolerate variation in their real consumption, accomplished by price increases, are sometimes tenaciously held. When prices rise suddenly, as they did in 1950 after the Korean War started, the percentage of personal saving dropped sharply. The ultimate resistance of people to cuts in their real consumption accomplished by higher prices or taxes may frustrate investment plans, if governments attempt to go beyond the zone of austerity which consumers will accept. Personal savings, which were 5 per cent of disposable personal income [7] in 1929 and a negative figure during the worst years of the depression, rose to 25 per cent during the war years, and since 1946 have ranged from 2.8 per cent in 1947, a year of rising prices and heavy purchases for replenishment, to 7.9 per cent in 1952. Fractions between 6 and 7 per cent have been most characteristic of this period. But such variations do not by any means imply stability of consumer spending. Disposable personal income was $305 billion in 1957, and a fluctuation of 2 per cent in the volume of personal savings involves a variation of at least $6 billion in consumption expenditure.

Variations in the share of national product used for consumption purposes can also be considerably affected by the availability of consumer credit. In the United States the volume of consumer credit rose from about $7 billion in 1939 to $14.3 in 1948, $17.3 in 1949, $42.0 in 1956, and $44.8 in 1957. In 1939, a year of moderate recession, slightly less than 11 per cent of all consumption spending was financed by consumer credits; in 1957, a year of boom, 16 per cent was financed in this way. Personal installment loans

7. Personal income less personal taxes.

of all types have risen from 1.4 per cent of disposable personal income in 1950 to 2.5 per cent in 1957. To the extent that the mechanics of the banking system permit such credit to be extended, either by sellers or by finance companies, in ways which enlarge the total flow of funds, its availability influences the size as well as the composition of the national product. Clearly, changes of $2–4 billion a year in the volume of consumer expenditure is not a negligible element in determining the flow of income. This is true even though such movements in consumers' credit generally follow, and do not lead, changes in employment: that is, a worker obtains credit for the purchase of a car or a refrigerator when he is reasonably sure of his job, not otherwise. American practice in extending credit to consumers is significant, however, in estimating the amount of gross national product which can be diverted to purposes other than consumption.

There is another short-run factor which may lead to fluctuations in the volume of consumers' outlay. When they fear higher prices, people may spend their money more rapidly than otherwise and hold a smaller fraction of their income as cash in their pockets or in bank accounts. Contrariwise, a general conviction that prices will drop may reverse the trend and cut consumption outlays for a time. Factors of this kind, however, seem to be less significant in the area of consumption than in spending for equipment, business plant, and especially for inventory. Nonetheless, consumer purchases in the second half of 1950 showed a definite spurt, apparently in response to the fear of shortages which spread when hostilities started in Korea. And in 1951, after the fear of price rises had been somewhat allayed, the proportion of personal incomes saved rose sharply. While the absolute amounts spent for consumption increased slightly, they rose far less than in proportion to the rise in personal incomes.

The fourth category of spending for the gross national product concerns transactions between the United States and other countries. The international circuit does not involve such large amounts as government finance or private investment, but the importance of variations in it as a causal element in fluctuations of the national income process cannot be exaggerated.

In the national income accounts, international transactions appear as a rather mysterious balance, or net item, called net foreign investment. It is calculated in this way: American exports of goods give Americans claims in foreign currency. American imports of goods give foreigners claims in dollars. The so-called "invisible" transactions are classified as they appear in the international balance of payments of the United States. Dollar payments to foreigners for insurance or shipping, the dollars spent abroad by American tourists, the remittances of immigrants to their relatives in the old country, dividends and interest on American securities owned by foreigners, and the other transactions in which foreigners acquire dollars are put on one side, with American imports. On the other side are listed the various transactions through which Americans earn foreign currencies—interest and dividends on foreign investment; wages and salaries earned abroad; profits from branch factories; and the earnings abroad of movies and musicians. If the net result of international transactions at the end of the year is that Americans have earned more foreign currency than the dollars earned by foreigners, the newspapers call the result an export surplus, or a "favorable" balance of trade and payments.

Viewed differently, such a result means that the United States has given foreigners more goods and services during the year than have been received from them. Whether the difference is paid for by foreigners in gold, which enters the American banking system, or by American loans or grants to foreigners, the immediate effect on incomes in the United States is approximately the same. The United States has made "unrequited" exports. People at home receive incomes for helping to produce and handle the goods and services provided to foreigners. But nothing corresponding to their income has been added to the flow of goods and services which can be bought and currently consumed at home with these money incomes.

In the United States, the effect of the "export surplus" is therefore exactly the same as that of expenditure on a domestic investment project with a long period of maturity, like a great dam. It enlarges money income without enlarging the flow of goods which can be used at home. If all current foreign economic transactions are put together, and as a net result it appears that the United States has earned more foreign currency all around than the dollars earned all around by foreigners, that surplus (the net export balance on goods and services, less the net outflow of gifts) is treated for national income purposes as a net investment abroad. "Net foreign investment" in the statistics measures the share of gross national product shipped abroad (apart from the amounts sent abroad as public or private gifts) in exchange either for gold or for some foreigner's promise to pay in the future. From the excess of exports, the statisticians deduct exports financed by government grants for European and Asian military assistance or economic aid, or by private contributions to relatives or charitable bodies abroad. This deduction is made purely as a matter of bookkeeping, since government aid had already been counted in the gross national product as part of the government's regular purchases of goods and services, and private gifts abroad as part of consumer expenditure. The resulting figure is the net foreign investment item of the gross national product series. If the figure is negative, it represents an addition to the volume of goods and services available for purchase at home, paid for either by drawing on the gold stock or by incurring American obligations to pay in the future. A negative figure means that, apart from governmental and private gifts, the American economy has in effect borrowed from foreign countries, by obtaining more goods and services from the rest of the world than it has currently supplied, and has paid for the excess in a way which does not directly reduce domestic national income in money terms.

In the last few years, the great export surpluses built up after the war have diminished, as foreign production has recovered, and regained its place in the world's markets.

Nonetheless, the United States has continued, except for a few months at a time, to operate at a small net export surplus on current account.

In 1950 the actual current surplus of exports, including both transactions involving goods and services, and "invisible" transactions, was $2.3 billion, having fallen from $11.5 billion in 1947, $6.7 billion in 1948, and $6.4 billion in 1949. At the same time $4.3 billion of American exports was financed under the European Recovery Program and other aid programs, $481 million by private gifts, and about $1.3 billion through the investment abroad of private funds, for a total of $6.1 billion. Something over $3.6 billion was therefore added to the gold and dollar balances of foreign countries during 1950, as American payment for what turned out to be an "unfavorable" current balance of payments, once grants and gifts were eliminated. The net foreign investment item in the gross national product series was therefore negative, in the amount of $2.3 billion. In 1951, the surplus of exports was far greater—about $5 billion, just about matched by government grants of $4.5 billion, $750 million of private investment abroad, and a small net loss of gold.

The stability of these relations after 1951 began to alter in 1957, and especially in 1958, when noticeable losses occurred in the gold stock. These were largely the consequence of adjustments to the measures taken in Europe and the United States to repair the financial damage of the Suez trouble of 1956, and to developing difficulties facing American exports after mid-1957, at a time of continued high military expenditures abroad, and of substantial programs of military assistance. In 1957, net foreign investment was $3.4 billion, representing imports of $20.7 billion, exports of $26.4 billion, and unilateral transfers of $2.3 billion. All three of these figures exclude transfers of goods and services under military grant programs. However, $3 billion of the "import" figures represent military expenditures abroad, through which dollars accrue to foreigners as they do from other forms of American travel abroad, and $1.6 billion of the unilateral remittances represent government grants. Against the net private foreign investment figure of $3.4 billion, there were net capital exports of $4.1 billion, of which the government provided nearly $1 billion. The balance of $800 million was met by small gold purchases and shifts in short-term balances. In 1958, as American exports dropped, the balance shifted, and gold was sold on a considerable scale.

The flows of spending through these four principal channels of the economy are closely connected. The amount spent in one area directly affects demand in the others. People who work for the government or for capital goods industries or for companies engaged in foreign trade all spend their pay checks in the same retail stores, and compete with each other for the same washing-machines, houses, and cars. On the other hand, the demand of private business for investment goods, like machine tools and electrical generating equipment, is based ultimately on the demand, and more particularly on the expected future demand for consumption goods. When the demand for clothing or electricity or travel is high, and profits are made and expected in those industries, limits of capacity appear. New textile machinery is ordered, new generating plants or hotels are built. A high level of demand for consumer goods generates a demand for capital goods. This demand may be met differently in different areas of the economy. A competitive industry made up of many relatively small firms, some efficient, some inefficient, some operating at capacity and others at far less than capacity, may well respond to this pressure differently from an industry consisting of a few large companies. The effect of the demand for consumer goods in inducing demand for capital goods is sometimes called the "acceleration" effect, or "the relation."

Some economists believe that to sustain the private demand for capital goods requires an ever-rising demand for consumer goods. Since capital expansion is needed only when capacity is inadequate, they argue, investment goods will be bought only when consumption is actually rising to or beyond the limits of existing capacity. Physical limits of capacity would require the rate of increase of output to slow down after a quick recovery from depression. It would therefore follow that a necessarily declining rate of acceleration could explain the fall in demand for investment goods at the end of the boom, and constitute the key to the trade cycle.

This position considerably overstates and oversimplifies the problem. There is no doubt, however, that high levels of demand for consumer goods, and high levels of profit in consumer goods industries, do give rise to a demand for capital goods—for expansion, for new firms, and for the replacement and maintenance of existing plant.

There is one particular time relationship between the process of production and the process of distributing income which is of striking importance in causing changes in employment, production, and prices. Wages are paid weekly or biweekly, and raw materials, transportation services, and other elements used in production are paid for at short intervals—usually a month or two at most. Thus in the course of building a new steel mill, a road, or an apartment house income will be received for work done on the mill or road or apartment house long before the new mill produces steel and long before the new road or apartment house can be used. The period of circulation of income, that is, is shorter than the period of production of many goods, and especially of many capital goods. This means that income distributed for work done or goods supplied in the course of a long period of production will reach the market as demand for food, clothing, cars and other current output; or will be paid as taxes; or saved in one form or another, before new production is added to the available flow of goods. It follows that all sorts of economic activities which require a long period of time to complete may exert a leverage effect on the economic system. If newly created funds are used to finance the expenditures, they will generate money income, and the demand for all the things people buy, long before they add to the flow of goods and services that people can buy. The wages of farm hands, for example, affect the market price of consumer goods long before the crop is harvested and sold. Perhaps the strongest leverage effect on the economy is exerted by expenditures which enlarge the flow of money income without ever adding to the flow of goods. In one sense, military spending, or payments for relief, have this character. So, of course, do the building of pyramids or other expensive monuments without economic value. It is this relationship between the flow of funds and of goods which has led some economists to advocate paying minimum personal or family allowances, or raising social security payments, especially during depressions.

If investment expenditure is financed by taxes or by previous savings, there will be no final expansion of the flow of money income, except on one condition. If the rate of saving and spending for investment purposes increases, even though the total volume of spending remains in balance, the change in the character of demand may result in some pressure for expansion during the period of production. The process of mobilization is perhaps the best example of how easy it is, while shifting resources from civilian to military use, to leave civilians with as much money as before with which to bid for a smaller volume of consumer goods.

The effect on income of spending newly created money or money withdrawn from "hoards," and more especially of expenditures incurred in the course of projects having a long period of production, is called "the multiplier effect." It implies that a given addition of spending to the stream of income—whether devoted to consumption, private investment, government services, or foreign investment—may increase the total flow of national income by several times its original amount before it exhausts its pressure for expansion, through increase in savings. Similarly, a reduction in the flow of spending, caused by private or governmental hoarding or by a failure of investment spending to return to the stream of incomes the amount previously withdrawn as saving, can lead to a net reduction of incomes which will be greater than the amount of the original cut in spending. The basic reason for this multiplier effect is that new spending becomes income, especially where investment is involved, more rapidly than output can be enlarged.

As the new spending becomes income in the course of

economic transactions, some of it is held as savings and some in the form of liquid balances. The speed and responsiveness of the economy to such stimuli may depend a good deal on how the form of spending affects businessmen's view of the future. New money added to income as armaments expenditure may lead to an altogether different over-all response than new money spent as an ordinary government deficit started by a tax cut, or by a special tax remission to encourage private investment, or by spending incurred to build a huge regional power development like the Tennessee Valley Authority project, or a publicly owned steel mill, or a subsidy for private housing. Similarly, a fall in incomes originating in a government surplus may show different symptoms from a fall beginning with a drop in private investment or a change in savings habits.

The responsiveness of the economy to a rise or a fall in the level of money incomes—that is, the size of the multiplier effect—varies also with the stage of the trade cycle at which pressure is applied. In the depths of a depression or at a period when people expect the worst, the economy may drop precipitately under the impact of any cut in incomes, and respond slowly and sluggishly to a rise. During a period of buoyant optimism and high levels of profit and employment, it may absorb even considerable cuts in income without breaking stride. At such times, on the other hand, even a small amount of additional income may drive up prices in such a way as to convince people that steep inflation of prices is ahead, thus precipitating a flight from money into goods which could aggravate the inflation.

These interconnections among the different forms of spending are basic parts of the process through which income and economic activity are controlled. The "acceleration" or "multiplier" effects of spending should be taken fully into account in attempting to predict the impact of economic events and in forming policy for the stabilization of income. If one concludes, for example, that the total of incomes and other money receipts by people will fall short by $10 billion of the amount required to maintain high levels of employment at stable prices, it does not follow that $10 billion of

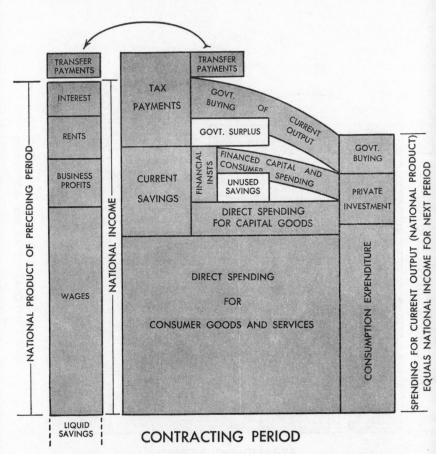

Chart 2 (continued on next page). Flow of spending through (imaginary) time intervals. See pages 101 ff., 144 ff.

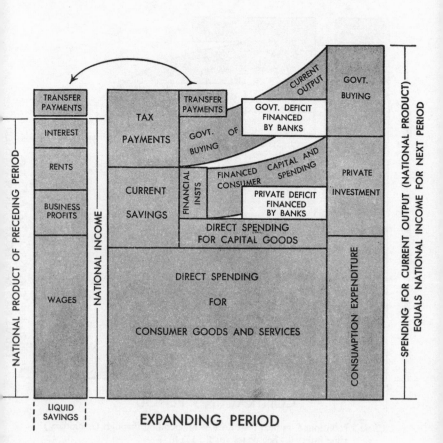

new private or public spending is needed to restore employment. A program for spending, or stimulating others to spend, $4 or $5 billion may be altogether adequate, depending on the size of the multiplier effect which could be expected under the circumstances.

The general character of these relationships is shown in Chart 2, which traces the total flow of spending of the economy through a contraction and an expansion. In the first period represented on the chart, people spend less than their incomes for current production, thus generating a lower income in money. A government surplus accrues, which may or may not be handled in ways which diminish the flow of spending. In the second period, that of expansion, people succeed in spending more than their incomes for current output, drawing on the banking system to finance the deficit. In the first period, financial institutions lend customers less than the savings they have received as deposits, premium payments, or securities purchases. Some income therefore accumulates as hoards of idle funds in their vaults. In the second period, the government and the public raise the total of spending. They may use idle balances, or speed up the velocity of circulation of money. Or they may draw on the banking system to finance their net deficits by creating new money.

The periods into which Chart 2 is divided are imaginary time intervals. The processes of production and of exchange are in fact continuous, and the periods into which they may be divided for analysis merge together. Nonetheless, this analytic device brings out some of the causal factors which can lead to depressions and booms.

Suppose that one could determine the total of all the funds available for spending in any period of time. As indicated on Chart 2, this total consists of a number of elements. First, there would be the national income paid out as costs of production in the preceding time interval—that is, the total amount previously received as wages, salaries, profits, rents, interest, dividends, and other payments for work done or services provided in producing the gross national product in the preceding period. Secondly, some of the funds which can be spent derive from social security

CARL A. RUDISILL LIBRARY
LENOIR RHYNE COLLEGE

and veterans' payments and other "transfer payments" received by individuals, and from interest on the national debt paid out to the public. Thirdly, there might be some new money to be considered, such as newly made bank loans or government loans financed with new money, and any liquid balances which people may have held idle before, and now decide to spend.

The money people have to spend may be spent in one of three ways. Within the period being considered, it may be spent directly for the "final" use of goods or services produced in the preceding period; or it may be paid to the government as corporate or personal income taxes, or other direct or indirect taxes; or it may not be spent for either purpose. If money is not so spent, there are again only three possibilities: it may be hoarded in peoples' pockets or in safe deposit boxes; or it can be put into savings or checking accounts in the banks; or it may be spent to purchase previously issued securities, old houses, second-hand cars, or other forms of property not produced in the preceding period—property, that is to say, which is not part of the gross national product of the preceding period.

By viewing the process of receiving and spending funds in an over-all way, the conditions through which the flow of funds affects the flow of production can be identified.

The first question in analyzing economic conditions at any moment is to determine the over-all relation between aggregate demand and aggregate supply: are the government and the public together spending enough to buy the flow of current output at prevailing prices, or too much, or too little? Suppose, for example, that in each period the government spent exactly the amount it received as tax payments for goods and services produced in the preceding period, and for interest, pension and social security benefit payments. And suppose that the banks, insurance companies, securities markets, and other financial institutions of society provided borrowers, who wished to purchase goods and services produced in the preceding period, with exactly the amounts not spent for that output by those who had hoarded or saved their income, or spent it on goods produced in some earlier period. In order to finance the purchase of newly produced raw materials, machinery, cars, houses, and the like, financial institutions would be lending their clients the amount of the national income not actually spent for the gross national product. If these two conditions as to the behavior of the government and of financial institutions were met, then the amount of money spent for the output of the preceding period would equal the incomes people had received for the contribution to its production they had made, in work or in property, plus the transfer payments they had received. Part of the gross national product would be sold in exchange for national income, part for money received as transfer payments. Financial institutions would have provided borrowers with exactly the amount hoarded or "saved," and in addition enough to balance any net shift of spending in the direction of Old Masters, old houses, or other existing property which was part of the output of earlier periods, but not of the current gross national product.

With these conditions satisfied, the flow of spending for the current gross national product would be in balance. The aggregate of demand for the gross national product, by the government and by private buyers, would equal its value at prevailing prices, and the total of costs incurred in producing it. There would be no pressure from the money side of the income flow to drive prices up or down. If the preceding period had been profitable and people had received profits, rents, dividends, and interest payments as part of their income, that degree of profitability would be maintained. If it was an unprofitable period, marked by unemployment, low profits, and default on interest and rent payments, conditions of balance in the government and financial accounts would not cure the unemployment, or aggravate it. The total of spending would just cover the value of the goods produced, at the same (relatively unprofitable) level of prices. If, starting either with a profitable or an unprofitable situation, the flow of funds were kept stable in this way through successive periods, prices would gradually fall as improved methods reduced costs of production, and more goods could be produced, and profitably sold, for the same total sum.

A good deal of confusion has been introduced into public

and even professional discussion of national income problems by the unqualified repetition of the proposition that national income, measured as the total of costs and earnings, must equal the gross national product, measured as the total value of goods and services. Actually, the statistical methods used by the Department of Commerce are such that national income is not quite the same as either gross or net national product. More important, however, the concepts used, and perhaps necessarily used, in the statistics, while they approach this identity between national income in money and in the value of production, tend to mask the elements which lead to changes in prices, employment, and production.

An analysis of the flow of goods and funds into successive periods, such as that portrayed in Chart 2, separates the process of production, which generates income, from the process of exchange, in which output is sold. Its advantage is to direct attention to the fact that the total of spending may exceed or fall below the prior level of incomes. The behavior of the government or of the financial system or of individuals who decide to change the amount of money they habitually hold idle, in one form or another, can make the total of funds spent for the purchase of currently produced output, and thus the value of that output, deviate from the amounts paid out originally as costs in the process of its production. The value of the output when sold is determined by the amounts of money people have at their disposal and by their willingness to spend such sums for it. In the continuous process of production and sale, through which national income in the technical sense is received, the value of output is altered. Prices rise or fall, because more or less money is offered for goods or services than had been paid out as the costs of producing them.

If these price changes are taken into account, the proposition that national income must be the same as the value of the national product is correct. Price increases increase profits, which are a part of income, and deprive people of the resources they intended to buy when they started for the store with their wages. These unanticipated profits, which arise as the consequence of a more rapid increase in the flow of spending than in the flow of goods, are sometimes called "windfall profits." They are the obverse of "forced savings." Price falls reduce profits and thus reduce national income by the amount of windfall losses corresponding to the fall in the value of the national product.

In this perspective, which is the basis for the statistics, the total value of output is always the same as the total income paid out as costs in producing it. If the government returns to the stream of income in expenditure exactly what it removed from it as taxes, then what is left is divided between consumption and the savings-investment circuit. The value of the current output of consumer goods and services is determined by the share of their incomes people devote to consumption. In terms of this approach, "investment" is defined as the value of the share of current output not consumed—that is, the value of capital goods produced and sold, and the value at current prices of changes in the level of inventories. Within the limits of these definitions, "investment" must be equal to the amount of income not spent for consumption purposes, or savings. This tautology is the meaning of the statement often met that "savings" always equal "investment."

The economists distinguish these two ways of looking at the national income and national product statistics. The method of viewing the process of production and the process of exchange as if they took place in successive periods of time is called *ex ante* analysis. It was developed most clearly by Knut Wicksell and D. H. Robertson. It provides a way of looking at the double process of production and exchange from the vantage point of its beginning. *Ex post* analysis, applied in the later work of Keynes, looks backward from the vantage point of the completed exchange, when goods have been sold (or left on the shelves), and price adjustments have created the corrections which bring about equality between the two sides of the equation. The only way so far discovered to construct national income statistics is on an *ex post* basis. In the *ex post* view, national income and national product are equal, or close to equal, in value. Changes in the volume of spending, whether caused by government policy, banking policy, or the desire of the public to change the rate at which it uses its cash balances, appear in the accounts *ex post* both as receipts and as expenditures —as a price paid for goods and services, and as somebody's income. As in any form of bookkeeping, double entries make the book balance. But the *ex ante* view is indispensable in policy-making. It is more important to isolate the forces which may lead the books to balance at the cost of unemployment, or of quick price rises or falls, than to confirm the fact that the books are always balanced. Hence everyone who attempts to forecast the future is in the difficult position of trying to use statistics based on one theory for the purposes of another.[8]

8. The classic introduction to national income accounting is Simon Kuznets, *National Income and Its Composition, 1919-1938*, New York, NBER, 1941. See also Richard Ruggles, *An Introduction to National Income and Income Analysis*, 2d ed. New York, McGraw-Hill, 1956; Ingvar Ohlsson, *On National Accounting*, Stockholm, Konjunkturinstitutet, 1953; United States Department of Commerce, *National Income, A Supplement to the Survey of Current Business*, 1954; United States Congress, Joint Economic Committee, 85th Cong., 1st Sess., *Hearings*, "The National Economic Accounts of the United States" (1957); Robert M. Biggs, *National-income Analysis and Forecasting*, New York, Norton, 1956; Harold C. Edey and A. T. Peacock, *National Income and Social Accounting*, London and New York, Hutchinson's University Library, 1954; Conference on Research in Income and Wealth, *A Critique of the United States Income and Product Accounts* Princeton, NBER, 1958.

Richard Downing, *National Income and Social Accounts*, Carlton, Melbourne University Press, 1951; *Problems in the International Comparison of Economic Accounts*, New York, NBER, 1957; Organization for European Economic Cooperation: *A Standardized System of National Accounts*, Paris, 1952; Paul Studenski, *The Income of Nations; Theory, Measurement and Analysis: Past and Present*, New York, New York University Press, 1958; United Nations Statistical Office, *National Income and Its Distribution in Underdeveloped Countries*, 1951, *National Income Statistics of Various Countries*, 1945, and *Yearbook of National Accounts Statistics*, 1958; Harry T. Oshima, "National Income Statistics of Underdeveloped Countries: Certain Shortcomings," *American Statistical Association Journal*, 52 (1957), 162-74; Christopher T. Saunders, "Current Trends in National Income Statistics," *Applied Statistics*, 4 (1955), 133-44.

6. Good and Bad Times [1]

EVEN THE MOST cursory glance at the history of output reveals two striking facts in every capitalist country which has successfully employed modern techniques in industry and agriculture. There have been alternating periods of boom and slump in economic activity, and, behind that process of variation, a steady and rather slow process of long-term growth in real output. The flow of money spending has varied a great deal more than the flow of actual production, but both have undergone sharp changes, in a pattern which shows both regularities and wide differences, from one period to another and from one country to another. The broad upward or downward movements of the economy, however they begin, are cumulative, in that they necessarily involve all aspects of economic activity, though with differing intensity. In all, fluctuation in the level of spending for investment goods—for machinery, for buildings, and for business inventories—is far greater than fluctuation in the level of spending for consumer goods. With some variation, spending for consumption seems to be a considerably more stable function of employment and the amount of income.

In addition to changes in output associated with depressions, the pace of long-term growth has itself been altered. The rates at which development takes place has varied greatly, from country to country, and even within the same country at different periods of its history. When a country starts to industrialize, its growth seems spectacular. A new factory will increase industrial output 50 per cent in a

1. While this chapter contains almost as much argument as definition of terms, it is intended primarily for noneconomists (see p. viii). Still, I hope a few economists will read it. And others are warned that it is crucial to the theme of the book.

country which has only two factories to begin with. It takes a great deal of capital formation to maintain even a constant rate of growth in an advanced economy. Moreover, the breakdown of the world economy after the first World War, and its even more complete collapse during the Depression of the thirties, the second War, and the postwar period, has for many countries appreciably increased the difficulty of maintaining earlier rates of investment and growth. The advantages of a world division of labor through trade were slowly eliminated, and international movements of capital were slowed down to a trickle by political insecurity, the experience of defaults, and the increasing autarchy of world markets. In many formerly colonial areas, as was pointed out in Chapter 4, political independence has automatically reduced the inflow of capital that had once permitted a relatively rapid expansion of production.

Many people have believed that the alternation of good and bad times was a necessary part of the process of growth. New industries and new firms displaced old ones. People moved from northern New England to the West, from Kentucky and Tennessee to Detroit. Rice gave way to cotton; the rise of the oil industry brought trouble to the coal fields; the automobile destroyed the carriage business and weakened the railroads. In some unexplained way, men have felt, the sometimes violent and dramatic changes of an expanding economy caused its occasional periods of paralysis and unemployment.

Chart 3 illustrates the main elements of the problem. Here the straight lines represent the rate of improvement in output which could be expected at different rates of technical progress and investment. The curved line measures the actual course of output in the United States, and the extent to which the economy has failed to achieve even its "normal" rate of economic growth. It reflects chiefly the impact of depressions on output—the value of the goods and services which were not produced during depressions. In a rough way, the difference between the curve and the line representing a 3 per cent annual rate of increase in output is an index of the minimal price of ignorance in the management of economic affairs. During the Great Depression of the thirties, for example, the people of the United States could have produced and used goods and services worth at least $275 billion in 1939 prices, more than three times as much as was produced and used in 1929, if the rate of employment had been kept at the 1929 level, and the rate of growth of output at 3 per cent. This figure is only the beginning of a measure of the cost of the Depression.

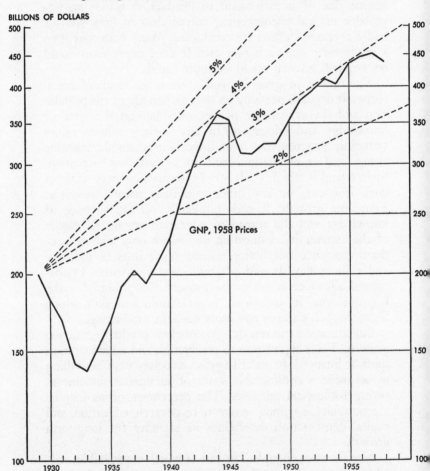

Chart 3. Changes in gross national product, in constant prices, with lines defining uniform rates of growth, 1929–58. Source: *Economic Report of the President,* 1959.

It does not take into account the effect of the American Depression on other countries, whose economies are invariably affected by the upward or downward movement of American business.

Estimates of this kind understate even the economic cost of depressions. If there were no prolonged slumps, the rate of progress would have been higher. A 3 per cent average annual rate of improvement in production is not an immutable natural phenomenon, independent of how well or badly economic affairs are conducted. Many countries have a lower rate, some a higher one. If deep depressions could be avoided, growth could be more rapid.

The rate of progress in production is the result of many forces. It depends not only on the size and age of the population and the availability of resources but on the state of knowledge and education. In any society which values economic progress, the most important economic resource is not land or population, iron ore or coal, but education. Switzerland is a highly advanced industrial country without coal, iron ore, or any other important natural resource. Economic growth depends ultimately on the advance of knowledge and the spread of education among all classes of the community. Education means not only a more productive science but better trained supervisors in industry and a more flexible and adaptable working force. Fundamental advances in education prepare the ground for the improvements in technique, organization, and skill which together spell cheaper and more efficient production.

But education and research do not alone produce economic growth. Their application to production and administration must be financed. In order to grow, a society must be willing to set aside a considerable share of its current income as saving for capital purposes. The percentage of its income a community is willing to devote to research, education, and capital construction determines its capacity for long-term growth.

Nor are these enough. The rate at which improved knowledge is used to reduce the cost of production depends on all the elements of a culture which influence the way people work, their willingness to take risks and to undertake new methods, their choice between security at a low level of production and earnings and insecurity at a higher one. The competitiveness of social and industrial organization plays a part. The freedom of people to change their status —to move from the proverbial log cabin to Wall Street or the White House—is a vital factor. In judging a society's potential for growth, one must take into account its entire structure and all the ways in which it conditions the drives and goals of the people who live in it. The insecurity and tension of life in a competitive society like that of the United States hardly satisfies the philosopher's ideal, from many points of view. Perhaps people were happier in the static towns and villages of the Middle Ages, where the sons of cabinet makers became cabinet makers, and life proceeded in an established pattern of craft and status. There is much to be said for the sleepy rhythm of the French provinces, with their ritual of good food and conversation, their time for the writing and reading of books and for the essential social act of sitting in a cafe. The push and bustle of getting on in the world destroys many values. Even the rich cannot enjoy leisure in America. And the pressure of commerce is deeply felt in science, art, religion, and public life.

But no society, whatever its structure, can have economic progress without investment, research, and education. The slumps reflected in the curved lines of Charts 1 and 3 were primarily slumps in investment activity, most notably in expenditures for machinery, machine tools, buildings, and other permanent instruments of production. Declines in investment spending spread themselves throughout the economy, cutting income and employment everywhere. For this reason, depressions do not involve merely an absolute waste of the output which might have been produced. In a thousand ways they slow up the process of learning and investigation, of experiment, training, and risk-taking, on which progress ultimately depends. A period of prosperity stimulates cumulative advances in science and in business procedure. The history of the patent system confirms the fact that prosperity is the mother of invention. A depression slows down all the factors that stimulate invention and other kinds of economic advance. While a depression puts business under pressure to produce more cheaply, to improve its organization and reduce costs, it also tends to reduce research and other expenditures too often regarded as "luxuries." And most important of all, by forcing much industry to operate below capacity levels, it eliminates any reason for expansion. Sustained periods of investment and development are bound to be more productive than development in fits and starts. They are not interrupted and disorganized at intervals, when a depression cuts all research budgets and destroys or postpones incentives for expansion. The straight lines of Chart 3 therefore understate the rate at which productivity could increase, if high levels of employment were sustained for long periods of time.

What lies behind the fluctuations in the general state of business mirrored in the curved line of Chart 3? Are they trade cycles, or merely fluctuations in trade? Is there a regular pattern of rhythmic, recurring changes, or only a random sequence of movements without a single plan? Whether these movements are erratic or rhythmic, are they subject to control, or must they be accepted as the consequences of some mysterious mechanical flaw in the working of the capitalist system?

Until lately, statistical ignorance about what happens during business cycles has given the economists a free field for speculation. Like everybody else, most economists are disinclined to learn from experience. They tend to find whatever happens strong evidence that they were right all along. The broad movements in the general level of economic activity spur them tenaciously and loyally to repeat the convictions they already hold—especially if they have already expressed their convictions in print. The Socialists among them argue that the alternation of good and bad times is caused by the private ownership of the means of production, and can only be cured by Socialism. Some purists find the Devil in state—and especially in banking—intervention. Once equilibrium in the relation of demand to

supply is disturbed, above all by acts of inflation, an investment boom is unleashed, and prosperity cannot be restored
until the consequent slump has "run its natural course."
Certain classical economists believe that monopoly is the
source of all economic troubles. Departures from perfect
competition make the economy sticky and unresponsive and
ruin the price mechanism, which otherwise would quickly
lead the economy back to full employment. Changes in the
pace of technological development impress some of the most
serious theorists as a fundamental cause both of investment
booms and of periods of investment paralysis. Variations in
the rate of change of technique in different parts of the
economy may produce an imbalance in the availability or
cost of factors which can only be used together—and hence
some unemployment. Men who specialize in labor problems
often conclude that wages are too low and profits too high
to sustain high levels of investment very long. Others contend with equal fervor that a society with strong unions
suffers chronically from wages that are too high and profits
that are too low to stimulate high levels of capital expenditure. Many banking specialists, on the other hand, contend
that the trade cycle is a monetary phenomenon, caused
primarily by mistakes in banking policy, which lead first to
excessive and then to inadequate levels of investment spending. One group of economists finds the clue to the trade cycle
exclusively in the fact that as full employment is approached,
after a period of depression, the rate of increase in consumption slows up, and thus reduces the demand for capital
goods. Economists with a flair for psychology and sociology
have produced other theories. The wavelike movements of
the economy, they say, are started by bursts of inventiveness,
the development of new industries, or variations in crops—
and thus ultimately by the weather, or the sun spots thought
to influence the weather. Mass movements of optimism and
pessimism drive businessmen and bankers along, sheeplike,
into alternate periods of manic investment activity and le-
thargic despair. With a weakness for biological metaphors,
some economists think that the economy has become stagnant
and mature. The passing of the frontier, the end of mass

immigration, and the increased average age of the population, they fear, mean that there are no longer enough investment opportunities in the United States to put savings to productive use. Therefore savings are chronically wasted in sterile hoards, and income has a tendency to fall. The economy is running down, getting old, and cannot be kept going without a great deal of adrenalin in the form of government spending. Or, others suggest, the development of business and legal institutions, with their sometimes irritating mixture of freedom and control, has produced a climate inhospitable to the effective working of the capitalist system. The energy and ebullience of entrepreneurs is held back by the hostility of the public and the government. Businessmen feel frustrated and sullen, scorned on the stage and in literature, and overtaxed and otherwise harried by suspicious bureaucrats. They fail to carry the burden of leadership and initiative in investment required to keep resources fully employed.

The most popular theories of fluctuation, among businessmen and labor leaders if not among economists, are the so-called "purchasing power" or underconsumption theories. These doctrines assume that chronic malfunctioning in the handling of saving and investment keeps the total of purchasing power below the value of output, so that the economy perpetually fails to sustain full employment. One meets propositions like this: "Our problem is not production, but distribution"; "The trouble with the capitalist system is underconsumption"; "Wait till we use up the money created by the war. You'll see then that we'll have another big depression, a hair-curling depression, worse than 1929." While this approach to the problem derives from Malthus and Hobson and has long been a hallmark of radicalism— even of something close to Marxism—it is deeply established among businessmen. The elder Henry Ford espoused the heresy in his time almost as warmly as Walter Reuther does today.

For men of this persuasion, the fatal flaw is associated with the level of profits and savings. Wages are too low and profits too high, they argue. Somehow large profits do not get spent, the total of purchasing power is therefore insufficient to clear the market, investment motives disappear, and the economy slows up.

Dogma of this kind is very hardy. It has a splendid capacity to resist the contrary evidence, in whatever volume. Over a generation, income and estate taxes have risen sharply, redistributing wealth and income; wages and social security payments have increased relative to other forms of income; despite the high profits of inflation, the proportionate number of millionaires has probably been cut. Since the end of the war the economy has gone through thirteen years of boom, marked by recurring shortages of savings, a clamoring surplus of investment opportunities, and rising interest rates. The trade cycle, someone has said, now consists of alternating periods of mild and intense inflation. Facts like these make no difference. The "oversaving," "underconsumption" arguments are repeated as a matter of almost religious conviction. While policy confronts the restless movement of full employment toward inflation, the underconsumptionists of all schools tell us that savings are excessive, purchasing power too low. The economy has an inherent tendency to depression, which can be cured only by higher wages and lower profits, more consumption and less saving, self-indulgence rather than thrift.

The advantage of considering this theory in the perspective of national income analysis is that it disappears. Chapter 10 will examine the most sophisticated version of the underconsumptionist view—whether one rate of investment spending is more likely than another to be self-sustaining, even if backed by adequate savings. But the simpler forms of the doctrine of underconsumption are all dispelled by the arithmetic of national income analysis.

If profits and other forms of savings are not hoarded but spent to finance private and public capital formation, the national income is large enough to purchase the current output of the economy at profitable prices, at least so long as the relationship between costs and prices remains unaltered. If the rate of investment spending outstrips the rate of savings, the aggregate of purchasing power becomes greater than the value of output at previous prices, unless the government offsets the rise by hoarding some of its tax receipts. Prices are pushed up by the rising tide of money demand, and profits increase. When money income rises faster than physical production, high profits make the economy suffer a tantalizing surfeit of investment opportunities. Even though the population is stable and no new industries appear, there are more profitable opportunities on hand than funds with which they can be financed. The economy suffers not from underconsumption, but from undersaving and overconsumption. It is only when the volume of investment spending in all forms is less than the previous volume of savings—that is, when part of saving is hoarded, in effect, either directly or through the banking system—that the level of money income falls below the value of output at previously profitable prices, and losses are made throughout the economy.

The factors which cause investment spending sometimes to outstrip and sometimes to fall behind savings are more complicated than the underconsumptionist view would suggest and, on the whole, have nothing to do with its premises.

The underconsumption theories are invariably arguments to justify higher wages and lower profits. But the case for a more equal distribution of wealth and income is one of ethics, not of stabilization policy—which is not to say it is unimportant, or to be put to one side. If the economy spends for capital purposes as much as has been saved out of income, then the level of saving and investing represents simply the policy choice of that community between present and future consumption—what Keynes once called the choice between having a good dinner now or a better one at some later time. A high level of saving and investing increases the rate of growth of the economy, if the capital is well used. But the rate of capital formation, for all its intrinsic importance, doesn't much alter the character of the problem of stabilization.

The most general version of the underconsumptionist doctrine is associated with the name of the elder Henry Ford —namely that high money wages provide the public with enough purchasing power to permit the mass sale of cheap cars and other things. The proposition is error, root and branch, and on the whole, dangerous error. The Ford wage policy helped to attract a large supply of labor from the Middle South and elsewhere to Detroit, and it was superbly effective advertising for the Ford Motor Company. But small cars could be sold to the working class public at that stage of American economic history because the productivity of labor had advanced, not because Mr. Ford pursued an unusually enlightened labor or business cycle policy. The countries of Western Europe are now actively experiencing the same phenomenon, without benefit of purchasing power theories. If Ford's money wages had been a little lower, the only consequence would have been a slightly cheaper Ford car, just as much within the means of the skilled factory worker, however, as the more expensive counterpart actually produced.

The underconsumptionist doctrine is well summarized in a story Walter Reuther told at Yale in 1958. While visiting a huge new mechanized plant with a Ford vice-president, Mr. Reuther was shown acres of massive machines, sprinkled with a handful of mechanics, where once there had been hundreds of laborers. "How are you going to collect union dues from them, Walter?" asked the vice-president, pointing at the machines. "I don't think that is the real problem," Mr. Reuther replied. "What I want to know is, how are you going to sell cars to them?" Mr. Reuther's view is as old as the impulse which for more than a century has led workers to resist new machines, and sometimes to destroy them. And it is as fallacious. The men who made the machines can afford to buy cars and to pay union dues, just as well as the men who previously had made cars. And if the machines have lowered the cost of making cars, market pressure should sooner or later lead to a reduction in their price.

If the argument of this chapter is correct, there is no one "true" cause of trade cycles. For this reason, like a good many others, I strongly prefer the term "industrial fluctuations," or the French and German words *conjoncture* and *Konjunktur*, to that insidious and misleading phrase "the trade cycle," with its implications of scientific rigor and implacability.

Industrial fluctuations may originate in any one of a number of sectors of the economy. They become cumulative and widespread when an appropriate combination or conjuncture of factors appears with sufficient intensity, leading the whole economy in the same direction. The volume of investment spending may fall below the prior volume of savings because rising wage costs or interest rates have made profit prospects unfavorable; because a speculative orgy and its aftermath have demoralized the securities markets; because political developments have induced a flight of capital to Switzerland or Canada. Or the total of spending may fall, thus making all business unprofitable, because the government has hoarded a large surplus at a time when other sectors of the economy were spending about as much as their incomes. On the other side of the equation, a dozen combinations of factors may induce a volume of spending which either balances or outstrips the prior level of spending, and thereby sets the stage for an expansion of incomes.

It is too late in the day, after the experience of two and a half wars and a whole series of industrial fluctuations, to wonder whether government spending is much different in its economic effect from private spending. Equally, it should be apparent that there is no special virtue in a boom which originates in the investment sector, as compared with one which starts with an outburst of consumption spending. An investment boom has the advantage, mentioned above,[2] of some extra momentum by reason of its phasing through time. But "trickle up" is inherently quite as stimulating to the level of national income as "trickle down." A sudden burst of consumers' expenditure, financed by the use of hitherto idle hoards, could have approximately the same expansionist effects as an increase in investment spending financed with newly created bank loans.

As a matter of experience, however, private investment spending and government spending are the forms of spending which chiefly determine whether times are good or bad.

2. Above, pp. 98–99.

Spending for consumer goods does not change appreciably of itself. On the whole, it responds rather passively to changes in the level of employment and earnings brought about by variations either in government or in investment spending. Consumption fell about 20 per cent between 1929 and 1932, while gross private domestic investment dropped more than 92 per cent. Net private investment became a negative figure, taking into account depreciation and maintenance requirements. From 1933 to 1937, consumption expenditures in constant dollars rose 45 per cent, while private gross domestic investment increased 575 per cent. Between 1937 and 1938, reflecting the depression of that period, consumption in constant dollars fell less than 2 per cent, while private domestic investment dropped by almost half. Between the first quarter of 1956 and the second quarter of 1958, gross private domestic investment fell 34 per cent, in constant dollars; during the same cycle, consumption fell only 2.2 per cent from its peak in the third quarter of 1957 to its trough in the second quarter of 1958. Along with changes in the level of government spending, changes of this magnitude in spending for houses, factories, inventories, and other newly produced investment goods drove the whole level of national income up and down.

Variations in the government's relation to the flow of income can lead the economy up or down just as dynamically as private investment. In a time of some unemployment, government deficits tend to make all business profitable, and stimulate investment as well as consumption. If they are not returned to the income stream, directly or indirectly, government surpluses cut down all forms of income, and may depress the economy as effectively as a shortage of private investment expenditure. Increases in government deficit expenditure during the Great Depression, and more sharply during the years of war and of war preparation, led all parts of the economy upward in response. Government surpluses in the postwar years and in the first year after the outbreak of war in Korea helped limit inflationary movements based on private investment in excess of savings.[3]

3. See below, Chap. 13.

The crucial significance of private investment in the normal movements of the economy becomes more sharply evident when one examines specific indices of activity. Certain series consistently anticipate general turns in the state of business, others change with them, while still others generally follow the larger trends in economic activity. Thus changes in the level of new orders for industrial equipment and machinery and in the record of contracts placed for new commercial, industrial, and residential building have usually come several months ahead of the peaks or troughs in business cycles; changes in indices of profits and employment have coincided with the general changes; and measures of retail sales and of personal income have tended to change afterward. Government action aside, that is, the economy is led upward or downward by changes in private investment, which spread income with cumulative force throughout the economy or cut income down when investment expenditures are insufficient to absorb or offset savings.

The responses of the economy to pressures of this kind have a wavelike quality. Such movements often start with a government deficit or surplus, or with a level of private investment spending that exceeds or falls considerably below the prior level of savings. Consider what happens, for example, when a recovery movement is begun after a depression. Recovery may start with a government deficit, spent for public works, armaments, or relief costs. The process will not be markedly different if recovery begins with a considerable burst of new private investment spending. Retail merchants suddenly discover that consumers have more than enough purchasing power to clear their shelves at prevailing prices. There is an upward pressure on prices and an increase in orders for wholesalers. Unemployed workers are hired; unused capacity is put to work. In many parts of the economy output rises quickly in response to the pressure of demand and the prospect of profits.

If businessmen expect the recovery to continue, with price rises in the offing, they seek to replenish their inventories. Buying for inventories is one of the most sensitive and volatile forms of business spending. It varies greatly at short intervals, almost always in anticipation of a general change in the level of trade. Inventory spending normally moves in the same direction as the general movement, and tends to give that movement a strong push upward or downward. The early stages of a recovery (or of a recession) gain momentum from purchases for inventory, one of the first forms of private investment to respond to changes in economic prospects. While the initial increases of business during an expansion may pull inventories down more rapidly than they can be replaced, thereafter inventories rise quickly and on a large scale. Since business tends to lack cash during a depression, a considerable part of the buying for inventory will be financed by new bank loans, which in turn help to expand the money level of national income, and further the recovery movement.

As the flow of money continues to outstrip the flow of goods, profits rise and generate optimistic views of the future. Investment opportunities appear. Orders for machinery begin to mount. Here and there bottlenecks of capacity appear, justifying outlays for new plant or plant expansion. Mining equipment, electric generating equipment, locomotives, and freight cars are ordered. Rents go up, inducing new residential building. New factories are built; office buildings and apartment houses are planned. Old equipment is replaced at an accelerating pace as the recovery drives up wages and makes cost-reducing investment in machinery more and more attractive. A sustained boom will force gas and electric companies, the railroads, and the telephone system into programs of long-term expansion on a large scale.

As the rising tide of money income draws the unemployed back into industry and as limits of capacity are reached in more and more sectors of the economy, motives for speculation change. Raw material prices may rise sharply as demand goes up, for the supply of many basic commodities cannot be increased quickly. The amount of rubber, tin, or wool available at any moment cannot be changed as rapidly as the output of cars, refrigerators, or television sets. Labor becomes short in many areas, as business competes for a limited number of hands. The wages of unskilled labor commonly rise more in such periods than the earnings of skilled labor, often under long-term union contracts. Industry, operating at advancing costs and with higher inventories, needs more and more credit to finance its operations. New issues of securities are sold to the public through the exchanges, and insurance companies and other lending institutions enlarge their loans. Profits as well as wages are higher, and the volume of private savings rises with the rise in income.

The process of boom develops some limits of its own. The shortage of labor, raw materials, and certain manufactured materials in the face of increased demand generates price rises that make some people decide to postpone their new houses, factories, or machines. The government tries to dampen the boom by collecting more taxes than it spends. As full employment nears, the banking authorities begin to tighten up on credit, because they fear an expansion of money income that could outstrip the possible expansion of output. The banks stop making loans. Interest rates rise. Money becomes scarce, as well as labor and raw materials.

At this point, businessmen turn cautious about their inventory position. They are no longer sure that prices will rise. The absorption of resources in inventory accumulation ceases. Unless other forms of spending increase correspondingly, income and output may fall. A speculative bubble or two may break on the commodities' markets or the stock market, creating uncertainty and even fear as to the future. With rising interest rates, new issues of securities may be hard to sell, or may even remain unsold in the hands of investment bankers.

The characteristic doubts of the peak of the boom can quickly become the panic of cumulative decline. Such a complete reversal of direction is by no means inevitable, however. When inventory booms peter out, construction booms, export booms, consumption booms, or booms based on government purchases may take over and sustain income. If the level of spending of all kinds can be kept high or restored after some drop, the national income in money will be large enough to absorb output at profitable prices. If aggregate spending falls short of the value of output at profitable prices, profits and then investment will begin to drop. What happens most commonly is that a combination of fears for the future affect first inventory and then other forms of private investment spending. Forward contracts are reduced. Backlogs fall off. While income, consumption, and actual investment spending are sustained for some time after the turning point, as existing contracts are completed, a dangerous drop in investment is foreshadowed. After an interval, such cuts in investment spending, coming at a time of high profits and high personal savings, reduce the flow of income and the general level of profits. What happens near this point will go far toward determining whether the downward movement will be quickly reversed, as a minor dip in the chart of economic activity, or be allowed to continue as a downward spiral.

The pattern of events would be more spectacular but not notably different if the government and the banking authorities did not try to restrain and control the boom. If money income continued to rise faster than output beyond the point of maximum possible employment, the erratic price increases of general inflation would soon bring the economy to a grinding halt. Everybody would have money and would want to spend it, in the face of price increases. People would try to build more houses, factories, bridges, roads, and schools than could possibly be made at the same time. They would be bidding hard for available credit and labor. New money created by the banks to finance private or public "deficit" spending, which helped to restore employment during the recovery period, would under these circumstances be a dangerous drug. It could no longer extract more production from the economy, for all resources would be employed. Its effect therefore would be to force up wages, prices, and interest rates rapidly, until their rise began to cut down on investment plans. The self-generated end of an inflationary movement can be among the most destructive economic experiences a society can suffer.

In the past, the level of investment spending usually fell

away after the season of boom had ended in a crash of some kind. The demand for a limited supply of credit, coming from every quarter of the economy, commonly led to severe increases in interest rates and therefore a stock market collapse. The process by which a highly speculative and psychologically sensitive stock exchange adjusts all its prices to a considerable change in the prevailing rate of return on money has often become a wild rout of pessimism, panic selling, and suicide. Energetic gloom on the stock market, in itself, helps to arrest the process of private investment spending, sometimes abruptly. The end of big programs of investment in roads, utilities, railway equipment, or houses may have coincided with a natural fall in inventory purchases. High tax collections may have produced government surpluses which were not returned to the stream of income. A variety of combinations of change in the different forms of spending initiated an over-all drop in investments and then in the total level of income. Such falls spread unless offset. Sometimes, although not always, price changes could help accomplish adjustments which would make investment attractive again. Particularly during the twenties, the banking system proved capable of influencing the level of interest rates and the volume of private borrowing from the banks and the securities markets, in ways which prevented deep depressions.

When a sharp decline in investment spending gains momentum, however, it proceeds with great force. To the public, it appeared as a deficiency of consumer purchasing power. Yet consumer purchasing, and therefore the profits of consumer goods industries, almost invariably fall *after* other indices. Even though the backlog of orders for investment goods declines, employment in the capital goods industries remains high until current orders are completed. Downward movements usually begin when consumer purchases, and profits throughout industry, are at a peak, and consumer spending commonly continues to be high, sometimes even to rise, for months after investment begins to fade.

When business begins to expect price falls, inventory changes again help to accelerate the movement. Sometimes inventories increase briefly at the beginning of a recession; businessmen are caught short by a decline in sales they had not anticipated; their unsold goods add to inventory, although business is falling. Such changes do not last long. Orders are cut sharply and inventories fall more than in proportion to the fall in income. Businessmen calculate that they can replace their stocks if necessary at lower prices. Between 1919 and 1938, the average changes in inventory investment were about 23 per cent of the average increase in gross national product during periods of expansion, and about half the decline in gross national product during periods of contraction. In periods of both expansion and contraction changes in spending for inventory were greater than the changes in other categories of investment spending —for construction, and for producers' or consumers' durable goods.[4]

With minor variations, this seems to be the pattern of fluctuations in the economy. Upward or downward movements start with levels of spending that increase or decrease the national income above or below its prior level. Changes in private investment spending or in the level of government spending are the main causative elements starting such movements. Their effects spread to every category of spending for consumption or investment. Movements of this kind are cyclical only in the sense that all economic activities are interrelated, so that additions to or substractions from the flow of income spread their effects throughout the economy. They are not cyclical, like some cycles in biology, in the sense of being beyond human control. Inventory movements powerfully reinforce the trend in the level of spending. But the crucial elements causing change are the many different factors which influence private investment spending for construction and equipment, or the behavior of the government budget.[5]

4. Moses Abramovitz, *The Role of Inventories in Business Cycles*, NBER, Occasional Papers, 26 (1948), 2; *Inventories and Business Cycles* (New York, NBER, 1950), chap. 21, and table 84, pp. 476–77.

5. For a general introduction to the subject of trade cycles see American Economic Association, *Readings in Business Cycle Theory*, Philadelphia,

From the point of view of policy, therefore, the first problems to be considered are what the government and the banking system can do to offset the tendencies for cumulative movement that are bound to develop from time to time in an economy so strongly affected by the vagaries of private decision.

A well-known economist used to preach that in economics cures were more important than causes. Quinine, he would point out, was a useful drug for centuries before the doctors found out about the habits of the anopheles mosquito. However booms and slumps may start, can they be stopped, once they have begun?

Blakiston, 1944; William Fellner, *Trends and Cycles in Economic Activity*, New York, Holt, 1956; Gottfried Haberler, *Prosperity and Depression*, Geneva, League of Nations, 3d ed. 1941; Alvin H. Hansen, *Business Cycles and National Income*, New York, Norton, 1951; J. R. Hicks, *A Contribution to the Theory of the Trade Cycle*, Oxford, Clarendon Press, 1950; J. M. Keynes, Vols. 1 and 2 of *A Treatise on Money*, New York, Harcourt, Brace, 1930, and *The General Theory of Employment, Interest and Money*, New York, Harcourt, Brace, 1936; D. H. Robertson, *Banking Policy and the Price Level*, London, King & Son, 3d ed. 1932; Kenneth K. Kurihara, ed., *Post-Keynesian Economics*, New Brunswick, N.J., Rutgers University Press, 1955; Knut Wicksell, Vol. 2 of *Lectures on Political Economy*, New York, Macmillan, 1935; Arthur F. Burns, and Wesley C. Mitchell, *Measuring Business Cycles*, New York, NBER, 1946; Robert A. Gordon, *Business Fluctuations*, New York, Harper, 1952; Erik Lundberg, *Business Cycles and Economic Policy*, Cambridge, Harvard University Press, 1957; Joseph A. Schumpeter, *Business Cycles*, New York and London, McGraw-Hill, 1939.

7. The Gyroscope of Fiscal Policy

TWENTY-FIVE YEARS AGO the notion that the federal budget should be managed as the ultimate gyroscope of the economy scarcely existed. A few voices urged large deliberate deficits as the means of recovery. They could hardly be heard in the babel of divergent proposals that promised to save the country. And when they were heard, they were regarded with repugnance as the lowest form of crackpot finance. Only two or three professors—Keynes in England, Hansen, Irving Fisher, and James Harvey Rogers in the United States—sponsored the new heresy. They were supported by occasional mavericks in the business and financial world, and the almost solitary roar of William Randolph Hearst among the journalists. Marriner Eccles, later Chairman of the Board of Governors of the Federal Reserve System, came up with the conclusion—on the basis of his observations as a banker—that the government could spend its way to prosperity. He has testified that he never read Keynes or the other radicals of the day.[1]

Head of a chain of banks in Utah, Mr. Eccles was almost destroyed by the banking deflation of the early thirties. When banks obtained cash with which to meet a run of depositors by selling their assets and calling their loans, he argued, they only made the depression worse by cutting the supply of money, reducing prices, and paralyzing business opinion. As early as 1930 and 1931 he began to urge the banks to fight deflation by expanding their loans. His colleagues thought his mind had been affected by the strain of his tremendous and successful efforts to keep his banks open. Somewhat later, Russell Leffingwell, a distinguished

1. *Beckoning Frontiers* (New York, Knopf, 1951), pp. 131-32.

member of the Morgan firm, expressed similar views, which were commonly taken as a symptom of the dangers to which international bankers are exposed by the intellectual character of their work and the questionable company they have to keep.

Throughout the early years of the New Deal, Eccles was the chief advocate of contracyclical fiscal policy in Washington. His view was not unanimously accepted even within the government, and sound newspapers thundered against it all over the country. Many government officials, including Secretary Morgenthau, continued to believe that a government could best stimulate recovery by inspiring business confidence in the soundness of its finance, and most notably by balancing its budget every fiscal year. President Roosevelt, who had campaigned for economy and budget-balancing in 1932, was a rather unwilling convert to the new idea, and he went through several periods of doubt and even of relapse into the older orthodoxy. So weak was the doctrine of deliberate deficits as the initiating factor in recovery that taxes were significantly raised not only in 1932 but in 1934, 1935, and 1936 as well. Eccles' policy had to be tested empirically, along with many competing plans for economic salvation, before it began to gain general acceptance toward the end of the thirties.

Today the principle of compensatory government deficits or surpluses as the ultimate control over the flow of national income is commonplace and respectable doctrine. It is no longer a hallmark of New Deal "radicalism." It has the support of conservative business and academic leaders; it appears in Congressional Committee Reports and the *National City Bank Letter* as well as in learned journals; in political speeches by Vice-President Nixon and Senator Flanders, almost as strongly as in those of Senator Douglas and ex-President Truman. Economists who differ deeply in their opinions on labor, monopoly, agriculture, and almost every other controversial problem of economic policy find a measure of common ground in supporting the general theory of compensatory fiscal policy. Senator Taft, one of the strong supporters of the Employment Act of 1946, said that government deficits were the "feather-bed" on which we could always fall back in stimulating private enterprise when everything else failed. Whatever might be said of the literary quality of his metaphor, his economic conclusion was clear. During the recession of 1957–58 the Committee for Economic Development, with impressive exactness, called for a tax cut that would produce a federal deficit of $7 billion in the fiscal year 1957–58, thus generating, in its prophecy, an increase of $30 billion in the gross national product.

The idea behind using the federal budget to fight depressions is appealingly simple. Private spending may be greater or less than the prior level of national income, thus causing changes in its flow. When such changes lead to depression or inflation, the federal budget can offset these movements by running at a deficit or a surplus. Balancing excessive dips and spurts in private expenditures, the federal budget could keep the total flow of spending high enough to assure most business a profitable level of demand, without permitting general price rises.

So, at least, the theory runs.

During the Depression President Roosevelt called the federal deficit a way of "priming the pump" of private spending. President Eisenhower, expressing pronounced distaste for the phrase, has accepted the theory. Deficits in bad years, inducing two or three times their amount in private spending, would after a time drive up national income, increase tax yields, and become government surpluses. The budget need not be balanced monthly or annually, but over the course of a trade cycle. Surpluses in good years would balance deficits in bad ones. Contracyclical fiscal policy would not only help to stabilize employment and support economic growth; it would be sound finance in the older sense as well. The government debt would not rise over the long run. The years 1947–57, for example, record a federal surplus of $11.3 billion on a cash basis, and a deficit of $10.7 on an accounting basis. This decade excludes the final phases of World War II and its immediate financial aftermath but includes the Korean War, two recessions, and two pronounced booms.

Of the cash surplus, President Truman contributed $12.4 billion, including four years of surplus and two of deficit, while President Eisenhower reduced the figure by $1.1 billion, with three years of cash deficit and two of surplus. On a budget basis the picture is comparable, President Truman showing a surplus of $3.3 billion, President Eisenhower a deficit of $14 billion. Over all, taking into account the events of the period, the budget record is certainly not a bad one, although the Eisenhower Administration might well have run higher surpluses and retired debt, notably between 1954 and 1956 or early 1957.

The theory of compensatory federal budgets includes another important element. As businessmen become convinced that the federal government will effectively react to bursts and slumps of private spending by budget adjustments, the argument proceeds, it will be less and less necessary for it to do so. Business will base its investment plans on the expectation of federal support for a high-employment level of national income. In that way, steadying business expectations and business spending would itself prevent excessive variations of national income. Experience with successful government stabilization policy would eliminate from business calculations the fear of indefinite expansions or contractions of the national income. That conviction would do a considerable part of the job of economic stabilization.

There is a good deal of disagreement as to when and how government action should be taken in the name of a compensatory fiscal policy. Some believe that the budget should be used as the first of government stabilization tools, others that it should be invoked last, only after banking action has clearly proved inadequate. Should action be taken when unemployment reaches 2 per cent, 5 per cent, or 10 per cent of the working force, on the down side, or when prices have risen 5 per cent, 10 per cent, or 15 per cent, on the up side? As soon as a significant drop or burst of inflation appears, or only after the economy has made supposedly desirable "structural adjustments" to the pressures of inflation or deflation? Should the government run a deficit by cutting taxes, by increasing expenditures, or by taking steps in both directions? Should it run a surplus by increasing taxes or by cutting expenditures? What should the government do with surplus tax collections—retire debt, accumulate deposits, or cut taxes at once?

The problems of conducting an effective contracyclical fiscal policy are only aspects of a government's general program for stabilization. Tactical issues of this order therefore merge inevitably into a series of larger problems. As it changes its tax collections in order to generate surpluses or deficits, as the case may be, the government must decide whether it wishes to have the burden of adjustment fall on consumption or on investment. Similarly, it must decide whether the general aim of its program is to keep "full" employment in the sense of a perpetual shortage of labor, or "high" levels of employment, allowing a small percentage of the labor force to be unemployed, while changing jobs, shifting to new industries, and the like. Should the target of its policy be to stabilize prices, which would permit the national income in money to rise slowly as productivity increased? To stabilize the total amount of national income in money, or the per-capita national income, which would require prices to fall slowly with increases in productivity? Or alternatively, should the government stand ready to use fiscal policy to drive national income and prices up to whatever level was necessary to ensure "high" or "full" levels of employment, taking into account the scale of wages achieved by collective bargaining?

The choice between varying tax rates and varying expenditures is in large part determined by the nature of the federal budgetary process and by the laws and customs which control it. The question of how to organize an appropriate federal deficit or surplus answers itself when one examines the maze of the federal budget and tax laws and the uses to which they have recently been put in the interest of employment stabilization. It is clear that while the federal budget is a powerful engine, it has a stubborn structure of its own. The impact of the federal budget on the economy can be varied quickly only by changing certain key tax rates, notably the withholding taxes of the social security system and the income tax.

The laws and practices governing the preparation of the federal budget have a long history. There are two principal themes in the story: the desire of Congress and the Executive branch to establish every possible safeguard against fraud on the part of those who spend federal funds, and the persistent efforts of Congress to control even honest officials of the Executive departments in the uses to which funds are put.

Both issues, of course, present fundamental problems in government. The second—the primacy of the Congress on money questions—is part of the greatest of all the conflicts that run through Anglo-American constitutional history. Representative government was won in an endless series of battles and skirmishes over the respective roles of King and Parliament, President and Congress, in the raising and spending of money. The American Revolution itself, after all, was precipitated by a quarrel over taxes. No governmental power is more passionately guarded than the legislative power over the purse. The centuries-long struggle of the House of Commons to wrest ultimate authority from the Crown and the feudal nobility of England is reflected in the American constitutional provision requiring all money bills to originate in the House of Representatives, as the branch of Congress in closest contact with the people. Many phases of the present-day problem of the federal budget are colored by the intense emotions of these tribal memories.

The extent to which the power to tax includes control over the power to spend has been a continuous source of friction between Congress and the Executive. After 160 years of imaginative and ingenious effort Congress, the presidents, and the assorted experts who have advised both Congress and the Executive have achieved a budget machinery so complex, so slow, and so thoroughly checked and balanced that it takes more than a year to prepare and pass a normal federal budget. This means that projects for which money is to be spent toward the end of June 1960 were first programmed sometime in the spring of 1958 and approved by Congress during the summer or even the early fall of 1959. On the basis of this procedure, prompt changes in the level and direction of federal spending are not easy to achieve, even by emergency or deficiency legislation.

The consolidated executive budget which the President now submits to Congress each January is a novelty in American government. It dates from the Budget and Accounting Act of 1921, which in turn derives from the Report in 1912 of President Taft's Commission on Economy and Efficiency. Before 1921 the Departments went separately to the committees of Congress most concerned with their work. Expenditures were authorized piecemeal, and there was more than a suspicion that committees competed for jurisdiction, so that Departments could to some extent shop around in the Congress, seeking a receptive forum. At the same time, it was extremely difficult for the President to control policy in his own administration. A strong Secretary of Agriculture, backed by determined Congressional committees, was not notably amenable to Presidential discipline. The present system began, therefore, in the interest of giving the President enough power to keep his house in financial order. At the same time, supervisory responsibility was centered in a single Appropriations Committee in each House, to eliminate conflicts of jurisdiction among Congressional committees and to permit Congress as well as the President to consider federal finances as a whole.

The Bureau of the Budget, the coordinating executive budget agency established by the 1921 act, was originally placed in the Treasury—a disposition reflecting British and French practice. Its strength developed gradually. In 1939, under the Reorganization Act of that year, it was transferred to the President's Office. There it became more than an instrument for coordinating departmental requests for money in behalf of the President's views on sound and economical administration. It has asserted strong positions on the substance of proposed legislative programs, exercising its power under the rule that prohibits any department from presenting its views on legislation to Congress without the prior written approval of the Bureau. And it began to present the budget not merely as a financial document but as a factor in economic stabilization policy, in the perspective of the over-all condition of the national economy. The pioneering work of the Bureau of the Budget during the thirties and early forties was the immediate precedent for the conception of the duties of the Council of Economic Advisers adopted by the Employment Act of 1946—a conception, be it said, which has since spread to Great Britain, France, and other countries.

The Congressional counterpart of the elaborate hearing and review procedures through which the Bureau of the Budget now coordinates the requests for funds of the Executive branch is centered in the work of the Appropriations committees of each House and their subcommittees. Under the Legislative Reorganization Act of 1946 these powerful committees are now equipped with considerable professional staffs. The highly paid and qualified assistants to the Congressional committees have powers of inquiry, and authority to make reports on their own responsibility. Like other features of the Congressional reorganization of 1946, the increase in the size of the Congressional staff seems to have intensified the inherent difficulties of conducting the American government. It has given Congress a more detailed grasp of problems raised by legislation, though not necessarily a better command of their essential policy aspects. At the same time, Congress has tended to rely on its own experts rather than on those of the Executive departments. Since the Congressional experts can most naturally assert their professional independence by disagreeing with the experts employed by the Administration, the result has frequently been to heighten the traditional friction between President and Congress.

In addition to providing the Appropriations committees with larger staffs, the Legislative Reorganization Act of 1946 called for joint meetings of both the Appropriations and the Tax committees of House and Senate. This group of about 100 legislators is admonished by the Act to consider the President's budget proposals and the state of federal revenues simultaneously. By February 15 of each year they are required by the law to recommend to Congress a fixed ceiling on all appropriations for the next fiscal year. So far it has been impossible to make this procedure work. While its laudable aim is to enforce self-restraint on legislators who always have a political interest in getting money spent for their own districts, it is difficult to see how the Congress can bind itself in February not to pass appropriation bills in June.

If an advance agreed limit on appropriations is hard to visualize in operation, the idea of considering taxes and appropriations together, and of reaching an over-all and consolidated legislative budget, has a good deal of merit. Congress has always to contend with the spirit of the late P. T. O'Connor, who explained as the secret of his longevity in politics that in forty years as a member of the House of Commons he had never voted against an appropriation or in favor of a tax.

Reformers have for years urged Congress to go further and adopt the procedure of voting funds through a single legislative instrument, which would correspond in character to the Executive budget submitted by the President. The proposal is long-lived and will certainly be presented again. In all probability it will be frustrated, as was the step in this direction under the LaFollette-Monroney Act, by the residual preferences of Congressmen and their committees for the more flexible habits to which they are accustomed.

The proposal for a legislative budget is considered by many to present grave dangers. It might undo the effects of the reforms of 1921, destroy the Executive budget, and restore Congressional supremacy in budget-making, or even establish Congressional supremacy in administration.

Other issues of budgetary reform have considerable bearing on the efficacy of the budget as an instrument of economic policy—most notably, perhaps, the various proposals to separate capital items from the ordinary budget. It is manifestly a paradox to insist that a dam, useful for a hundred years, be paid for in full out of current taxation. Separate treatment and financing of capital items in the budget should lead to more realistic appraisal of the role of federal expenditures in the economy.

The historic development of the budget-making process

reflects the assertion of several vital policies of government
—the reach for effective Presidential control over the Executive branch, the interplay of Presidential and Congressional prerogatives with regard to the federal purse, and
the development of meaningful administrative procedures
for protection against fraud, the misuse of funds, and waste.
These are realities which dominate the choice among possible alternatives in efforts to use the federal budget as a
means of stabilization.

There has been some development of the practice in appropriation statutes of granting the President discretion as
to the timing and amount of expenditures for specific purposes, in the light of changing economic conditions. Some
housing and highway legislation, for example, has authorized
the President to accelerate or decelerate federal expenditures,
as the state of the economy may indicate to be desirable.
Presidents have sometimes ventured in the same direction
without specific Congressional authority. One of the more
intriguing unresolved problems of the Constitution is the
recurring assertion by presidents that they have discretion
not to spend funds appropriated by Congress when in their
judgment such spending would be unwise. Every time the
claim is made, Congressmen explode with rage: sometimes
the dire word "impeachment" is even spoken. Nonetheless,
the conflict survives, both in fact and in principle, despite
a 1950 revision of the law, which purports to grant the
Executive a limited power, save as to certain reserved subjects, to apportion appropriations and set up reserves for
contingencies, or for savings which become possible because
of "changes in requirements, greater efficiency of operations,
or other developments subsequent to the date on which" the
appropriation was made available.[2] In 1958, in fact, the Pres-

2. General Appropriation Act, 1951, §1211, 64 Stat. 765 ff. (1950), 31 U.S.C.
§665(c)(2)(1954). See, generally, chapters by T. I. Emerson and Gerhard
Colm, in Max F. Millikan, ed., *Income Stabilization for a Developing Democracy*, New Haven, Yale University Press, 1953; A. Smithies, *The Budgetary
Process in the United States*, New York, McGraw-Hill, 1955; Lewis H. Kimmel,
Federal Budget & Fiscal Policy, 1789–1958, Washington, D.C., Brookings Institution, 1959.

ident faced the problem in several areas, most notably in atomic energy and defense, where Congress appropriated more funds than had been requested.

While developments along these lines may well make for somewhat more flexibility in federal expenditure policy over the long run, the division of power between Congress and the President is a fact of such central importance to our political theory as to make radical change in the pattern most unlikely, and most undesirable.

The federal revenue now rests on three primary groups of taxes: the corporate and personal income taxes, producing about 75 per cent of the total; employment taxes, under the social security system, providing a little more than 10 per cent; and customs and excise taxes, which yield approximately 15 per cent. The others, including the much discussed gift and estate taxes, yield only minor fractions of the whole revenue.

All three of these basic tax devices are sensitive to changes in the level of national income. A fall in employment and profits reduces income tax liability. With the development of pay-as-you-go tax collection methods, such a drop in tax liability is quickly reflected in tax payments. Payroll tax revenues fluctuate, of course, with employment. Many of the excise taxes also vary with the state of business. And since American imports of basic raw materials and other imported goods are sensitive to the state of the trade cycle, customs receipts likewise rise in good times and fall off in bad.

The built-in responsiveness of the federal tax system to cyclical change will probably not be sufficient for stabilization purposes under most circumstances without the help of effective monetary action, further fiscal action, or both. If national income falls sharply in response to a cut in private investment spending, and if people expect a severe recession, the deficit arising as a result of the fall in incomes would rarely be big enough to reverse the trend without a change in tax rates. The new money raised to finance the deficit by bond sales to the banking system would be exactly as inflationary as bond sales to finance a public-works program or a military deficit. Its psychological effect might be weaker. Much of it would go for relief or unemployment benefit payments, or subsidies to farmers.

It is sometimes contended that earnings at this level could arrest the depression but hardly turn it into recovery as effectively as actual employment at prevailing wages. While these considerations may affect business calculations and the size of the "multiplier" response to the deficit, if any, they miss the central point. The effectiveness of the deficit as a pressure for recovery depends first of all on its size in relation to the deflationary gap it is designed to fill. Many, including the Committee for Economic Development at an early point in its history, have proposed that these relationships are sufficiently predictable to permit the development of a "Fixed Rule" of fiscal policy. Under such a rule Congress could determine in advance the size of the deficits or surpluses that would be needed to assure a full employment economy without more. This approach is attractive, and the calculations which lie behind it are useful. But the phenomenon of unemployment is a function of too many variables to permit any such degree of automaticity in policy. Richard Musgrave of Michigan and others have the better of the argument in concluding that the magnitude of built-in variations in tax receipts and expenditures are unlikely, without changes in tax rates or unusually effective monetary policy, to reverse downward trends, or to arrest upward trends.[3]

There have been several proposals for delegating to the President a limited power to change tax rates within a specified zone, in the event that inflationary or deflationary pressures develop too fast for full-dress Congressional action. There are analogies supporting the constitutionality of such procedures. The Board of Governors of the Federal Reserve System can alter the reserve requirements of member banks, within statutory limits. And in the field of tariffs the Tariff Commission and the President have long had authority to change customs rates and affect their applicability, on certain

3. R. A. Musgrave and M. H. Miller, "Built-in Flexibility," *American Economic Review, 38* (1948), 122. See Bent Hansen, *The Economic Theory of Fiscal Policy*, London, Allen & Unwin, 1958.

conditions. Some have wondered whether such a delegation would be possible, in view of the constitutional provision that money bills originate in the House of Representatives. The force of this reasoning is doubtful, since it would apply equally to Congress' delegation of some of its tariff powers to the President and to the Tariff Commission.

But in this field, as in others, the issue of constitutional power is not the most important aspect of the problem. The level of income taxes or social security taxes is an extraordinarily sensitive political problem. The President's present power to reduce tariffs has been grudgingly given by the Congress in successive short-term renewals, amendments, and extensions of the Tariff Act and the Trade Agreements Act of 1934. The power of the Federal Reserve Board over interest rates and reserve requirements, great as it is, has the backing of accepted central banking tradition. From the point of view of Congress the delegation of power to the Federal Reserve Board has a further advantage. The powers of the Federal Reserve Board, after all, are not exercised directly by the President, but by a body partially insulated from his influence, and that of his powerful Treasury. There would be far greater resistance to giving the President a weapon so politically appealing as the power to reduce taxes in an election year, no matter how carefully it was hedged about. Congress has been more jealous of its prerogatives in the tax field than in any other. Indeed, it has been the custom to regard tax statutes as so exclusively a Congressional problem as to be all but immune from the President's veto power.

It should not be beyond the limits of reason to reach the goal of flexibility in tax receipts by developing the practice of changing tax rates through a joint resolution of both Houses, or by simple statute. At whatever time of the year such a resolution or statute were passed, it could apply to subsequent withholding tax collections and to final tax settlements for the calendar year, or even to the final tax settlement for the previous year. It could use varying procedures, depending on the situation—a seemingly permanent change in rates, or a tax holiday such as that proposed in 1958 by Henry C. Wallich and others.

The goal of flexible tax rates may be difficult to attain. During the latter part of 1957 and the first six months of 1958, strongly-urged proposals to reduce taxes were beaten back by an inarticulate but powerful coalition of forces, including the Treasury and the principal financial experts of the Congress. The New York *Times* thundered in vain. The Committee for Economic Development issued statements; spokesmen for unions and business demanded action. Economists in high regard, including Arthur F. Burns, formerly Chairman of the Council of Economic Advisers under President Eisenhower, made stern speeches and wrote vigorous Letters to the Editor. All these efforts failed. The remedy of prompt tax cuts, which had proved helpful in dealing with the recessions of 1949 and 1954, was not invoked to shorten the recession of 1957–58.

The President said, "Wait and see." Neither he nor other spokesmen for the Administration advanced systematic reasons to explain their course to the public. In part, their views seemed to be a reaction to the prospect of massive deficits at existing tax rates in the fiscal years 1959 and, perhaps, 1960. Despite the Administration's considerable talent for resistance, military expenditures were clearly rising, in spasmodic response to Sputnik and other public demonstrations of Soviet military and scientific progress. If there would be a big deficit in 1959 anyway, the unstated argument ran, why go to the trouble of cutting taxes in 1958, since it might be necessary to raise them again during the next year? The economic and social cost of the continued recession was not regarded as of sufficient importance to overcome the forces of inertia, and the risks of further inflation a quick surge of recovery might involve. There was a pronounced distaste in some quarters for taking the initiative, and especially for taking a New Dealish initiative.

This positive preference for inaction as a political principle was fortified by certain aspects of the tax problem as a matter of Congressional dynamics. The Ways and Means Committee of the House is in a state of siege. Year after year, powerful lobbies seek plausible changes in the tax law— changes which would favor the interests of influential charities, educational institutions, particular regions, and business and professional groups. The tax authorities of Congress protect themselves, and the fisc, by trying to follow the rule of "no change." Any amendment, however desirable, would put Congress on a slippery slope, they argue. It would be the entering wedge. It would open Pandora's box. Where would it end? Congress would cut taxes ruthlessly if given an opportunity, and no pressure short of war could lead it to raise them. The safer course, therefore, is to stand pat and hope for the best.

The tax policy followed in 1958 is hardly the basis for an adequate and responsible long-run program. The economy requires a counterpoise—a net change in expenditure which can rise when private spending falls, and drop when private spending rises. The administration of federal deficits and surpluses should permit this function to be performed with reasonable ease. Expenditure programming can hardly be carried out quickly enough to permit variations in federal spending to accomplish the larger part of the task of compensation. It follows that the economy requires legal procedures for arranging reasonably prompt changes in tax collections. If Congress remains for long in the mood of paralysis about tax policy which characterized its session in the spring of 1958, it will be necessary seriously to consider the possibility of delegating limited powers over tax rates to the President. A Presidential power to change certain tax rates, which could be exercised only to offset measurable trends toward inflation or deflation, would have at least one attraction to Congress. It could not be charged with opening the Pandora's box of far-reaching statutory amendment. The existence of such a power would protect Congressional committees from having to consider hundreds of attractive proposals for tax reduction, all offered in the interest of curing inflation or recession, as the case might be. A President, of course, is quite as capable of inaction as a Congress. But his failure to exercise a statutory power would be far harder to explain, or to blame on others, than comparable failure on the part of a diffuse Congress, which does not run for office as a single body.

Many economists believe that the federal government should depend entirely on tax increases and tax reductions, rather than on variations in expenditure, whenever a deficit or a surplus is required to keep the national income at the level most likely to produce full employment without inflation. In that way, they contend, the federal government will not spend for the sake of spending, but will undertake only projects regarded as desirable on some assumedly fixed scale of values. Taxation and expenditure policies would be independent. Spending would be fixed by what the community considered it appropriate for the government to do. But taxes would be high or low, depending on the state of trade. During a depression, tax cuts would release funds to the hands of individuals. Their choice of spending goals would direct development into more economic channels than the postoffices, swimming pools, and other monuments which the federal government might build in the course of an anti-depression public works program.

While there is everything to be said in favor of doing part of the job of contracyclical fiscal policy by means of tax changes, on grounds of speed as well as of principle, even severe tax changes could not always do the job of stabilization. If a depression psychology should gain real headway before a tax cut took effect, people might fail to spend that part of their income released by the tax cut, partially frustrating the intended effect of the deficit. Direct increases in government spending in depression may sometimes be necessary in order to be certain that new money actually enters the stream of income payments in sufficient volume to reverse the trend in national income.

Some of those who strongly favor accomplishing the goals of fiscal policy by varying taxes rather than expenditures also feel that if the level of private spending is high enough to support full employment, federal or other governmental projects should be deferred or postponed as a matter of principle. While the general rule of a market economy is that resources should be allocated according to market criteria of profitability, the rule easily becomes a sterile dogma. Quite apart from its basic functions of defense, administration, and public order, many of the tasks allotted to modern government are highly productive. Such a rule of fiscal

policy would carry the dangerous implication that government activities be considered economically less legitimate
than private forms of spending. This attitude can lead, both
in good times and in bad, to a socially inadequate allocation
of funds for education, research, health, conservation, and
other goals not readily submitted to the market calculus.
Some grandiose and imaginative proposals for federal spending, like the Tennessee Valley and other flood control and
power projects, would probably never have been accepted
in the first place had it not been for the fact that in a depression, when men and resources would otherwise have been
unemployed, the real cost of undertaking such programs was
low. Yet many enterprises of this kind, which have made
incalculably valuable social and economic contributions,
could never have overcome the initial resistance to their acceptance except under depression conditions. This is not, of
course, an argument for depressions. But it does illustrate the
risk implicit in regarding the federal budget exclusively as
a device for balancing the flow of national income. Federal
spending has to fulfill many social and economic purposes
beyond its contribution to employment stabilization. There
is much to be said for the regular planning of desirable public
works, which could become more acceptable during even a
mild recession than at the peak of a boom. And there is even
more reason to back Kenneth Galbraith's recent powerful
plea, in *The Affluent Society*, for direct and conscious
support of higher levels of public expenditure for education,
conservation, and the protection of urban capital as good in
themselves.

8. The Flow of Money and the Banks[1]

UNTIL THE RECENT PAST, controversy about the character
of the monetary system was an inflammatory issue in political
life. "Paper money" versus "sound money" was a vital theme
in the debates through which the Constitution itself was
drafted, and narrowly ratified. Jackson and Cleveland, greenbacks and specie payments, Bryan and the "Cross of Gold,"
Black Friday, the price of silver, and "the Crime of 1873"
were passionately argued at every level of politics. The
money system has always been regarded by large bodies of
opinion as a possible cause of the booms, panics, and prolonged and catastrophic depressions which punctuated
American economic history in the nineteenth and early twentieth centuries.

The Constitution establishes the supremacy of Congress
and the national government over the states in this field.
Article I, Section 8 declares that "Congress shall have the
power . . . To coin money, regulate the value thereof, and
of foreign coin." This provision in the Constitution had been
strongly resisted in the name of states' rights. It was regarded
with suspicion by those who feared that the national government would naturally be the ally of creditors against debtors,
and of commercial and financial interests against farmers and
traders. The nominal victory won by the advocates of uniform national law in the drafting of the Constitution was
not followed up by legislation carrying out their purposes.
A truly national currency was not to exist for many years.
The opposition to such action was powerfully based both
on principle and on accident. In this realm the triumph of

1. A good deal of this chapter is an expository exercise intended for noneconomists and nonlawyers. See p. viii.

the Federalists is still incomplete. The banking system, long dominated by local banks operating largely under state law, is to this day a mixture of state and federal elements. Half the banks of the United States—holding, it is true, only 15 per cent of all deposits—are not members of the Federal Reserve System. Their existence and competition in many parts of the country establishes a limit, however, upon the possible range of policy which the Federal Reserve Board may adopt for controlling the supply of currency and bank credit. Moreover, the policy against branch banking has strongly influenced the structure of the banking system, and strengthened the forces of localism in banking.

Since the passage of the Federal Reserve Act in 1913, however, the money issue has changed in political character. No one could now campaign, as Jackson did, to abolish the national banking establishment. The basic machinery of the banking system is universally accepted, although the American Bankers Association attacked the Federal Reserve proposals in 1913 as "Socialism." Controversy has been transferred to issues of policy and structure in its direction.

On the other hand, a conviction has been developing during the last ten years that the Federal Reserve System should be restudied from the beginning, to consider what reforms, if any, are required in its structure to make it a fully adequate instrument of monetary policy in a world of full employment. The President has recommended the establishment of a National Monetary Commission, like the Aldrich Commission, whose labors fifty years ago led to the passage of the Federal Reserve Act in 1913. In default of Congressional action, the Committee for Economic Development, supported by a grant from the Ford Foundation, has now undertaken to make such a study, which should prove to be an act of basic importance in the evolution of the public law. The Federal Reserve System, after all, was established without much concern for the purposes which have now been declared in the Employment Act of 1946. The prevention of "crises of credit" was certainly among the goals which the founders of the Federal Reserve had in mind. But their approach was dominated by other issues, and it would not be surprising if their work, constructive as it has proved to be, required amendment, even basic amendment, in order to adapt the Federal Reserve System to the needs of our time.

The legal structure of the banking system determines the limits of monetary policy. The federal government and the Federal Reserve Board can use the banking system as an engine to pump new money into the stream of income or to suck it out of the income flow, when desirable in the interests of stability. The essential mechanism of the system for accomplishing this result centers on the relationship between the Treasury, the Federal Reserve System, and the commercial banks that are members of the System.

The Federal Reserve System consists of twelve regional Federal Reserve banks, each operating in a designated district of the United States, under the general guidance and direction of the Board of Governors of the Federal Reserve System, which sits in Washington. The members of the Board of Governors are appointed by the President and confirmed by the Senate. They have staggered fourteen-year terms and cannot be reappointed, in practice a most undesirable rule, although it expresses part of the effort of Congress to ensure their independence of political influence. Unlike the officers of the Reserve banks, the staff of the Board of Governors are government employees. The divided structure of the Federal Reserve System was supposed to prevent Washington or Wall Street from dominating banking policy throughout the country. It was hoped that the several Federal Reserve banks would be able to pursue somewhat different policies, if necessary to meet local conditions, and to accommodate the special commercial, agricultural, and industrial interests of the people in their districts. In the great debate which preceded the passage of the Federal Reserve Act, and in the successive debates accompanying each of its major amendments, the banking community has by and large resisted attempts to increase the statutory powers of the Board of Governors. This conflict between local autonomy and centralized authority remains a constant if somewhat diminishing stress in the life of banking policy. In both 1935 and 1945 amendments were adopted increasing the powers of the Board, and correspondingly cutting down those of the twelve Reserve banks.

The Federal Reserve banks are nominally private corporations whose stock is owned by the member commercial banks. However, their stock ownership does not carry the usual consequences of stockholding. They may vote for 6 of the 9 Directors of their own Reserve bank, 3 being appointed by the Board of Governors; but their nominations of Directors may be vetoed by the Board of Governors. They receive dividends on their stock, but since 1947 90 per cent of profits after dividends have been paid to the Treasury as interest on Federal Reserve notes. And it is provided that if the banks were liquidated, their surplus would revert to the Treasury, not to their stockholders. The Federal Reserve banks are run with a view not to maximizing their profits but to carrying out the monetary policies laid down by the Board of Governors and its important Open Market Committee, which includes representatives of the Federal Reserve banks.

There are about 7,000 member banks in the Federal Reserve System. Of these, 5,000 are National banks, organized under the federal statute of 1863, passed during the Civil War to facilitate the war-financing problems of that day. The rest are state banks, whose charters are granted under the banking laws of the various states. State banks may or may not join the Federal Reserve System, as they see fit. These member banks—the familiar First National or Butchers' and Drovers' banks on every main street of the country—constitute the most important part of the commercial banking facilities of the United States. Most of the checks used in payment of personal and business debts are drawn against demand deposit accounts in the member banks. The bulk of the bank loans which business uses to finance its working capital needs are made by them. The member banks make loans to individuals in large amounts to finance the purchase and construction of houses and other buildings, and the purchase of cars and other consumer durable goods. Many of their loans finance members of the securities exchanges, and brokers and dealers who operate on them. Under the Securities Exchange Act, passed in 1934, brokers, dealers, and members of the exchanges must do their borrowing within certain limits fixed by the statute and by Federal Reserve Board regulations adopted to carry out its purposes. They are allowed to borrow only from member banks, or from nonmember banks which formally agree in this respect to comply with the provisions of federal law.

There are other important banking and financial institutions in the country. The Federal Land banks, established in 1917, handle a considerable share of farm mortgages, and were used during the depression to refinance farm mortgages which ordinary banks and insurance companies considered hopelessly frozen. The Home Owners Loan Corporation, set up in 1933, served an emergency function during the depression in financing private home building and providing commercial banks the inducement of a federal guarantee in making such loans. Almost thirty federal financial institutions are now functioning, of more than sixty which have been established from time to time. They provide or guarantee an important part of the credit used in agriculture, small business, and especially housing, where federal finance is a crucial factor in home building, real estate mortgages, and urban renewal and redevelopment programs.[2] The Export-Import Bank makes loans to help finance the foreign trade of the United States, and the Rural Electrification Administration makes loans to encourage the use of electricity and telephones in rural areas. Building and loan associations, savings banks, and personal finance companies operate on a large scale in their respective spheres, and insurance companies are an increasingly important source of industrial loans. Industrial financing through factoring and other forms of commercial credit has expanded greatly during the last twenty years.

But none of these institutions has the flexibility of policy possible within the Federal Reserve System. Almost all of

2. These institutions are ably surveyed in R. J. Saulnier, H. G. Halcrow, and N. H. Jacoby, *Federal Lending and Loan Insurance*, Princeton, NBER, 1958.

them utilize the services of the Federal Reserve System. The System is not merely the major banking institution in the United States—it is the only banking institution through which the volume of money can be directly influenced by national policy.

The twelve Federal Reserve banks have various service functions which they perform for the member banks. They clear checks between banks, a technical but important job which has greatly reduced the time and cost involved in presenting checks received in one part of the country for payment in another. Before the Federal Reserve System was established, it was common for a check on San Francisco to be received in New York at a discount, representing the uncertainties of previous clearing arrangements. Today checks are automatically received at par throughout the country.

For all practical purposes, the Federal Reserve banks have taken over the function of issuing paper currency, with the exception of silver certificates and some older forms of banknotes issued by the Treasury. The once common types of currency issued by individual banks throughout the country have largely disappeared from circulation. The Federal Reserve notes are printed, signed, and turned over to the Federal Reserve banks by the Treasury, at the order of the Reserve banks, which pledge part of their gold or other approved assets to secure their redemption. But the notes are obligations of the nation as well as the Reserve banks. They bear a rather mysterious inscription: "The United States of America will pay to the bearer on demand five [or ten, or fifty] dollars. This note is legal tender for all debts, public and private, and is redeemable in lawful money at the United States Treasury, or at any Federal Reserve Bank." Since gold coins can no longer be circulated, however, no one knows what the "Lawful Money" now is into which the Federal Reserve notes purport to be redeemable. Semifrivolous attempts to redeem the Federal Reserve notes have led merely to circuitous and rather puzzled correspondence with the Treasury and the Federal Reserve banks.

For all practical and legal purposes, the Federal Reserve notes are themselves "lawful money of the United States."

The silver certificates, on the other hand, bear the legend: "This certifies that there is on deposit in the Treasury of the United States of America one dollar [or five dollars] in silver payable to the bearer on demand." The anomaly of silver certificates aside, along with a few other surviving reminders of the monetary past, the Federal Reserve banks are the sole banks of issue for paper money in the United States, and they provide the member banks with the paper money their business requires. The thought behind this provision is that it permits both greater economy in the use of reserves, and better coordination of control over the volume of paper money circulating throughout the economy.

The issuance of notes was and is one of the important banking tasks of the Federal Reserve System. The plan of the statute was to provide a more elastic volume of currency, so that booms would not be choked off or panics precipitated, as they had been in the past, by a shortage of paper money. The Federal Reserve System itself ran into a bottleneck in 1932, when the demand for currency became epidemic. But legislation in 1933 broadened the types of collateral the Reserve banks could use as backing for notes to include government bonds, and only the gold reserve now seriously limits the System's capacity to supply currency. Since 1945, 25 per cent of the collateral against notes must be gold.

Another of the banking purposes of the Federal Reserve System was to economize reserves by pooling them. The member banks no longer hold gold as a reserve against their liabilities. All the gold reserves are held by the Federal Reserve banks, and the commercial banks keep their reserves in the form of noninterest-bearing deposits with their Reserve banks. Smaller banks also keep accounts in correspondent banks in the larger cities, to facilitate their financial transactions and to serve in a sense as secondary reserves. But for practical purposes the only reserve required of the commercial banks by law is that they hold a specified fraction of their deposit liabilities in their accounts at one of the Federal Reserve banks.

These banking functions of the Federal Reserve System are collateral to its main task—helping to regulate the volume of money spending in the interest of over-all economic stability.

The direct money supply of the United States consists of the demand deposit accounts of member bank customers— the ordinary checking accounts at commercial banks through which most payments are made; the volume of currency outside the banks; and time deposits in savings banks and in the postal savings system. At the end of March 1958 the total of "Deposits Adjusted and Currency" in the Federal Reserve Board's series was $224.5 billion, of which $104.6 billion, or 46 per cent, were customers' demand deposits.[3] $27.4 million was currency in the pockets of the public— currency outside the banking system, a factor of secondary importance in the strategy of banking policy but still one of importance. Of the currency outstanding, it is estimated that $6 billion is held abroad in private hoards. The amount of paper money outstanding fluctuates a good deal during the course of a year, rising to peaks for vacation and holiday periods when people require unusual amounts of cash. There is a third element in the money supply—the volume of deposits in savings accounts, either at commercial banks or mutual savings banks or in the postal system. While legally these accounts are often payable only on thirty or sixty days' notice, in fact they are payable on demand and can readily be used to enlarge the flow of means of payment. At the end of March 1958 time deposits were $92.5 billion, almost 41 per cent of the total. Beyond these three forms of money are forests of "near money"—liquid assets so readily transferable that they are often used as money substitutes or as sources of "money" in the conventional sense—government bonds, the cash surrender value of insurance policies, and the like.

The maximum total volume of demand deposits or cash which can exist at any time is fixed by law, through requirements that both the Reserve banks and the member banks keep part of their assets idle as reserves against their liabilities in these two crucial forms.

The Federal Reserve banks are the banks for the Treasury,

3. Excluding government and interbank demand deposits.

for member banks, and for foreign central banks, but not for members of the American public.

The three-way relationship between the Treasury, the Reserve banks, and the member banks is one of the key mechanisms of the law governing the size of the money supply. Checks sent out by the Treasury to members of the public are drawn either on its deposit accounts in one of the twelve Federal Reserve banks or in accounts which it keeps in member banks. And each member bank has a deposit account with the Federal Reserve bank in its district. When a member of the public receives a Treasury check, or any other check on a Federal Reserve bank, he treats it as he would any other check. He deposits it to his account in a member bank, or cashes it with someone who does. For his bank, however, the deposit is altogether different from the deposit of a check received by a customer drawn against another member bank. For the Reserve bank check builds up the member bank's credit with its Reserve bank without reducing any other bank's credit—that is, it increases the reserves of the particular member bank, and of the member banks as a whole. Similarly, a payment to the Treasury by a member of the public transfers a claim against a commercial bank to the Treasury, and then usually to a Federal Reserve bank, cutting member bank reserves in the first instance. In order to minimize and control the impact of tax payments on the reserve position of member banks, the Treasury in recent years has handled a large part of its routine business through accounts in member banks rather than in Federal Reserve banks.

Treasury transactions are not the only means by which commercial banks gain or lose reserves, in the form of credits to their accounts at the Federal Reserve bank. Such balances may be created or destroyed in a variety of ways—most typically by the immobilization of member bank claims on other member banks, by loans from a Reserve bank to a member bank, or by Reserve bank purchases or sales of securities on the open market.

For the Reserve banks, the ultimate limit of expansion is the gold reserve of the United States. The law now requires that the Reserve banks keep a 25 per cent reserve in gold certificates both against deposits and against the Federal Reserve notes they issue. This reserve requirement was reduced to 25 per cent in 1945 from 45 per cent for notes and 35 per cent for deposits. Under the present statute the total of Federal Reserve notes outstanding and of member bank (and other) deposits with the Reserve banks cannot exceed four times the value of the gold reserve owned by the Treasury and normally kept as a basis of Treasury deposits with the Reserve banks. Gold therefore fixes the capacity of the Reserve banks to issue notes, to make loans to member banks or the Treasury, or to draw checks to pay for securities they purchase. In May 1958 the Federal Reserve banks held about $21 billion in gold certificates, against deposits of $19.4 billion, and notes outstanding of $26.5 billion. The gold reserve was 45.7 per cent—enough to support an expansion of almost 88 per cent in outstanding liabilities without changing the law. Against these figures, however, must be counted the short-term dollar balances and dollar assets held in the United States to foreign account. Largely as a result of United States government financial policy during and since the war, such holdings have risen abruptly, while gold reserves have been more widely distributed than during the interwar period. In mid-1958 foreign dollar deposits and holdings of short-term Treasury bills and certificates and of commercial paper reached nearly $17.6 billion, as compared with $8.2 billion in 1949. In the unlikely event that foreign owners should wish to convert these holdings into gold, the Federal Reserve System would be under severe strain, for the first time since 1932.

Since 1934, when Congress abolished the circulation of gold and gold certificates in the United States, all the gold not used in dentistry, the arts, or industry must be sold to the Treasury for $35 an ounce. When the Treasury buys the gold, it does two things. It pays for it with check, usually drawn on a Treasury account in a Reserve bank. Its normal practice used to be to issue a gold certificate—legally about equivalent to a warehouse receipt—attesting that it holds a given amount of gold in Fort Knox. It would then deposit this certificate to its account in one of the Reserve Banks. Now the Treasury no longer goes to the trouble and expense of issuing gold certificates. The Reserve banks credit the Treasury's account on the basis of a far less formal obligation of the Treasury to issue the certificates if necessary. In this way the deposit of gold builds up the Treasury's deposit balance to where it was before the gold purchase, and the Reserve bank receives a new reserve asset.

The purchase of gold is an entirely different kind of transaction, both for the Treasury and for the banking system, than a Treasury purchase of guns or steel or wheat or any of the other commodities the government may buy. In monetary terms, the gold purchase is "costless," since the Treasury's bank account is not reduced by the check it draws to buy the gold. It does not need to raise taxes or borrow money to pay for the gold; it draws a gold certificate, which it then deposits to its credit in its checking account.

This aspect of gold purchase transactions has given rise to some confusion. A congressman, faithfully trying to get to the bottom of the mystery, engaged a Secretary of the Treasury in the following colloquy before a Congressional committee:

Congressman F. C. Smith: "Up to June 30, 1940, the Treasury had acquired, nearly all from foreigners, roundly $13,000,000,000 of gold at $35 an ounce. By August 6, 1941 it was carrying on its books approximately $16,000,000,000 worth of gold at $35 an ounce, which represented the gold stock that was added to the amount held at the time of gold debasement, January 31, 1934.

"What did the Treasury use to pay for this gold? In section 8 of the Gold Reserve Act is prescribed what shall be used to pay for it. It reads in part as follows:

" 'With the Approval of the President, the Secretary of the Treasury may purchase gold in any amounts, at home or abroad, with any direct obligations, coin, or currency of the United States authorized by law, or with any funds in the Treasury not otherwise appropriated.'

"This is plain. It means the Treasury shall use money from its ordinary receipts, taxes, customs, and so forth, or direct Government obligations to pay for the gold it acquires.

"But does it pay for the gold it acquires with any of these payment media? The following colloquy took place between myself and Secretary of the Treasury, Mr. Morgenthau, at the hearings on the price control bill (p. 1152). It will be noted that Under Secretary of the Treasury, Mr. Bell, answered most of my questions, but specifically at the request of Mr. Morgenthau. Also it will be seen at the end of the colloquy, as shown here, that Mr. Morgenthau fully subscribed to all Mr. Bell said. Therefore, the answers to my questions are those of Mr. Morgenthau, as well as of Mr. Bell.

" 'Mr. F. C. Smith. What do you use to pay for this gold?'

" 'Secretary Morgenthau. Could Mr. Bell go through the operation of going to the bank and everything else?'

" 'Under Secretary Bell. If a country imports gold into the United States it is presented to the assay office, we will say in New York, and the New York assay office gives the importer or the bank or whoever it might be, a check on the Treasury, what we call a gold-fund check, and that check is cashed just like any other Government check. It is deposited by the recipient in his bank and creates a deposit.'

" 'Then, when that check goes around the circuit and comes into the Federal Reserve Bank it is charged to our account. It depletes the Government's balance with the Federal Reserve banks, and then in turn we issue gold certificates against that gold, and receive a credit for the gold certificates with the Federal Reserve Banks, thereby replenishing our account.'

" 'Mr. F. C. Smith. And you pay for the gold with gold certificates?'

" 'Under Secretary Bell. The gold pays for itself; it is money; it is just an exchange of one form of money for another.'

" 'Mr. F. C. Smith. What does the law say on that?

Section 8 of the Federal [Gold] Reserve Act of 1934 reads: "With the approval of the President, the Secretary of the Treasury may purchase gold in any amount at home or abroad, with any direct obligations, coin, or currency of the United States, authorized by law."

" 'That is what the law prescribes you shall use to pay for this gold. What do you use?'

" 'Under Secretary Bell. We use a Government check which is payable in any coin or currency. Anybody can present that check to the Treasurer of the United States or a Federal Reserve bank and he can get currency or silver coin.'

" 'Mr. F. C. Smith. That is quite enigmatic. I am just wondering, is the cost of this gold reflected anywhere on the books of the Treasury? Does it enter into the debt?'

" 'Under Secretary Bell. The gold does not enter into the debt. It enters into the monetary system, and is shown on the daily statement every day.'

" 'Mr. F. C. Smith. Well, it does resolve itself into this, that you pay for it with a gold certificate.'

" 'Under Secretary Bell. We get a credit for the gold certificate that we issue to the Federal Reserve bank, which is backed by the gold.'

" 'Mr. F. C. Smith. But in the end, that is all that the United States Treasury gives out for this gold, is that true or not? Has it anything else to show that it paid for this gold except the gold certificate?'

" 'Under Secretary Bell. That is all that we have to show, but the importer of gold has a bank credit to show, or bank deposit to show for it.'

" 'Mr. F. C. Smith. But you have set up a deposit in the banks?'

" 'Under Secretary Bell. That is right; it increases the deposits. Gold earmarked in favor of a foreign government does not, of course, enter our monetary system.'

" 'Mr. F. C. Smith. But you printed the gold certificate, so you paid for the gold with fiat, did you not?'

" 'Under Secretary Bell. No; a gold certificate

backed by gold is not fiat currency, if I understand the word "fiat." ' . . .

" 'Mr. F. C. Smith. When you issue currency that is a temporary proposition until you get the transaction adjusted, until you make your so-called gold-certificate deposit, and then your check transaction is canceled out. It is through the gold certificate that the credit in the bank is set up.'

" 'Under Secretary Bell. That replenishes our account and in fact the gold has paid for itself.'

" 'Mr. F. C. Smith. Would you say, Mr. Secretary, that the United States Government is carrying the cost of this gold?'

" 'Secretary Morgenthau. If you mean, are we carrying it on our books at cost, yes; but there is no cost to carry it.'

" 'Mr. F. C. Smith. Somebody paid for it; who paid for it?'

" 'Secretary Morgenthau. Mr. Bell tried awfully hard to explain it.' " [4]

The bearing of gold movements on the monetary system is one of the most important factors in monetary policy. Gold movements between countries are the classic means of settling international debts, and keeping price movements together in all countries which engage in international trade. The older theory of the gold standard has more vitality and application than people sometimes think.

Both before 1914 and today, the gold standard depends ultimately on international trade and capital movements to set the limits of internal monetary policy. If prices rise faster in one country than another, its exports become expensive and decline. At the same time, its high prices make it a favorable place in which to sell. As imports rise, and exports fall, the country loses gold, cutting down its internal money supply. Credit restrictions become necessary, and the total volume of money and of money payments is reduced, often at the expense of unemployment, until prices among coun-

4. *Cong. Rec.*, Vol. 87, Pt. VIII, p. 9105 (77th Cong., 1st Sess.), Nov 25, 1941.

tries are once more in step. On the other hand, if price levels in one country are low in relation to prices abroad, exports are encouraged and imports discouraged. Gold flows into the country. Credit is eased domestically, and prices at home rise. Similar effects are experienced when capital moves. When, in the nineteenth century, Britons, Dutchmen, and Frenchmen bought American railway bonds, the United States acquired more foreign currencies than it earned with its exports of wheat and cotton. These loans permitted the nation rapidly to build up its industrial base, by importing more foreign goods than had been currently earned in trade.

In this perspective, there is nothing surprising in the conclusion that a gold purchase by the Treasury should enlarge the monetary base on which the entire credit structure rests, while a gold sale by the Treasury contracts it. Gold transactions of this kind represent one of the vital functions of a central bank—the conduct of the international relations of the economic system.

Since 1917 the only permissible form of reserves for the member banks has been deposits with the Reserve banks. Reserve requirements differ for different banks, and for different classes of deposits. They are customarily less for time deposits than for demand deposits. And they differ depending on the location of the banks. The National Bank Act of 1863 and the Federal Reserve Act were built upon prevailing banking practice, under which banks in smaller outlying communities cleared their obligations to other banks with checks on accounts they kept in larger centers. They also used such "correspondent" banks to hold reserves for them. Therefore the reserve provisions of the Federal Reserve Act specify that banks in "central reserve" cities have somewhat higher reserve requirements than banks in "reserve" cities, and that "country" banks have still lower reserve requirements.

The Board of Governors of the Federal Reserve System now has the extremely important power to alter the reserves member banks are required to hold against demand deposit liabilities, between the amounts set in the 1917 legislation and twice those figures. This authority was first given in

1933 as an emergency power, only to be invoked after Presidential proclamation. It was established by the Banking Act of 1935 as a regular feature of the system. The Board can change reserve requirements in order to prevent "injurious credit expansion or contraction." The emergency anti-inflationary legislation of August 1948, which expired on June 30, 1949, enlarged the discretionary limits within which the Board could alter member bank reserve requirements. But Congress was unwilling to give the Board so much permanent power.

The structure of the money supply is often represented as an inverted pyramid. A given volume of gold permits the Reserve banks to have outstanding four times that amount in Federal Reserve notes or in deposit liabilities. The permitted maximum level of Reserve bank deposits, taking into account the outstanding volume of notes, in turn permits the member banks a much larger volume of ordinary customers' demand and time deposits. The limits of expansion are set by the reserve requirements of the law and the regulations issued under the law by the Reserve Board.

Originally, reserve requirements were established, both by custom and by law, to protect customers against the risk that when they came to their bank for their money, the bank would not be able to pay in cash. Under any system that calls for cash reserves calculated as a fraction of deposit liabilities, the banks would in fact be unable to meet their demand deposit obligations if all their customers came in at once to withdraw their deposits in cash. On the other hand, if all a bank's assets were kept in the form of idle cash in its vaults, it could earn no money. It would be a safe deposit box for its customers, not a bank. Reserve requirements were therefore calculated against the normal habits of the community in requiring part of their deposits in the form of cash. These requirements almost invariably broke down during a panic, when large parts of the community, fearing bank failures, lined up outside the banks to withdraw their deposits in cash. The banks were unable to convert their non-cash assets quickly enough to meet a panicky demand for cash.

Since the passage of the Federal Deposit Insurance Act in 1934 and the extension of its provisions to all accounts of $10,000 or less, both in member and in nonmember banks, the risk of a panic demand for cash has disappeared as a factor in American banking. Reserve requirements today have two functions. They should be related to the variable share of deposits which the public requires for payments by cash rather than by check. And they are used more and more deliberately by the Federal Reserve Board to limit or to expand the banks' collective power to make loans and buy securities, and thereby to "create" money in the form of demand deposits.

There is inevitably something mysterious in the idea that commercial banks can by their own actions enlarge the volume of their deposits and thus the amount of money in all forms available to the public. Nor does it help to produce clarity if one adds that the banks enlarge the volume of deposits by making loans to their customers, or by buying securities or supplies with their own checks. It is true that a bank loan of $1,000 will permit a customer to draw checks for $1,000 or take $1,000 in bank notes from his bank, which he would not otherwise have been able to do. And it is equally true that if a bank issues its own check in payment for a bond, the person who sells the bond deposits the bank's check he has received for the bond to his account, raising the total of his own deposits. The seller of the bond has shifted part of his property from the form of a bond to that of a bank deposit.

But can banks do more than lend out to their customers, or pay out with their own checks, money which has been left with them on deposit by others? Many bankers grow purple at the suggestion that they "create" money. They receive money on deposit. And they endeavor to put that money to work in the best interests of their stockholders and of the community by making ordinary loans to customers, by making mortgage loans, or by purchasing government securities or other securities in which they may be allowed to invest by law. A part of their assets must be kept as cash, to take care of the cash needs of their customers.

Part is always tied up in a floating volume of checks being cleared, since they normally credit their customers with the amount of checks deposited but do not themselves receive credit for such checks until they have been presented for payment at the banks on which they were drawn. And finally, a part of their assets must by law be kept as a reserve against their own deposit liabilities in the form of a deposit by the bank with a Federal Reserve bank.

Member bank reserve requirements define the total volume of deposits which can be based on a given volume of reserves. But they do not explain the commonly made assertion that a given change in reserves can permit banks to expand their loans and deposits by four, six, or even ten times the amount of the reserves. Suppose that a member bank in Keokuk is operating under the requirement that it hold a 24 per cent reserve against its demand deposits, and the Federal Reserve Board cuts the requirement to 20 per cent. If the bank has $10,000,000 in deposits, the effect of the change is to release $400,000 of its assets which it previously had to keep in the form of a reserve deposit with a Federal Reserve bank. The member bank can now use its new excess reserve credit of $400,000 in either one of two ways: it can buy securities or it can use its improved reserve position as the basis for making additional loans to customers. Those loans will give rise to additional deposits, against which the $400,000 could be used as reserve.

If the bank buys securities, it must pay for them with its own check, which may be presented for payment at its Federal Reserve bank. When that check is presented, its reserve balance will drop by the amount of the check. Thus the bank can buy up to $400,000 in securities. The purchase would in effect transform its $400,000 excess reserve credit with its Federal Reserve bank from a noninterest-bearing balance in its Reserve bank account into interest-bearing bonds. If it does this, it transfers its excess reserve credit to the bank from which (or from whose customer) it has purchased the bonds.

On the other hand, it may use its credit as the basis for making loans to its customers. By how much can the bank in

Keokuk expand its loans and deposits? It would be easy but wrong to calculate that since the bank has $400,000 in excess reserves, and since reserve requirements are now 20 per cent, the bank could make an additional $2,000,000 in loans. If there were only one bank in the country, it could expand loans at once by almost $2,000,000. But the fact that there are many banks introduces complications. If the bank made $2,000,000 in new loans, its customers would draw some of their deposits out in the form of cash, hold some idle, and for the balance draw checks which would in the main be received by customers of other banks, and then deposited at those banks. The bank making $2,000,000 in loans on the basis of its new reserve of $400,000 would soon find itself in grave difficulty, for it would almost surely have to meet claims from other banks for something close to $1,250,000 or $1,500,000, while it had a reserve credit of only $400,000 with which to pay them. If the bank makes loans, it cannot expect to keep the full amount of $400,000 as a reserve. The loan is an asset embodied in a customer's note, for which the bank must pay as clearly as if it had bought bonds. In making loans, the bank must take into account prevailing banking practice. It must calculate that some of the deposits it creates by making loans would require additional cash, which it would have to obtain with part of its $400,000 credit; that part would remain idle as a deposit with it; and that the rest would be drawn out and deposited in other banks. The maximum amount of loans it could safely make would be $400,000, which might all be drawn out, either as cash or in the course of paying checks presented by other banks. As a result of such loans, it would have turned the amount of its nonearning Federal Reserve deposit into an earning asset.

But would it have "created" new money? Yes, but only in the amount of $400,000. The act of the bank either in buying securities or in making loans gives rise to $400,000 in ordinary member bank demand deposits which did not exist before. In the case of a purchase of securities, the bank's check for $400,000, paid to the vendor of the securities, is deposited by him in his bank account, increasing the total of deposits by $400,000. In the case of expanding loans, the bank empowers its own customers to draw checks for $400,000, or to draw out cash in that amount. If all the cash and checks were taken out and deposited in some other bank, that bank would gain additional deposits of $400,000. As reserves against its new deposits, the second bank would need only $80,000 as reserves. It therefore would have $320,000 of newly acquired excess reserves which it could use in turn to buy securities, or to make mortgage or other loans, exactly as the first bank did. Again, even if all the $320,000 were immediately withdrawn from the second bank in cash, or by the process of drawing checks, which would be deposited in accounts at a third bank, the third bank would acquire $320,000 in new deposits, of which it could use all but $64,000 (20 per cent of the $320,000), or $256,000, as excess reserves for the acquisition of new earning assets. The net effect of the process of expansion for the whole banking system would be to permit the creation of deposits of almost $2,000,000, five times the original amount of excess reserves, since the reserve requirement is set at 20 per cent. The total expansion would be less than this, depending on how much of the additional demand deposits is kept in peoples' pockets as cash, or in the vaults of banks as additional cash held to meet cash claims against the new deposits. Of course, if the banks could not find suitable securities to buy, or suitable customers to whom to make loans, the process of expansion would fall short of its maximum. In that case, as sometimes happens, the banks would hold excess reserves, and the expansionist purposes of the original step would be frustrated.

But in general, these are qualifications in the arithmetic of the process. The process itself is simple enough. The creation or destruction of reserves sets in train a series of reactions which give the banks an incentive to acquire earning assets, and in that way to create or destroy deposits—that is, money —in proportion to the reserve requirements. Fractional reserve requirements therefore can lead to the creation or destruction of money on a massive scale. If reserve requirements for member banks are 20 per cent, newly created reserves can become the basis for a fivefold expansion of the money supply in the banking system as a whole.

These twin reserve provisions of the law—of gold as the reserve limiting Federal Reserve operations and of deposits with the Reserve banks limiting member bank operations—are the determining structural elements of the system.

Certain transactions have special significance, in terms of the legal machinery for controlling the volume of money. Any purchase of securities by the Reserve banks from member banks or from the public gives the member banks a check on the Reserve banks—i.e. new reserves. Any payments by the Treasury made with checks on its account in the Federal Reserve banks have the same effect. On the other hand, when a Reserve bank sells securities to the banks or the public, it receives checks on member banks. The receipt of such checks by the Reserve banks automatically cuts member bank deposits in the Reserve banks, and their reserve position. And when people pay their taxes or buy bonds, the Treasury receives checks on commercial banks, which it may deposit to its accounts in Federal Reserve banks and again cut down member bank reserves.

The increasing weight of government transactions in the monetary system has led to the development of a practice according to which the Treasury keeps part of its receipts on deposit with member banks rather than with Reserve banks. This procedure was used during the first World War and was revised to aid in handling the financial problems of the second World War. It has been continued since, both for convenience and in order to control the impact of Treasury operations on the reserve position of member banks. Since January 1, 1950, the Treasury has permitted member banks to hold special "Treasury Tax and Loan Accounts," if they qualify as depositories. In these accounts, employers can pay withholding taxes to meet both income and social security tax liabilities, and the banks can keep the proceeds of government bonds sold to the public. The banks can earn small amounts on the assets they receive in these accounts. And the Treasury can time its transfers from these deposits to its Reserve bank accounts to avoid disrupting either the money market or the reserve position of the banks.

The traditional ideas of Federal Reserve policy and its later refinements simply manipulate various aspects of the structural relationship involving the Treasury, the Reserve banks, and the member banks. When the Federal Reserve Board decides that credit conditions are too tight and that it would be desirable to put the banks into a position where they could make more loans, it can undertake "open market purchases"—that is, purchases of government securities on the public securities market from the public or the banks. Such purchases directly increase the reserves of the member banks. If the Federal Reserve bank buys securities from an individual, his deposit of the Federal Reserve check he receives to his own account increases member bank deposits as well as its reserves. If the Reserve bank buys from a member bank, the member bank has in effect shifted one of its assets from the form of a government bond to the form of a Reserve Bank credit. In either case the member bank now has both the capacity and a profit incentive to make more loans to its customers. On the other hand, "open market sales" by the Federal Reserve banks quickly eliminate reserves, by giving the Reserve banks checks on member banks which cut down member bank balances with the Reserve banks.

In the same way, the Reserve banks can control the reserve position of the member banks, and their capacity to make loans (which create deposits) by buying and selling assets other than government bonds. Certain forms of commercial obligations called bills and acceptances, private short-term promises to pay—often secured by bills of lading or warehouse receipts or by the endorsement of a bank—are traded in relatively small amounts in New York and some other cities. Under the law, assets of this type can be purchased or sold by the Reserve banks. When the Federal Reserve Act was passed, it was thought that the market in such obligations would grow as it had in London, and offer a desirable facility both for trade and for central banking operations. This development has not taken place in the United States on the scale expected. But bills and acceptances in this form do constitute part of the portfolio of the Reserve banks, and purchases or sales of these banking assets have the effect of other open market operations on bank reserves and deposits.

Open market purchases or sales by the Reserve banks operate on the investment flow in another way. They not only change the level of commercial bank reserves: they influence the rate of interest on government bonds or commercial paper, and the prices charged for money on the securities markets of the country. Suppose the Reserve banks step in to buy government bonds, both short and long term. The price of government bonds may well be forced up as a result. Since the bonds yield a fixed contractual return in dollars, calculated as a percentage of their face amounts, an increase in their price means a decrease in their yield. But all securities prices are closely related. People can hold their funds in alternative forms. They can own government bonds, corporate bonds of various degrees of risk, or stocks. Or, if they expect prices to fall, they may shift their portfolios heavily to cash. The decisions of investors as to the purchase of differing types of securities depends upon their evaluation of the risks of each, as compared with their yields. Naturally, one expects a higher return from a risky corporate debenture or stock than from a government obligation, which could hardly go into default. Therefore a rise in the price of government securities almost invariably leads some investors to buy corporate bonds or stocks rather than governments. Through these shifts of funds, the various financial markets tend to influence each other. A rise in the market price of government bonds leads to some increase in the market level of corporate bonds and of stock. A fall in government bonds weakens other securities markets, as people are induced by the higher yield and greater safety of government securities to shift some funds to them from corporate securities. In this way, open market operations influence the price that must be paid for new capital.

The demand for capital, like the demand for most other things, is sensitive to its price. A higher interest rate usually cuts down the demand for funds. A lower interest rate is at least one factor stimulating the demand for capital. Hence open market operations are a powerful instrument for influencing the flow of capital, both through the securities markets and through other financing institutions.

The price of securities has other and less direct effects on the demand for capital. The level of stock market prices is an important element in the formation of business opinion. Through their effect on the securities markets, open-market operations can influence general expectations as to the future, and help to crystallize moods of optimism or pessimism that deeply influence the rate of spending and the flow of national income.

When the member banks have loans and therefore deposits outstanding that are close to the limit set by their reserve position, they can get additional reserves in several ways.

They can sell some of their assets which earn less money, like government bonds, to other banks, or to insurance companies or other members of the public, and deposit the checks received as the proceeds of such sales to their account in a Federal Reserve bank. A deposit of that kind would increase the reserve position of the bank that sold its securities but would cut down the reserve position of the bank that bought them, or of the bank whose depositor bought them, by the same amount. It would not increase the reserve position of all banks as a whole. Sometimes the member banks accomplish the same result by lending one another their excess reserve balances with the Reserve banks.

There is another technique which can be used to increase reserves under these circumstances. A bank can "rediscount" with the Reserve banks certain kinds of eligible commercial paper it owns; in effect, the bank borrows from the Reserve banks, for a rate of interest, on the security of notes signed by its customers, and endorsed by it. A rediscounting increases the reserve position of all banks. It was the idea of the statute that the Federal Reserve banks could make rediscounting attractive or unattractive by varying the rediscount rate—the rate of interest it would charge for the service. When the Reserve Board wished to contract credit, to keep the flow of funds from outstripping the flow of goods, it could raise its rediscount rate and discourage banks from seeking additional reserves. On the other hand, it was thought, a low rediscount rate would make it easy for the banks to enlarge their loans in periods of slack business. Whether money was cheap or dear, the banks could always get additional reserves by rediscounting their customers' obligations, and then accommodate their customers' urgent needs. Rediscounting enabled the banks—for a price—to use the same reserves over and over again.

These two instruments of control—open market operations and rediscounting—can be effective only under certain conditions. The first condition is that the banks are "loaned up"—that is, they have expanded their loans and deposits to the limits allowed by law. The second is that business conditions permit the banks to use the excess reserves the Reserve bank authorities may force upon them, either by buying securities or by making loans to good credit risks among their customers. During the depression years neither condition was fulfilled; the banks, unable to find outlets for their funds, habitually kept more of their assets in the form of deposits with the Reserve banks than were required by law. They did this even though their deposits at the Reserve banks earned nothing, while they could have earned some return on the funds by holding government securities. Bankers were willing to pay for the privilege of not being dependent on Reserve bank authorities or too heavily loaded with government bonds, whose prices they regarded as abnormally high. Under depression conditions all business loans looked doubtful.

The banking system was in the position of the horse duly led to water but quite unable to drink. This factor defines a basic limitation on the capacity of the banking system to control business fluctuations by its own actions. During the Great Depression of the thirties, unusual factors made the member banks willing for protracted periods to refrain from making money by using their excess reserves. The uncertainties of Federal Reserve policy, doubts as to the future prices of government bonds, and the difficulties experienced by the banks in obtaining discounts at the Reserve banks in the early thirties led to extraordinary liquidity and caution on the part of the banks. There is every reason in terms of banking history to suppose that this pattern of behavior will be rare. The banks normally respond to the opportunities of their reserve position by buying securities if not by making loans.

Difficulties and limitations on the effectiveness of open market operations and of rediscounting practice as devices to control member bank reserves have led to the development of direct controls over certain bank lending policies. Fear that bank credits are used to finance disturbing speculation on the exchanges persuaded Congress in the Securities Exchange Act to authorize the Federal Reserve Board not only to fix the terms on which brokers and dealers could borrow on the security of stocks but to fix margin requirements in ordinary stock market purchases. The regulations of the Reserve Board establish the amount which members of the public must pay their brokers when they purchase securities on the broker's credit. The margin requirement was fixed at 20 per cent for several years before the war; it rose to 75 per cent during the war, and between January 1946 and February 1947 it was 100 per cent, thus powerfully limiting the amount of demand for securities, and perhaps limiting a possible downward movement on the stock market by eliminating the risk of panic liquidation to cover margin requirements in a falling market. In recent years margin requirements have varied between 50 and 90 per cent, being changed relatively often.

The terms of instalment buying and other consumer credit, and of real estate loans, have also come within the regulatory power of the Reserve Board from time to time, although Congress has not given the Reserve System permanent power in this sensitive field. By fixing downpayment requirements and the possible term of loans, the Board has been able to limit the volume of credit extended to finance consumers' purchases of cars, refrigerators, and other goods normally bought on credit, and to limit the demand for new houses, in periods when demand was outstripping possible supply.

In the final analysis, the modern view of the trade cycle makes the control of depressions depend ultimately on the federal government's capacity to finance a deficit by creating new money. While it could do so under the Constitution by printing greenbacks—as it did during the Civil War—public abhorrence of such practices has led the government in recent years to finance its deficits by selling bonds.

There is much to be said in pure theory for financing deficits, if they must be incurred, by printing money. No interest has to be paid on greenbacks, and their existence on a large scale would not complicate the problems of central banking for the indefinite future, as does the current volume of government debt. But there is a universal and on the whole justifiable fear of fiscal devices that would make it too easy for politicians to spend money without voting for taxes. And inherited taboos about the wickedness of fiat money leads us to prefer more complicated ways of expanding the volume of money.

When the federal government incurs a deficit, it can raise money in one of three ways: it can sell its bonds to the public, to the commercial banks, or to the Federal banks. The effect of these three procedures on the quantity of money in the community is sharply different.

A sale of bonds to members of the public, through one of the Victory Bond programs or otherwise, means that the Treasury acquires checks on member banks in payment for its bonds. The people who buy the bonds give up some current purchasing power, exactly as if they had paid taxes. The Treasury, depositing these checks in its accounts at Federal Reserve banks, cuts down member bank reserves, which are restored to their previous level only when the Treasury spends its newly acquired funds and spreads its own checks on the Reserve banks throughout the commercial banks of the community. A sale of bonds to the public—whether individual savings bonds or bonds sold to insurance companies and other nonbanking corporations—is neutral in its monetary effect. Purchasing power is initially transferred from the public to the Treasury. When the money is spent, the reserve position of the member banks and the quantity of deposits in the member banks are at their previous levels. The only result of the series of transactions is that there are more bonds outstanding and the government, rather than the public, has been able to purchase part of current output. Instead of buying goods and services the public has bought bonds, releasing goods and services to the government in a noninflationary way.

If, however, the bonds are sold to commercial banks, the monetary consequences differ. If the banks have no excess reserves, they could buy the bonds only by cutting down on other investments—an unlikely step, since most other assets held by banks earn more than government bonds. If they hold excess reserves—and the Federal Reserve System can force excess reserves on the banks either by cutting reserve requirements or by buying government bonds or commercial paper on the open market—the effect of the sale would be to activate their excess reserves as deposit currency. The banks acquire bonds in exchange for their excess reserves, and the Treasury acquires checks drawn by member banks either on themselves or on their Reserve bank accounts. In either case the effect is the same: member bank reserves are reduced and member bank investment increased by the amount of the bonds purchased. *But the volume of member bank deposits—that is, the volume of purchasing power held by the public—has not been decreased in order to pay for the bonds. The bonds have been bought with reserves, not with customers' deposits.* On the contrary, the volume of deposits held by the Treasury has been increased. When the Treasury spends the money it has acquired by selling its bonds to the member banks, and thus distributes checks on its Federal Reserve accounts to the public, the member banks gain back the excess reserves they had used to purchase the bonds. Their deposits increase in the same amount, as people receiving government checks deposit them to their accounts. The quantity of money—the volume of demand deposits in the member banks—has been increased, and the reserve position of the member banks is what it was before the bond sale was begun. Considering the banking system as a whole, the transaction creates the new money the government needs, by transforming excess reserves into holdings of bonds. The bonds are paid for by member bank checks, which become Treasury deposits, then member bank deposits, finally restoring the member banks' reserves. The reserves are no longer fully "excess," since the volume of deposits has increased, increasing the level of required reserves. But a considerable fraction of the reserves are still excess and can serve as a base for further expansion of deposits, either by way of bank security purchases or an expansion of loans.

Law and custom forbid, at least in its direct forms, the practice of direct borrowing by the Treasury from the central bank—the historic symbol of debauchery in public finance, sure to send shudders throughout the markets and board rooms of the world. Since 1942, Section 14(b) of the Federal Reserve Act has authorized direct purchase and sale transactions between the Treasury and the Federal Reserve, up to a limit of $5 billion. This power is regarded as emergency authority, to be used for short periods of time in periods of market disturbance or of lean tax receipts. It has rarely been invoked, and rarely for more than a month at a time. It has been renewed by Congress for two-year periods, as a kind of extreme safety valve for the Treasury, to be kept in reserve for situations of genuine short-term distress. When the Treasury does sell bonds directly to the Federal Reserve banks, the potential expansion of deposits arising from the transaction is even greater, for the transaction increases both deposits and reserves. The Reserve banks acquire bonds and give the Treasury credits in its Reserve bank accounts in exchange. Treasury deposits increase *without cutting down member bank reserves, even temporarily*. The Reserve banks can do this only if their gold position is sufficiently high (as it has been for almost thirty years) to produce what are in effect unused or "excess" gold reserves of their own. When the Treasury spends deposits created in this way, not only are member bank deposits increased; member bank reserves are also increased beyond their previous level by the amount of the Treasury spending. Approximately the same double-expansion effect, both in reserves and in deposits, is accomplished if bonds sold to the public or to the member banks are then resold to the Federal Reserve banks.

One can observe this process of inflating the money supply via bond sales to the banking system in recent wartime experience. On December 30, 1939, the total money supply was $63.2 billion, the volume of government bonds held by commercial and savings banks was $19.4 billion, and by Federal Reserve banks $2.5 billion. On December 31, 1945, the money supply had risen to $150.8 billion, commercial and savings banks held $101.3 billion in government bonds, and Federal Reserve banks $24.2 billion. While many billions in government bonds had been sold to the nonbanking public in the first instance, a considerable fraction of these bonds had subsequently been resold either to commercial banks or to Federal Reserve banks, which, until March 1951, were committed to purchase certain classes of government bonds at prices that kept their yields constant.

The capacity of the banking system to finance a deficit by creating new money in this way depends on the reserve position of the Federal Reserve banks and of the member banks. The extremely favorable international position of the United States in recent years has given the Reserve banks almost unlimited freedom to accommodate the government. And Congress has proved, in case of a stringency arising from shortage of reserves, that it is willing to change the price of gold, or the reserve requirements applicable both to the Reserve banks and the commercial banks, in order to retain flexibility in domestic monetary policy. The freedom to pursue a domestic banking and price policy without regard to its effects on exports and imports is a luxury the United States and the Soviet Union are almost alone in possessing. For the United States, at any rate, this luxury has limits implicit in both the international obligations of the nation and the social policy it wishes to pursue in regard to the price level over the long run. Both elements in this boundary for American monetary freedom became visible in 1958, for the first time in many years.

9. The Interplay of Monetary and Fiscal Policy

THOSE WHO CONTROL the federal budget can influence the flow of the national income most directly and effectively by operating at a cash surplus or deficit. The Treasury has other, less potent techniques at its disposal for affecting the state of trade. Its program of debt management has far-reaching impacts on the money markets, and on the portfolios of financial institutions. And the movement of its deposits within the banking system can alter the reserve position of commercial banks—that is, their ability to make loans or to buy securities. All three of these procedures depend upon the several statutory powers of the Federal Reserve System, and utilize its structural relationships with the financial markets and the member banks. It would be difficult if not impossible for the Treasury to carry out policy in any one of these areas without the agreement and cooperation of the Federal Reserve System.

In its turn, the Board of Governors of the Federal Reserve System has some authority which it is at least nominally free to assert without the concurrence of the Treasury. As Chapter 8 explains, the Federal Reserve Board can influence the level of employment in the United States, and the international position of the American economy, in three principal ways: by controlling the reserve position of the member banks, the main source of variation in the money supply; by ordering the Reserve banks to buy or sell government securities of different types; and by helping to manage the finances of its chief client, the United States government. In taking action to control commercial bank reserves or to affect the securities markets, the Federal Reserve is in principle an independent authority. Even in working with the Treasury on the administration of its financial affairs, the Federal Reserve is free to have views of its own.

Actually, it is almost inconceivable that the Reserve System would undertake policy steps of any consequence without consulting the Treasury and the President. The normal rule, visible under layers of polite silence, almost certainly goes further, to give the President and the Treasury something close to a veto over Federal Reserve policy. Sir Montagu Norman, a most powerful Governor of the Bank of England, once defined the effective practical relationship between the Central Bank and the Treasury in these terms: "I look upon the Bank as having the unique right to offer advice and to press such advice even to the point of nagging; but always of course subject to the supreme authority of the government." [1] Sir Montagu's definition does not follow the lines of legal authority in the United States, nor indeed the line of legal authority in England in 1926, when his comment was made. It would not satisfy many who yearn for a more complete separation of banking power from political responsibility. But it corresponds reasonably well to the pattern of reality. It rings altogether true in reflecting an Englishman's ingrained deference to government, not quite so true as a statement of the characteristic attitude of Americans. In dealing with their government, Americans are all from Missouri, whether they are private citizens or civil servants. Nothing is more striking in government experience than the American official's refusal to accept policy, even on the highest authority, until he is personally convinced it is sound. Nonetheless, in the electric relationship between treasuries and central banks, Sir Montagu's remark comes pretty close to identifying the larger battalions.

Of course there are no absolutes, especially in the realm of public and quasi-public bodies, like central banks. The

1. R. S. Sayers, *Central Banking after Bagehot* (Oxford, Clarendon Press, 1957), p. 35.

statutes give the Federal Reserve Board a great deal of discretion, and many legislators have hoped the Board would be free of—that is to say, "reasonably" free of, and "not unduly" influenced by—political pressures, executive or Congressional. The Board has exercised its discretion, sometimes—though not on great matters—acting against the strong preferences of Congress or the President. The degree of independence enjoyed by the System has varied a good deal, depending upon the nature of its problems, and the capacity for battle of the people necessarily involved—the Chairman of the Board, the Secretary of the Treasury, the President, and the leading members of the relevant committees of the Congress. Some chairmen have been especially skillful in achieving elbow room for the Board by playing Congress against the President and financial opinion against both. No chairman of the Federal Reserve Board can, however, enjoy the quantum of power exercised by the heads of the Bank of England or the Bank of France. They are beyond a significant frontier, for they can no longer be deterred or restrained by the threat of nationalization.

There has been a good deal of debate in recent years as to the relative weight that can and should be given to banking and to fiscal policy in the administration of programs designed to control the size and flow of the national income.

Some would keep the Treasury neutral, save in dire emergencies. They would remit almost the entire task of stabilization to the supposedly cool and detached experts of the Federal Reserve. Those who hold such views might be called the Banking party, a coalition including both Rockbound Old Mossbacks and Bright Young Intellectuals. By and large, they believe devoutly that the "Art of Central Banking" can deal subtly and surely with almost every disequilibrium likely to occur in a capitalist economy. Their views recall the fond hopes of senators who looked to the governors of the Federal Reserve System as a Supreme Court of Banking, far above the sweat of battle. For them, deliberate federal deficits or surpluses are not quite respectable. They would be more comfortable in an older financial universe of "sound" money, "sound" finance, and "sound" principles, with discreet bankers to keep the economy on an even keel, and politicians confined to less important work.

On the other hand, there are many who regard central banking as a narrowly limited tool, or a dangerous one. Somewhat inconsistently, they conclude that banking action is both ineffective and powerfully discriminatory in its impact on the economy. They would prefer fiscal policy to be the principal means of stabilization. Identifying this party by name presents a delicate problem in semantics, for the several wings of the party make odd bedfellows. It is a party of Pure Views, and No Compromise. Some members would trace its doctrines to Keynes, others to Henry Simons. All branches of the party would agree that there is something undemocratic about delegating responsibility for economic stabilization to a central bank. They would contend with equal fervor that the banking system should be a neutral and rather passive servant of democratic government, which has inescapable responsibility for developing and executing a full-employment, optimum-output program. According to the platform of the party of Fiscal Policy, government surpluses or deficits should be the normal, not the exceptional compensatory devices used to keep the flow of national income at an appropriate level. Some members of the party would strip the central bank of all discretionary powers. They assume they know what "money" is:—that is, what the economy uses to make payments, and to hold resources in liquid form with reasonable safety. They would have the quantity of "money," or at least of bank notes and commercial bank deposits, fixed by law. Under their rule, the money market would function freely and competitively, without manipulative intervention by the Federal Reserve. Others—the left or the right wing of the party, depending on how one defines these elusive terms—would preserve the convenience of the Federal Reserve's discretionary powers but would not use them much, save as auxiliary features of stabilization programs resting mainly on fiscal action.

Like many debates over public policy, this controversy has meaning principally for the Ideologues, who are unhappy unless on every issue they can claim a position labeled "liberal" or "conservative," "radical" or "reactionary," as may best suit their temperaments and their view of themselves.

The use of the federal budget as a tool of stabilization policy is not only legitimate; it is inevitable. Whatever one's inherited views, the federal budget is far too big to be ignored. One can hardly program the raising and spending of $70 to $80 billion without considering the impact of the process on the economy as a whole.

Equally, it would be irresponsibly foolish to give up the flexibility, resourcefulness and promise of the Federal Reserve System, one of the most useful achievements of our legal and political history.

Fashions change in economics as in other arts. During the thirties many tended to ignore central banking as a futile exercise, incapable of moving a sluggish economy. The wheel has turned several times since the war. Central banking has been in and out of favor, at least as a matter of style.

Whether or not at any given moment banking policy is a popular theme for doctoral dissertations, the Federal Reserve System has never ceased to be a vital part of the machinery for economic action. Federal Reserve operations have been effective on certain occasions, ineffective or even harmful on others. Sometimes they have been well conceived, occasionally badly planned or executed. At best, they can be expected to function with varying degrees of impact at different stages of the trade cycle. They are capable of extremely direct and even abrupt application in bringing a boom to a halt. During the early stages of a recession they have been used with moderate success to induce increases in spending, and a restoration of prosperity. In the depths of the depression, however, when people expect prices to keep falling, there is no reason to expect the manipulation of reserves and of interest rates to constitute a sufficient influence to stimulate expansion. If a businessman expects the price of raw materials or buildings to drop 10 per cent, only a rare combination of circumstances could induce him to borrow from the bank in order to buy them at any interest rate above zero. At no stage of the cycle, however, can one conceive of a stabilization program that would not in considerable part utilize and depend upon the skills and powers of the Federal Reserve System.

In the planning and administration of stabilization programs, fiscal and monetary policy should be viewed as joint instruments, not alternative ones or rivals. They should normally be employed together, not separately. And they should be studied, perfected, and improved as correlative means for carrying out the difficult feat of economic stabilization. Together they have more strength than either could have alone. The emphasis given to each in programs of action should depend upon the occasion. The same combination of procedures should not be expected to work equally well at the height of a speculative boom, in the early stages of a recession or recovery, or in the pit of a slump. And in this regard, experience amply confirms the expectation of theory.

The evolution of policy must take into account more than the inherent reach and the inherent limitations of banking and fiscal institutions, viewed separately and in tandem. Their potential utility should be appraised also against the background of a financial world whose contours are changing rapidly. The scope of banking policy was not the same in 1933 as in 1958. The federal debt has been revolutionized both in size and in composition. The tax laws have been amended many times, altering investment incentives in a variety of ways. Commercial banks are now relatively less important than they were, compared with other institutions for deposit and for lending. The international position of the United States is different. Comparable developments establish new perspectives for fiscal policy. The federal budget offered the policy-maker one kind of leverage when national governmental spending, in all forms, absorbed some 2.5 per cent of the gross national product, as it did in 1929. It has quite another when the government claims 18 per cent or thereabouts, as it does today.

These factors define the field for effective stabilization by fiscal and monetary action, and set changing limits for what it might accomplish under ideal conditions. Above all, the possible uses of fiscal and monetary policy have been redefined by the changes which have occurred during the last twenty-five years in public thought and opinion. The spread of ideas and the accumulation of experience have developed new signals for economic responses and new sensitivities to government policies, which identify a new financial environment.

The issues of policy in this realm are on the whole practical, not ideological. Both flexible central banking and flexible budget policy are legitimate instruments of Liberal Planning, as the term has been defined here. The battle between the Banking party and the party of Fiscal Policy offers little reasonable opportunity to play the popular game of labeling one position as that of liberalism (of virtue or vice, depending upon one's outlook), and the other that of reaction (of vice or virtue, as the labeler prefers).

At this point we should seek to review the functions of the Federal Reserve System somewhat more closely, in the perspective of proposals for its reform. As we have seen, these functions can be classified into three overlapping groups: the direct control of commercial bank reserves, the direct and indirect manipulation of prices on the securities markets, and the management of government finance. In all three areas policy is acquiring new accents, as the banking system and the Treasury adapt themselves to the growth of new financial institutions and practices and to the pressures of cold-war full employment.

The first function of the Federal Reserve—its direct control over the reserves of member banks—involves several aspects of its armory of powers. First, the Reserve System depends upon its discretionary power to alter the reserve requirements of the member banks, within limits fixed by law. Secondly, it looks to the Federal Reserve's capacity to alter the terms on which certain selected classes of loans are extended. Finally, it alters the rediscount rates at which member banks can borrow from the Reserve banks, and replenish their reserves. These aspects of Federal Reserve action can make it cheap or dear for businessmen to borrow from the commercial banks. Even more important, they can control within considerable limits the amount of bank money available to be lent. Banks and their customers have been skillful in recent years in economizing on money and the use of reserves, and in shifting various assets to and from the banks in ways which seem for a time to escape the long arm of Federal Reserve policy. A more rapid turnover of funds has been thought occasionally to have frustrated the restrictive aims of the Federal Reserve authorities. In fact, however, the Reserve has been able, at least since 1951, to fix something close to a ceiling for the quantity of bank money, and to enforce it, at least after an interval of adjustment. While the denotation of the word "money" is not always clear, in an economy of "money substitutes" and "near monies" the surprising thing about Federal Reserve policy during the postwar period has been not weakness but strength. Over and over again Federal Reserve action has had far-reaching consequences. One could argue that the Federal Reserve was wrong, that it should have done not what it did but something else. Yet it has rarely been possible to contend that the System was beating the air in vain. It is a tribute to the pinch of the System's monetary policy that the American Bankers' Association is now proposing changes in the historic pattern of reserve rates that would free the banks to lend more, require them to hold a smaller proportion of assets as idle reserve balances, and reduce the discretionary power of the Federal Reserve System to control the quantity of money.

One of the consequences of Federal Reserve action in maintaining a limit on the quantity of money the banks can create by lending is that in any period of money stringency the banks naturally prefer their stronger customers. The interest rates of banks, even when they rise by conventional increments, do not behave with anything like the freedom of prices in open markets. For this reason, the banks have to ration credit by other means in a time of high demand. As a result, the impact of recent periods of tight money has been felt most keenly by the weaker borrowers—smaller business, state and local governments, and those who cannot finance themselves from retained earnings or by loans from insurance companies, pension funds, and other large-scale lenders. It is by no means obvious why society would be better off if these potential borrowers were protected against the temptations of debt rather than the larger and more opulent candidates whose applications prevailed.

The second general power of the Federal Reserve Board is to order the Reserve banks to buy or sell government securities. Open market operations do more than govern the reserve position of the member banks, although they accomplish that end most drastically. Open market operations may and often do exercise a broad and compelling influence over the level of security prices, the state of opinion, the general level of all money and interest rates, and the ease with which new issues can be sold to the investing public. These effects of Reserve intervention in the market for government securities are heightened by reason of the fact that it is a market of fixed supply, at any one time, so that Federal Reserve purchases and sales influence both sides of the mechanism of exchange.

Through open market operations, the Federal Reserve directly affects the liquidity preference of the investing public —that is, the ratio of their assets people hold at any time in liquid form. Keynes' emphasis on this aspect of investment opinion was one of the most important of his insights into the functioning of the economy. Investors' views as to the future of the market induce them to shift funds to or from stocks, or bonds, or cash. The net impact of these decisions helps fix the prevailing mood of the market, and the prevailing pattern of charges for funds of various types. In the United States, at least, it strongly influences the horizon of business expectations. Not the least interesting conclusion of the studies of industrial fluctuations carried on under the auspices of the National Bureau of Economic Research is that the stock market is one of the most consistently accurate forecasters of economic change. Whether in this respect the stock market acts as earthquake or seismograph is not clear. But its significance to the economy is distinctly a major one.

The powers of the Federal Reserve System include both

"quantitative" or "general," and "qualitative" or "selective" controls, to use the special vocabulary of the banking world. "Quantitative" controls are those which affect the banking system and the economy generally, by altering the price and the availability of money. These controls rely primarily on the mechanism of market competition to ration funds among all possible bidders. Open market operations, changes in the rediscount rate, and, perhaps less clearly, changes in reserve requirements are general or quantitative controls. Through the use of these procedures, the Federal Reserve System alters the level of bank reserves, the mood and price level of the securities markets, and the pattern of interest rates thoroughout the economy. "Selective" controls, on the other hand, influence, or indeed directly regulate, the terms on which credit is extended to given classes of borrowers or to any borrowers for designated purposes. Selective controls are usually intended not to affect general conditions in the money markets. The Federal Reserve Board may regard stock market speculation as too active, or too depressed. It may therefore change the margin requirements, enlarging or restricting the volume of bank credit which can be used to finance the purchase of securities. Or selective controls of this kind, whether administered by the Federal Reserve Board or by other agencies, may be used to set the key terms for real estate mortgages, consumer credit contracts, and credit extensions for other purposes. If building activities lag or spurt, if the sale of goods on installment seems to present special problems of instability, selective controls may accomplish much without completely transforming the pattern of prices for every sector of the money market. Of course no one can prevent some leakage, if funds are advanced for one purpose but used for another. Nonetheless, selective controls have sometimes succeeded in stimulating or restraining housing, the sale to consumers of heavy durable goods, and stock market trading.

The general, quantitative controls of the Federal Reserve System, on the other hand, have pervasive, cumulative, and far-reaching effects on the economy, extending over relatively long periods of time. They are clumsy instruments for dealing with the affairs of a region, an industry, or a sector of the economy which may be out of step.

Arthur F. Burns and others have recently stressed the fact that changing practice has changed the sensitivity of the economy to Federal Reserve policy, and has perhaps reduced the potential influence of the Federal Reserve System. I fully agree that recent developments in finance have altered the channels through which the impulses of banking policy are conveyed to the economy as a whole. The economy now responds to central banking in somewhat different ways than was the case a generation ago. But I doubt whether central banking is now notably less useful than it was then. It is perhaps desirable to stress the danger of regarding the past as a Golden Age and its great men as giants. Banking policy is not in itself a sufficient method of stabilization today. But it was not all-powerful in the twenties, either. If anything, I am inclined to think that a full-employment economy, chronically dependent upon the availability of marginal funds, may be more rather than less tractable, from the point of view of the central bank, than the economy of the twenties or thirties. In any event, I fully agree with Burns that it would be wrong now, as it was a generation ago, to expect the Federal Reserve System to stabilize the economy single-handedly.

First, let us briefly review the changes that have occurred in the institutions through which the guiding pressures of central banking are transmitted to the economy. The percentage of retained corporate earnings has increased in a generation, and depreciation and obsolescence reserves have become relatively larger. Corporations depend on external financing for a smaller share of their funds than they did during the twenties. And a larger fraction of corporate external financing is now accomplished by insurance company loans and other directly negotiated loans rather than by the flotation of new issues. As a consequence, a smaller part of the task of allocating capital among its possible users is carried out by the direct judgments of a competitive securities market. To this extent the process of capital allocation is partially insulated—although only partially—from the influence of the Federal Reserve System over long- and short-term interest rates. On the other hand, insurance companies, commercial banks, and corporations themselves all keep liquid funds in government securities, and often hold longer-term funds in that form as well, so that their investment decisions are sensitive to the yield for alternative uses of money.

Furthermore, several students have concluded that the development of new types of loan amortization contracts tends to make interest rates both less visible and less significant in the businessman's decision to borrow. The transformation by federal legislation of the market for construction finance has operated to limit the power of the Federal Reserve over the availability of funds for this important class of users. And the enlarged area of tax-financed governmental activity is to a considerable extent immune from general monetary controls expressed through interest rates. Some bond-financed capital projects of state and local governmental units, and of highway authorities, are thought to depend on the prevailing level of interest rates. But the case is hard to demonstrate. Furthermore, the tax laws favor debt financing, since interest paid (but not dividends) is a deductible corporate business expense. In that way the Internal Revenue Code reduces the significance of interest rate changes in the investment decision.

Then again, financial institutions other than commercial banks have grown far more rapidly in recent years than the banks. Insurance companies, finance companies, savings banks, and building and loan associations have assembled funds and lent them out again on a large scale. Their interest rates are not directly subject to the policies of the Federal Reserve Board, although they are necessarily affected by what it does elsewhere. And finally, the vast holdings of government securities by corporations, banks, and other financial institutions limit the freedom of maneuver of the Federal Reserve System, and permit the commercial banks at least to delay their compliance with its commands. In recent years, the banks have been able to sell government securities on a considerable scale in order to replenish their reserves and make loans, at a time when the Federal Reserve authorities were seeking to restrict credit. They have not been quite so free to do this as they were before 1951.[2] But despite the penalties which sales of government securities may involve nowadays, they are bought and sold in large volumes, as funds are shifted from less to more profitable forms, and as banks and insurance companies seek to meet the demands of their customers for loans. Although the Federal Reserve Board in recent years has allowed the market for long-term government bonds freedom not merely to fluctuate but to gyrate, there are limits beyond which even principle will not take the Board. It cannot indefinitely ignore the Treasury, which must go to the market regularly to refinance its debt, and to finance its deficits. And when the market gyrates too exuberantly, its movements begin to threaten the equilibrium of opinion upon which the willingness of business to invest, and therefore the future, depends.

In consequence of these developments, Arthur Burns concludes, "the economic power of the Federal Reserve System —that is, its ability to restrain the expansion of credit with reasonable promptness and yet without shock—[has] been eroded in some degree by the narrowing of the economic base on which its policies impinge." [3] The burden of Federal Reserve action falls unequally, he finds, on different segments of the economy, and bears with particular directness on small competitive business, which tends to be far more dependent on commercial bank loans than other forms of enterprise. While the system has power to restrict credit, and ultimately to bring the whole vast network of financial activities to heel, he wonders whether it could gain control of a strong movement of expansion without precipitating a depression.

While there is much strength in Burns' analysis, his con-

2. See below, pp. 343–44.

3. *Prosperity without Inflation* (New York, Fordham University Press, 1957), p. 81, also p. 54. Joseph Aschheim, "Commercial Banks and Financial Intermediaries, Fallacies and Policy Implications," *Journal of Political Economy*, 67 (1959), 59, reviews the literature on the relationship of the Federal Reserve System to financial intermediaries, and makes various proposals for change in the area.

clusion seems excessive, and the general issue he poses is relatively academic. There is no special virtue in having the Federal Reserve Board carry out a stabilization policy all alone. And it is by no means clear that even in the halcyon times of Governor Strong the Federal Reserve System could have gained control over a strong forward movement without risking some recession. Events between 1928 and 1931 would not suggest that the job was easy. In any event, the restraint of an inflationary volume of spending is by no means the only function of the Federal Reserve System, nor the only criterion by which its usefulness is to be judged.

The more pertinent question is what the central bank should do, and whether its powers are sufficient for the responsibilities it can reasonably be expected to meet, both alone and as part of a comprehensive governmental program, at various stages of the trade cycle.

The first task of central banking is to influence what Lundberg has called the "credit climate" of the economy. By its controls over bank credit and its interventions in the securities markets, the Federal Reserve effects the prices paid for money throughout the economy. Beyond its action on the supply and price of funds, both for long and for short period investment, monetary policy plays on opinion. Lundberg remarks that it "achieves its success through the delicate mechanism of its influence upon future expectations and upon the feelings of uncertainty among lenders and borrowers concerning interest rates, liquidity, and cyclical changes." [4] The mechanism of monetary policy is not always delicate. In recent years the Federal Reserve has released forces that have sometimes swept over the securities markets with the impact of a buffalo herd.

The securities markets are a connected series of markets, linked both regionally and functionally. They include not only the organized exchanges on which stocks and bonds are sold in various parts of the country and the world, but the totality of transactions, organized and unorganized,

4. Erik Lundberg, *Business Cycles and Economic Policy* (Cambridge, Harvard University Press, 1957), p. 163.

through which investment decisions are made. Credit is extended. Real estate mortgages or short-term loan contracts are made, and then sometimes traded, at prices which may or may not be reported and published. All parts of the money market are joined, imperfectly but effectively, by the fact that funds may shift. If the yield of bonds becomes attractive, in comparison to that of stocks, people sell stocks and buy bonds. The commercial banks, pension funds, insurance companies, and other large financial institutions keep large and variable amounts of money in every major sector of the market for government securities, moving funds freely from one to another, when they think it will pay.[5] Similarly, funds may be sought, both by the government and by other borrowers, through contracts in differing forms, of different terms, and for different periods of time. In that way, borrowers adapt themselves to conditions of ease or of shortage in varying parts of the market. A panorama of prices emerges, reflecting differences of risk and maturity on investments of different kinds and in different places. In the end, this range of interest rates is built around the "pure price of waiting" —the yield on riskless government securities, the central interest rate from which all others deviate in proportion to the risks they involve.

What factors would determine this price, and hence influence the whole related network of prices for money, in the absence of central banking intervention?

We can visualize the money markets in this sense as a host of savers and borrowers. The supply of funds provided by the savers measures the force of thrift in the economy. The demand for funds on the part of borrowers measures their views as to the present and future productivity of capital in various uses. Is the price of money determined merely by the balancing of these two elements, thrift and productivity —on the one hand, peoples' habits in making provision for the future, and on the other the changing contribution that technique can make to returns on the use of resources? Would such a balance in a free market yield a "natural" rate

5. See Winfield W. Riefler, "Open Market Operations in Long-term Securities," *Federal Reserve Bulletin, 44* (1958), 1264.

of interest, assuring society that all savings will in fact be spent for investment purposes, and that no funds will be created by the banking system, and supplied for investment use, in excess of the amount of voluntary savings?

The time dimension of the financial market prevents it even in theory from reaching so neat a short-period equilibrium between the forces of thrift and those of productivity. The liquidity preference of investors represents a powerful force playing on interest rates. When investors conclude that the actual level of prices has become "too high" in some sense, they sell, and hold cash, in large enough volume to drive prices down again. When the market rate of interest is "too low," in their view, they use liquid funds to buy securities and drive up their price. The judgments leading speculators to intervene in the market embrace more than their view as to the future of thrift and of productivity. Some have thought that the norm toward which speculation forces market rates of interest is a conventional idea as to the just price of money, lurking in men's minds as a survival of older times.[6] More probably, the peg to which the market is attached is a variable norm, representing the composite of what people think at any time about future prospects for the profitable use of money, taking into account the full range of relevant guesses. With varying degrees of certainty and uncertainty, they will have views as to the future supply of savings, the future productivity of capital (in both real and monetary terms), the expected future rate of inflation or deflation, and the future of Federal Reserve policy, to mention a few key points. Whatever the elements that enter the speculative view of the future—and they are numerous, complex, and quite volatile—there is such a view, which expresses itself in purchases and sales of securities. In this way, speculation keeps the market at any time from being a simple scale, weighing the supply of savings against the demand for them. The immediate price—the "spot" price—of money is constantly being influenced by uncertainty as to its expected future price. There is no reason to suppose that the norm

6. See, e.g., Thomas Wilson, *Fluctuations in Income & Employment* (3d ed. London, Pitman & Sons, 1949), chaps. 1–2, esp. pp. 20–26.

toward which speculation pushes the price of money at any given moment has any particularly close relation to the "natural" rate of interest which would ensure the full utilization of all savings as investment expenditure.

There is nothing unusual in this confrontation between the present and the view the present takes of the future. The spot price of cotton or wheat openly measures like forces, since for such commodities there is organized futures trading. The speculative element appears, equally, in the market for any commodity that can be stored. There, however, its effect is felt through purchases for inventory, or sales from inventory—in many cases, highly significant factors in the market.

If the forces governing the price of money are not unique, their combination is. In no market is the future so strong, compared to the present. In one sense, transactions in money are exclusively concerned with the future. As Keynes said, "Money in its significant attributes is, above all, a subtle device for linking the present to the future." [7] The speculative factor is necessarily powerful in fixing the immediate prices of money, as compared with others.

These facts define the general problem of a central bank seeking to maintain employment, keep prices from rising, and protect the international solvency of the economy. The money markets are marvelously reticulated institutions. But they are not well adapted to achieve a "natural" rate of interest and in that way ensure full utilization of the savings of the community. They are as likely to permit too much investment spending as too little. It would be an accident if at any moment of time an *ex ante* equilibrium between savings and investment were the upshot of all financial transactions.

It follows that the central bank must be prepared to intervene in the money markets to counter, to influence, and ideally to lead the forces of speculation. These interventions should reflect its own judgments as to what is required in order to maintain employment, international equilibrium,

7. *The General Theory of Employment, Interest and Money* (New York, Harcourt, Brace, 1936), p. 294.

and tolerable prices. And they should be made steadily and moderately, if the Board is to avoid the development of extreme pressures that would require it to intervene on a drastic scale and therefore take grave risks. There can be no reality and much danger in a policy that leaves the Treasury free to manage the public debt, and confines the central bank to short-term issues of government debt and "pure" commercial banking. Without central banking guidance, liquidity preference is likely to frustrate the efforts of savers and of borrowers to reach agreement. The money markets may fluctuate around a speculative rate of interest too low or too high to maintain a full-employment, noninflationary rate of spending. The central bank is entitled cautiously to assert its own view as to the pattern of interest rates best calculated to serve the national interest in the future. In that way it may help make the future conform to its desires.

This conclusion is emphatically not intended to suggest that monetary management has a free field to choose an interest rate and then to impose it on the economy. The marginal efficiency of capital sets one powerful limit on monetary policy in this sense—both in real and in money terms. And the savings habits of the society, the laws affecting saving, and the effectiveness of institutions for mobilizing savings help define another. It may be, too, that speculation itself has an autonomous aspect, as people guess not about the future course of events but about the future course of opinion about events. If the interest rate the central bank seeks to achieve is too much at variance with these underlying forces, the market will have its revenge, and the bank will be frustrated.

On the whole, underlying forces seem to be giving an upward movement to the whole network of interest rates, even at full employment equilibrium. The schedule representing the real marginal productivity of capital at different volumes of capital formation is probably rising, and may well continue to rise for long periods of time, as a consequence of scientific advance. At most, weighing together the various relevant influences, it is apparent that the percentage contribution which new capital makes to output is not falling, despite the obvious downward influence of huge volumes of new capital.

It used to be thought that an implacable tendency toward diminishing returns would force the marginal productivity of capital, and therefore profits and interest rates, down along a declining curve as economies advanced. Over moderately long periods of time, if not forever, it is now clear that science may postpone the impact of this iron law, or conceivably repeal it altogether. Even in agriculture, more and more capital seems to yield more returns in proportion over the years, not less. The apparent bias of full-employment economies for inflation exaggerates the impact of this influence on the money markets. As investors come to expect a long-term rise in prices, the expected marginal efficiency of capital in money terms is correspondingly affected. On the other side of the market, that of the supply of funds, while savings are available in large volume, they have certainly not outstripped the rate of increase of investment opportunity. On the contrary, both in the United Kingdom and in this country the volume of savings seems to have been too low during the postwar period as a whole to permit all capital needs to be satisfied at the prevailing pattern of interest rates, although that pattern is much higher than it was during the thirties. Some of the most perceptive economists, like Nicholas Kaldor, have therefore been exploring possible means for increasing the supply of savings at the expense of consumption, and thus the community's capacity for growth.[8]

There is another reason, beyond the inherent instability of the market for money, which requires the Federal Reserve System to participate broadly and regularly in the workings of the money markets. Perhaps that reason can be brought out most clearly by examining one class of proposals for the reform of the System: that advanced by the late Henry Simons and some of his students and colleagues.

Simons, Milton Friedman, and others have advocated the adoption of fixed rules rather than discretionary authority

8. See Mr. Kaldor's *An Expenditure Tax*, London, Allen & Unwin, 1955.

for the Reserve System, as the only appropriate basis for its action in the jurisprudence of a society ordered by law.[9] Indeed, Simons urged that the entire process of creating money be socialized, as an essentially governmental function, which should not be left even partially in private hands.

The legal status of the Federal Reserve System is certainly anomalous. It is a curiosity in our legal system—a group of corporations private in form and atmosphere but directed in essentials by an independent federal agency and accustomed to pay 90 per cent of their profit after dividends to the Treasury. There is surely logic in the proposal to nationalize the Reserve banks. Extensive governmental powers have been delegated to them, in seemingly rigid form. But as Holmes pointed out long ago, the life of the law has not been logic alone. Nothing significant could be accomplished by nationalizing the Federal Reserve System—certainly nothing to justify the immense effort that would be required to bring it about. And a good deal could well be lost. Countries which have recently nationalized their central banks have discovered that the change generally increased the powerful autonomy of the central bankers in their relation with elected officials, rather than the reverse. It is hard to see which of the difficulties the System has experienced over the years would be cured by the legal act of making the Board and the banks direct agencies of the federal government in form as well as in fact.

There is a wisdom of long experience, echoed in every governmental structure, that counsels the preservation of semidetached institutions for financial control, like the Federal Reserve System. They cannot long defy popular government. But they can delay it, argue with it, sometimes even persuade it. Their power really is that of a Second Chamber, which should survive because on these matters a well-informed second opinion is a good thing to have. Of course

9. H. C. Simons, *A Positive Program for Laissez-faire,* Chicago, University of Chicago Press, 1934, and "Rules versus Authorities in Monetary Policy," *Journal of Political Economy, 44* (1936), 1, reprinted in *Economic Policy for a Free Society,* Chicago, University of Chicago Press, 1948; M. Friedman, "A Monetary and Fiscal Framework for Economic Stability," *American Economic Review, 38* (1948), 245.

the Federal Reserve has been and is more than an advisory chamber. Under the statute it has the final power to decide many questions. And in fact it has a fair chance to argue for its view and to translate it into policy, unless the government objects too vigorously.

But the question of nationalizing the banks was only one phase of Simons' central argument—that a democratic society should have fixed rules, not broad discretion, to govern the exercise of banking powers. Simons would separate the depository from the lending function in banking. He would eliminate fractional reserve banking, keep the banks out of the securities markets, and eliminate every vestige of their discretion. The government would control the business cycle by varying its tax collections. It would run a deficit or a surplus, as the case might be, according to equally fixed rules of fiscal policy, intended to preserve price stability as well as full employment.

I agree with Simons that stability of prices over time should be an explicit goal of national policy—stability of prices rather than a fixed quantity of money, a fixed national income, or any alternative combination of targets. But I conclude that the central bank must have considerable discretion in seeking that goal by varying the quantity of money—buying and selling government securities and inducing the commercial banks to do likewise.

Any system needs a safety valve. The Simons-Chicago proposals rest on the premise that if only the economy could be made competitive enough, it would reach full employment equilibrium by itself, with the help of occasional federal deficits or surpluses. In such a world, monetary authority could be relatively passive, confined to its narrow task by responsibly established legal doctrine.

It is hard to disagree with Simons' proposition that the Federal Reserve should be kept a responsible part of the system of law, both by a clarification of the authority delegated to it by the Congress and the President, and by the active interest of Congress and its committees. Mr. Martin cannot justly complain that he has been ignored by Congress in recent years.

But the premise of the Chicago proposals—that a competitive economy would remain fully employed, almost unaided by government—is wrong, as a matter both of theory and of fact.[10] In this instance at least a mistaken premise leads also to a mistaken conclusion. The repercussive adjustments of prices and wages under the pressure of full employment could never be so readily accomplished by competitive forces alone as to permit us the luxury of a really free market for money, even if we had genuinely competitive markets for goods and labor.

We do not, of course, have such free competitive markets. In one perspective, it seems fair to describe the work of the Federal Reserve System as that of "managing" or at least influencing the price of money throughout the economy, in the interest of compensating for the recurring failures of the pricing mechanism elsewhere to maintain full employment. For all the risks of this kind of action, it is a small price to pay for comparative freedom in the product markets of the economy. While the quantity of money does not determine the quantity of spending, it certainly exerts an influence, both through interest rates and otherwise. And if part of the task of central banking can be done by altering the quantity of money, fractional reserve banking is as convenient a means as any for carrying out its purposes. In this perspective, the Chicago reforms promise more rigidity than we can afford.

If this is an accurate description of the central bank's role, it follows that the Federal Reserve should be as much interested in the level of stock prices as in the volume of commercial bank loans, and that all the interrelated parts of the financial market are of direct concern to it. In recent years the Federal Reserve has put renewed stress on confining itself to commercial loans, short-term credit, and short-term government securities. This attitude recalls the views of the day when central banking was an appendage of commercial banking, and central bankers harbored the illusion that they could pursue a neutral role while the money market found its own level.

The "bills only" policy of the Federal Reserve Board was

10. This proposition will be considered in Chap. 10.

adopted in 1953. It confines open market operations to short-term government securities, particularly Treasury bills, save on the rare occasions when the market for long-term securities becomes "disorderly," in the Board's judgment. The rationale of the rule is as follows: [11] The market for long-term securities is a delicate, sensitive mechanism, reflecting long-term trends and expectations for the economy at large; the Federal Reserve System should not interfere with it directly, lest it create "unjustified" expectations among dealers and investors as to the future of yields, or the future of Federal Reserve policy; intervention in the long-term market would have the further disadvantage of making it harder for the System to differentiate between trends and tendencies originating in the economy and those which reflect the consequences of its own actions. The next step in the argument is paradox confounded. Since all parts of the market are connected by the fluidity of money, Mr. Winfield Riefler says, speaking for the Board, Federal Reserve intervention in the bills sector of the market is quickly translated into pressure on long-term bonds. Indeed, he indicates that more frequent changes in reserve requirements would probably do all that is necessary by way of open market operations, since the commercial banks use excess reserves to buy government securities in *all* sectors of the market. Thus the policy of "bills only" is defended both because it leaves the vital market for long-term government securities free to reflect economic forces originating outside the Federal Reserve System, and because it keeps the long-term market under the influence of Federal Reserve policy almost as quickly and directly as if the System had bought or sold long-term bonds in the first place.

At this late date there is no hiding place from the obligations of monetary management. Riefler is of course right in saying that funds flow from sector to sector of the market, and that borrowers, too, move from part to part, as may seem profitable and convenient to them. But the parts of the money market are not joined by a law of hydraulics. There is nothing automatic about the way in which yield patterns

11. See Riefler, "Open Market Operations in Long-term Securities" (above, p. 188, n. 5).

change, in roughly parallel lines, as the market responds to a variety of pressures, both of events and of policy. Fears of inflation, set off by Congressional action or by a wage settlement, may affect short- and long-term prospects quite differently. One sector may be far more vulnerable to speculative raids than another, far thinner, far more susceptible to changing expectations. A thousand factors—the timing of a refinancing, the failure of a government or a private issue, the stage of the inventory cycle, crop reports—can touch the long view differently from the short.

"Bills only" is a dangerous policy precisely because it commits the authorities not to intervene where intervention may be most needed. While the market certainly links long-term rates and those in the bill market, the link is more elastic than is desirable, given the equilibrating ends of monetary policy. As has been apparent in recent years, the turbulent flow of funds in a full-employment economy is not so easily kept in channel. The pressure of funds may distort market relations, on which the "bills only" policy depends. Then an outcry develops to invoke the traditional remedies for "disorderly conditions," i.e. Federal Reserve purchases of securities (even Treasury purchases, in extreme cases), more reserves, easier money. Those potent medicines may not, however, be exactly what the economy needs. On the other hand, if the markets are allowed to crash, a depression may develop, and then easy money will be needed on a larger scale. "Bills only" sharpens both horns of the central bank's dilemma.

The Federal Reserve should plan to include the full spectrum of government securities in its open-market operations. It will not always be necessary for it to function in all markets. For long periods of time it may not be essential for it to move outside the customary range of Treasury bills. What is indispensable, however, is that it be known to stand ready to intervene in any relevant market, in the interest of carrying out its basic work of helping to maintain employment and stable prices, and to carry out the nation's international financial policies.[12]

The greatest obstacle to the government's freedom of ac-

12. See, for an acute comment, R. S. Sayers, *Central Banking after Bagehot* (Oxford, Clarendon Press, 1957), chap. 10, esp. pp. 137–45.

tion in using fiscal and monetary policy as weapons of stabilization is the composition of the federal debt. The division of the debt into instruments of varying maturity, and of diverse contractual character, has no doubt permitted the government to borrow pools of money that might not otherwise have been available to it. But the consequence is that the Treasury must sell astronomic volumes of securities every year merely in order to stand still. On June 30, 1955, the Treasury had outstanding $49.7 billion in securities that would mature within a year. On the corresponding date in 1956 the total was $58.7 billion; in 1957, $71 billion; and on March 30, 1958, $72.6 billion.

The necessities of this process cannot fail to influence the tenor of banking policy. It would be inhuman for the Chairman of the Federal Reserve Board to allow a Treasury issue to fail. No Secretary of the Treasury enjoys paying needlessly high interest charges. The Reserve Board has more than enough power to maintain "orderly" conditions in the market, by buying or announcing that it will buy. The combination of these elements is familiar and irresistible. The pressures inherent in the task of "rolling over" the government debt delay restrictive action by the Federal Reserve Board and encourage expansionary action. One partial remedy would be to refund considerable parts of the debt as "consols"—that is, perpetual issues. If it proved impossible for any reason to develop this practice, certainly a degree of liberation could be achieved by shifting a considerable part of the debt into securities of reasonably long maturity.

If central bankers must have discretion, both to discipline the forces of speculation and to compensate for shortcomings in the performance of the product markets of the economy, how should their discretion be defined? The society yearns to satisfy certain economic goals simultaneously—full employment, high rates of growth, steady prices, exchange stability without excessive loss of gold. At different times these goals will have different degrees of urgency. Sometimes they will be incompatible: policy may have to sacrifice one in order to satisfy others. Central banking can assist in reaching these goals by its influence on the rate of spending for investment purposes, and on the extension of credit to finance consumers' purchases. That influence can be felt equally through the securities markets and through the commercial banks, through long-term and through short-term transactions of finance. The means through which this influence could become effective is to encourage or to limit spending—that is, to keep the aggregate of all demands for current production close to the value of potential output at a level of prices deemed appropriate. The particular forms of spending most sensitive to the influence of central banking are those financed by loans, or the proceeds of new securities issues, and those in which the decision to go forward represents a balance of pros and cons, which could be altered by a change in the financial atmosphere.

It is true, of course, that many firms can finance themselves with undistributed profits, and that banks can often expand their loans by selling government securities. But a period of sustained prosperity, sooner or later, creates opportunities for expansion beyond the limits of undistributed earnings. Firms must come to the securities markets, or to the institutional lenders, for large capital needs. And as the boom runs its course, internal liquidity declines, making it more and more necessary for firms to return to the commercial banks for working capital. Meanwhile, the banks and insurance companies have sold large parts of their government bonds and can no longer expand loans at will. Thus the financial system falls under the control of the Federal Reserve at the point where such control really becomes important.

From the viewpoint of stabilization policy over the long run, it makes little difference whether the commercial banks or the insurance companies—internal or external sources of money—finance the period of economic recovery up to the point of close-to-full employment. The period of high employment may continue, sustained by effective government policies; it may become an inflationary boom, with or without speculative explosions; or it may be followed by a sharp or a mild slump. What came before cannot usually be decisive, nor even particularly important, in determining the course of events from this point forward. What is crucial is the way the government uses the whole of its armory to deal with events and opinion as they develop.

If this analysis is correct, it follows that the Federal Reserve System does not require basic structural reform. Like other institutions of policy, it needs the assistance of thought —the studies of its own staff and the criticism of others—to keep its work closely addressed to the world of reality. Central banking is a highly intellectual sport. It can be well played only by men of high intuitive talent, or by commoner mortals who have thoroughly considered first-class intelligence about the markets they are trying to influence.

The traditional proposals for banking reform would make little contribution, or none, to the process of rational thought about central banking, or to the improvement of our capacity to achieve its goals.

The case against gold as the reserve base of the system has been written many times. No doubt reserves more logical than gold could well be devised. Several, of course, have been earnestly urged, most particularly the various "commodity-reserve" plans.[13] But I doubt whether their adoption would be worth the trouble a campaign of persuasion would require. These proposals are in a class with Plantagenet Palliser's charming dream of decimal coinage for England. As Keynes once said of another reform: If we were sensible enough to adopt it, we should not need it, for in such a state of rationality we should be able to manage with existing institutions.

One of the most interesting ideas for monetary reform would require reserves to be held against member bank assets, not deposit liabilities. This approach to the problem was put forward during 1948–51, first by Jacob Viner of Princeton.[14] The advantage of Viner's idea would be to separate the Federal Reserve System's policy toward the quantity of money from its open market operations. At the time he

13. See Benjamin Graham, *World Commodities and World Currency*, New York and London, McGraw-Hill, 1944.

14. Letter to the Editor, *New York Times* (April 22, 1951), p. 10, col. 7. For background of this era, see below, pp. 330–37.

wrote, debt management and interest-rate support policies kept forcing the Federal Reserve to inflate member bank reserves when it wanted to reduce them. The stormy course of government security markets in 1957 and 1958 may revive interest in such plans or in their equivalent, the more drastic manipulation of existing reserve requirements.

Some of the substitute reserve plans aim to free the world from the deflationary pressure of a gold shortage—the old, familiar Cross of Gold argument. There has been precious little evidence since the war, however, that the world is suffering from chronic deflation. The trend has all been in the direction of inflation, despite the fact that many countries have been operating with what would once have been considered dangerously skimpy gold reserves.

This is not to say that all is well with our international monetary arrangements. Robert Triffin has been the Cassandra calling attention to certain dangers implicit in the general success of postwar monetary policy.[15] Since the end of the war a massive redistribution of the world's gold reserves has occurred, and the reserve base of the free world's monetary system is now divided more usefully than has been the case in many years. American policy for financing aid to other governments, from the time of Lend-Lease, is the basic cause of this series of changes, both encouraging a rapid increase of trade in the postwar world and financing much of it through grants. The net result has been not merely an increase in foreign gold holdings but a most striking rise in foreign holdings of short-term dollar assets. If such assets are deducted from our monetary gold stock, the United States reserve in June 1958 stood at $4.7 billion, compared with $16.3 in 1949 on the same basis, while the gold and dollar holdings of foreign countries totaled $31.5 billion, compared with $15.8 billion in 1949. Foreign-held dollar balances in the United States rose from $2.2 billion in 1938 to $8.2 billion in 1949, $16.6 billion in 1957, and $17.6 billion in 1958.

15. See *Europe and the Money Muddle*, New Haven, Yale University Press, 1957; *The Future of the European Payments System*, Wicksell Lectures (1958), Stockholm, 1958; "The Return to Convertibility: 1926–1931 and 1958–, or Convertibility and the Morning After" (in press).

As a consequence of these enormous shifts, convertibility of the key Western currencies has become distinctly possible.

Quite apart from these developments, there is another reason to doubt the long-run viability of the system, on its present reserve foundation of gold, dollars, and sterling. The primary function of reserves now is not merely to establish a disciplinary rule of thumb for linking internal monetary policy to external economic events; it is to provide a cushion of liquidity, permitting a country to finance a transition period, during which it survives a nonrecurring shock, like Suez, or adapts itself to a long-run change in its international position—the impact, for example, of a round of wage increases, the loss of an export market or a major colony, or some other event of long-range implications. According to Triffin's calculations, the gold and dollar holdings of countries other than the United States and the United Kingdom constituted in 1958 a distinctly smaller fraction of their annual imports, taken as an index of their foreign trade, than was the case in 1928. They were then at the same relatively low level as in 1913, and were falling as a fraction of imports. These reserves are by no means equally divided among the nations in proportion to their needs for international liquidity. It is assumed that since reserves are primarily required to facilitate international economic transfers, they should grow in rough proportion to the volume of world trade, unless the development of new institutions for clearing and the control of reserves should permit further economy in their use. But a growth of reserves at the rate of growth of trade is now almost impossible to visualize. Gold production is relatively low in the West, and the gold-producing countries complain that it is unprofitable. Newly produced gold now provides only about one-fifth or one-sixth of the new reserves required each year to keep pace with the healthy expansion of world trade. The United States cannot continue indefinitely to finance world trade by providing other countries with short-term dollar balances "without eventually undermining confidence in the dollar itself." [16] The present size

16. Triffin, *Europe and the Money Muddle*, p. 297. "A continuation of this movement would inevitably undermine the international position of the dollar

of these balances and their rate of increase in recent years impose a check-rein on the freedom of the Federal Reserve Board to pursue cheap money policies, if such policies should prove desirable. And like the huge foreign-held sterling balances of the late twenties and the postwar period, the magnitude of foreign dollar holdings in relation to our gold reserve exposes the United States, and thus the entire world monetary system, to the risk of collapse in the event that rational or irrational doubts develop about the future of the dollar. The unwillingness of foreigners to continue their accumulation of dollar balances led in 1958 to a loss of $2.3 billion in the gold stock of the United States, much the largest such fall in recent history.

This kind of risk is an inherent weakness of the gold exchange standard. As Triffin says, "The basic absurdity of the gold exchange standard is that it makes the *international* monetary system highly dependent on individual countries' decisions about the continued use of one or a few *national* currencies as monetary reserves." [17] The spread of questions about even the strongest currency can precipitate a flight to gold that would bring the whole structure down. Confidence is the essence of international as it is of national banking. Increases in the customary fraction of banking assets held in liquid form can be carried out only at the cost of forced sales, deflation, and monetary restrictions, on the one hand, or by devaluation on the other.

The most important reform of the Federal Reserve System for the immediate future, therefore, is the strengthening and development of institutions for international monetary cooperation and integration. Unless we soon develop more effective devices for economizing and institutionalizing existing reserves and eliminating the chance that flights from key

---

and ultimately endanger its acceptability as a safe reserve medium for other countries, just as the excessive growth of short-term sterling indebtedness during the War led to the post-war downfall of sterling as a means of international payments and as a normal component of international monetary reserves": Triffin, *The Future of the European Payments System*, pp. 35–36. See, however, Per Jacobsson, "International Liquidity," Federal Reserve Bank of New York, *Monthly Review*, Supp., Dec. 1958.

17. "The Return to Convertibility," p. 66, n. 29.

currencies to gold destroy the world's banking system, the growing shortage of reserves will lead either to a general financial crash or to a new wave of planned or unplanned devaluations. Certainly recent financial history demonstrates that central bankers and legislators are quite willing to use modern forms of an ancient remedy—coin clipping, through changes in the price of gold, and changes in the statutory or administratively determined fractions that determine the ratio of gold to the volume of notes and deposits.

The emergence of the International Monetary Fund as a strong and effective Reserve Bank for central banks could facilitate the shift of the free world to more normal procedures for long-term finance without risking general deflation. The level of foreign-held dollar balances could then be kept within tolerable limits by American imports, full employment, and considerable private capital exports, to utilize foreign currencies earned by American exports, current borrowings, or the repayment of loans.

Confronting this series of phenomena, certain proposals for the future of the Federal Reserve System aim to impose on central banking more automatic rules than the rather comfortable accommodations of international to national forces that characterize the present stage of development in the conduct of the gold standard. While I favor measures that would more effectively integrate national economies into a world economy, the attempt to do so through rigid rules of central banking is futile. Discretion is the essence of central banking—persuasion, not coercion; parallel movements; not abrupt, autonomous actions. This was true even before 1914, when there were fewer cushioning layers between most central banks and the pressures of international economic life. The reform of the Federal Reserve System should involve more discretionary powers, not more rigid rules.

All things considered, there is little point in seeking a radical change in the status of gold reserves as they are administered under modern legislation, in the light of the evolving rules of the International Monetary Fund and the habits of central bank cooperation. Save for the prospect of a shortage of reserves, discussed earlier, the contemporary gold standard serves reasonably well to translate the underlying international realities into signals and pressures the banking community has learned to understand and usually even to accept. Gold reserves and gold movements represent a mechanism through which the monetary policies of different nations can be roughly coordinated with some hope of success. The same function would have to be performed by any other reserve scheme. The "real" economic problems are there to be coped with, so long as a country participates in international trade: the effect of domestic monetary policy on domestic prices; that of its domestic prices on its international trade; and finally, the impact of international trade on the reserve position of the nation and the implication of changes in reserve for domestic prices. The connection between exchange rates and capital movements would exist whether the world used gold or bundles of wheat to settle international accounts. On the whole, it has not been shown that another system would make it easier for nations to adapt their national economic aspirations to the tides of international economic life. Short of putting monetary policy under supranational control, the present-day gold standard serves about as well as any alternative could in facilitating day-to-day adjustments and encouraging international cooperation in the making of monetary policy. There are many areas that promise higher marginal returns for the expenditure of energy in behalf of reform.

This survey is not intended to imply, however, that certain improvements are not needed in the statutory basis for the domestic functioning of the Federal Reserve System. The most important step that could be taken to improve the banking law would be to confer on the Federal Reserve Board greater power than it now has to vary reserve requirements for member banks. This authority has proved to be one of the most pervasive and effective of its instruments for influencing the credit climate of the economy. It should be re-established in a way that would make it easier to use.

The last generation has witnessed the development of a series of devices intended to supplement general monetary controls through direct regulation of the terms on which money can be loaned on certain kinds of security or for certain purposes. The regulation of margin trading on the stock market is characteristic of these "selective" regulations of credit extension. Except for the regulation of credit advanced on the security of stocks, however, vested interests have tenaciously, and so far successfully, resisted the permanent extension of Federal Reserve authority to the field of consumer finance or real estate mortgages. Nonetheless, it is desirable that the Board have permanent discretionary powers to fix down payments and other key terms of real estate mortgages and other forms of financing used in the construction industry, and comparable powers in the field of consumer credit. Selective controls of this kind should give the Board some capacity to limit the availability of funds for particular uses without greatly altering the level of interest rates or the credit climate for the economy as a whole. Such controls would probably not be invoked for long periods of time. They are unpopular and hard to administer, and do not fully succeed in governing the flow of credit to finance the demand for particular products. Nonetheless, they have proved to be useful devices both for restricting and for encouraging large volumes of borrowing. They will often prove useful adjuncts to central bank policy. And national policy in this regard should be coordinated by the Federal Reserve Board, not left in the hands of officials charged with housing programs, or programs of assistance to veterans.

The scope of Federal Reserve jurisdiction deserves careful consideration. What advantage is there to the nation in the fact that half the banks in the country are not members of the Federal Reserve System, and that state law complicates national efforts to prescribe uniform policies for the merger of banks, and their combination into local or regional groups? For purposes of monetary policy, the United States should be a nation, not a federation of states. The Constitution authorized Congress to "coin money and to regulate the value thereof." In this realm, the survival of state power defers to the appearance, not the reality of federalism. New legislation should go beyond the progress so painfully made in 1913, and advance the amalgamation of the nation's banks into a single system, not a congeries of centripetal forces. By the same token, mechanisms of control should be developed to bring nonbanking financial institutions within reach of Federal Reserve policy.

Secondary Tools of Control:
Free and Regulated Markets

ONE of the major gaps in contemporary economics has been a relative neglect of the relationship between the flow of national income and the functioning of markets.[1] Studies concerned with the over-all level of economic activity, on the one hand, and those analyzing the behavior of single firms or single markets, on the other, have typically proceeded in separate channels. Except in a few notable instances these two lines of inquiry have not so far come together. The failure to integrate aggregative and market analysis has weakened the literature of economics as a source of policy. It has permitted confusion to develop and to persist about the terms on which it should be possible to maintain high levels of employment at reasonably stable prices.

Industrial fluctuations are not governed by Archimedes' law. The effect of fiscal and monetary policy on the actual employment of men and the production of goods is not a simple matter of so much additional spending automatically producing so much more employment and production. The final result of fiscal and monetary action depends upon what happens to prices and wages and profits in the rough and tumble of ordinary business life. The government and the Federal Reserve System can do much to alter the volume of funds and the volume of spending. But the flows of spending for consumption or investment have their impact on production through markets, industries, and individual firms. Successful stabilization is not a trick to be carried out in the quiet offices where financial experts practice the black arts of banking, budget, and tax policy. The success or failure of fiscal and monetary policy as weapons of stabilization depends in the end not only on the skill and insight of a few wizards of high finance but on the structure and behavior of many markets, and on the policies of the law in regulating them.

1. William J. Fellner, "Employment Theory and Business Cycles," in Howard S. Ellis, ed., *A Survey of Contemporary Economics* (Philadelphia, Blakiston, 1948) pp. 49, 75.

In the first place, some problems of unemployment cannot be reached by programs of general stabilization that attempt to balance aggregate spending and aggregate output at an acceptable price level. Programs of this kind can assure the economy at large an appropriately high level of demand for aggregate output. But the notion of aggregate output is precisely that—an aggregate. Certain firms, industries, or regions may decline even when the economy as a whole is flourishing. Some of the problems of agriculture and the railroads are of this character. And all studies of particular industries show a pattern of widely variable rates of growth, reflecting changes in the technology of an advanced industrial economy. It may be, at times, that the growth of particular forms of capital may outstrip demand or the availability of labor or other resources which may be necessary, at certain prices, before they can be used. Special dispensations are often required to deal with such problems, even when policy has achieved a general balance between over-all demand and full-employment supply. In such instances, policy may, in the alternative, relieve hardship by facilitating a shift of resources to more profitable employment, or subsidize sectors of the economy that could not otherwise hold their own.

Secondly, all forms of spending added to the stream of income do not have the same "multiplier," or secondary effect on total income.[2] Some deficit spending may discourage more spending than it stimulates in the first instance. The same observation applies to the reverberations of cuts in spending which reduce the national income. A fall in income starting with a government surplus may have different consequences from a fall beginning with a drop in private investment in inventories, building, or equipment, or with a change in savings habits. Attempts to measure these repercussions of changes in the level of spending on national income have been inconclusive thus far. Doubt is developing about whether in fact such multiplier effects have high values, even under favorable circumstances.

Problems of this sort aside, however, the main factors determining the effects of fiscal and monetary policy on em-

2. See above, pp. 98–100.

ployment are those of market structure and behavior. Of these, the most significant are the presence or absence of competitive and speculative forces in markets, their strength, and the ways in which various degrees of monopoly power are used in the making of prices and wages. Especially in recent years, experience indicates that it is quite easy for price and wage policy to frustrate the intended effects of fiscal and monetary action or greatly to increase both its costs and its effects on the class structure of society. After all, it would hardly advance the ends of policy to have the government's antidepression budgetary deficit translated into a rise in prices rather than in output and employment.

Part III will be concerned primarily with three questions of market organization and market policy in relation to stabilization:

1. Could either competition or monopoly, as a rule for organizing markets, in itself protect society against booms and slumps? To this question, the answer offered here is no. This conclusion is probably correct in theoretical terms, and is certainly correct as a practical matter, in view of the extent to which private monopoly, public regulation, and custom have established lags and rigidities in the prevailing pattern of price adjustment.

2. Should policies of enforced competition, such as those of the antitrust laws, play an important part, where they are at all feasible, in government programs of stabilization and growth? To this question, the answer given is yes.

3. How adequate is our present law for the control of free markets, regulated industries, and labor, in the light of the several purposes of the Employment Act of 1946? To this question the answer proposed is "not very adequate." All these bodies of law need amendment or reinterpretation, to a greater or lesser degree, before they can be expected to complement fiscal and monetary policy in helping to keep a growing economy fully employed at prices that are approximately stable over long periods of time.

10. Market Organization and Stabilization Policy

THE EFFECTS of changes in the level of spending upon output, employment, and prices differ not only with the structure of markets but with the stage of the business cycle. The problems of stabilization policy presented by market behavior are different, at least in magnitude, during a depression, a period of recovery, a period of gross inflation, and a situation of reasonably full employment—the ideal we seek but probably can never quite realize.

Analysis might well begin with the case of developing depression. A depression is a period in which the total of spending for current output—that is, the gross national product—falls below its previous level, and continues to fall significantly below that level for some time. The drop may start for any one of a number of reasons. The government may be effectively hoarding some of its tax receipts. Businessmen and consumers may borrow from the banks and other financial institutions, and then spend, less than the volume of savings which those institutions have received. Corporations may fail to spend all their undistributed profits or depreciation allowances. Any one of these factors, or all of them in combination, may result in a sizable drop in the total of spending.[1]

For present purposes we are more concerned with the effect of the downward movement in money income than with its origins. Because spending for current output has fallen, the level of demand is too low to clear the market at prevailing prices. Stress appears in all markets, save those few, if

1. These relationships are described and discussed above, Chap. 5.

any, where demand is independent of the level of income. Demand for different products and services falls off irregularly. The pattern of declining spending and demand reflects the relative intensity of consumer preferences for different products in a period of falling income, and the differential impact of the depression on the various sectors and regions of the economy. The decline is felt first and most strongly in those sectors of the economy associated with investment in plant, equipment, and inventory. But it spreads. For most products, demand is reduced—that is, in each market buyers will take less at any given price than before. At the new, lower schedule of demand, buyers would continue to take more at lower than at higher prices, although probably in a different pattern than before, and perhaps in one more sensitive than before to cheaper alternatives.

There has been a good deal of controversy as to how competitive and monopolistic markets respond to downward shifts in the schedule of demand for their products. Several careful studies support the popular impression that at least in the short run price seems to fluctuate proportionately more than output under these circumstances in competitive markets, whereas in markets characterized by the presence of a good deal of monopoly power, price seems to hold firm in the first instance, or to drop proportionately less, and output correspondingly more.[2]

2. F. C. Mills, *Price-quantity Interactions in Business Cycles*, New York, NBER, 1946. See also Saul Nelson and Walter G. Keim, *Price Behavior and Business Policy*, TNEC, 76th Cong., 3d Sess., Monograph 1 (1940); A. C. Neal, *Industrial Concentration and Price Inflexibility*, Washington, D.C., American Council on Public Affairs, 1942; Gardiner C. Means, *Industrial Prices and Their Relative Inflexibility*, Senate Document 13, 74th Cong. 1st Sess. (1935); National Resources Committee, *The Structure of the American Economy*, Pt. I (1939), Pt. II (1940); Edward S. Mason, *Economic Concentration and the Monopoly Problem* (Cambridge, Harvard University Press, 1957), pp. 6–10; Don Patinkin, *Money, Interest and Prices*, Evanston, Ill., Row, Peterson, 1956; T. De Scitovsky, "Prices under Monopoly and Competition," *Journal of Political Economy*, 49 (1941), 663; J. Kenneth Galbraith, "Monopoly and the Concentration of Economic Power," in Howard S. Ellis, ed., *A Survey of Contemporary Economics* (Homewood, Ill., R. D. Irwin, for the American Economic Association, 1948), pp. 99, 109–15; Ellis, "Monopoly Power and Price Rigidities," *Quarterly Journal of Economics*, 50 (1936), 456, and "Market Structure and Stabilization Policy," *Review of Economics and Statistics*, 39 (1957), 127; R. F. Harrod, "Imperfect

In theory, these observations present a puzzle, and perhaps a paradox.

The word "monopoly" literally means "one seller." The idea of monopoly in its simplest form implies no more—only that a single seller provides the full market supply of the given product or service. There may be substitutes, to which buyers may shift more or less comfortably, or other limits upon the monopolist's price power. But the heart of the matter is that the monopolist can choose the price he charges, taking into account both his judgment as to the state of demand for his product, and his knowledge of his own cost conditions. The buyer must accept this price or do without. The result is a capacity to make higher profits than in competitive sectors, by providing less than would be forthcoming under competition, and at higher prices. The seller in such a position is insulated from pressures for cost reduction. Resources are not used as fully as in competitive situations. And the distribution of income does not correspond to competitive norms. This is the essence of the popular and economic objection to monopoly, so deeply rooted in our legal history.

The idea of competition means, in contrast, the absence of such power over price on the seller's part. Typically, competition reigns as the determinant of price, output, and resource use in markets of many sellers, each producing a small share of output, without power to bar the entry of rivals. The identification of monopoly power is a question of degree.

Competition and the Trade Cycle," *Review of Economic Statistics, 18* (1936), 84; Don D. Humphrey, "The Nature and Meaning of Rigid Prices, 1890–1933," *Journal of Political Economy, 45* (1937), 651; James Tobin, "Money Wage Rates and Employment," in Seymour E. Harris, ed., *The New Economics* (New York, Knopf, 1947), p. 572; Rufus S. Tucker, "The Reasons for Price Rigidity," *American Economic Review, 28* (1938), 41; Donald H. Wallace, "Industrial Markets and Public Policy," in Carl J. Friedrich and Edward S. Mason, eds., *Public Policy* (Cambridge, Harvard University Press, 1940), p. 59, and "Monopoly Prices and Depression," in *Explorations in Economics: Notes and Essays Contributed in Honor of F. W. Taussig* (New York and London, McGraw-Hill, 1936), p. 346; Ralph C. Wood, "Dr. Tucker's 'Reasons' for Price Rigidity," *American Economic Review, 28* (1938), 663; Richard Ruggles, "The Nature of Price Flexibility and the Determinants of Relative Price Changes in the Economy," in *Business Concentration and Price Policy* (Princeton, NBER, 1955), p. 441 (includes a critical review of most of the prior literature).

Some sellers have a great deal of discretion over the price they receive, others less, some none at all. In an effectively competitive market, since one seller does not provide a significant share of supply, he cannot without collusion control his rivals' offerings. He must therefore accept the market price and adjust his own production to that price, with reference to his own costs. There are a number of other cases, typical and atypical, which ring changes on these themes, but for present purposes it is unnecessary to spell them out.

In any market, competitive or noncompetitive, economic theory would expect sellers to enlarge their output in the short run so long as it paid them to do so—that is, so long as the extra revenue added by selling another unit, their marginal revenue, exceeded or equaled the extra out-of-pocket costs actually involved in its production, their marginal costs.

In a competitive market, where the seller has no discretion over the price he receives, each additional unit brings in the same amount, the price charged for all units, so that the sensible limit of production for him is that at which marginal cost equals price as well as marginal revenue. For the competitive market as a whole, the available supply is the sum of these separate offerings. It can be sold at a price fixed by the state of demand in the market. The market will be cleared of all offerings at the price indicated by the schedule representing the quantities people would take at different prices at that moment. If, as may happen for short periods when supply cannot be increased, market price is above the industry's marginal cost, output will rise and price will fall. If it is less, output will fall and price rise, until price and industry marginal cost are equal again. This reasoning does not suggest that in a competitive market at any time profits cannot be earned. Price equals the seller's marginal cost, but may well be more than average cost at that scale of output, for exceptionally efficient or well-located producers, or indeed for all producers, if demand is high for the product or service. Such profits are signals for expansion in the market, through the entry of new firms or otherwise, so that competitive markets tend toward an equilibrium, even though they probably never reach it, defined by the equality of price and industry marginal cost.

A seller with significant market power, on the other hand, can sell more units only by charging less. The sale of extra units at a reduced price—through a secret rebate, for example —reduces the average revenue received for all units. Marginal revenue is different from price, and always lower. The sensible limit of production, that at which marginal cost equals marginal revenue, does not therefore also define price, which in terms of the prevailing schedule of demands will always be above marginal revenue and marginal cost at this scale of production.

In short, *output* is a function of the relation between *marginal cost* and *marginal revenue; price,* however, is a function of the relation between *output* and the schedule of *demand,* or average revenue. Against this background, in either a competitive or a noncompetitive market, a fall in demand, perhaps changing the shape of the demand curve, may affect both price and output, depending upon the schedules representing the amounts that will be offered and bought at different market prices at the new and lowered level of income.

At this point, the distinction between the long and the short run becomes important. As economists use these terms, the long and short run are not fixed periods of time. The "short period" is the interval for which the basic capital and productive arrangements of the firm are fixed, the "long period" that in which capital plant, machinery, and permanent staff can be adjusted to market conditions. The short run, generally speaking, is the period during which supply can be changed only by varying the number of workers or the volume of raw materials used, the long run that during which capital and managerial factors can be added or withdrawn. In the short run the firm has "fixed" and "variable" costs, costs which do not vary with output, and those which do. In the long run, all costs are variable, in that shifts of capital and other permanent resources can and do occur.

As the total of spending falls off, the demand for different commodities and services declines in a variable pattern. In the very short run, prices in competitive markets fall at once; those in noncompetitive markets may or may not fall, depending upon the price policies of sellers. The price of stocks or of wheat on the Chicago Board of Trade drop. The price of tomatoes in the wholesale vegetable market near the railroad station in New Haven fall, until the market is cleared. Clothing is marked down, unless sellers are willing to carry it in inventory for another season. On the other hand, many products are produced only after they are sold—bituminous coal, for example, or fabricated steel. For such products the relation of demand to short-run variable costs is decisive, fixed costs being irrelevant, unless the seller can pursue price policies of some discretion. In general, for competitive markets the shorter the period, the more completely price is determined by demand, whereas in noncompetitive markets the response of price to a fall in demand may be resisted or postponed. The contrast between the short-run behavior of steel prices and steel scrap prices, or those of bituminous coal, bring out the point.

Both in the short period and in longer periods a fall in demand often reduces market price. Then each seller adjusts his output to the reduced price in terms of his own cost conditions. Frequently, he discovers that a reduction in price or a weakening of the market stimulates cost economies not hitherto suspected to be available. For this reason some economists comment that price is a far greater influence on costs than costs on price.

Over a period during which some adjustment of output to market conditions can occur, the fall in demand might well be met differently in competitive and noncompetitive markets. In a competitive market, if the industry is able to produce a considerable part of its output under conditions of constant marginal costs, the reduction in demand would not reduce price, although output would fall, since according to the new demand schedule less would be taken at the price which equaled the prior marginal cost. If marginal costs were rising—that is, if marginal costs would fall as output was reduced—the fall in demand would reduce both price and output.

The mechanism of expected short-period adjustment in the situation of considerable monopoly is the same, although the results are different. In such a market, the previous equilibrium was one at a higher price and lower output than would have prevailed had the market been competitive. Under conditions of constant marginal cost, the fall in demand would reduce both price and output, whereas only output would fall had the market been competitive. The relative change in price and output would be determined by the shape of the two curves representing technique and demand. If marginal costs were rising, again both price and output would be expected to fall, the proportionate fall in each being determined by the shape of the schedules.

Thus the theoretical image of expected short-run adjustments to a fall in the schedule of demand would not lead one necessarily to expect a greater fall in price than in output in competitive industries, or a greater fall in output than in price in situations of significant monopoly. Indeed, where marginal costs for the industry are constant over a considerable zone of possible outputs a competitive market would react to a fall in demand without price changes, whereas monopolies would adjust by reducing both price and output. The relative impact of the fall in demand on prices and output would depend, even in the short run, on the relationship of cost and demand conditions within the industry.

So far this analysis has been concerned only with the expected theoretical effect of falling demand in competitive and noncompetitive markets. The same kind of responses could be anticipated in circumstances where costs changed while demand remained fixed. Again, such a shift would work itself out in price and output, with the proportionate changes dependent upon the shape in each case of the respective cost and demand schedules. Several suggestive attempts to verify these hypotheses empirically have been made, notably those of Ruggles, Neal, and Mills, using various theoretical premises and statistical procedures.[3] While they are inconclusive, they tend to show prices moving in rough correspondence to indices of changing marginal cost, without conspicuous variation between competitive industries and those with a high degree of concentration, save where prices are regulated by administrative agencies. On

3. Works cited above, pp. 215–16, n. 2.

the other hand, individual industry studies often reveal patterns of considerable price inflexibility during depressions, although such individual variants tend to disappear into the aggregates of large statistical series.[4]

In common sense terms there is nothing startling about this analysis. It suggests what ordinary experience would anticipate, that in a world of changing cost and demand price rigidity in an industry over long periods of time, including a general industrial fluctuation or two, would be significant evidence that effective competition is absent, save in most unusual combinations of cost and demand schedules. On the other hand, it would pay the most pig-headed monopolist to change his price if his cost conditions changed. It is hardly revolutionary to suppose that changing cost conditions should have an effect first on offerings of supply, and then on price. Nor should it cause surprise to discover that where the opportunity is available, sellers charge different prices for the same product in different markets, adjusting to the differing intensity of demand for alternative uses of the product, the pressure of substitutes, or the character of local market situations. It is commonplace to have different export and domestic prices, to have one price norm for steel products in the automobile industry and another in construction, or for milk to be priced at one level for liquid consumption, and quite another when used in the paint industry.

But this is an elementary textbook picture, useful as it is as a starting point for analysis. The main difference between this image and the real world centers on the assumption that the seller with a considerable degree of monopoly power actually knows the shape of the demand schedule he confronts. In actual fact, his uncertainty about this essential market fact exercises a far-reaching effect, in the short run and in the long run, reinforcing tendencies toward price inflexibility in many noncompetitive sectors of the economy. Both

4. See Mason, *Economic Concentration and the Monopoly Problem*, chap. 6; A. D. H. Kaplan, *Big Enterprise in a Competitive System*, (Washington, D.C., Brookings Institution, 1954), pp. 170–73. In *The Structure of American Industry* (New York, Macmillan, 1954), Walter Adams finds evidence of price rigidity in chemicals (pp. 219, 220), in steel (pp. 180–84, 194–96), and in tin cans (pp. 424–28).

the competitive and the noncompetitive seller, if they are taking full advantage of their opportunities, will carry forward production so long as marginal revenue equals or exceeds marginal costs. But the competitive seller knows his marginal revenue, the noncompetitive seller only guesses what his might be at alternative prices. And powerful fears and interests color his guesses.

Here we should distinguish the case of monopoly for some purposes from the closely related but distinguishable situation that prevails in many industries where the bulk of output is provided by a few large sellers, the so-called "administered price" industries. In these industries "of the few," as Fellner calls them,[5] each seller is acutely conscious both that he has some discretion over the price he charges and that his discretion is shared with rivals. No one seller can gain a larger share of the market by cutting prices openly, for others would follow his lead. Hence the prevalence in these markets of intense rivalries in advertising, packaging, minor product variation, and the like. "Nonprice competition," of the kind represented by the new-model craze in the American automobile industry, is competition through higher costs rather than lower prices, and involves a dubious use of resources, from the point of view of society as a whole. A seller in such a situation is concerned about the possibility that high prices and profits in the short run would attract new firms into the industry, an eventuality to be feared as a threat to the firm's profit position in the long run. High profits also attract the responsive interest of trade unions, Congressional committees, and ambitious members of the Department of Justice staff. They create an unfavorable climate of public opinion. These are anxieties which do not impinge upon the lives of sellers in an effectively competitive environment. The monopolist, and especially the seller in a market "of the few," worries whether more sales today might make for fewer sales tomorrow, and whether price reductions would be irreversible, thus "spoiling the market" indefinitely. A regime of stable prices, or well understood patterns of price leadership and price response, make it easier to achieve that degree

5. William J. Fellner, *Competition among the Few*, New York, Knopf, 1949.

of tacit or overt coordination of price policy which the government often unkindly calls collusion. And they permit both an easier life and more agreeable opportunities for the pleasures of industrial statesmanship than are open to men engaged in the tough struggle of full-blown competition.

In monopoly situations, and in the cognate markets of oligopoly, considerations of this order play an important role in price formation, perhaps even more important in markets "of the few" than in complete or near monopoly. They reflect long-run price policies deemed most appropriate for each firm, in the conduct of its complicated relationship with its rivals. These views of the market tend to dominate the opinion sellers have about the responsiveness of demand to price change. The result is that prices often persist in such markets for some time even though demand falls and costs have not changed. The price mechanism tends to be "sticky," since every price move has strategic and tactical implications for the market's pattern of interdependent rivalry. No one seller can change his price without taking into account the response of his competitors. In such markets, price stability is the safe rule of "live and let live," since few sellers believe they could gain an advantage from independent price action. During the depressed early months of 1958 when the steel industry was operating at less than 60 per cent of capacity, a well-informed observer noted little or no secret price-cutting, even among smaller companies in the industry. All the companies had finally learned, he concluded with relief, that each had a stake in the prevailing level of prices: they realized that since any open price cut would be met, an announced price cut would reduce profits without increasing volume enough to make the cut attractive to the whole industry. Each concluded that it would be more profitable in the long run to weather the recession without sacrificing the present level of prices, than to set sail on a sea of risky confusion, while prices bobbed about, price wars threatened, and customary patterns of price leadership were broken up. The industry believes firmly that a price cut could not change the volume sold significantly enough to increase profits. This conviction is a characteristic business myth, especially favored in industries of large sellers. For such industries it is almost indispensable to a safe and stable price regime. The impulse to "wait and see" is strongly rooted, even though extended delay may make the ultimate adjustment to falling demand more severe.

The strength of motives of this order, sometimes purely spontaneous, sometimes cultivated by arrangements of cooperation, makes it doubtful whether monopolies or markets "of the few" react to falls in demand exactly as they do to falls in cost. No one would have any interest in misjudging his economic interest if costs fall while demand remains unchanged. It does not follow, however, that the same condition obtains if demand falls while cost remains unchanged. For this reason studies of the response of prices to reductions in cost may not be fully applicable in situations where changes in demand initiate the adjustment.

If this observation is correct, it follows that industries characterized by a good deal of monopoly power may misjudge the demand curves they face. In that sense they fail to behave according to the textbook model. They do not always maximize the immediate, short-run profits they could have gained from a more realistic probing of demand, at least in periods of developing depression; they may sacrifice short-period profit in this sense, often for some time, in favor of the stable price policies they deem more favorable to maximum long-run profits. The conviction that recessions will be short and that government will do something to reverse them tends to reinforce this tendency in monopoly pricing.

Monopoly is not the only source of price rigidity and lagging response in the adjustment of markets to changes in demand, or equally, to changes in costs. Some prices are fixed by contract, like rents or many hourly wage rates, and only change at intervals. Others are regulated by government or established by custom. The wages of civil servants, for example, which can only be changed by elaborate public action, customarily move long after most others in the economy.

In competitive industries, on the other hand, no one seller

can translate his uncertainty about the future into price policy. He takes what he can get—the market price, or he reduces his output if market price is below his marginal costs. He does not have the option of waiting, even for a short period. There is no lag in the rate at which the reduction in demand is translated into reductions in price or output or both, according to the schedules representing the amounts that will be offered and bought at different market prices. The market has no choice but to adjust promptly to the fall in demand. This pattern is visible even in industries like bituminous coal, where the schedule of demand for the product is closely linked to investment activity and shifts greatly with changes in investment. Results of the same general character may obtain in a monopoly situation where the seller pursues aggressively flexible price policies or, in labor markets, where wage contracts contain cost-of-living escalator clauses.

Both in competitive and in noncompetitive markets, whether prices fall or remain the same, the fall in national income reduces profits, since the over-all position of the economy is that the total of spending is less than the value of output at the previous level of prices. The success of any one seller in holding the line of demand for his product would merely shift the downward pressure of reduced spending to less protected sectors of the economy. And any firm which managed to maintain considerable profits in the face of generally falling demand might well make unemployment worse by not spending undistributed income, or by not spending it promptly. While higher-than-normal profits or expected profits are the normal signals of the economy for investment, generally declining demand would lead even the rare firm which maintained its profits to reduce inventory, not to enlarge it. It would have no motive to buy new plant or equipment. Throughout the economy, cumulative pressures develop to reduce investment spending of all kinds, thus tending to multiply the initial reduction in income. These trends *are* the depression.

Some contend that if only prices and wages were flexible enough, if only markets were competitive enough, market forces would of themselves produce a new equilibrium at full employment, but perhaps at lower levels of prices and wages.[6] It is this reasoning that lies behind the suggestion, frequently heard still, that recessions should be allowed to "run their course," at least for some time, in order to produce desirable "structural adjustments" in wages and prices. Others urge, on the contrary, that if prices or wages were pegged, by private or public action, that fact would itself be "stabilizing."[7] Businessmen would not anticipate price falls in the face of declining demand, and would therefore have no reason to postpone their purchases in expectation of cheaper prices to come.

These two points of view are both popular. They are, of course, incompatible. And, on the whole, both are more wrong than right. No degree of effective competition could guarantee re-employment without more. Nor could full employment be restored by price stabilization, whether accomplished by private monopoly or by public action. Such a

6. Notably Gardiner C. Means, *Industrial Prices and Their Relative Inflexibility*, above, n. 2. See also A. C. Pigou, *A Theory of Unemployment*, London, Macmillan, 1933, *Employment and Equilibrium*, London, Macmillan, 1941, "The Classical Stationary State," *Economic Journal*, *53* (1943), 343, *Lapses from Full Employment*, London, Macmillan, 1945, and "Economic Progress in a Stable Environment," *Economica*, new ser. *14* (1947), 180; Don Patinkin, "Price Flexibility and Full Employment," *American Economic Review*, *38* (1948), 543. Further, and more generally, consult George W. Stocking and Myron M. Watkins, *Cartels or Competition?* (New York, Twentieth Century Fund, 1948), chap. 7; Howard S. Ellis, "Monopoly and Unemployment," in *Prices, Wages and Employment*, Board of Governors of the Federal Reserve System, Washington, D.C., Postwar Economic Studies, No. 4 (1946); Corwin Edwards, "The Relation of Price Policy to Fluctuations of Investments," *American Economic Review*, Supp., *28* (1938), 56; Henry C. Simons, "Economic Stability and Antitrust Policy," *University of Chicago Law Review*, *11* (1944), 338, reprinted in *Economic Policy for a Free Society* (Chicago, University of Chicago Press, 1948), p. 107; Paul H. Douglas, *Controlling Depressions* (New York, Norton, 1935), p. 64; Rendigs Fels, "The Effects of Price and Wage Flexibility on Cyclical Contraction," *Quarterly Journal of Economics*, *64* (1950), 596.

7. Alvin H. Hansen, *Fiscal Policy & Business Cycles* (New York, Norton, 1941), chap. 15; J. R. Hicks, *Value and Capital* (Oxford, Clarendon Press, 1939), chap. 21, and *A Contribution to the Theory of the Trade Cycle* (Oxford, Clarendon Press, 1950), pp. 127–35; Joseph A. Schumpeter, *Capitalism, Socialism, and Democracy* (New York, Harper, 1942), pp. 92 ff. Cf. Alvin H. Hansen, *Economic Policy and Full Employment* (New York and London, Whittlesey House, McGraw-Hill, 1947), pp. 64–66, 132–34.

policy would probably make the depression worse, and subsequent adjustment more difficult.

Once a downward movement in the flow of the national income has begun, it can be reversed in only two ways: prices may be pushed up when demand rises faster than costs, or costs may fall faster than prices. In either case, profitability will be restored, and motives for investment reestablished. Put more exactly, there are two policy choices: to enlarge the flow of spending for current output, which could restore full employment at or near the previous level of costs and prices, as unemployed resources are put back to work; or, contrariwise, to seek full employment at a lower level of costs and prices, by seeing to it that costs fall more than prices in response to the initial fall in demand. In either case, real profits gain at the expense of real wages, so that investment may be resumed.

It is difficult to accept the persuasiveness, even in the abstract, of the theory that competition could of itself restore full employment after a drop originating in a reduction of the national income. And of course such a miracle of adjustment would be unthinkable in the economy as it is, containing trade unions and large corporations, and prices fixed for long periods of time by contract, convention, and public and private regulation.

A decline in national income means that available funds cannot buy available current output at previous prices. As we have seen, the result may be a decline in price or output or, most normally, both. In almost every such case profit falls, perhaps more in competitive than in monopoly sectors, but substantially everywhere. The decline in income may have started with a fall in business spending for investment. It will in almost every conceivable case involve a fall in business spending for inventory, plant, and equipment, however the downward movement began. As profits fall, incentives to invest in plant, equipment, or inventory are affected. If the scale of output falls, only the most unreasonable optimist would consider enlarging capacity. A businessman rarely builds an additional plant if he is only half using the plant he has. Futhermore, on short time the volume of inventory needed for operations will decline, and cost-reducing innovation, while appealing, will seem expensive as compared to its alternatives, or unavailable, in the absence of current profits. Even if one could conceive a frictionless economy, a fall in costs that was exactly proportionate to the fall in prices would not reverse and could hardly arrest the fall in output and employment. Such patterns of fall were common during the Great Depression, as Ruggles' recent study has shown again.[8] But that fact hardly shortened its life. Price and output fell with declining cost curves. These responses did not, however, convert depression into recovery.

To restore investment motives and substantial investment spending, both prospective profit and close-to-capacity output must be restored. And to restore profitability after a fall in demand, costs must fall more than in proportion to the fall in prices (or prices be pushed up more than costs by rising demand); for the previous relation of costs and prices, in the case of developing depression, was by hypothesis one that produced less than full employment of the community's investment resources.

But there is no reason either in the workings of the competitive market or in the facts of life to expect costs to fall more than prices. At best, they might fall miraculously together. Then nothing would be changed but the value of the dollar. Such a flexible adjustment might restore the previous relation of prices and costs and thus perhaps slow up the rate of decline. But it could hardly do more, even in the model world of pure and perfect competition. Yet only by achieving a more profitable cost-price ratio or its prospect could competitive adjustments lead to increases in output that might, in turn, restore incentives to replace equipment and then to expand capacity.

Nor would one expect an improvement in the cost-price ratio from the responses of the real-world American economy to a fall in national income. Even if the producer of a

8. Richard Ruggles, "The Nature of Price Flexibility and the Determinants of Relative Price Changes in the Economy," in *Business Concentration and Price Policy*, p. 441.

commodity had a greater degree of monopoly power than the trade union with which he deals, it could hardly help him or the economy in the face of falling demand, unless the relationship were general. It is hardly likely that commodity markets are sufficiently more monopolistic than labor markets to permit businessmen to translate downward movements of the national income into *increases* of profitability. In an economy of trade unions and large-scale industry, while both prices and wages are more flexible than is sometimes assumed, a greater drop in costs than in prices is even more unlikely than under the theoretical conditions of pure and frictionless competition.

If this is the case, there is no reason to suppose that a downward movement of the economy would promptly or even necessarily come to an end of itself; there is no apparent advantage in a self-generated restoration of spending. Nor is there a goal of policy to be served by delaying governmental intervention intended to reverse it. Society has little or nothing to gain from allowing a recession to continue very long. The economy seems to have lost even the capacity to shake down the level of prices and costs during a depression, which used to occur rather regularly. Business and labor have weathered the short postwar recessions—each about a year long—without appreciable price changes. It is shocking but no longer surprising to see great basic industries operating at 50 per cent of capacity or less without changing their prices. It is poor policy, I am convinced, for the companies as well as for the economy, but we seem to have become reconciled to it.

If competitive adjustments promise little help in shortening or curing depressions, neither does monopoly. Yet several excellent economists have urged that monopolistic price stability would be a constructive force arresting the possible extent of a downward movement in national income. They argue that businessmen anticipate considerable price movements in the more competitive parts of the economy. Therefore, when a downward movement begins, they hold off on purchases from such markets, expecting further price falls. Prices respond rapidly to changes in the level of ag-

gregate demand, and price movements are exaggerated by
speculation and changes in inventory policy. Thus Dean
Mason doubts if it would be desirable to have a really sensitive competitive adjustment of industrial prices to the
swings of the business cycle, since such price movements
would complicate business planning and labor relations.[9] If,
on the other hand, businessmen knew that price movements
were to be limited by private or public price policy, that fact
alone would be stabilizing.

It is hard to accept the conclusion. Surely the relevant
expectation for the investment decisions of businessmen is
their own expectation of profit, in terms of the expected level
of the national income. Investment decisions are governed
not by the expected course of prices, as such, but by the expected course of prices in relation to costs and, equally, by
the expected relation of aggregate demand to capacity, given
the expected cost-price ratio. Investment decisions, like many
others in a dynamic economy, are influenced most directly
by the expected course of the national income. A rising national income is the most powerful engine of initiative we
have; a falling one suffuses the economy with gloom. Holding prices stable against the tide of falling aggregate demand
could not materially increase the volume of investment or
otherwise help reverse the trend.

If the decline in profitability has come about because of
a substantial fall in the flow of national income, the issue is
whether a policy of maintaining prices by private or public
action could be expected to restore profitability, in the absence of government or central banking action to reverse the
trend in the money volume of national income itself. The
crucial question, therefore, is whether keeping prices pegged
could lead the industry to sell enough, at a profitable price,
to justify it in maintaining or expanding its capital. The most
perfect control of prices—for example, in the field of utility

9. Edward S. Mason, "Competition, Price-policy and High Level Stability,"
in *Economic Institute of the United States Chamber of Commerce* (Sept. 18,
1947), pp. 19, 29, reprinted as chap. 8 of his *Economic Concentration and the
Monopoly Problem* (Cambridge, Harvard University Press, 1957), pp. 168,
178. See also A. C. Neal, "Pricing Aspects of Business Cycle History," ibid.,
p. 32.

rates—would introduce a stable element into business planning, in that no one would expect the price of utility service to fall further. But such expectations of stability could hardly influence expectations as to the general level of national income, on the one hand, or of cost-price relations for particular industries, on the other. While it is true that no one would have the incentive to postpone purchases of utility services in anticipation of a price cut, it is equally true that no one would have an interest in buying more utility service, in a period when demand was falling, merely because its price was not expected to fall further. Since other prices fall, utility service has become more expensive than before in real terms. The utility industry may remain profitable by reason of its price policy, but at a less than capacity output. Profits, which in the theory of capitalist development should lead to expansion, can under these circumstances merely add to the hoard of unused funds, thus further reducing the flow of income.

It seems almost a pun on the word "stability" to contend that monopolistic policies of price stability in the face of falling general demand contribute stability to business anticipations *of profit at levels of output which strain capacity*, and hence to business expenditures for investment purposes.

It was thinking along this line, perfectly natural for individual businessmen and quite unreasonable for the economy as a whole, that stimulated great increases in monopoly and equivalent protective arrangements during the Great Depression. Tariffs were raised to prevent prices from being pushed down further by the cumulative fall in income. Enforcement of the antitrust laws was relaxed, as businessmen sought in combination to arrest the pressure of falling national income on their prices.[10] Such arrangements often stopped the fall in particular prices, at least in public. Higher tariffs may have shifted unemployment from less efficient domestic producers to more efficient foreign suppliers. But they did nothing to restore general profitability, because they did not increase or even maintain the aggregate flow of spending. Even when

10. See, e.g., Appalachian Coals, Inc. v. United States, 288 U.S. 344 (1933); United States v. Republic Steel Corp., 11 F. Supp. 117 (N.D. Ohio, 1935)

they succeeded in adding to immediate profits, those who received such profits would rarely have had any incentive either to use them for investment purposes or, more important, to seek new funds on the basis of having earned them. Yet national income as a whole could have been maintained and expanded only if the price changes led to such results. Finally, in the experiment of the NRA we embraced the remarkable doctrine that if prices and wages could be raised by decree and enforced by the closer and more monopolistic organization of industries and markets, the course of recovery would thereby be advanced.[11] We found, of course, that so long as the national income remained unchanged, the raising of prices merely reduced the amount that could be sold, and that as national income rose the effect of NRA was to frustrate the aim of reflation by absorbing the increase in aggregate demand more by monopolistic price rises than by commensurate increases in output and employment. Under the circumstances of prolonged depression, when businessmen see no reason to expect an increase in the level of aggregate demand, a price rise made possible by increased monopoly control could hardly lead to increases in spending and thus to an increase in national income itself.

Actually, monopoly industries do not seem in general to practice anything like the degree of price stability for which they are often complimented, or accused. While conspicuous cases of absolute price stability over time can be found, the general pattern of monopoly pricing, revealed in a study like Neal's, is that monopoly prices move in correlation with changes in unit cost, although at a level (during depressions at any rate) somewhat more profitable than the prices prevailing in more competitive parts of the economy. Of course, where the degree of monopoly control is altered—by the

11. C. F. Roos, *NRA Economic Planning*, Bloomington, Ind., Principia Press, 1937; Kenneth Boulding, "In Defense of Monopoly," *Quarterly Journal of Economics*, 59 (1945), 524; Comments, *Quarterly Journal of Economics*, 60 (1946), 612, 615, 619; Lionel Robbins, *Economic Planning and International Order* (London, Macmillan, 1937), chap. 6; A. C. Pigou, "Stabilization in Particular Industries" (1927), in A. C. Pigou and D. H. Robertson, *Economic Essays and Addresses* (London, King, 1931), p. 34.

organization of a combination, or by law—prices tend to be raised, at least while the combination or law remains effective.[12] Later studies, especially Ruggles', indicate a similar pattern.[13]

But such studies do not support the view that policies of price stability in the face of falling demand help to create business anticipations of profit at levels of output that strain capacity and therefore help to generate business spending for investment purposes. Such stability of prices would normally mean lower output and somewhat higher profits than in competitive industries, but hardly profits as high as before, or near-capacity operations. Yet nothing less than improved profits, or the expectation of improved profits, could begin to revive business spending.

Thus while monopoly industries react to depression differently from competitive ones, neither can by its own responses be expected to correct and offset declines in the level of national income in such a way as to restore full employment. The reversal can come about only when the level of spendings starts to increase again, either as a result of private or public decisions. Usually, such reversals have come about in the past as a result of factors external to the working of markets themselves—outbursts of speculative enthusiasm for new projects, industries, or regions; discoveries of gold; effective changes in banking policy; war spending or other inflationary acts on the part of government. It is not inconceivable that market forces could of themselves reverse a downward movement, if people concluded that prices had fallen too far and would rise, and if for that reason they began to spend either their idle balances, or money borrowed from the banks. In this rather exotic case, the sum of private decisions would have a "positive monetary effect," inducing people to hold goods or securities rather than liquid funds. The result would be the same as that of government inter-

---

12. Neal, *Industrial Concentration and Price Inflexibility*, p. 134.

13. Richard Ruggles, "The Nature of Price Flexibility and the Determinants of Relative Price Changes in the Economy," in *Business Concentration and Price Policy*, pp. 441, 489–94.

vention. It would lead to a rise in the level of spending, the indispensable condition of recovery—in fact, its definition.[14]

During a recovery movement, however initiated, the problems are comparable to those of a recession, but not the same; the recovery is not the mirror image of the depression. For one thing, a recovery movement has a limit, although a rather flexible one, at or near the level of full employment, but the depression has no theoretical limit at all, short of a chilly zero. Whether the recovery starts in the consumer goods sector of the economy, in government, or in private investment is immaterial. The impact of increased spending spreads, producing rising profits, prices, and employment, in varying combinations reflecting the intensity of demand for different products, differing patterns of cost, and the way in which monopoly power is in fact exercised.

Will the structure of the market organization affect the response of the economy to the pressure of increased spending? Will the "multiplier" be higher in a competitive than in a monopolistic economy?

The textbook answer to the question is simple, and partially correct. The resilient response of competitive markets should be, and usually is, quick and active in meeting the rising tide of demand by expanding output rapidly, borrowing and spending on a considerable scale to finance the effort, and thus adding further new spending to the forces of recovery. In the textbooks, however, monopoly is assumed to be ready to raise prices as much as it can and to meet the

14. Oscar Lange discusses the conditions of this response in his *Price Flexibility and Employment* (Bloomington, Ind., Principia Press, 1944), reviewed by Milton Friedman, *American Economic Review*, *36* (1946), 613, as does Don Patinkin, from a slightly different viewpoint (real rather than money balances) in "Price Flexibility and Full Employment," *American Economic Review*, *38* (1948), 543, reprinted with some revisions in American Economic Association, *Readings in Monetary Theory*, (Philadelphia, Blakiston, 1951), p. 252. See also A. C. Pigou, *Employment and Equilibrium*, both 1941 and the revised ed. of 1949; Herbert Stein, Comment, *American Economic Review*, *39* (1949), 725; Thomas C. Schelling, "The Dynamics of Price Flexibility," *American Economic Review*, *39* (1949), 911, Comments, Lawrence R. Klein, Don Patinkin, and Thomas C. Schelling, *American Economic Review*, *40* (1950), 605; Richard M. Bissell, Jr., "Prices, Costs and Investments," *American Economic Review*, Supp., *30* (1941), 200.

pressure of increased demand more in price rises than in rises in output, employment, and capacity.

Actually, since the war at least, many industries having some degree of power over the prices they charge have tended for a variety of reasons to charge less, in all probability, than the market would bear in the short run.[15] Prudence and a bias in favor of long-run price stability; the twin mottoes of "wait-and-see" and "live-and-let-live"; a concern for the firm's relations with government, labor, and the public; a fear of new entrants and of excess capacity—all these combine to persuade the firm and the industry that the upward movement is temporary, that demand is weaker than it is, that it would be better, on the whole, to pursue a cautious line than to risk being wrong about the new shape of the schedule of demand.

Many economists and public officials have praised the great companies in markets of the few for their statesmanship in keeping prices low, or raising them relatively slowly, during periods of recovery. Indeed, President Eisenhower has preached this doctrine both to business and to labor as their highest social duty.

Viewed against the background of the flow of national income as a whole, a policy of profit abstinence seems neither tenable for extended periods nor sound, especially during a recovery period of rising total spending.

The first consequence of such moderation in pricing is that demand is unusually high for the product of such industries, but prices rise less than in others. Relatively low profits are earned. The pressure of rising demand is diverted to other sectors of the economy, where prices and profits rise more rapidly. Thus capital is attracted to areas which would have claimed less if the market mechanism had been more accurate in measuring the comparative intensity of consumers' desires for different products. On the other hand, since demand for the product is high, public policy may intervene, as it has through accelerated depreciation and other policies,

---

15. See F. C. Mills, *The Structure of Post-war Prices*, NBER, Occasional Papers, 27 (1948); J. Kenneth Galbraith, "Market Structure and Stabilization Policy," *Review of Economics and Statistics, 39* (1957), 124.

to subsidize expansions of capacity within existing firms despite their relatively low profits. Big firms, having very great advantages in any event in their access to both long- and short-term capital, may be able to finance expansion without subsidy, despite their relatively low profits during such periods. The result, as is perhaps the case now in the steel industry, may be the paradox of low profits and capacity which is genuinely if temporarily excessive in the real sense —that is, excessive even at full employment levels of demand, and at the prices that would prevail under competitive conditions.

This kind of policy, in either of its aspects, records a failure of the market as the chief instrument for guiding the allocation of capital and labor. If long continued, policies of self-restraint may result in a serious distortion in the pattern of resource use. The classic example of French rent control represents an extreme case of this phenomenon. Rents in France have until very recently been frozen at their World War I levels. The result is that tenants pay less rent for their Paris apartments than they do for cigarettes. Leases, of course, are sold, and sold at high prices. But landlords have no incentive to build new apartment houses or repair old ones. After forty years of this pressure, the housing situation is almost insoluble, save through public action.

I do not suggest that we have yet reached this point in the great oligopoly industries that have been so widely applauded for price moderation during the postwar inflationary boom. But the phenomenon has been visible in varying degrees, signaled by the appearance of occasional "gray" markets for certain key products. And it has been a major barrier to the possibility of entry by new firms, since the earnings of existing capital resources have often been lower than the return to be anticipated at prevailing prices on investment in totally new capacity.

One of the consequences of so-called moderate price policies has been to delay and prolong the process of adjustment to episodes of inflation—that is, to periods when demand was excessive in relation to full employment supply. During such periods, competition for scarce resources bids up prices, as businessmen persist in optimistic views about the future of demand, price, and profit in their bailiwick. Raw material prices rise, inventories are accumulated, and the wages of junior executives, foremen, and good machinists are pushed up by the offers of unusually efficient, productive, well-located, or optimistic firms. The entire economy must adapt its system of notations to the impact of such changes in the marginal productivity of labor in money terms—that is, the value of the marginal product of work, the norm around which the general wage structure is crystallized. Price moderation, like other lags in the process of market adjustment, prolongs the agony. Long, slow, rolling movements of prices and wages have characterized the response of the economy to the pressure of such inflation-induced changes in the general wage level. The length of time required for these adjustments explains the apparent anomaly of costs and prices rising slowly during the early part of a recession, as they did in 1957 and 1958.

Of course even latter-day policies favoring price stability in markets of the few cannot indefinitely postpone action to bring short-run profit at a maximum. Pessimistic views about the nature of demand schedules do not survive indefinitely. It is difficult for a firm or even for an industry to buck the tide. The result is that companies in this position take every opportune excuse, such as a labor negotiation, to raise their prices and catch themselves up to the position which gives them as much as they could earn in their market. Guided by experts in public relations, the companies make matters worse by trying to blame others for their own mistakes of price policy.

Many have proclaimed these lagging and erratic price practices of some large firms and large trade unions as the dawn of a better day. The great managers of industry and labor, thay have assured us, free at last of the outworn maxims of Adam Smith, have abandoned selfish profitseeking for the higher virtue of responsible citizenship. Corporations and trade unions now have consciences, we are

told.[16] A literature has grown up, which Mason has recently
characterized as "the apologetics of managerialism." [17] We
find our great corporations concerned almost as much with
aid to education, foreign policy, and public relations as with
their basic job of conducting the business enterprises society
has entrusted to their control.

There are dangers in the course, quite apart from the
vagueness of the standards of statesmanship that have so far
been announced. I certainly do not object to corporate management which takes a civilized and democratic interest in
the morale of its employees, treats them with dignity and
respect, and deals with them as equals, through collective
bargaining procedures and otherwise. Nor do I oppose trade
union leadership that is willing to acknowledge the common
humanity of management. But the basic service for which
society looks to business and labor is the production of goods
and services at the lowest possible cost, and at prices which
measure the comparative pressure of consumers' choices. This
is a hard and demanding task. The literature of "managerialism," from Commons and Veblen to Drucker, Burnham, and
Berle, suggests no criteria to replace the standards for judging
the propriety of wages and prices which the economists have
painfully developed during the last century or so.

We have tended to misconstrue the fascinating sociology
of the modern corporation, with its divorce of ownership
and management and its hierarchical features. There is a rich
literature which describes corporations and trade unions as
institutional entities. These studies have much to contribute
to our understanding of the dynamics of economic life. They
raise fundamental questions of accountability, since the

16. Adolf A. Berle, Jr., *The 20th Century Capitalist Revolution*, New York,
Harcourt, Brace, 1954. See also George W. Stocking, "Institutional Factors in
Economic Thinking," *American Economic Review*, 49 (1959), 1. Kaysen goes
further, attributing "soul" as well as "conscience" to the modern business
enterprise. See Carl Kaysen, "The Social Significance of the Modern Corporation," *American Economic Review*, Supp., 47 (1957), 311, together with
Earl Latham, "Anthropomorphic Corporations, Elites and Monopoly Power,"
ibid., p. 303, and Comments, pp. 320–27.

17. *Journal of Business of the University of Chicago*, 31 (1958), 1. I have
recently discussed this problem in the perspectives of corporation law, in a
paper referred to above, p. 34, n. 3.

bodies they describe seem to become more and more autonomous, free of any but the most nominal reference to their legal source of authority, the votes of stockholders and union members.

But these studies of social and human relations, however valid, do not provide a substitute for the competitive norm in defining an acceptable social goal for the process of price-making. Indeed, the literature of managerialism has not so far squarely faced the issue. I doubt very much whether we can produce a standard for pricing which expresses the idea of efficiency in the use of resources otherwise than in the familiar guise of the concept of competitive equilibrium. It is an ironic comment on the problem that many of the younger Socialist economists, especially in England, propose procedures for pricing under Socialism which would in fact achieve the classic purposes of competition, both in distributing goods and in determining which branches of the economy expand or contract. Their effort comes perilously close to the thought that the first task of a Socialist society should be to restore competitive markets—the traditional hallmark of capitalism, and its most characteristic institutional ideal.

These paradoxes about the differing response of competitive and noncompetitive sectors of the economy to rising national income become more pronounced as full employment is approached. Key resources are short, expensive, and hard to find throughout the economy. The relative profitability of smaller industry becomes conspicuous. Capital is strongly attracted to retail trade, consumer goods, and service industries, rather than to basic manufacturing capacity.

That resources are not employed according to the preferences consumers would have expressed had the market been competitive saddens economists. It implies a waste of resources and a failure of the market as a device for allocating capital. But we are used to wastes of this kind. We have always employed resources in ways that offend the thrifty instincts of economists. The problem presented by monopoly during periods of continued inflation beyond the point of maximum effective employment is more serious than waste.

When the national income in money rises more rapidly than the "real" national income in goods, although the economy is fully employed, the economy is buffeted by explosive forces. The unremitting pressure of excessive purchasing, which can no longer elicit more production from the business system, drives up prices, wages, and profits in different sectors of the economy.

If all wages and other prices followed suit, the result would be serious enough—a continued depreciation of the dollar internationally, an increase in imports, a decline in exports, perhaps a flight of capital, and a loss of gold, until we decided to call a halt and once more sought internal price stability, or at least coordination with world price movements. Even that pressure for stabilization might be lacking if, as is not unlikely, most other countries followed our inflationary lead.

The domestic aspect of the problem is at least as serious, however. All wages and other payments do not and cannot promptly follow the trend. Some are fixed by custom or contract—pensions, some wage rates, trust income. Others are earned in sectors of society which do not share fully in the boom—municipal government, universities, social agencies, and the like. They find it difficult to pay the wages and salaries required to hold their staffs against the pull of the upward trend. Groups may be impoverished while others make feverish advances. The dangerous tensions of general inflation cloud every part of social life.

If the expectation of further price advances becomes firmly established, people become unwilling to hold cash balances. When this happens, the demand for commodities and property is increased further, at a time when supply may be fixed or even falling.

Under these circumstances of general inflation past the point of full employment, some economists have found monopoly policies of price restraint highly constructive. Viewing the comparative moderation of price rises in big business as compared with small business, in the period immediately after the war, Mason said "Whatever the nature of the monopoly problem at other times and places, at this particular juncture of incipient inflation public authorities should thank heaven for a substantial degree of concentration in the American economy." [18]

The difficulties with the argument, however strong its practical appeal, are deep-seated. If the economy is under the pressure of a flow of spending for current output which exceeds the value, at previous prices, of all the goods and services that can currently be produced, self-restraint in price policy cannot shorten the inflation or protect society against its consequences; it can only divert the flow of excessive demand to other parts of the economy, where double profits will be made in consequence. These profits, in turn, will lead to even more exaggerated distortions in the pattern of new investment spending. It is hard to see what goal of policy beyond the stability of particular prices for their own sake is served by such a policy. Insofar as higher prices tend to encourage a demand for higher wages, monopolistic price stability might serve a useful purpose if it could help prevent the long-drawn-out and costly readjustment of the economy to an entirely changed system of costs and prices—that is, a permanently changed value of the dollar. But this goal could be realized only if fiscal and monetary authorities were struggling at the same time to cut the flow of funds down to the level of the value of output at or near previous prices. In actual experience, the process seems to work the other way. Stable "key" prices in industry lulled the fiscal and banking authorities into relative inaction during the early years of the postwar inflation. They contended that restrictive measures were not needed because certain vital prices were not rising.

What has been said of prices applies also to the making of wages under conditions both of recovery and of boom, through collective bargaining and through more open market procedures. It is often asserted, with vehement conviction, that wage increases are "inflationary" or that we have endured a "cost-push" not a "demand-pull" inflation. The moral is drawn that unions should be abolished or regulated, col-

18. Mason, *Economic Concentration and the Monopoly Problem*, p. 171.

lective bargaining limited to the single firm, and the antitrust laws "applied" to collective bargaining.[19]

"Higher" wage rates are no more inflationary than "higher" interest rates or "higher" steel prices.[20] If interest rates exceed the expected yield of capital—the marginal efficiency or productivity of capital—they result in a decline in the demand for money. If wage rates exceed the expected marginal efficiency or productivity of labor, they result in a decline in the demand for labor. In a frictionless economy, where work and labor are uniform and one worker can substitute for another, there would be one wage rate, that measured by the marginal efficiency of labor. In fact, of course, labor is divided into many markets by differences in skill and location, by ignorance, by habit, and by peoples' unwillingness to move. But the pull of alternative employments is strongly felt over time, nonetheless. Schoolteachers get jobs in factories or offices. New candidates for police departments fail to appear. The wages of domestic servants rise, as more and more money is required to keep them from the temptation (and higher productivity) of factory work. Wage differentials are the device through which labor is drawn from less to more productive work.

Wage rates rise initially in areas of labor shortage—that is, where the marginal productivity of labor in money terms is unusually high, or is expected to be high. They may be new industries, or industries for whose products demand is rising rapidly. They may not necessarily be the industries in which costs are coming down most rapidly. If wages go up in such parts of the economy to the full limit under the pressure of inflationary expectations and inflationary demand, the increase spreads. The *average* wage rate in the country cannot rise faster than the *average* increase in productivity without shifting all cost curves and thus affecting output, prices, or both. A rise in the average wage rate more rapid than the average rate of improvement in productivity does

19. See, e.g., Edward H. Chamberlin, *The Economic Analysis of Labor Union Power,* Washington, American Enterprise Association, 1958.

20. By wage rates I mean the effective hourly wage rate, not the weekly, monthly, or annual wage earnings paid for variable quantities of work. The wage rate in this sense is a measure of the cost of additional labor.

not of itself raise prices. Like other increases in prime cost, however, it makes an increase in prices necessary before the same amount of labor can be hired at the higher wage, and as much supply as before be offered to the market.[21] Wages can be won on paper by strikes or successful negotiations. They will be paid by industry only if the general level of incomes permits them to be paid.

If a rise in wage rates increases marginal prime costs, it is deflationary, not inflationary, in every meaningful sense. In the first instance, its effect would normally be to reduce the number of workers employed. The subsequent impact of a rise in the wage rate would depend upon whether the spending to which it led would be greater than the spending it discouraged or prevented—that is, whether the employed workers, receiving higher wages, would increase their spending more than higher prices and reduced profits would cut the spending of other consumers, the direct spending of businessmen, and the pace of investment. It may be realistic in many situations of depression to assume that wages earned will be spent more promptly and more completely than profits. But no such assumption is tenable in the postwar world of full employment. During periods of boom or near-boom the economy is more likely to suffer from an excess of investment over saving than from the excess of saving over investment characteristic of a depression.[22] The fact that the gross national product in dollars is rising under these circumstances measures the impact of a shortage of savings in this sense. High corporate profits or other forms of saving are therefore likely to be spent, or offset by spending, for the economy's current output of capital goods. There is no reason at such times to suspect corporations or those who receive dividends of hoarding more than wage-earners. It would be desirable, however, if they did. Nor is there any reason, save in cases of considerable price increases, to suppose that employed work-

21. As D. H. Robertson once put it: "To say that price is determined by marginal cost is always bad theory," "A Survey of Modern Monetary Controversy," *Manchester School*, 9, No. 1 (1938), 1, reprinted in American Economic Association, *Readings in Business Cycle Theory* (Philadelphia, Blakiston, 1944), pp. 311–17.

22. As these terms are defined and used above, Chap. 5, esp. pp. 87–89, 102–6.

ers reduce their savings and increase their consumption expenditure proportionately, as prices rise, in order to preserve the same standard of consumption as before. Much of the saving of the working class is contractual, through welfare programs and insurance policies. And a shift from saving to consumption would not in any event increase the total of spending, during a period when savings were being fully utilized. Taking these factors into account, the net effect of abrupt and large-scale wage increases is likely under most circumstances nowadays to be unfavorable to employment. The usual experience near the upper turning point of a boom emphasizes the importance of rising wages and other costs in discouraging investment spending. Wage increases can be inflationary only if the government and the banks choose to offset their intended purpose by further acts of monetary expansion, or by private action having the same effect, through increased velocity of circulation of funds.

When average wage rates go up faster than the average increase in productivity, businessmen will be interested in paying them if, but only if, they expect their revenues to rise at least as fast. Making this assumption, they would be willing to finance the higher wage rate from profits, idle balances, or the newly created money of bank loans. Since all firms are not equally profitable, even at full employment, and many are at the margin of no-profits, financing wage increases at the expense of profits is neither feasible nor likely to happen, save at high costs in unemployment. Nor is it more likely that a general wage increase can be financed by the activation of idle balances, either during a boom, when cash balances are low, or during a slump, when they do not exist. The most practicable source of such financing, therefore, even when businessmen think prices will be pushed up by rising demand at least as rapidly as costs, is borrowing, and especially borrowing on reasonably short term from the commercial banks.

Under these circumstances a wage increase can lead to inflation, on two conditions: that businessmen expect prices to go up, and that the Federal Reserve authorities are willing to validate and underwrite any wage bargains employers care to make. If these two conditions are met, collective bargaining makes monetary policy. As has often been remarked, we should then be on a Labor Standard, not a Gold Standard. The wage increase is not of itself inflationary, but it may induce the government or the banking system to enlarge the money supply. The wage increase requires society to choose between unemployment and a rise in all prices sufficient to make production profitable at the higher wage rate. It is important in such a case to be explicit that in the general interest of full employment, monetary inflation has frustrated the earnest and often costly effort of the trade union to secure a higher real wage. It is not an irony but a tragedy to see zealous men and their families live through the bleak tension of a strike only to find their painful victory wiped out by higher prices.

Actually, most of the cost-push elements in the recurring cycles of postwar inflation have not originated in the collective bargaining process. Both in the United States and in other Western countries wages rise most rapidly when the authorities have permitted the rate of spending to advance more rapidly than the output of goods and services, or perhaps more accurately, when they have not prevented this from happening. Then actual earnings, as overtime or otherwise, are often higher than contractual wage rates, and wages outside the zone of collective bargaining frequently increase faster than wages influenced by union action. Wage increases spread from areas of the economy where optimistic price assumptions are widely and securely held. In such industries, attracting a suitable labor supply is an urgent matter, and rising wage costs not a significant deterrent. The trouble, however, is that such wage increases spread.

Whether the upward movement in wages begins with collective bargaining or with a condition of excess aggregate demand, however, the next round under most circumstances presents the same issue of policy: should the monetary system undo the intended effect of the wage increase by further monetary expansion?

Part of the confusion which characterizes the heated debate on the role of wages in inflation arises from a misunderstanding of Keynes. Keynes did his major work as an economist between 1920 and 1936 or 1938. It is inevitably shadowed by the great policy problems of that period—rates of exchange and unemployment. He argued that in the world as it is, *money* wage *cuts* could not cure a *depression*, both because they could not be put into effect quickly enough and because their net effect on aggregate spending would probably be negative during most depressions, taking into account their impact on consumption, profits, interest rates, and the relative demand for capital and labor as substitutes. For this reason he advocated curing depressions by reducing *real* wage rates, rather than *money* wage rates, through fiscal and monetary action to inflate spending, and thus force prices up faster than wages. But Keynes thoroughly understood that the problems of inflation and deflation were not entirely symmetrical. It hardly followed from his argument that employment would *increase* if *money* wage rates rose *faster* than prices. On the contrary, he clearly saw the danger of unemployment or monetary collapse in such a process, and that of social tension as a result of redistributing income in favor of wages and profits, at the expense of interest, rent, pensions, fixed incomes, and dividends paid out.

For this reason he advocated stable rather than flexible wage rates as a general policy. Flexible wage rates he thought were appropriate only to authoritarian societies, where they could be made effective by decree. In Western communities, during both inflations and depressions, wage flexibility presented great dangers.

> I am now of the opinion, [he wrote] that the maintenance of a stable general level of money-wages is, on a balance of considerations, the most advisable policy for a closed system; whilst the same conclusion will hold good for an open system, provided that equilibrium with the rest of the world can be secured by means of fluctuating exchanges. There are advantages in some degree of flexibility in the wages of particular industries so as to expedite transfers from those which are relatively declining to those which are relatively expanding. But the money-wage level as a whole should be maintained as stable as possible, at any rate in the short period.

This policy will result in a fair degree of stability in the price-level;—greater stability, at least, than with a flexible wage policy. Apart from "administered" or monopoly prices, the price-level will only change in the short period in response to the extent that changes in the volume of employment affect marginal prime costs; whilst in the long period they will only change in response to changes in the cost of production due to new technique and new or increased equipment.

It is true that, if there are, nevertheless, large fluctuations in employment, substantial fluctuations in the price-level will accompany them. But the fluctuations will be less, as I have said above, than with a flexible wage policy.

Thus with a rigid wage policy the stability of prices will be bound up in the short period with the avoidance of fluctuations in employment. In the long period, on the other hand, we are still left with the choice between a policy of allowing prices to fall slowly with the progress of technique and equipment whilst keeping wages stable, or of allowing wages to rise slowly whilst keeping prices stable. On the whole my preference is for the latter alternative, on account of the fact that it is easier with an expectation of higher wages in future to keep the actual level of employment within a given range of full employment than with an expectation of lower wages in future, and on account also of the social advantages of gradually diminishing the burden of debt, the greater ease of adjustment from decaying to growing industries, and the psychological encouragement likely to be felt from a moderate tendency for money-wages to increase. But no essential point of principle is involved, and it would lead me beyond the scope of my present purpose to develop in detail the arguments on either side.[23]

The most important cause of price and wage increases since World War II has been the pressure of excessive demand— that is, a level of spending persistently higher than the value

23. J. M. Keynes, *The General Theory of Employment, Interest and Money* (New York, Harcourt, Brace, 1936), pp. 270-71.

of full employment output at previous prices. This level of spending was financed both by the creation of new money and by the increasingly rapid and economical use of existing money stocks. It resulted in the bidding up of prices and wages throughout the economy, as industry after industry faced shortages or the loss of personnel and had to match, as best it could, the high wages achieved in certain key areas of unusual productivity or exceptionally determined unions. The pull of excess demand in this sense has been a far greater factor in inflation since the war than the push of wage and price increases caused by monopolistic exploitation.[24]

Many studies substantiate this conclusion. To take a simple illustration, the salaries of young lawyers on their graduation from law school have risen almost 50 per cent in the last two years, without benefit of a trade union. According to James Tobin's analysis, for example, average hourly earnings rose between 7 and 9 per cent a year during the period of rapid general inflation, from 1945 to late 1950. Between 1950 and 1955, however, they rose between 4.6 and 5.7 per cent a year.[25] Even such a rise, however, is serious. No index of productivity change shows improvements of more than 2 or 3 per cent a year, either for industry as a whole or for manufacturing alone. Increases in productivity are by no means uniform or regular in their incidence. If changes in the real marginal efficiency of labor are translated into higher money wages rather than lower prices for the product, average wages can easily be driven well beyond the average increase in productivity—the factor which measures the "elbow-room" for money wage increases without general price rises.

This view of the inflationary process does not minimize the fact that monopoly power presents serious problems for

24. See, e.g., Council on Prices, Productivity and Incomes, *First Report*, H. M. Stationery Office, 1958; Richard T. Selden, "Cost-push versus Demand-pull Inflation, 1955–1957," *Journal of Political Economy*, 47 (1959), 1; F. W. Paish, "Inflation in the United Kingdom, 1948–1957," *Economica*, new ser. 25 (1958), 94. Note, however, Robert Ozanne, "Impact of Unions on Wage Levels and Income Distribution," *Quarterly Journal of Economics*, 73 (1959), 177.

25. James Tobin, "The Interdependence between an Effective Stabilization Policy and the Attitudes of Labor," in Gerhard Colm, ed., *The Employment Act, Past and Future* (Washington, D.C., National Planning Association, 1956), p. 114.

stabilization policy, either in business or in labor. Such problems are fundamental, and difficult. All I mean to say at this point is that if policy persists for long in keeping the economy under the pressure of large volumes of excess demand, the problems of monopoly, both in labor and in industry, will become insoluble.

If businessmen are convinced that in the end government will step in to make their wage bargains good, there will be little restraint in their bidding for the existing labor supply in periods of boom or expected boom. If excess demand keeps business profits high, then nothing can prevent unions from pressing for wage increases. And if unions find that their nominal wage gains are regularly stolen from them by acts of monetary inflation, bitter feeling may be expected to develop about policies of full employment that involve so serious a price.

The consequence of such programs, if they go on for extended periods, will be the development of direct government controls over wages and prices. Long experience with excessive demand in this sense would mean the end of free trade unions, and the end, too, of the dominance of private decisions as to price and output in business.

American tradition, it is true, has favored inflation almost as a deliberate choice. At least since the Revolutionary War, we have not experienced galloping, pathological inflation. Our middle classes, unlike those of Europe, have depended far more on profits, salaries and capital gains than on interest, rent, or even dividends. They lack the intense faith in price stability as a social policy that is so notable a feature both of public opinion and of academic thought on the Continent.

There is, however, a limit. The question is, how much inflation will we tolerate, and how rapidly. A well-known economist used to say that "coin-clipping" had always been used, and always would be necessary, to slough off the burden of debt and permit the world to get on with its work. There is a good deal of truth in the observation. But it is not the whole truth.

If excess demand kept up an unremitting pressure on wages and prices for a period of five or six years, distorting the pattern of rewards and incentives; putting many regions, classes, industries, and occupations into serious trouble; enriching those who live on wages and profits, and making life miserable for those who depend on pensions, fixed incomes, social insurance, or compensation which cannot readily be varied—confronting an economy of this kind, we should surely opt for "order," not flexibility in our price mechanism, and supersede the market as our chief instrument for determining prices and wages.

In a regime of overfull employment, where inflationary pressure forces the adoption of direct government controls over the ordinary detail of business decision, the problem of industrial and market organization has a completely different aspect than in situations of falling national income, or of recovery from a depression, and in situations of attempted stabilization at high but noninflationary levels of employment. In a war economy or an economy under inflationary pressure, one expects the rationing of goods and the allocation of resources to be accomplished not by the market but by coupons and government orders. The aim of policy is to keep prices stable—so as to minimize the cost of its orders to the government and prevent any change in the relationship of prices and wages on which the stabilization structure is precariously built. Under these circumstances, the quality one wants in markets is not resilience and responsiveness, but discipline. We care more about whether there will be a black or gray market than whether the market extracts the last ounce of production from industry at minimal prices.

With this object in mind, the public and the government will inevitably prefer monopoly to competition, and insist on organizing the equivalent where it doesn't exist. Experience in two wars and in the depression adventure of NRA is altogether convincing evidence that it is far easier to control a monopoly industry in this sense than a competitive one. Fixed prices, allocations, quotas of production, divided markets, limitations on the entry of new competitors, and prices high enough to reward the least efficient will necessarily be the order of the day. There would be few incentives to reduce costs under such a regime, and few, if any, of the traditional economic justifications for private enterprise.

Is there any chance for a program of considerable price stability at high levels of employment and growth? Can we expect to walk the tightrope of full employment without price inflation, and without giving up market freedom in labor and in business?

Let us suppose that the government and the Federal Reserve System announced that they were tired of full employment at the cost of rapidly rising prices. The country needed a period of price stability, they might say, in order to adapt itself to the strenuous changes of the last eighteen years. Full employment would be financed, but only at a reasonably stable price level. Congress might underscore the point by accepting Senator Bush's amendment to the Employment Act, declaring that reasonable price stability is a goal of policy under that statute, which has generally been assumed to be the case in any event. The government might undertake to keep the total of aggregate spending fixed, or allow it to rise no more than 3 or 4 per cent a year, the expected pace of increasing output.

What would be the chances and conditions of success for such a program? At the end of a long boom, can the economy continue in a regime of full employment and sustained growth, or must policy choose between an upward or a downward spiral? If price stability and full employment are compatible goals, would there be advantages in policies of competition for the product markets of the economy, and of freedom for collective bargaining in the labor markets?

If businessmen and labor leaders were convinced that a dominant majority favored such a policy, horizons would alter both for business and for labor. The easy assumption of perpetual sellers' markets would disappear. Men would realize that all increases in cost would not necessarily be offset sooner or later by increases in aggregate demand, driving up prices, and justifying all earlier bargains. Business would begin to take a more calculating approach both to price-making and to wage-making. Management would be encouraged, indeed forced, to economize, in order to confront competitive forces, and forego the luxury of reckless bidding for available supplies of labor and management.

But no such policy has a chance of success if it is limited to the level of pious words. American business cannot hope to persuade labor or the public to accept harder wage bargaining so long as it continues to indulge in what Arthur B. Van Buskirk, Chairman of the Federal Reserve Bank of Cleveland, has called corporate abuses, weakening the system of free enterprise: exorbitantly high salaries and bonuses, and "the practice of regarding age as of no concern in the case of corporate directors." He cites instances of corporate salaries of $600,000 or $700,000 a year, in some instances to executives over eighty years old. And he refers to great corporations, almost half of whose directors are over seventy. In one case he cites, eight of thirty-six directors were seventy-five or older. "Is it any wonder," he concludes, "that big business comes in for criticism and in the coming years may be under severe attack?" [26] Nor could a dogged restriction of the flow of spending, in the spirit of Sir Stafford Cripps, do the job for long unaided. The political pressures for full employment and the fears of unemployment are too real and too acute to be met by negative means.[27] They will prevail—and should prevail—against any purely negative policy.

The policy of monetary and fiscal restriction would have a chance to achieve its purpose of full employment without price inflation only if it were supplemented by an entirely new approach to the other side of the equation of money and goods—the side of goods. Achieving long-run stability of the price level depends on the outcome of the race between output and the pace of spending. Monetary and fiscal restraint can do only part of the job of achieving balance, and then at serious costs of output foregone. The government should embark on an imaginative program designed to speed and

26. Speech at dinner of the Federal Reserve Bank of Cleveland (October 10, 1956), pp. 7–8.

27. For another view see James E. Meade, *The Control of Inflation,* Cambridge University Press, 1958.

facilitate the growth of output, both for its own sake and for the sake of long-term stability.

With an optimism rooted in our national experience, we take an expectation of economic growth for granted. It is almost the rule of our nature. Actually, it is a new and revolutionary phenomenon in human history, which began to appear only with the explosion of the world after 1492. It was accelerated by the application of science to industry during the seventeenth and especially the eighteenth and nineteenth centuries. At the moment we assume that science has relegated Malthus to the gallery of discredited men. There are signs, however, that the cheerful premises of the age of science may be in for some rough tests in the years ahead. The rate of population increase, accomplished by improved public health and even more mysterious forces, raises difficulties for many societies. Certain raw materials will soon be in short supply, or available only at increasing cost. Above all, the disorganization of the economy of the free world and the plight of the so-called underdeveloped countries will make it hard to achieve steady improvements in the standard of living throughout the world during the years ahead.[28]

It is essential, however, that American policy confront these issues and take a variety of steps to accelerate the rate of growth of output, particularly in sectors of urgent social importance.

Ending the fear of great depressions should of itself do much to provide a favoring climate for growth. The spread among businessmen of the conviction that no prolonged depression will be allowed to develop encourages long-term capital commitments. Sustained expenditure on research, possible only in prosperous times, should begin to yield significant returns. And high employment leads to dramatic increases in population and in the percentage of the population being trained and educated to higher levels of ultimate productivity.

These automatic stimuli of growth are not, however, sufficient. Gross private domestic investment, the key index of increasing capacity in the private sector of the economy, was

28. See above, Chap. 4.

just short of 20 per cent of the gross national product in constant dollars in 1929, 15.6 per cent in 1956, and 14.2 per cent in 1957. This drop of between 20 and 30 per cent in the rate of private capital formation is an ominous fact, from many points of view. It is conservative to assume that the rate of capital formation in the Soviet economy is of the order of 25 per cent of gross national product. And of course Soviet capital is not going into houses, swimming pools, roads, and factories producing consumer goods, but into the foundations of their military effort. Even if we add 2 or 3 per cent to the figure of private domestic investment, to represent the share of our public expenditure which might be classified as long-term capital formation, it is apparent that the Soviet rate of growth is now almost 40 per cent ahead of our own.

We shall not for long be able to afford guns and butter too, and to act in addition as the free world's banker, unless we prepare to save and invest more of our current income, and to take a variety of other steps to facilitate economic expansion.

Any attempt to draw up a balance sheet for the American economy ten or twenty years hence reveals how hard pressed we shall be in seeking to satisfy all the claims which now seem inescapable. A deficit in available output looms up even if the projection is based on the optimistic hypotheses that full employment can be maintained throughout the period, and an average rate of growth of 4 or 5 per cent in real output achieved. The consumption requirements of a rising population are formidable even if no leeway is given for improvement in the standard of living. A full-employment economy generates huge capital demands, which must be met if a constant rate of growth is to be sustained. As we saw earlier, the nation will have to export capital on a much larger scale than in recent years, for both economic and political reasons. Urgent public works are desirable—schools, roads, hospitals, and educational and welfare institutions. The social security programs have built-in features of rising cost, even if they are not extended to the field of medical care, because of the aging of the population covered by social insurance. And it seems likely that a military program adequate to the needs of our diplomacy will claim more money rather than less in the immediate future.

Two general lines of policy are indicated in the interest of facilitating growth: policies designed to eliminate waste, and those intended to encourage growth more directly and positively.

As to waste, we should readjust our thinking to the fact that we are no longer living in the upside-down world of the depression, when savings were a menace, spreading-the-work was a sensible idea, and tariffs and monopolistic restraints on investments were tenable policies. Saving, economizing, and hard work are as virtuous now for us as they were for Poor Richard.

There are traditions of waste built into our economy.

Perhaps the most important is the process of destroying the enormous capital of our cities, which is going on all around us.

The nature of the economic issue at stake in the condition of our cities is illustrated by the fate of Warsaw. Hitler ordered the city razed, after the heroic uprising of its people and their army in 1944. He is supposed to have said that whatever the outcome of the war might be, Warsaw would not live again. The Poles, however, decided to rebuild their capital on its old site. The decision was not merely an act of pride and defiance. Despite the enormous costs of clearing the rubble, they found that it was cheaper to restore Warsaw than to build elsewhere. By using the old site, they had the advantage of the city's underground capital—its costly mains for gas, electricity, water, and sewage.

The process of urban decay is quantitatively the largest economic problem in the country. It offers the nation its most considerable single opportunity for economizing in the use of its resources. The fate of the cities has many vital political and sociological aspects, as well. The mass movements of people and industries to suburbs involve wasteful duplications of expensive capital facilities, as well as the premature abandonment of houses, schools, utilities, roads, police stations, and the other expensive capital items of city life. Much of this needless expenditure on new capital could be prevented by vigorous programs of urban renewal. These are complicated affairs, but healthy ones, for they require the cooperative efforts of whole communities, backed by state, local, and national authority.

Such programs promise social dividends more important even than their economic advantages. The growth of suburbs often weakens a city by detaching some of its most active leaders. Migration affects the city's population unevenly. Many cities are becoming more and more completely communities of a single class, or of a single ethnic group. When trends of this kind appear, they can become epidemic as fears spread, reinforcing the impulse to depart.

Secondly, in the interest of preventing waste, we should give renewed attention to programs for minimizing monopoly. Monopolies, restrictive business practices, and combinations in restraint of trade remain a significant source of waste in the economy, more significant in a setting of full employment than in any other. I will return to this theme in some detail (below, pp. 258).

Thirdly, the patent laws require fundamental review. There is serious question whether they adequately serve to encourage both the development of real innovations and the public disclosure of new ideas.

If we turn to more positive measures for encouraging growth, we find a closely related panorama of issues, largely neglected in the making of policy.

In this area, policy could contribute the largest possible increment of output to the nation by concentrating on a series of problems related to organization of the labor supply. The economy produces less than might well be produced because neither the working force nor the market for managerial talent is effectively organized. Restrictions on apprenticeship create genuine bottlenecks in many parts of the labor market. Pension plans and seniority rights, and the stock option and pension plans of management, tend to prevent the movement of manpower to its most productive possible employment. We are in danger of creating a new feudal system of employment, with gains of security at the cost of efficiency. I do not, of course, suggest that such plans be prohibited. But the law should begin to consider the step taken long ago in insurance legislation, of insisting that the beneficiaries of such plans be recognized as having a vested right in the capital value of their interests, so as not to discourage their shift to other jobs. Plans of this kind present difficult problems of investment policy and management practice. Financial legislation is certainly required to enforce suitable concepts of trusteeship in administration and investment. From the point of view of labor policy, legislation might also contemplate arrangements for some pooling of these welfare programs. Coordination could reduce their costs, which are now often unduly high. And it could help prevent them from restricting the mobility of labor and of management.

Much can and should be done to create a truly national market for labor. The national employment service should be re-established, to spread knowledge of work opportunities throughout the country. Transfer payments could remove barriers that now inhibit the shift of workers from less to more productive occupations. Serious retraining programs could yield high dividends, both in encouraging transfers and in up-grading the skills of the entire working force, including management. The laws and working agreements affecting older workers constitute an artificial and a socially cruel and harmful limitation on the employment of older people, and thus on the effective size of the working force. It is sometimes forgotten that one of the motives of social security legislation during the Great Depression was to remove older people from the labor market. All traces of that philosophy should be systematically removed from the law. It is economically foolish and socially wrong. Men and women should be free, if they wish, to continue in gainful employment whatever their age. In order to balance the traditional prejudice against the employment of older workers, tax inducements could readily be devised to encourage their employment. Finally, the labor force should be enlarged by liberalizing our immigration laws. Save under the exceptional pressures of war, the rate of growth of the economy has never quite recovered from the shock of the restrictive immigration laws of the twenties. Manpower shortages are endemic in a full-employment economy. They can best be offset, if we wish to preserve the looseness of our present market system, by increasing the labor supply. Canada, Australia, Brazil, Mexico, and other countries seeking rapid growth rates are profiting from immigration programs. The main secret of Germany's postwar recovery was the influx of refugees West Germany received from the East.

Finally, as an essential element in a program for growth, I should stress the importance of education. We are interested in education for its own sake, as a stage in the formation of civilized and responsible men and women. Nonetheless, education has economic consequences. Improving educational standards is an indispensable part of any effective long-term effort to improve productivity.

The country has recently become familiar with reports of Soviet superiority in the training of scientific manpower. Other countries also have educational systems decidedly better than our own in certain respects. It has become a national obligation to see to it that we train our most promising children, and all our children, in the skills upon which the future of society depends.

This goal can be sought and achieved without revolutionizing the pattern of local responsibility for the schools to which the nation is historically so attached. The means to this end is a system of federal grants, through which higher standards could naturally be developed. Americans used to shudder at the story of the French Minister of Education, who looked at his watch and remarked to a visitor that at that moment in a given grade throughout France, its territories, and the French schools of Tunisia and Morocco every child was studying Cicero. How terrible, we thought, to have such centralization of control over everything in Paris. Nowadays, however, the story has a different aspect. Its real point, it would appear, is that every child was studying Cicero, not home economics or radio broadcasting.

A few pages above I put aside the issue of competition and monopoly as part of a comprehensive program for achieving stabilization through growth, as well as through an appropriate restraint in monetary and fiscal policy. It was suggested earlier that the policy of competition would not survive prolonged periods of excessive demand, and that during depressions neither monopoly nor competition could help much to restore full employment. The competitive principle can make its most useful contribution as part of an effort to sustain high levels of employment without substantial price increases. In such periods, the economics of competition come into clear focus as an essential aspect of the philosophy of the Employment Act of 1946. There are two classes of reasons for this conclusion: those of resilience, and those of productivity and economic welfare.

A policy of removing restraints on business and competition should make it easier and cheaper to manage fiscal and monetary programs addressed to maintaining employment. Reasonably competitive responses of price and output to movements in the general level, and especially in the direction of demand should be advantageous. Fiscal and monetary policy should be the more effective as instruments of planning if new firms can be organized with some chance of success, if capacity increases quickly in response to increases of demand, and if price adjustments clear markets promptly in the face of minor shortages and surpluses.

No program for stabilizing a dynamic economy could or should keep all industry equally profitable at all times. Many forms of investment will vary in volume from year to year, even under conditions of overfull employment. Some industries should expand faster than others—housing at one point, steel at another, road-building and utility construction at still a third. The flexible price movements of an effectively competitive market should prove useful in directing the endless redeployment of resources required to permit steady growth in the production of the goods and services the economy can produce most cheaply.

Stabilization can never be achieved automatically in an economy which devotes a considerable fraction of its national income to capital purposes. Investment spending is inherently variable. From the point of view of stability alone, there is no magic division of output between consumption and investment that would be safer and more nearly self-sustaining than any other. The choice of an appropriate level of investment—the choice between work and leisure, higher consumption and growth—is a choice each society and each generation must make in the light of its sense of social justice, and of the claims upon it. Upon that choice depends the rate of possible progress against poverty, and the degree of the nation's security in the world. Whatever the share of its production a community undertakes to invest, it will have to manage its banks, stock markets, and interest rates in order to be sure that the volume of investment is high enough to assure full employment. But the problem of controlling the variable investment process is not simply to achieve an arithmetical balance between saving and investing habits, so that the level of national income remains constant. In primitive societies and in societies without much capital equipment the level of national income scarcely varies. Capital construction is the only way to achieve long-term improvements in the standards of living. As an economy develops and matures, its capital needs appear to become greater, not less. Depreciation and maintenance alone require prodigious amounts of capital, and in periods of rising prices conventional depreciation allowances do not maintain productive capacity. There seems to be no limit to the number of industries inventiveness can generate in a highly mechanical economy, from the production of Coca-Cola to the manufacture of deep-freeze units and even more ingenious household appliances. The problem of achieving stability at high levels of employment would not be notably different in an economy devoting 10 per cent of its production to future uses and in one investing 25 per cent of its gross national product. Western societies, including that of the United States, are now suffering in general from a shortage of capital, and from interest rates which do not rise rapidly enough to reflect changing patterns of efficiency, demand, and anticipation. This is more likely to be their prevailing economic difficulty than the capital glut and the excessively high interest rates, against which we were frequently warned during the depression of the thirties.

Thus the ultimate problem of policy is not what level of investment to choose as self-stabilizing but how to achieve high levels of investment and employment without endless inflation. The inherent variability of many forms of investment will probably require offsetting action by government from time to time, whatever level of investment is chosen as appropriate. The number of times such offsetting action is required and its cost should be less in an economy where prices vary in response to changes of demand in a reasonably competitive way.

The second class of reasons for a policy of enforcing competition—those of welfare—are even more important than the considerations of resilience we have just reviewed. More competition should enlarge the real income of the community by reducing many of the wastes of nonprice competition and by facilitating a more rational allocation of resources and a more defensible distribution of income. And under most circumstances it should increase both the rate at which productivity increases and the pace at which improvements in productivity are applied throughout the economy.

Productivity is not of course a simple function of competition. No one could contend that small business is invariably efficient and big business inefficient, or that monopoly power in the contemporary American economy invariably stifles technical advances.

Schumpeter argued that monopoly power was essential to progress. He criticized the literature of economics for ignoring what he regarded as the obvious fact that big business had accomplished the immense improvements in technique which have increased the standard of living in the United States during the last two generations. He contended that the promise of monopoly profit was necessary to induce the investments required for modern mass industry and that only monopoly industries could afford the research indispensable to economic progress. He also urged (inconsistently) that the power of monopoly industries to control, slow up, or postpone innovations was a good thing, since it reduced the social cost of destroying the value of existing capital, a net loss which in his view almost inevitably takes place when

a new technique displaces an old one.[29] From the viewpoint
of the economic welfare of society as a whole, no innovation
should be adopted unless average *total* costs, using the new
technique, are no greater than average *variable* costs, using
the old. It does not pay to commit new capital to replace
old capital, that is to say, unless one expects a return on its
use sufficient to attract it from other paths. The old capital
should be employed so long as it earns its average variable,
or out-of-pocket, costs. William Fellner's analysis suggests
that where monopolists and oligopolists have perfect foresight and rationally seek to maximize their revenues, they
will adopt cost-reducing innovations at exactly the same rate
that would obtain automatically under conditions of pure
competition.[30] Under these circumstances, barriers to entry
do not alter the pace of technological progress. While
monopoly has no advantage over competition in this regard,
considerations of progress through time do not constitute a
separate objection to monopoly. But, Fellner points out,
the foresight of monopolists and oligopolists is often incor-
rect, and they may well fail to pursue policies of profit
maximization, because of the distorting influence of noneconomic business objectives: freedom from worry, prestige,
popularity, etc. "The influence of market structure on the
rate of progress," he concludes, "depends primarily on factors of this sort." [31] Viewing the spectrum of possible cases,
he finds "the case for broadening narrow market structures
remains fairly generally valid on the dynamic as well as on
the static level of economic analysis, even though on the
dynamic level no general case emerges for atomistic competition. The case also remains valid from a general sociological point of view for any society that considers freedom
of opportunity a desirable objective." [32]

Assuring society the long-run advantages of the most

29. Schumpeter, *Capitalism, Socialism, and Democracy*, chap. 8. See also
G. Warren Nutter, "Monopoly, Bigness and Progress," *Journal of Political
Economy*, 64 (1956), 520.

30. "The Influence of Market Structure on Technological Progress," *Quarterly Journal of Economics*, 65 (1951), 556.

31. Ibid., pp. 573–74. This point is of course closely linked to the argument
of pp. 221–24, above.

32. Ibid., p. 575.

rapid possible advance in efficiency is or should be a central preoccupation of our law regarding industrial organization. Technological advance has been the most important single factor in economic progress—more important, in all probability, than either the rate of capital formation or the economies of scale in the organization of business units. The problem of discovering and attaining improvements in technique is far more significant than some of the short-run wastes of monopoly or monopolistic competition.

The development, application, and adoption of new ideas by agriculture and industry is a process of many facets. A conditioning factor is the level of general education among the working force, and the state of higher technical education in the research centers where technical innovations originate. There are crucial cultural elements as well. The insecurity and competitiveness of American life, which is shared by all classes, strengthens the restless drive of American industry for mechanical improvement. On the other hand, the relative lack of originality of American science, and of American cultural life generally, has condemned much of our technology to the role of vigorous adaptation rather than creative innovation. Looking back at the list of truly original changes in technology over the last generation, it is clear that for all our research expenditure, few originated in this country, and of those several were developed by innovators who were originally trained abroad. Jet engines, atomic science, the cracking of petroleum, penicillin, new processes for manufacturing steel, radar, cellophane, dacron—the list suggests the greatest of all challenges to our culture—the recognition and release of the creative potential of our people, who are, after all, the same people as those of Europe.

Thus far, and I stress the point, this view is not a judgment but a doubt. It is difficult, at least for me, to reach more categorical conclusions about the relative originality of American thought. Certainly in those literatures I know best —those of history, economics, and law—there have been many American contributions of genuine excellence, but few with the revelatory power of genius. A sobering comment on the problem is the number of American industrial corporations which have located their research laboratories abroad. A thoughtful executive of one such corporation recently said that the reason for his company's decision in this regard was that American science in his field was not original, and that it was an economic necessity for his company to maintain direct contact with the laboratories of Europe.

Can the form of economic organization—the degree of competition or monopoly in economic life—make any difference to the complex and far-reaching process whereby increases in efficiency are sought? We have examples of advanced technology and management in monopoly situations, and of retarded management and technology in competitive ones. We know that to a certain extent management can be an independent factor in economic behavior. Skill, energy, and imagination sometimes appear as a tradition in the most unlikely places. By and large, however, observation confirms theory in supporting the conclusion that the pressure of effective competition, which gives industry strong motives for reducing costs, is the most reliable foundation for a policy of dynamic development, even though it is not alone a sufficient condition for assuring that goal. Society should get a better return in steady advance when an industry has a pressing economic interest in competitive cost reduction.

It is often claimed that using the antitrust laws to bust trusts would turn back the clock to horse and buggy days of industrial technique. It is widely believed that the size of American corporations is a technological necessity, required in order to gain the advantages of scale in manufacturing and distribution. The available evidence is to the contrary. The history of many corporations shows that the motives for merger were to gain positions of monopoly, or to float new securities profitably.[33] Several suggestive studies

33. See Donald H. Wallace, "Industrial Markets and Public Policy," in Friedrich and Mason, eds., *Public Policy*, pp. 59, 101, and passim; *Relative Efficiency of Large, Medium-sized and Small Business*, TNEC, Monograph 13 (1941); Eugene V. Rostow, "The New Sherman Act," *University of Chicago Law Review*, 14 (1947), 567, 568; Simon N. Whitney, *Antitrust Policies; American Experience in Twenty Industries* (2 vols. New York, Twentieth Century Fund, 1958), passim.

indicate that in many industries small- and medium-sized firms function at lower costs and have higher profits than extremely large ones, especially during periods of rising national income and high employment.[34] Such studies must be treated cautiously, since smaller firms often have advantages precisely because they operate under umbrellas held up by their larger brethren. Still, there is much to be learned from them. And it is a common experience to find huge firms saddled with a burden of heavy extra costs because of their size. The decentralization movement in many large national companies is a revealing response to the diseconomies of bigness. These companies are seeking advantages of autonomous management and of rivalry within the firm, which sound a great deal like the Socialist competition much discussed by Soviet economists.

Certainly firms can have all the economies of scale in production, and finance serious competitive programs of research, without being as large as some of the giants of American industry. We could do a great deal of antitrust enforcement without losing any advantages of technique. The presidents of small steel and oil companies have testified

34. See Wallace, "Industrial Markets and Public Policy," pp. 100–5; FTC, *Report on the Divergence between Plant and Company Concentration, 1947* (1950), and *Rates of Return for 529 Identical Companies in 25 Selected Manufacturing Industries, 1940, 1947–49* (1950); William L. Crum, *Corporate Size and Earning Power*, Cambridge, Harvard University Press, 1939; Ralph C. Epstein, *Industrial Profits in the United States,* New York, NBER, 1934; Corwin D. Edwards, *Maintaining Competition* (New York, McGraw-Hill, 1949), pp. 113 ff.; Roy A. Foulke, *Expansion from Retained Earnings, 1940–1944,* New York, Dun and Bradstreet, 1946; G. Warren Nutter, *The Extent of Enterprise Monopoly in the United States, 1899–1939* (Chicago, University of Chicago Press, 1951), pp. 29 ff.; R. C. Osborn, *Effects of Corporate Size on Efficiency and Profitability*, Urbana, University of Illinois Press, 1950; J. M. Blair, "The Relation between Size and Efficiency of Business," *Review of Economics and Statistics, 24* (1942), 125, and "Does Large Scale Enterprise Result in Lower Costs?" *American Economic Review*, Supp., *38* (1948), 121; R. N. Anthony, "Effect of Size on Efficiency," *Harvard Business Review, 20* (1942), 290; J. L. McConnell, "Corporate Earnings by Size of Firm," *Survey of Current Business, 25*, No. 5 (1945), 6; Clair Wilcox, *Competition and Monopoly in American Industry*, TNEC, Monograph 21 (1940), pp. 309–13. The more recent literature is reviewed in M. A. Adelman, "The Measurement of Industrial Concentration," *Review of Economics and Statistics, 33* (1951), 269, and "A Current Appraisal of Concentration Statistics," *Journal of the American Statistical Association, 53* (1958), 56.

that they are quite big enough to get along, both in costs and in research.[35] The steel industry would be quite different if it consisted of ten or eleven companies no bigger than National or Republic. And in that industry, firms even smaller than National or Republic have pioneered in technical advance.

In the oil industry and some others technology is now generally available to all comers on the same contract terms. One of the most important consequences of judicious antitrust enforcement in basic industries might be to reduce or to eliminate the present advantage very large firms have in raising capital, whether for long or short periods—a most important subsidy the organization of the money market now gives to monopoly. And the whole history of technology bespeaks the importance of free, competitive, unorganized research. Over and over again the experience of science attests the advantage of having many minds independently pursuing different approaches to knowledge. Fred Hoyle recently commented that if the best minds in the field of medical science had been assembled during the nineties, as a committee to coordinate research and make grants, not one man would have anticipated the development of the X-ray.

It is sometimes contended that only monopoly industries can afford the cost of research programs capable of yielding practical results for industrial technique. Too little is known about the history of important technical innovations to permit generalization, and perhaps no generalizations will ever be possible about a process so distinctive and individual.[36] In many instances, however, the important tech-

35. Testimony of S. D. Williams, "Study of Monopoly Power," *Hearings* before Subcommittee on Study of Monopoly Power of Committee on the Judiciary, House of Representatives, 81st Cong., 2d Sess., Serial No. 14, Pt. IVA, Steel (1950), pp. 755 ff. See also *Report* of Subcommittee on Study of Monopoly Power of the Committee on the Judiciary, House of Representatives, 81st Cong., 2d Sess., The Iron and Steel Industry (1950), pp. 69–77; Editorial Note, *Fortune* (Aug. 1949), p. 16.

36. See W. Rupert MacLaurin's valuable work, *Invention and Innovation in the Radio Industry*, New York, Macmillan, 1949, "Patents and Technical Progress, A Study of Television," *Journal of Political Economy*, 48 (1950), 142, and "The Process of Technological Innovation," *American Economic*

nological advances seem to start with the independent research of universities, government bureaus, or smaller companies. The great laboratories of larger companies then frequently perfect the techniques of applying the new ideas on an industrial scale. They are often delayed by the conservatism, vested interests, and habitual methods of established industrial practice. The history of the introduction of the tank, rejected by the British Army and finally developed by the British Navy, on Churchill's personal instructions, has many parallels in the world of industry as well as of warfare. In some industries, like the railways, advances in administration and technique seem to respond to the spectacular introduction of competition, such as developed for the railways during the Depression. And all too often, as in that case, the response of the older industry is to seek protection against the newer and cheaper forms of competition by legal restrictions on their growth. Thus we find legal limitations on the entry of new firms into the trucking business and into air transport, prohibitions against the use of express highways by busses and trucks, and similar arrangements in a protectionist spirit.

Competitive industries meet the problem of research in different ways. Research in agriculture is largely, although not entirely, socialized in the United States, and is conducted in state and federal agricultural stations, colleges, and research establishments. In bituminous coal mining, a competitive industry of advanced technique, private companies and privately supported research groups do a great deal of

---

Review, 40 (1950), 90; John Jewkes, David Sawers, and Richard Stillerman, *The Sources of Invention*, London, Macmillan, New York, St. Martin's Press, 1958; C. F. Carter and B. R. Williams, *Industry and Technical Progress*, London and New York, Oxford University Press, 1957; "A Spark in Steel," *Fortune* (Dec. 1948), p. 95; Robert Schlaifer, "Big Business and Small Business: A Case Study," *Harvard Business Review, 28*, No. 4 (1950), 97, and *Development of Aircraft Engines*, Boston, Division of Research, Graduate School of Business Administration, Harvard University, 1950; S. D. Heron, *Development of Aviation Fuels*, Boston, Division of Research, Graduate School of Business Administration, Harvard University, 1950; Robert E. Wilson, "Competitive and Cooperative Research in the American Petroleum Industry," *Journal of the Institute of Petroleum, 37* (1951), 407; Sir Frank Whittle, *Jet*, London, Pan Books, 1953.

work on actual mining and combustion methods, although important pioneer work is also done by the Bureau of Mines of the Department of Interior and by many university schools of engineering. The clothing industry and other branches of the textile industry seem to progress at a rate which compares favorably with that of other industries, and draw for new ideas and procedures on the work of many small laboratories, inventors, and research units, both within and outside the textile industry itself.

Even in industries characterized by the presence of relatively few large firms, however, it hardly follows that society must put up with the existing degree of monopoly power in order to enjoy the advantages of research. The size of enterprise capable of supporting adequate research facilities is far smaller than the dominant huge corporation of many of our major industries. The essence of advance in science is not concentration of research facilities under a single direction but the encouragement of independent study by persons of diverse views, most of whom tend to regard each other as highly unsound. In many industries—petroleum, steel, and construction, for example—independent research firms have undertaken important work, often the crucial development of real innovation. The arts of management themselves, usually a most important sphere for possible reductions of cost, have latterly been invaded with some success by the management consultant, who offers his ideas for a fee to all comers. The history of important technological innovations, insofar as it is yet available, hardly supports the view that a somewhat more competitive organization of industry would require us to sacrifice the advantages of industrial research. On the contrary, in instance after suggestive instance, it indicates that rivalry in this realm is perhaps the most important rivalry of all.

The development of a sensible national policy for scientific research goes far beyond the question of monopoly and competition. A recent study by Henry H. Villard contends that the minute scale of research expenditures is the most important resource misallocation under capitalism.[37] He es-

37. "Competition, Oligopoly and Research," *Journal of Political Economy*, 46 (1958), 483.

timates that total research is currently absorbing about 2 per cent of the national income, civilian research one per cent, and fundamental research not more than one-sixth of one per cent. Industrial research is concentrated heavily in larger companies and in a few industries connected with defense—notably aircraft, electrical equipment, and chemicals. Villard proposes a tripling of national spending for basic research and a doubling of expenditure for applied research as the most productive possible use of the funds over the long run. He starts with the premise that the organization of industry that maximizes the rate of increase in productivity over time is socially most desirable. And he concludes that what he calls "competitive oligopoly" [38] would be the ideal form of industrial organization, since it would include firms large enough to carry on research programs yet sufficiently numerous in each market to feel the goad of severe competitive incentives to reduce costs and to innovate. He deems government sponsorship, and indeed government financing of research, essential if widely diffused programs of competitive research are to be developed and the general advantages of competition preserved. In his view, society will have to choose between government-sponsored research and increasing industrial concentration, since in his judgment they offer the only possible roads to a tenable rate of improvement in productivity. I should differ only in doubting whether increased concentration would in fact lead to a more satisfactory investment in basic research.

The argument of the preceding sections of this chapter is that effective competition has much to contribute as an auxiliary instrument of fiscal and monetary policy in programs of stabilization under two sets of circumstances: those of recovery, while some unemployment exists, and those of stabilization at high levels of employment. On the other hand, some forms of disciplined monopoly are inevitable if we mismanage fiscal policy in such a way as to indulge in inflation beyond the point of close-to-full employment, so

38. Which I do not read as greatly different from the norm for antitrust enforcement in basic industries mentioned below, pp. 293 ff.

that the economy is always under the pressure of excess purchasing power, rising prices, and costs. The same choice may well be made if certain key prices, notably wages, are advanced so rapidly by the exercise of monopoly power as to require considerable compensating doses of inflation and hence increases in prices generally, in order to permit employment to be maintained. Extremes of depression are pathological cases which society should not and need not tolerate for any reason. Although a substantial falling of national income always provokes the protective reaction of monopoly, as people seek to hold their own prices against the falling tide of demand, heightened monopoly power cannot help to shorten or reverse a downward movement. It may make it more intense and more expensive to control by effective action in the fiscal field. On the other hand, while a competitive economy can and does react flexibly to mild downward movements of national income, flexible prices as such cannot often cure a serious recession and may make it worse, where expectations of further price falls become widely held. Cumulative depressions can be cured only by government action to increase the flow of spending, or by a combination of private decisions that has the same effect.

The economic reasons that generally lead economists and the public to support the policy of competition are basically long term in character and have little to do with the reactions of the economy to cyclical forces. Competition should serve society better than monopoly in directing resources to the uses consumers prefer; it should give industry and commerce strong incentives for reducing costs and developing cheaper methods of manufacture, management, and distribution; it should result in a distribution of income more nearly based on differences in productivity; and it should minimize both the classic offense of monopoly exploitation and the wastes of monopolistic competition. Resources would be more fully used under competitive than monopolistic circumstances, and investment opportunities should therefore be greater. These are the general economic justifications for a system of free markets.

The ultimate elements in the American credo of competition are not, however, economic at all. The antitrust laws are a monument to our fear of concentrated power and our yearning for a society in which economic power is at least widely scattered. In such a world, we hope, we should be protected against an oligarchy of the rich. Equally, opportunity would be open to talent, and men could enter the middle classes at their own will and risk. The privilege of enterprise would be shared by those who wished to try it.

These themes, economic and noneconomic alike, are the aspirations of the American law of markets.

11. Some Notes on the Law of Market Organization

THIS CHAPTER is an exercise in perspective. It offers some descriptive background, of possible assistance to nonlawyers, although it does not attempt to put the law of markets into a proverbial nutshell. Principally, it proposes to define a few major features of the process through which the law seeks to carry out its policies for the organization and conduct of markets.

The larger part of the economy, involving activities which originate approximately 75 per cent of the national income, are subject to the antitrust laws as private business, largely affecting interstate commerce and not directly regulated by government through administrative agencies. This estimate follows the interesting observations made by Messrs. Wilcox, Nutter, and Stigler a few years ago.[1] Something like one-third of the companies in this sector, originating perhaps 20–25 per cent of the national income, can be classed as private monopolies or oligopolies. Unresolved questions of antitrust policy, of varying degrees of seriousness, are raised by the structure and behavior of these industries. According to Nutter's study, some 40 per cent of manufacturing production was accounted for by effectively monopolistic industries during the thirties. This percentage may be slightly higher now, as a result of subsequent mergers; but the increase has in all probability not affected the figure by more

1. Clair Wilcox, *Competition and Monopoly in American Industry*, TNEC, Monograph 21 (1940); G. Warren Nutter, *The Extent of Enterprise Monopoly in the United States 1899–1939*, Chicago, University of Chicago Press, 1951; George J. Stigler, *Five Lectures on Economic Problems* (New York, Macmillan, 1949), lecture 5.

than a few percentage points at most. If one uses the measure of persons engaged in production in the business sector of the economy, excluding government, nonprofit organizations, and the like, Stigler's estimate for 1939 is that 76.5 per cent of the work force was in competitive industries, 19.7 per cent monopolies, and 3.8 per cent in compulsory cartels, a classification that includes airlines, highway transportation, the dairy farmers, and, at that time, bituminous coal.[2]

Controversy has raged in recent years as to whether the monopoly sector of the economy is increasing or decreasing in size. It is reasonably clear by now that the degree of monopoly in American business is substantial, and worth talking about, but that it has changed only slightly since 1900.[3] The influences weakening monopoly have for some time roughly balanced those which favor it. Many forces make for increasing competition in the economy. The development of transportation has opened local markets to wider and wider zones of competition, and to penetration by new methods of distribution. It has also permitted labor to move more freely and thus to reduce the power of local employers in their protected labor markets. The multiplication of substitute commodities and services, too, has been a force mitigating monopoly influence in many situations of importance. And the flexibility of many companies in switching from the manufacture of one commodity to others has sometimes helped. The railroads, to take a familiar example, do not have the immense monopoly power of their position fifty years ago. Steel, coal, and many other products face an array of competitive pressure from substitutes—aluminum, oil, plastics, glass—which has transformed their status. The slow influence of the law has not been unimportant, through enforcement efforts, the development of judicial doctrine, and the improvement of the statutes themselves. On the other hand, the attractions of arrangements to reduce competition are always real, and they

2. Stigler, p. 50.

3. See Nutter; M. A. Adelman, "The Measurement of Industrial Concentration," *Review of Economics and Statistics*, 33 (1951), 269, and "A Current Appraisal of Concentration Statistics," *Journal of the American Statistical Association*, 53 (1958), 568.

have from time to time been encouraged or at least tolerated by the state. The popularity of mergers in recent years has been significant in this connection. It has been stimulated by many factors, including the capital gains and other features of the tax laws, and the weakness, until 1957, of Section 7 of the Clayton Act.[4]

Enough careful studies of the history and structure of industries are already available to permit one to dismiss the plausible proposition that competition is dead or dying; that monopoly is technologically inevitable; and that efforts to achieve more competition in many industries, including some of those now subject to direct regulation, are futile or worse.[5] If the argument of the preceding chapter is correct, competition can make a greater social contribution in an economy of stabilized full employment and rapid growth than at any other stage of the trade cycle. Under such circumstances, programs for removing restraints on competition offer much, both in themselves and in providing a favorable setting for labor negotiation. The presence of high monopoly profits is inevitably an invitation to extreme wage demands. The maintenance of competitive levels of profit in industry is a necessary if not a sufficient condition precedent to obtaining tenable wages from the system of collective bargaining.

The law does not, however, take the simple view that the object of national policy is competition *à outrance*. Nor does it even go so far as to demand all the competition of which the economy is capable. The law of markets includes, of course, the Sherman Act and a considerable mass of related statutes, which purport to forbid a variety of acts in "undue" or "unreasonable" restraint of competition. But the American law of markets has other panels. In the field of labor, for broad social reasons, it encourages the formation of trade unions and the process of collective bargaining, in order to redress the historic inequalities of labor's bargaining position

4. 38 Stat. 730 (1914), 15 U.S.C. (1952).

5. A most useful, revealing, and judicious appraisal of the economic consequences of antitrust appears in Simon N. Whitney's study, *Antitrust Policies; American Experience in Twenty Industries,* 2 vols. New York, Twentieth Century Fund, 1958.

vis-à-vis employers. The law with regard to agriculture has supplanted competition with syndicalism, in the interest of assuring farmers minimum prices or minimum incomes. In the case of public utilities, like railroads, gas and electric companies, and the communications system, there are state and national administrative bodies, with variously defined powers over the prices and earnings of companies engaged in this considerable sector of the economy. And the production of oil is limited by state and national action, that of several other minerals by subsidies and programs of stock-piling.

Nonetheless, American law makes a greater effort than that of other capitalist countries to counter monopoly, and enforce competition. The relative success of that effort has encouraged developments in the same general direction on the part of other countries, especially since the war.

The point of departure for the body of law we have developed for preventing restraints of competition is the Sherman Act, passed in 1890 by a vote of both parties, in response to a social development that had widely alarmed public opinion.[6] The vigorous and enterprising business leaders of that era were putting together industrial empires. In many fields their companies had realized complete monopoly power or come close to it. The barons of the railroad industry particularly seemed to threaten the country with combinations too vast and too ominous to be tolerated. Tactics of coercion were freely used. Discriminatory advantages were obtained in transport costs and other facilities.

6. 26 Stat. 209 (1890), 15 U.S.C. 1608 (1952). The historical background of the statute appears in Hans B. Thorelli, *The Federal Antitrust Policy: Origination of an American Tradition*, London, Allen and Unwin, 1954; Eliot Jones, *The Trust Problem in the United States*, New York, Macmillan, 1921, and "Historical Development of the Law of Business Competition," *Yale Law Journal*, 36 (1926), 42, 207, 351; William Letwin, "The English Common Law Concerning Monopolies," *University of Chicago Law Review*, 21 (1954), 355, "Congress and the Sherman Antitrust Law: 1887–1890," *University of Chicago Law Review* 23 (1956), 221, and "The First Decade of the Sherman Act: Early Administration," *Yale Law Journal*, 68 (1959), 464; Rush H. Limbaugh, "Historic Origins of Antitrust Legislation," *Missouri Law Review*, 18 (1953), 215.

Indeed, in one famous instance competitors were ultimately forced to pay a tithe to the dominant company on every sale they made. Organizations of farmers and of laborers were effectively heard for the first time in American politics. Along with other groups and other leaders they sought the protection of national policy against these threats, which were beyond the control of any state. The Sherman Act stands with the Interstate Commerce Act, passed in 1887, as the first great achievements of the movement to reform modern industrial society.

The Sherman Act contains two essential provisions. It declares illegal every contract, combination, in the form of trust or otherwise, or conspiracy in restraint of interstate or foreign trade, and it provides that every person who shall monopolize, or attempt to monopolize, or combine or conspire with other persons to monopolize any part of interstate or foreign trade or commerce shall be deemed guilty of a misdemeanor.

The Sherman Act built upon certain common law ideas drawn from the law of torts, crimes, and contract.[7] And it established new and practical remedies for activities previously difficult to correct by legal action. Four modes of enforcement are provided. Violations of the Act are criminal offenses, and criminal enforcement has been used from time to time—usually resulting in the imposition of rather small fines. The courts naturally tend to resist criminal proceedings against respectable businessmen, and in any case criminal convictions cannot alter the fundamental economic structure of an industry, nor materially change trade practices. Secondly, public officials can bring civil proceedings to halt activities violative of the statute. Civil suits of this character are the most important and most frequently used of all enforcement devices. The powers of the courts in equity cases are far-reaching. Flexible decrees can be developed, requiring action on the part of defendants, or permitting

7. Arthur L. Corbin, *A Treatise on Contracts*, 6 (West Publishing Company, St. Paul, Minnesota, 1951), pars. 1379-1403; Donald Dewey, "Common-law Background of Antitrust Policy," *Virginia Law Review*, 41 (1955), 759; John C. Peppin, "Price-fixing Agreements under the Sherman Antitrust Law," *California Law Review*, 28 (1940), 297, 667, and material cited in note 6, above.

court officers to carry out the wishes of the court. And the courts can retain jurisdiction indefinitely, investigating from time to time to see how their orders are being carried out. In the third place, individuals injured by conduct that violates the law can sue privately, without the help or permission of a public official, and recover three times the amount of the damages they have sustained. Finally, the law provides that goods produced under conditions which violate the act can be seized, in effect as contraband. This interesting feature of the law has almost never been used and remains a curiosity on the statute books.

It is worth noting what the Sherman Act is not. It did not pursue the suggestive line of the Massachusetts corporation law, which until late in the nineteenth century fixed an absolute limit on the value of the property a corporation could possess.[8] Nor did it accept the view of the British courts of the time, and of the later British and German statutes, that the law should tolerate the existence of monopolies and monopoly arrangements and condemn only their abuses or adverse effects. It thus launched the American law on a distinctive line of its own, which the courts, the Congress, and the Federal Trade Commission, faithful after their changing fashions, have pursued to this day.

The early years of the Sherman Act were years of experiment, but also of remarkable achievement. Save for one decision involving the sugar trust in 1894, a decision subsequently ignored, the government won every important case it took on appeal to the Supreme Court of the United States between 1890 and 1918.[9] In that period the antitrust law stopped the process of railroad amalgamation, which threatened to put our entire railway network under the ownership of a single group.[10] It required the dissolution of

8. E. Merrick Dodd, *American Business Corporations until 1860, with Special Reference to Massachusetts*, Cambridge, Harvard University Press, 1954; Brandeis, J., dissenting, in Liggett v. Lee, 288 U.S. 517, 548 ff. (1933).

9. United States v. E. C. Knight Co., 156 U.S. 1 (1894). Walton Hamilton and Irene Till, Antitrust in Action, TNEC, Monograph 16 (1940), 121–43.

10. Northern Securities Co. v. United States, 193 U.S. 197 (1904); United States v. Union Pacific R. R. Co., 226 U.S. 61, 470 (1912, 1913). See also United States v. Southern Pacific Co., 259 U.S. 214 (1922).

gigantic holding companies which had brought together substantially the whole of the petroleum industry,[11] the powder industry,[12] and the tobacco industry.[13] And it had a notable impact as well on meat-packing,[14] naval stores, and a number of other markets of the economy.[15] The example of these basic decisions served as a powerful negative factor in business affairs. Certain lines of development were denied to ambitious men. The United States Steel Corporation, which at one time had between 80 and 90 per cent of American steel capacity in its hands, pursued a course of prudence and restraint which had many followers.[16] It won the suit which the government brought against it. But it was so impressed by the closeness of its escape that it has given up all attempts to gain complete control of the market. As in the oil industry, and others, new companies have grown in strength, and the United States Steel Corporation now possesses less than one-third of American steel capacity.

The most important achievement of the first generation in Sherman Act enforcement, however, was to clarify its premises. The judges, commentators, and congressmen who considered the Act entertained a variety of theories about how the statute should be construed. For twenty years or more controversy raged as to the fundamental meaning of the words used in the Act, and its scope. It was a dramatic debate, with Judge Taft and Justice Peckham, stalwart

11. Standard Oil Co. of N.J. v. United States, 221 U.S. 1 (1911). The effect of the decree and its subsequent history are reviewed in Whitney (above, n. 5), *1*, chap. 3.

12. United States v. E. I. DuPont de Nemours & Co., 188 Fed. 127 (D. Del., 1911), consent decree, United States Department of Justice, Decrees and Judgments in Federal Antitrust Cases (1918), pp. 193–206. The subsequent history is reviewed in Whitney, *1*, chap. 4.

13. United States v. American Tobacco Co., 221 U.S. 106 (1911). See Whitney, *2*, chap. 11, for literature and subsequent history; William H. Nicholls, *Price Policies in the Cigarette Industry*, Nashville, Vanderbilt University Press, 1951; Richard B. Tennant, *The American Cigarette Industry*, New Haven, Yale University Press, 1950.

14. Swift & Co. v. United States, 196 U.S. 375 (1905); see also Whitney, *1*, chap. 2.

15. Most notably perhaps, anthracite coal, United States v. Reading Co., 226 U.S. 324 (1912), 253 U.S. 26 (1920).

16. United States v. United States Steel Corp., 251 U.S. 417, 439 (1920).

"conservatives," fighting hard for a vigorous antitrust law [17] against Justice Holmes, a Darwinian "liberal" who thought the Act was humbug and interpreted it accordingly.[18] The debate was officially resolved by Chief Justice White's Delphic opinion in the *Standard Oil* case of 1911, announcing the "rule of reason" as the official canon of Sherman Act construction.[19] Vehemently attacked at the time, this opinion now stands as the most comprehensive exegesis of the Act the Supreme Court has ever issued.[20] On the whole, it has served the law well.

Chief Justice White was a Louisianan trained in the civil law, a Confederate veteran, and a figure of substance in the history of the Court. His literary style was one of the most ornate, and most obscure, ever to appear in the United States Reports. His opinions were dictated, and in form are distinctly kin to the later novels of Henry James. They have been unfashionable for some years. But his star has been rising, as judges, lawyers, and students have come to realize again how solid some of the work is, behind the heavy, gelatinous flow of the words.

The Attorney General's National Committee to Study the Antitrust Laws, which issued its Report in 1955, made an unexpected discovery. The sixty diverse members of the group found that there was an antitrust law, and not merely a vast heap of cases and statutes, rules and exceptions. With refreshing unanimity, they concluded that on the whole they knew what the law was. And they found the decisive

17. United States v. Addyston Pipe & Steel Co., 85 Fed. 271 (C.C.A. 6th, 1898) (Taft, J.); United States v. Joint-Traffic Ass'n., 171 U.S. 505 (1898) (Peckham, J.).

18. Northern Securities Co. v. United States, 193 U.S. 197, 400 (1904) (Holmes, J., dissenting); Dr. Miles Medical Co. v. John D. Park & Sons Co., 220 U.S. 373, 409 (1911) (Holmes, J., dissenting). See *Holmes-Pollock Letters*, ed. Mark De Wolfe Howe (Cambridge, Harvard University Press, 1941), *I*, 163: "I don't disguise my belief that the Sherman Act is a humbug based on economic ignorance and incompetence, and my disbelief that the Interstate Commerce Commission is a fit body to be entrusted with rate-making . . ."

19. Standard Oil Co. of New Jersey v. United States, 221 U.S. 1 (1911).

20. Report of the Attorney General's National Committee to Study the Antitrust Laws, Stanley N. Barnes and S. Chesterfield Oppenheim, Co-Chairmen (1955), pp. 5 ff.

elements of the law they knew stated, or at least foreshadowed, in Chief Justice White's much abused opinion in the *Standard Oil* case.

The members of the Committee read White's classic opinion with all the legitimate advantages of hindsight. They unanimously found in it pregnant definitions of the reach and boundaries of the "rule of reason." They said with White that the central theme of the Sherman Act and of the statutes that amend and amplify it was to forbid "undue limitations on competitive conditions." [21] This phrase, the Court had said, took its original meaning from the common law but was not restricted by the tradition of the common law. It had been redirected and redefined by the Congress to effectuate a statutory policy of protecting the public against situations popularly known as those of monopoly, from which certain wrongs might be expected to flow. Situations of this kind ranged from those of monopolization, prohibited by Section 2 of the Sherman Act, at one end of the spectrum, to some of the lesser restraints on competition dealt with by Section 1 of the Sherman Act, where the issue is the same but the test of the Act required a lesser showing of the extent or amount of the limitation on competition involved or threatened. While all monopolizations violated Section 1, as restraints of trade, Section 1 could be violated even though the restraint of competition did not amount to a monopolization. And a situation of monopoly could offend Section 2, as a monopolization, although the defendant did not otherwise violate Section 1.

Thus it gradually became clear that all phases of the antitrust law are addressed to interferences with the competitive potential of markets, the varying prohibitions of the law being reconciled as applying to differing *degrees* of such interference.[22] This identification of antitrust policy puts to one side varying competing doctrines that had currency in the past and have currency today. The antitrust laws do not distinguish between good and bad trusts. They allow the judges no discretion to condone monopolies or restrictive

21. Ibid., p. 7.
22. Ibid.

arrangements that pursue low price policies, or can otherwise be described as well managed, progressive, or socially well adjusted and well oriented. The serious remedies of the law are not invoked only when a showing is made of "coercive," "ruthless," "predatory" or other behavior that the judges may deem unethical or antisocial in terms of some vague and undefined standard of their own.

This statement of the scope of the rule of reason, as the universal principle for interpreting the law in the light of its statutory purposes, brings antitrust into revealing focus. The antitrust laws are concerned with monopoly, which the law opposes, and competition, which it favors. And in distinguishing the two concepts, the law relies on an essentially practical and economic definition of the crucial words. This approach, explicit in Justice White's opinion, permits all the antitrust laws to be read together, as concerned with several aspects of a single issue.

These implications of the *Standard Oil* opinion were not, however, to be fully accepted for a long time. The opinion in *Standard Oil* was obviously a totem to which obeisance was expected. But for many years it seemed to permit almost as much ambiguity about the Sherman Act as had prevailed in the rancorous period before 1911.

During the twenties, years in which American life was largely dominated by the attitudes and ideas of business, the doctrinal base of the Sherman Act was weakened somewhat in the courts. Despite several important defeats, the Government gained vital victories as well. And the pressure of the Sherman Act spread steadily throughout the business world, becoming an increasingly important dimension of business decisions.

With the Great Depression, business lost a good deal of its prestige in American opinion. More progressive and even radical attitudes became dominant. The Supreme Court, with new justices appointed during the Roosevelt regime, returned to an earlier and more stringent application of the antitrust laws. During recent years it has handed down an extraordinary number of increasingly severe decisions, which are having an unmistakable impact on economic life.

The antitrust laws had meanwhile been amended and enlarged. During Wilson's first term two new antitrust statutes were passed, reflecting the upsurge of liberal opinion his election symbolized and responding to the experience in antitrust administration under Presidents Theodore Roosevelt and Taft.

The Clayton Act [23] prohibited price discrimination, where its effect might be to lessen competition, thus ending some doubts as to whether this practice fell under the prohibition of the Sherman Act. It should be noted that this provision of the Clayton Act, like other of its clauses, has a different test of legality from the Sherman Act. It applies not merely when a given practice actually has restrained competition, but where there is a substantial probability that it might have such an effect. The purpose of the law is said to be preventative and "therapeutic." It recognizes that it is always more difficult to undo combinations than to prevent them from being born.

The discrimination clause of the Clayton Act has had a curious history. For some years it was invoked in vain by the old-fashioned system of retail distribution to limit the growth of department stores, chain stores, mail order houses, and other competitive methods of distribution. During the Great Depression, always a force which favors protection, this section of the Clayton Act was amended in the interest of the small retailer, the grocer, and the local pharmacy, to help him against the large chain stores, which could buy, and therefore sell, more cheaply than he could.[24] The Supreme Court is wrestling with this paradox, of a section of the antitrust laws being used to restrain competition rather than to encourage it.[25] The price-discrimination fea-

23. 38 Stat. 730, chap. 323 (1914), as amended, 15 U.S.C., pars. 13–26 (1952).

24. Robinson-Patman Act, 49 Stat. 1526, chap. 592, pars. 1, 3, 4 (1936), as amended 15 U.S.C., pars. 13, 13a, 13b (1952). For an introduction to the vast literature on this much discussed statute see F. M. Rowe, "The Evolution of the Robinson-Patman Act: A Twenty Year Perspective," *Columbia Law Review*, 57 (1957), 1059, and "Discriminatory Sales of Commodities in Commerce," *Yale Law Journal*, 67 (1958), 1155.

25. Standard Oil Co. of Indiana v. Federal Trade Commission, 340 U.S. 231 (1951). See Note, *Harvard Law Review*, 67 (1953), 294; J. S. McGee, "Price Discrimination and Competitive Effects," *University of Chicago Law Review*,

tures of the Clayton Act have also been employed in a variety of industrial situations, most notably in the cases in which the courts have prohibited any system employed by competitors, of basing their price quotations on agreed delivery points.[26] This practice, which has greatly facilitated the predictability of prices among competitors, was held to be discriminatory, in that consumers were denied in effect the natural advantage of their geographical position.

The Clayton Act also prohibits any sales or other transfers of goods, whether patented or unpatented, on condition that the purchaser refrain from dealing with a competitor of the seller, where such arrangements have the possibility of restraining any substantial part of the national commerce. This provision has been interpreted quite consistently in a most severe way.[27] Almost every attempt to use an advantage

23 (1956), 398. See also United States v. New York Atlantic & Pacific Tea Co., 173 F.2d 79 (7th Circ., 1949); Comment, *Yale Law Journal, 58* (1949), 969; M. A. Adelman, "The A. & P. Case: A Study in Applied Economic Theory," *Quarterly Journal of Economics, 63* (1949), 238, "Effective Competition and the Antitrust Laws," *Harvard Law Review, 61* (1948), 1289, "Integration and Antitrust Policy," *Harvard Law Review, 63* (1949), 27, "The Consistency of the Robinson-Patman Act," *Stanford Law Review, 6* (1953), 3; Joel B. Dirlam and Alfred E. Kahn, *Fair Competition—the Law and Economics of Antitrust Policy* (Ithaca, Cornell University Press, 1954), pp. 202–56.

26. Federal Trade Commission v. Cement Institute, 333 U.S. 683 (1948). See George J. Stigler, "A Theory of Delivered Price Systems," *American Economic Review, 39* (1949), 1143; J. M. Clark, "The Law and Economics of Basing Points," *American Economic Review, 39* (1949), 430; Fritz Machlup, *The Basing-point System*, Philadelphia, Blakiston, 1949; George W. Stocking, *Basing Point Pricing and Regional Development*, Chapel Hill, University of North Carolina Press, 1954; Comment, *Yale Law Journal, 58* (1948), 426.

27. International Business Machines Corp. v. United States, 298 U.S. 131 (1936); International Salt Co. v. United States, 332 U.S. 392 (1947); Northern Pacific R.R. Co. v. United States, 356 U.S. 1 (1958). Cf. Times-Picayune Publishing Co. v. United States, 345 U.S. 594 (1953). See John P. Miller, *Unfair Competition*, Cambridge, Harvard University Press, 1941; Arthur R. Burns, *The Decline of Competition*, New York and London, McGraw-Hill, 1936; Louis B. Schwartz, "Potential Impairment of Competition," *University of Pennsylvania Law Review, 98* (1949), 10; R. W. McLaren, "Related Problems of 'Requirements' Contracts and Acquisitions in Vertical Integration under the Antitrust Laws," *Illinois Law Review, 45* (1950), 141; W. B. Lockhart and H. Sacks, "The Relevance of Economic Factors in Determining whether Exclusive Arrangements Violate Section 3 of the Clayton Act," *Harvard Law Review, 65* (1952), 913; W. S. Bowman, Jr., "Tying Arrangements and the Leverage Problem," *Yale Law Journal, 67* (1957), 19.

in one market as a "lever" to gain an advantage in the market for another commodity has been struck down. For example, gasoline stations linked to their major oil company suppliers cannot be bound by contract to buy their requirements of gasoline, lubricating oil, tires, tubes, and batteries from their chief source of gasoline.[28] Manufacturers of film projectors attempted by a patent license to prevent motion pictures made by others from being shown on their projectors. The International Business Machine Company, the leading firm in its field, once tried to prevent users of their products from buying the indispensable perforated cards from any other source.[29] Devices of this kind have been frequently held illegal, especially where a patent was involved. The courts are sensitive to the danger of allowing the monopoly conferred by the patent for the invention itself to be extended to another area.

Another section of the Clayton Act attempted to limit the process of corporate growth by stock purchases. A technical flaw in the statute was discovered by the Supreme Court, which made it almost entirely ineffective for almost thirty years. After many cycles of agitation, this loophole was corrected in 1950,[30] and in 1957 the *Du Pont* case foreshadowed a rejuvenation of this most important provision.[81]

28. Standard Oil of California and Standard Stations, Inc. v. United States, 337 U.S. 293 (1949).

29. Motion Picture Patents Co. v. Universal Film Mfg. Co., 243 U.S. 502 (1917); International Business Machines Corp. v. United States (above, n. 27). See also Carbide Corp. of America v. American Patents Development Corp., 283 U.S. 27 (1931); Oxford Varnish Corp. v. Ault & Wilborg Corp., 83 F. 2d 764 (6th Cir., 1936); Mercoid Corp. v. Mid-Continent Investment Co., 320 U.S. 661 (1944).

30. P.L. 899, 81st Cong., 2d Sess., H.R. 2734, Dec. 29, 1950, 64 Stat. 1125 (1950), 15 U.S.C., par. 18 (1952). See *Report* 1191, House of Representatives, Committee on the Judiciary, 81st Cong., 1st Sess., Aug. 4, 1949; "Amending Section 7 and 11 of the Clayton Act," *Hearings*, Subcommittee No. 3, House of Representatives, Committee on the Judiciary, 81st Cong., 1st Sess. (1949); Arrow-Hart & Hegeman Electric Co. v. Federal Trade Commission, 291 U.S. 587 (1934); Comment, *Yale Law Journal*, 57 (1948), 613; J. W. Markham, "Merger Policy under the New Section 7: a Six-year Appraisal," *Virginia Law Review*, 43 (1957), 489.

31. United States v. E. I. DuPont de Nemours & Co., 353 U.S. 586 (1957). The *DuPont* case was decided under Section 7 of the Clayton Act as it stood

Apart from the substantive new provisions of the Clayton Act, there were several clauses of considerable significance. One purported to exempt labor unions and cooperatives from the scope of the antitrust laws. Another fortified the triple-damage provision of the Sherman Act, thus encouraging the enforcement of the law by private litigation and adding to the deterrent force of the statute. Still another specified that if a decree under the antitrust laws was entered by consent of the parties, such a decree could not serve as the basis of subsequent private suits for triple damages, whereas an adverse decree entered after a fully contested proceeding was to be given the status of prima facie evidence in a private damage suit. Thus a powerful inducement was created to persuade businessmen to accept compromise settlements without a struggle. Consent decrees have in fact been an extremely important enforcement device, which has permitted the government, with its limited manpower, to deal with many more situations than would otherwise have been possible.[32]

At the same time another procedure of enforcement was established in the Federal Trade Commission, an administrative body that can make extensive studies and investigations in the field of trade policy, and enforce the antitrust laws in administrative proceedings through which respondents can be required to "cease and desist" from committing violations of the Act.[33] Its decisions in particular cases are sub-

---

before its amendment in 1950. But the interpretation made will be applicable to the amended Act. See also Hamilton Watch Co. v. Benrus Watch Co., 114 F. Supp. 307 (D. Conn., 1953), aff'd. 206 F.2d 738 (2d Circ., 1953), Note, *Yale Law Journal*, 63 (1953), 233; American Crystal Sugar Co. v. Cuban-American Sugar Co., 152 F. Supp. 387 (S.D.N.Y., 1957), aff'd. 259 F.2d 524 (2d Circ., 1958); United States v. Bethlehem Steel Corp., 168 F. Supp. 576 (S.D.N.Y., 1958).

32. M. S. Isenbergh and S. J. Rubin, "Antitrust Enforcement through Consent Decrees," *Harvard Law Review*, 53 (1940), 386; M. Katz, "The Consent Decree in Anti-trust Administration," *Harvard Law Review*, 53 (1940), 415; Comments, *Yale Law Journal*, 51 (1942), 1175, *Michigan Law Review*, 55 (1956), 92.

33. 38 Stat. 717 (1914), as amended, 15 U.S.C., pars. 41–77 (1952). "Functional Operation of the Federal Trade Commission," *Hearings*, U. S. Congress, Select Committee on Small Business, 81st Cong., 2d Sess. (1950), and *Final Report* (1951); Comment, *Yale Law Journal*, 65 (1955), 34.

ject to a limited review on appeal to the higher courts but are treated with considerable deference in court and are in fact difficult to overturn. The Federal Trade Commission deals with a variety of problems apart from the antitrust laws proper. Its position has been much strengthened in recent years, and it has become a rival of the Department of Justice in the general enforcement of the antitrust laws.

The antitrust philosophy extends to a good many other statutes of the federal system. For example, the banking laws prohibit commercial banks from being connected with investment banks. Since 1907 railroads have been denied the right to engage in most other forms of business, although they had been deeply involved in mining, oil, and other industries before that time. A separation has been required also between shipping and air transport, between air transport and the manufacture of planes, and a variety of other connected types of business. The laws governing radio express a similar viewpoint, and the distribution of government-owned surplus property after the war proved an effective instrument for increasing the competitive character of several markets. And the public utility holding companies have been reorganized under a special statute into simplified regional systems.

In approaching this panorama of problems under the antitrust laws, it was suggested earlier that the courts have gradually defined their initial task under the rule of reason as an economic one. The first step nowadays in most cases before the courts and the Federal Trade Commission is to describe the market where the defendant or defendants actually do business.[34] Then the courts or the Commission seek to discover whether the defendants' conduct in that market constitutes a "monopolization" or an "undue" restraint of competitive conditions under the Sherman Act

34. See David Macdonald, "Product Competition in the Relevant Market under the Sherman Act," *Michigan Law Review*, 53 (1954), 69; Note, *Columbia Law Review*, 54 (1954), 580; George W. Stocking, "Economic Tests of Monopoly and the Concept of the Relevant Market," *Antitrust Bulletin*, 2 (1957), 479; D. F. Turner, "Antitrust Policy and the Cellophane Case," *Harvard Law Review*, 70 (1956), 281; Note, *Minnesota Law Review*, 41 (1958), 498; *Harvard Law Review*, 70 (1956), 95, 168.

or a probable restriction of competition, within the ambit of the Clayton Act.

In identifying the market for antitrust purposes, the courts concentrate on the pattern of the defendant's actual business. The commodity or service he sells must be distinguished from its direct substitutes, the geographical boundaries of the market fixed in terms of his own experience.

Consider, for example, the analysis in *Columbia Steel*, where the Court determined the legality of the purchase by United States Steel of Consolidated Steel Company, an 8 million dollar rolled-steel fabricator on the West Coast.[35] The merger eliminated competition between United States Steel and other large companies in selling rolled steel to Consolidated. Is "rolled steel" a commodity sufficiently distinct for the purposes of the Act, or must the Court examine the effect of the merger on the national or international market for all steel products, or all primary steel products? Should it include aluminum, copper, plastics, wood, and other commodities that compete for steel in one use or another?

In determining whether the particular merger before the Court violated the Sherman Act, or the policy of the Clayton Act,[36] the Court was content to take rolled steel as the relevant commodity in this branch of the case, and the region where Consolidated functioned as the geographical market. The first question it had to answer, therefore, was "what fraction of the rolled steel sold on the West Coast did Consolidated consume?" The government contended for a narrower definition, which would have made the fraction larger. The defense urged a wider geographical market, which would have resulted in a smaller fraction. The Court, framing the question in this form, found that the merger would eliminate competition as to only 3 per cent of the local business in rolled steel, and concluded that this reduction in competition was so small that it could be per-

35. United States v. Columbia Steel Co., 334 U.S. 495 (1948).

36. The form of the transaction at the time of trial—prior to the 1950 amendment of the Clayton Act—precluded direct recourse to that statute. But the Court said its policy was "to be taken into consideration" nonetheless. 334 U.S. at 507.

mitted, especially in view of the business and public policies involved in other aspects of the case.

The *Columbia Steel* case raised several cognate problems that illustrate the intensely functional character of the market issue in antitrust cases. Consolidated was not only a customer of United Steel, it was also a rival, in the sale of two classes of fabricated products—structural shapes and pipe. The effect of the merger in eliminating this competition was also measured in quantitative terms. Consolidated sold structural steel only in twelve western states. But it sold pipe in competition with United States Steel and others wherever oil was sought, throughout the world. The relevant market was therefore defined differently for these two aspects of the case.

Defining the market has been a hotly contested matter in recent years, and properly so. Although the Supreme Court has recently divided three times in answering the question in specific factual situations, there is no division among the Justices as to the relevance of the problem, or the terms in which it should be framed.[37] In the *Cellophane* case, the Court found, for purposes of determining responsibility under Section 2 of the Sherman Act, that cellophane competed directly with other transparent wrapping materials.[38] The Justices who spoke for the Court concluded that purchasers could and did choose among these products in individual transactions, and that their choice among competing materials was responsive to their relative price. The minority found otherwise, but without challenging the Court's formulation of the issue. The problem was dealt with in a similar way in the *DuPont–General Motors* case to reach a rather different conclusion.[39] The Court viewed that case as a challenge to the legality of a merger under the Clayton Act, before its 1950 amendment. A plurality of the Court found that in all probability the merger adversely

37. United States v. E. I. DuPont de Nemours & Co., 351 U.S. 377 (1956); United States v. E. I. DuPont de Nemours & Co., 353 U.S. 586 (1957); Times-Picayune Publishing Co. v. United States, 345 U.S. 594 (1953).
38. United States v. E. I. DuPont de Nemours & Co., 351 U.S. 377 (1956).
39. United States v. E. I. DuPont de Nemours & Co., 353 U.S. 586 (1957).

affected competition in the sale of fabrics and finishes to the automobile industry, such fabrics and finishes having "sufficiently peculiar characteristics and uses to constitute them products sufficiently distinct from all other finishes and fabrics to make them a 'line of commerce' within the meaning of the Clayton Act." [40] The dissenting Justices were not convinced that DuPont's advantage in selling General Motors these two classes of products reflected an influence emanating from DuPont ownership of General Motors stock. And they believed that there was not enough evidence in the record to support the conclusion that fabrics and finishes used by the automobile industry were in fact sufficiently distinct from other fabrics and finishes to constitute a separate market. The reasoning in this case throws considerable doubt on the standing of the earlier *Cellophane* case as a guide to analysis.

Once the Court has defined the relevant market, it must face the question whether the defendants' conduct, in fact or in prospect, "unduly" restrains competition within that market, in violation of one or another of the provisions of the Sherman or Clayton acts. In dealing with this issue, cases divide into two broad classes that are closely related but distinguishable: those concerned directly with the process of price formation, and those involving restrictions upon the possibility of entry into a market. The first group of issues includes price-fixing and price-leadership programs, open-price plans, various schemes involving price manipulation, and the merger of competitors; the second group includes exclusionary devices, boycotts, market division agreements, long-term supply contracts, some vertical integrations, and other arrangements that effectively limit the competitive opportunity of business rivals. In both groups the courts find some practices (like boycotts or price-fixing plans), which they consider anticompetitive "in character" —that is, as having no possible function or effect save the elimination of competition. Others, like mergers, may or may not restrict competition, depending upon circumstances, so that they would not normally be classified as conclusively

40. Ibid., pp. 593–94.

anticompetitive. In handling the first category of problems
—those of price formation—the treatment of the courts is
now almost entirely one of economic analysis; in dealing
with the second group—those of competitive opportunity—
the approach of the courts, while strongly economic, is
tinged also by the feeling that limiting a rival's chance to
compete is an unfair assertion of economic power, to be
condemned on moral as well as economic grounds.

What has been the pattern of decision in handling substantive problems of this order?

In the first place, a long series of decisions on certain key
business practices has meant that behavior which is common-
place in many countries hardly exists in the United States.
The easy techniques of combination are denied, and those
who wish to organize monopolistic combinations must depend on other and often more difficult procedures. For
example, agreements among competitors to fix or to agree
on prices, or to divide markets, have been consistently held
to be illegal since 1897.[41] The reasoning of the Court has
been that it will not consider whether the prices themselves
are reasonable. The existence of the power to fix or control
a price must of itself be denied, since a price which is reasonable today may be unreasonable tomorrow. Neither the
courts nor the Federal Trade Commission can continuously
supervise the market and pass on the transient "reasonable-
ness" of prices. Authority of this kind, the Supreme Court
has frequently remarked, can be exercised by the state but
never by a private group.[42] Cases of this order, the Supreme
Court said as early as the *Standard Oil* case of 1911, present
situations that will be "conclusively presumed" to be unreasonable under the rule of reason.[43] The defendants'
conduct substantially limits competition, in view of the
"character" of the conduct or its "necessary" or "actual"

41. United States v. Trans-Missouri Freight Ass'n, 166 U.S. 290 (1897);
United States v. Joint-Traffic Ass'n, 171 U.S. 505 (1898); United States v.
Trenton Potteries Co., 273 U.S. 392 (1927); United States v. Socony-Vacuum
Oil Co., Inc., 310 U.S. 150 (1940).

42. See n. 41, above, United States v. Socony-Vacuum Oil Co.; Fashion
Originators Guild v. Federal Trade Commission, 312 U.S. 457 (1941).

43. Standard Oil Co. of New Jersey v. United States, 221 U.S. 1, 65 (1911).

effect. Conduct of this kind, the Court said later, is unreasonable per se for its actual or assumed effect on competition.[44]

The hostility to price-fixing, as illegal in itself, has had a far-reaching development. It applies not only to horizontal combinations among competitors but to vertical arrangements as well. Once a manfuacturer has sold his product to a wholesaler or retailer, he gives up all power to control the price at which it can be resold.[45] Under the pressure of the depression an amendatory law passed in 1937 permits a limited exception to this principle, the one authorizing resale price maintenance under the appealing label of state "Fair Trade" laws.[46] The Supreme Court and other courts have interpreted the Fair Trade laws unsympathetically, limiting the possible scope of Fair Trade contracts. Congress, however, influenced by lobbies of retailers and other "small" businessmen, has on several occasions sought to undo the effect of adverse judicial decisions and to restore the possibility of using the practice in distribution.[47] Fair trade apart, however, the general principle remains. In recent decisions it has been extended to cover not only agreements to fix prices but arrangements which are thought significantly to influence price or narrow the market in any way, or limit the fullest development of competitive forces. Thus trade associations

44. United States v. Socony-Vacuum Oil Co., Inc., 310 U.S. 150 (1940); United States v. Columbia Steel Co., 334 U.S. 495, 522 (1948).

45. Dr. Miles Medical Co. v. John D. Park & Sons Co., 220 U.S. 373 (1911); Federal Trade Commission v. Beech-Nut Packing Co., 257 U.S. 441 (1922).

46. 50 Stat. 693 (1937).

47. McGuire Act, 66 Stat. 631 (1952), 15 U.S.C., par. 45(a) 1952). See W. S. Bowman, Jr., "Resale Price Maintenance—a Monopoly Problem," *Journal of Business of the University of Chicago,* 25 (1952), 141. For a defense of the laws see Walter Adams, "Resale Price Maintenance: Fact and Fancy," *Yale Law Journal,* 64 (1955), 967; E. S. Herman, "A Note on Fair Trade," *Yale Law Journal,* 65 (1955), 23, and Reply by Adams, *Yale Law Journal,* 65 (1955), 196. See J. A. MacLachlan, "A New Approach to Resale Price Maintenance," *Vanderbilt Law Review,* 11 (1957), 145. For situations in which the Fair Trade Laws have been invoked see United States v. Bausch & Lomb Optical Co., 321 U.S. 707 (1944); Pepsodent Co. v. Krauss Co., 56 F. Supp. 922 (D. La., 1944); United States v. Frankfort Distilleries, 324 U.S. 293 (1945).

are forbidden to collect and circulate statistics and estimates
of future production and consumption, or future prices,
which might well influence production plans and thus market
prices.[48] And competitors cannot agree to install uniform systems of cost accounting, the effect of which might lead to
uniform price quotations. It is a complex issue of fact to determine whether a trade association plan, a rule of the Board of
Trade, a basing-point system, a "code of ethics," or some
other arrangement among competitors actually involves
price-fixing, or a substantial noncompetitive effect on pricing,
within the policy of the antitrust laws. These questions cannot be answered in the abstract, but often depend upon their
factual setting. Many, perhaps most, of the cases litigated
under Section 1 of the Sherman Act turn on this question.

Secondly, all forms of boycotts, or collective refusals to
buy or sell, are severely dealt with. A famous case concerned
the problem of what is called style "piracy." [49] Certain manufacturers of ladies' dresses made it a practice to copy the expensive creations of *haute couture* for the stenographers' and
housewives' market. Outraged by this flattery, the manufacturers of the more expensive clothes agreed not to sell to
merchants who sinned in this way, and circulated a list on
which the style "pirates" figured in red ink. The Supreme
Court upheld an order of the Federal Trade Commission

48. American Column & Lumber Co. v. United States, 257 U.S. 377 (1921);
Maple Flooring Mfgr's Ass'n. v. United States, 268 U.S. 563 (1925); The
Sugar Institute, Inc., v. United States, 297 U.S. 553 (1936). See J. L. Fly,
"Observations on the Anti-trust Laws, Economic Theory, and the Sugar
Institute Decisions," I, *Yale Law Journal*, 45 (1936), 1339, and II, ibid., 46
(1936), 228; S. Marmin, "Sugar : A Rugged Collectivist," *Illinois Law Review*,
31 (1936), 320; George W. Stocking, "The Rule of Reason, Workable Com-
petition, and the Legality of Trade Association Activities," *University of
Chicago Law Review*, 21 (1954), 527; Report of the Attorney General's
National Committee to Study the Antitrust Laws, S. N. Barnes and S. C.
Oppenheim, Co-Chairmen (1955), pp. 12–24; H. Kemker, "The Legality of
Trade Association Statistical Reporting under the Anti-trust Laws," *Vander-
bilt Law Review*, 11 (1958), 361.

49. Fashion Originators' Guild v. Federal Trade Commission, 312 U.S.
457 (1941). See also United States v. Frankfort Distilleries, 324 U.S. 293
(1945). See C. F. Barber, "Refusals to Deal under the Federal Antitrust
Laws," *University of Pennsylvania Law Review*, 103 (1955), 847.

against this plan to improve the ethics of the dress business. Whether it was legal or illegal, as a matter of civil law, to copy dress designs, it was illegal under the antitrust laws to restrict competition among manufacturers of dresses.

Thirdly, the scope of the protection given in American law to trade-marks and trade names and to patents has been extraordinarily restricted by the antitrust philosophy of the federal judges. Such topics are favorite subjects for litigation, and the courts strike down these statutory monopolies on all sorts of grounds with something approaching enthusiasm. One might cite an instance involving the word "cellophane," originally a trade-marked name for which the DuPont Company paid a French inventor a large sum of money. The success of the product, the court said, had made the word part of the language, and not an indication of the source of a product. Therefore, all protection was lost and other manufacturers were allowed to call their goods cellophane.[50]

Fourthly, there has been a striking development in the effectiveness of the monopoly section of the Sherman Act, which was for many years neglected, or employed only in connection with cases involving combinations in restraint of trade. The defeat of the government in the *Steel* and the *International Harvester* cases of the twenties seemed to establish the proposition that neither "size" nor "unexerted" power were offenses under the Act.[51] Those cases apparently called for evidence that defendants provided close to 90 per cent of market supply, even for purposes of Section 1 of the Sherman Act, and that they engaged in "predatory," "ruthless," or overtly coercive behavior. For twenty years these precedents made it virtually impossible to stop the combination of competitors by merger.

But a series of decisions beginning with the *Pullman* case

50. DuPont Cellophane Co. v. Waxed Products Co., 85 F. (2d) 75 (2nd Cir., 1936); E. I. DuPont de Nemours & Co. v. Sylvania Industrial Corp., 122 F. (2d) 400 (4th Circ., 1941). See Rudolph Callmann, *The Law of Unfair Competition and Trade-marks*, Chicago, Callaghan, 1945; R. S. Brown, Jr., "Advertising and the Public Interest," *Yale Law Journal*, 57 (1948), 1165.

51. United States v. United States Steel Corp. 251 U.S. 417 (1920); United States v. International Harvester Co., 274 U.S. 693 (1927).

in 1943 and including *Alcoa, Paramount,* and *United Shoe Machinery* have given Section 2 of the Sherman Act an altogether new vitality.[52]

In perhaps twelve decisions, involving both small local markets and national industries, the courts have all but buried the earlier *Steel* and *Harvester* decisions. They have held the Act violated where a company or a group of companies in combination possesses a high degree of market power, although they supply a good deal less than 90 per cent of output in the market. The existence of the power is illegal, the newer cases say, unless the defendants meet the burden of proving that their market position has been "thrust upon them" solely by reason of their superior skill, by circumstances of nature beyond their control, or by accident. In

52. United States v. Aluminum Company of America, 148 F. (2d) 416 (2nd Cir., 1945); American Tobacco Co. v. United States, 328 U.S. 781 (1946); United States v. Paramount Pictures, Inc., 334 U.S. 131 (1948); United States v. Griffith, 334 U.S. 100 (1948); Schine Chain Theatres v. United States, 334 U.S. 110 (1948); United States v. Columbia Steel Co., 334 U.S. 495 (1948); United States v. Pullman Co., 50 F. Supp. 123 (E.D. Pa., 1943), 53 F. Supp. 908 (E.D. Pa., 1944), 55 F. Supp. 985 (E.D. Pa., 1944), 64 F. Supp. 108 (E.D. Pa., 1946), aff'd. without opinion by equally divided court, 330 U.S. 806 (1947); United States v. United Shoe Machinery Corp., 110 F. Supp. 295 (D. Mass., 1953), aff'd. without opinion, 347 U.S. 521 (1954). See Carl Kaysen, *United States v. United Shoe Machinery Corporation,* Cambridge, Harvard University Press, 1956.

On the doctrinal issues behind these cases, see Report of the Attorney General's National Committee to Study the Antitrust Laws, S. N. Barnes and S. C. Oppenheim, Co-Chairmen (1955), pp. 43–61; Edward H. Levi, "The Anti-trust Laws and Monopoly," *University of Chicago Law Review, 14* (1947), 153; E. V. Rostow, "The New Sherman Act: A Positive Instrument of Progress," *University of Chicago Law Review, 14* (1947), 567, and "Monopoly under the Sherman Act: Power or Purpose?" *Illinois Law Review, 43* (1949), 745; M. A. Adelman, "Effective Competition and the Antitrust Laws," *Harvard Law Review, 61* (1948), 1289; Edward R. Johnston and John P. Stevens, "Monopoly or Monopolization—a Reply to Professor Rostow," *Illinois Law Review, 44* (1949), 269; John R. McDonough, Jr., and R. L. Winslow, "The Motion Picture Industry: United States v. Oligopoly," *Stanford Law Review, 1* (1949), 385; Lawrence Wood, "The Supreme Court and a Changing Anti-trust Concept," *University of Pennsylvania Law Review, 97* (1949), 309; David M. Wright, "Toward Coherent Anti-trust," *Virginia Law Review, 35* (1949), 665; R. Callmann, "The Essence of Anti-trust," *Columbia Law Review, 49* (1949), 1100; G. E. Hale and Rosemary Hale, *Market Power: Size and Shape under the Sherman Act,* Boston, Little, Brown, 1958; Milton Handler, *Antitrust in Perspective,* New York, Columbia University Press, 1957.

the absence of such a showing, the defendants' dominant market position becomes "monopolizing," in violation of Section 2, if it was deliberately obtained or maintained. The element of purpose needed to satisfy Section 2 in such cases is carefully limited. It will often be inferred or assumed, especially in the friendly atmosphere of established, cooperative oligopoly. It is sharply distinguished from the "specific intent" required to establish other offenses. The requirement will be satisfied by a showing that the monopolist engaged in restrictive practices which violated Section 1 of the Act, although no such extrinsic violations need be shown, as Chief Justice White remarked in 1911, as part of the cause of action under Section 2.

Where monopolizing is found, the normal remedy seems to be the dissolution or partial dissolution of the offending business unit.

For example, there were eight large manufacturers of motion pictures in the United States, five of whom also owned theaters, including the majority of the first-run theaters. First-run theaters are the larger, better-located theaters, to which distributors lease films for their initial showing. They charge higher prices than at other theaters, which can show a film only after a marked delay. Together, the eight companies occupied a considerable share of the market, both as producers and as exhibitors of films at first run. Without an express agreement, the policies of these companies followed parallel lines, and they engaged in a variety of practices that the courts found illegal in themselves, devices to keep up admission prices in theaters—block-booking, and the like. Apart from these practices, however, the court said that the combination of theater ownership and film manufacture under these circumstances restricted competition among films. The companies were required to sell the larger share of their theaters to third persons.[53]

In 1945 the Aluminum Company of America, which before the war manufactured 90 per cent of the virgin aluminum on the American market, was held to have monopolized

53. University States v. Paramount Pictures, Inc., 85 F. Supp. 881 (S.D.N.Y., 1949).

the market for virgin aluminum in the period before 1940. The court refused to consider the scrap market as part of the field, although scrap competes with virgin aluminum, or to enlarge its measure to include processed aluminum. While the case was pending, the government sold to other companies the aluminum plants built on government account during the war, with the result that the Aluminum Company had only 50 per cent of national capacity in this field in 1950. In that year a lower court decided in an opinion of broad scope that although Alcoa probably did not then have a monopoly position in the American industry, the fact that it did have one in 1940, coupled with the fact that in 1950 it had a "dominant" influence in the market, required the court to retain jurisdiction, in the interest of ordering whatever acts were proved practicable to achieve "effective competition." After a lengthy factual review of the state of the industry, the court required a complete dissolution of the stock-owner-ship connections between the American and the Canadian companies, and certain steps designed to weaken Alcoa's hold on improvements which might be developed by other companies using its patents under licenses. This approach of the lower court, coupled with the policy followed by the government in selling the bulk of its wartime aluminum plants to independent companies, has significantly transformed the structure of the American aluminum industry.[54]

At the other extreme the monopoly section of the Act has been used against an unfortunate man who happened to be the only manufacturer of a certain type of rugs made of linen. A merchant wished to buy his product in order to be able to compete with him for a government contract. He refused to sell, in order to be able to bid alone for the contract. He was held guilty in a criminal proceeding.[55] Simi-

54. United States v. Aluminum Co. of America, 91 F. Supp. 333 (S.D.N.Y., 1950). See E. V. Rostow, "Problems of Size and Integration," in Commerce Clearing House, *Business under the Federal Antitrust Laws* (New York, 1951), 117, reprinted in J. G. Van Cise and C. W. Dunn, eds., *How to Comply with the Antitrust Laws,* (New York, Commerce Clearing House, 1954), pp. 311, 317–22.

55. United States v. Klearflax Linen Looms, Inc., 63 F. Supp. 32 (D. Minn., 1945).

larly, the proprietor of an area's only newspaper in which local merchants were virtually forced to advertise, was held to have violated the law by refusing to accept advertising from those who advertised on a radio station.[56]

This cycle of decisions suggests a doctrine that threatens the existing structure of several large industries in the United States. In many fields, two or three or four big companies occupy crucial market positions. Together, they produce 60 or 70 per cent of the particular product. They follow each other's prices out of self-interest and without overt agreement. Each one knows that any move on his part would provoke a response from the others, and that a price cut could not change his share of the market. Hence, prevailing policies in such markets are those of price leadership, on the one hand, and advertising and other marketing efforts, on the other. There is competition not through price reductions but through increases in cost. Each seller has an equal distaste for what he calls "cut-throat competition," an equal interest in the policy of "live and let live." When an industry is organized in this way, price, output, and opportunities to enter the field are akin to those which would obtain under conditions of monopoly; in many instances the amount of social waste involved may be greater than that which would prevail under conditions of monopoly. The ordinary consequence of the market structure is that the dominant large companies, if they have a decent regard for their own interests, will act as if they had combined, even though their officers may never have talked to each other, even on the phone or the golf course. The market power of the dominant group is used collectively—pooled, in fact, for price purposes.

This pattern represents the expected norm in situations where a large part of market supply comes from a few large firms. The dynamic elements in this model are altogether familiar in practical life. They often appear in the guise of information programs, customs of price leadership, nominal product differentiation, and other devices whose function is to reduce uncertainty and build up consumer loyalties and preferences moderately insensitive to price.

56. Lorain Journal Co. v. United States, 342 U.S. 143 (1951).

Oligopoly does not always take so cooperative a form. For one reason or another, great uncertainty may prevail, or be encouraged by public action. A member of the group, for example, may be a congenital maverick, like Ford, Firestone, or Pew. Uncertainty about his policy and about the expected responses of the other rivals to his policy may throw the whole group's conditioned reflexes askew. It is hard to play the game sensibly if a different card, quite unannounced, becomes wild with every deal. In markets of this kind it is easy to understand, if not to sympathize with, the aversion businessmen feel for the "price-cutter," the "chiseler," the "unethical" seller who engages in price competition and thus "spoils" the market for all.

Two possible lines of approach to the problem of "cooperative oligopoly" are emerging from the decisions of the Court. One would be to deal with the cooperating group as a "combination" or "conspiracy" monopolizing the trade, in violation of Section 2 of the Sherman Act. The other would be to bring suit only against the one or two giant companies in the field, individually, as "combinations" in continuing restraint of trade, offensive to Section 1 of the Sherman Act.

The first approach, that of collective monopolizing, would follow the lead of *American Tobacco Co. v. United States* [57] and *United States v. Paramount Pictures, Inc.* [58] In both those cases, the "major" companies in an industry of the few were found to have joined together informally and without express agreement, in consciously making parallel decisions as to important aspects of their market policy. The evidence of "combination" accepted by the courts was in most respects indistinguishable from the kind of behavior to be expected in a situation of rational, well-established, well-informed, cooperative oligopoly. The effect and result of the companies' parallel action was to give the group a considerable degree of power over the price they charged and over the possible entry and prosperity of new and old rivals in the field. That power was treated as on a par, legally, with the power exercised by single firms in cases like *United States v. Aluminum Com-*

57. 328 U.S. 781 (1945).
58. 334 U.S. 131 (1948).

pany of America and *United States v. United Shoe Machinery Company*.

The Court has warned about the limits of such proofs. It is always good evidence of combination or conspiracy to show that in a situation of oligopoly the defendants behave in uniform and parallel ways, as if they had tacitly agreed to coordinate their price policy. If, on the basis of such evidence, a jury, a lower court, or the Federal Trade Commission finds that the defendants have reached an understanding, that finding will not be disturbed on appeal. On the other hand, guilt and responsibility under the law must be individual, and not imputed by association, or even without it. If the trial tribunal is satisfied, despite such evidence, that the defendants' decisions were independent and not collective, and did not stem from a collusive agreement, tacit or express, the appellate courts will not usually reverse that finding of fact.[59]

It is an open question whether the Supreme Court would now apply the precedent of the *Paramount* case to order the competitive realignment of a major oligopoly industry, where market power is shown to be shared by a small group and used in common to minimize uncertainties and avoid price competition. The doctrinal basis for such a suit is well established. Several industry-wide cases now pending raise the issue. They may soon settle it.

The second legal approach identified above—that of suing a single large firm as a "combination" under Section 1 of the Sherman Act—may well turn out to provide a simpler and more discriminating means for increasing the degree of competitiveness in many situations of oligopoly. The theory of actions of this kind would build on the word "combination," in Section 1 of the Sherman Act. That section makes illegal "every contract, combination in the form of trust or otherwise, or conspiracy, in restraint of trade or commerce among

59. Theatre Enterprises, Inc. v. Paramount Film Distributing Co., 346 U.S. 537 (1954). See also Eastern States Retail Lumber Dealers Ass'n. v. United States, 234 U.S. 600 (1914); Interstate Circuit, Inc. v. United States, 306 U.S. 208 (1939); Federal Trade Commission v. Cement Institute, 333 U.S. 683, 716, n.17 (1948). See Report of the Attorney General's National Committee to Study the Antitrust Laws, pp. 36–42; M. Handler, "Annual Review of Antitrust," *The Record, 10* (1955), 332, 343.

the several states, or with foreign nations." The scope of the word "combination" in this setting, as distinguished from "contract" or "conspiracy," has never been seriously considered. It is clear, however, that for more than fifty years the idea of "combination" in this section has been called into play not only by "trusts" in the form of trusts, but also by "trusts" established through mergers, holding companies, and other devices which achieve a permanent or semipermanent association among competitors.[60] Any company whose history includes an episode of merger therefore faces the risk that it is a "combination" for purposes of Section 1 of the Sherman Act, and a perpetual, standing, and incurable "combination," to boot. The mark of Cain is upon it.

Next, the argument would proceed to the words "restraint of trade or commerce," in Section 1 of the Act. This phrase defines an offense different from the "monopolization" condemned by Section 2. The *Standard Oil* case of 1911, as the Attorney General's Antitrust Committee recently interpreted it, viewed "restraints of trade and monopolization as two phases or degrees of the same phenomenon." [61] Both at common law and in ordinary speech, the Court had said, the words "monopoly" and "restraint of trade" referred to situations where competitive conditions were "unduly" limited. The two sections of the Act were therefore interpreted to supplement each other, in the interest of making the prohibitions of the Act all-embracing, whether the forbidden end— monopoly—was achieved, partially achieved, or merely sought, and whether it was pursued by a single entity or by a group. In two leading cases of great importance it was de-

60. Northern Securities Co. v. United States, 193 U.S. 197 (1904); United States v. Union Pacific R.R. Co., 226 U.S. 61, 88 (1912); United States v. Southern Pacific Co. 259 U.S. 214, 229–31 (1922); United States v. Reading Co., 253 U.S. 26, 48 (1920). See Report of the Attorney General's National Committee to Study the Antitrust Laws, p. 32 ("several of the corporations grew out of mergers of previously independent competitors, thus making them 'combinations' within the meaning of the Act"), and discussion, pp. 30–36.

61. Report of the Attorney General's National Committee to Study the Antitrust Laws, p. 7.

cided that groups of sellers acting in concert had "restrained trade" in violation of Section 1 of the Act, by significantly influencing prices, although they were expressly found not to have "monopolized" by conspiring to fix prices and to dominate the market.[62] The power they had over price in the market, while significant enough in each case to suppport the conclusion that they were violating Section 1, fell short of the quantum required to justify a finding of monopoly, for purposes of Section 2. Section 2 of the Act calls for a higher degree of monopoly power than Section 1, just as the Clayton Act deals with lesser degrees of monopoly power than either section of the Sherman Act. In Judge Learned Hand's phrase, certain contracts in restraint of trade within reach of Section 1 are "only steps towards that entire control that monopoly confers: they are really partial monopolies." [63]

This line of reasoning would recognize the final burial, even in the most technical sense, of the Supreme Court's famous opinion in *United States v. United States Steel Corp.* That decision has been discredited, qualified, and ignored, and its incidental philosophy has been repudiated. But the exact issue decided there has never been squarely confronted again, save in *United States v. Socony Vacuum Oil Co., Inc.*[64] In its *Steel* opinion of 1920, the Supreme Court treated the case as if the charge were realized monopolization rather than combination in restraint of trade, or as if the two issues were the same. The Court agreed that the holding company had been formed for the express purpose of monopolizing the industry, and that for a while it came close to doing so. But the Company's share of the market dropped. It could not control prices save by devices of collusion. It provided only half the market supply, and lacked the power of monopoly as "a continually operating force." "Whatever there was of wrong intent could not be executed; whatever there was of

62. United States v. Reading Co., 226 U.S. 324, 343-46 (1912), 253 U.S. 26, 53 (1920); United States v. Socony-Vacuum Oil Co., 310 U.S. 150, 221, 243-48 (1940).

63. United States v. Aluminum Company of America, 148 F.2d 416, 428 (2d Circ., 1945).

64. Cited above, n. 62.

evil effect was discontinued before this suit was brought, and this, we think, determines the decree." [65] The dissenters protested that in a case of combination or conspiracy it was erroneous to require complete monopolization. "To insist upon such result would be beyond the requirements of the statute and in most cases practicably impossible." [66] The manifest influence of the United States Steel Corporation in the steel industry of 1920, they thought, was "too plain to require extended argument." One great integrated company, embracing half the industry and dealing with competitors then much smaller than itself, was strong enough, the dissenters thought, to come within the prohibition of Section 1, if not of Section 2.

In the light of subsequent history it is fair to conclude that the dissenting opinion represents the law as it now stands more accurately than that of the plurality. If this view is correct, the word "combination" may well become an increasingly familiar word in the federal courts, in suits seeking to break up large corporations not in themselves "dominant" firms in their markets, or "monopolizations," but entities whose power and influence in some of the markets where they buy or sell might reasonably be considered unduly restrictive of competitive conditions.

This line of reasoning is the obverse of that accepted by four justices of the Court in deciding the recent *DuPont* case, holding DuPont's 23 per cent holding of General Motors' stock to be a violation of Section 7 of the Clayton Act.[67] DuPont has held a substantial minority interest in General Motors' stock since 1917, and has been strongly represented on the General Motors Board. It had actively participated in some of the difficult financial and managerial crises of the General Motors company, immediately after the first World War. And it had sought and procured a good deal, though by no means all, of General Motors' business in the purchase of paints, fabrics, and other products manu-

---

65. 251 U.S. 417, 452 (1920). See discussion of case above, Report, n. 60, pp. 48–52.

66. 251 U.S. at 465.

67. United States v. E. I. DuPont de Nemours & Co., 353 U.S. 586 (1957).

factured by DuPont. General Motors' needs and DuPont's ability to meet them were rather freely discussed not only by the directors of General Motors but by officers and employees of both companies. The suit started in 1949 and was tried largely under Section 1 of the Sherman Act, on a theory of conspiracy. But the Supreme Court disposed of it only under Section 7 of the Clayton Act, on the ground that the effect of DuPont's ownership of General Motors' stock "may be to . . . restrain . . . commerce in any section or community or tend to create a monopoly in any line of commerce." The primary issue, Mr. Justice Brennan said, was "whether DuPont's commanding position as General Motors' supplier of automotive finishes and fabrics was achieved on competitive merit alone, or because its acquisition of the General Motors' stock, and the consequent close intercompany relationship, led to the insulation of most of the General Motors' market from free competition, with the resultant likelihood, at the time of suit, of the creation of a monopoly of a line of commerce." [68]

The case has occasioned an outcry. [69] Some have criticized the application of the pre-1950 Clayton Act to vertical integrations. I can find no plausible way to avoid applying the complicated sentence structure of the Act to vertical integrations, despite the contrary views of the Federal Trade Commission. And the Supreme Court did so, in effect, in *Columbia Steel*, ten years before, a Sherman Act case which the Court said, however, "took into consideration" the policy of Section 7. [70] Others have complained because of the lapse of

68. Ibid., pp. 588–89, and see p. 607.

69. G. W. Stocking, "The DuPont–General Motors Case and the Sherman Act," *Virginia Law Review*, 44 (1958), 1; Symposium, *Georgetown Law Journal*, 46 (1958), 561–702; M. A. Adelman, "The DuPont–General Motors Decision," *Virginia Law Review*, 43 (1957), 873; J. W. Markham, "The DuPont–General Motors Decision," *Virginia Law Review*, 43 (1957), 881; J. B. Dirlam and I. M. Stelzer, "The DuPont–General Motors Decision: In the Antitrust Grain," *Columbia Law Review*, 58 (1958), 24; H. G. Manne, "The Perplexing DuPont Case: Additional Confusion in the Law of Mergers," *University of Pennsylvania Law Review*, 106 (1958), 385; Comments, *California Law Review*, 46 (1958), 266; *Yale Law Journal*, 66 (1957), 1251.

70. *United States v. Columbia Steel Co.*, 334 U.S. 495, 507 (1948).

thirty years between the stock purchases, in 1917–19, and the time of trial, and because the Court seemed to take the position that a merger might be legal when made, but become illegal later. In the Court's opinion, the tests of Section 7 concern the business situation at the time of trial, not that of the date of acquisition.

The *Steel* case of 1920 supports this view; it decided that while the company was illegal when formed, it did not violate the Act at the time the issue came before the courts. That decision under the Sherman Act should apply *a fortiori* to the Clayton Act, in view of its preventive purposes. Long delays always present an issue of fairness in the administration of justice. But the economic potentialities of a merger may not appear for some time. The market may change. And there is little point in enforcing a law whose object is to prevent monopoly as an instrument for punishing the sins and errors of the remote past.

Justice Burton's dissent concedes that the Court may consider what happened between the acquisition and the trial as evidence confirming or disproving an inference that the anticompetitive consequences of the merger were reasonably probable at the time it was consummated.[71] As Stedman has remarked, Justice Burton

> seems to be telling a trial court—or even worse, a jury —that it shall take the circumstances as they exist on a given date and predict what effect these will have upon competition five, ten, fifteen or twenty years hence; that in making this prediction, however, they may go beyond the facts upon which they base their guesses and consider what actually happened later—being careful, however, not to use these later facts as the basis for improving their guesswork in terms of the earlier facts. To some people, this could become quite confusing.[72]

It has been said, with some heat, that this aspect of the Court's decision introduces an element of risk into the merger process. It plants a time bomb in the offices of the merged

71. 353 U.S. 625–26.

72. John C. Stedman, "The Merger Statute: Sleeping Giant or Sleeping Beauty?" *Northwestern Law Review*, 52 (1957), 567, 582.

companies, one which may not explode for many years. This charge is true. But it was the purpose of the Clayton Act to discourage mergers whose effect might be to lessen competition or tend to monopoly in any market. Congress passed the Clayton Act because it thought that the prolific merging habits of American business had dangerous potentialities for competition. Congress was right. The antitrust law does distinguish and has always distinguished between growth through merger and growth through the internal development of the corporation itself. As we saw a few pages ago, in discussing the law's concept of "combination," merger may have serious consequences long after it has occurred. This phase of the DuPont decision seems realistic and inevitable.

Perhaps the weakest part of the opinion and the strongest part of the dissent is that concerned with the definition of the relevant market. There the subsequent discussion in the law journals buttress Justice Brennan's opinion.[73] The "market" for General Motors' custom is a separate market not because the paint and fabrics it used were physically different from those used by other possible customers, but because such products sold to automobile manufacturers are sold under quite distinct economic circumstances—just as milk is sold in different "markets" when sold for human consumption, and for the manufacture of cheese, ice cream, or casein. In this case the adverse effect on competition in a market, which the statute requires to be proved, is inferred as a matter of common sense from the evidence that the defendant has a business advantage not otherwise available, and not based on his superior efficiency. At least the courts are willing to do so where a significant part of the market is "foreclosed" or blocked off to competitors.[74] While the antitrust laws are probably not violated if a steel company owns a "captive" coal mine, since the other coal companies have plenty of prospective customers, putting General Motors partly beyond the reach of DuPont's rivals for sales of paint and fabrics was a different matter.

But this phase of the case, over the long run, is its least

73. Particularly the article by Irston R. Barnes in the Georgetown Symposium and that of Dirlam and Stelzer, cited above, n. 69, and Stedman's, cited above, n. 72.

74. See, e.g., Standard Oil Co. of California v. United States, 337 U.S. 293 (1949).

important feature. Every judicial definition of a market depends upon an analysis of its particular economic setting. The *DuPont* opinion will contribute to that process the example of strictness, at least where great corporations are involved.

Justice Burton was on sounder ground in calling attention to the inconsistent nature of the evidence showing DuPont's actual advantages in selling to General Motors. While DuPont sold a large fraction of General Motors' paint and fabric requirements, it sold little of other products General Motors purchased, and DuPont made. "Thus," Justice Burton commented, "the alleged nefarious influence arising from DuPont's stock interest apparently affects the Oldsmobile antifreeze buyer, but not the Oldsmobile paint buyer; the paint buyers at Chevrolet, Buick and Pontiac, but not the antifreeze or electroplating buyers; and the electroplating buyer at Cadillac, but not the Cadillac paint buyer." [75] To this thrust the only answer can be a simple, practical one, inherent in the prospective theory of the case: that the justices, as men of the world, treated DuPont's position on the General Motors Board of Directors as a potentially restrictive advantage in influencing General Motors' purchasing policy, like the influences found illegal in the *Benrus* and *American Crystal Sugar* cases. [76]

In that sense, the case means that Section 7 has regained the vitality it was intended to have from the beginning, as the principal weapon of the antitrust law for dealing with problems of merger. Thus it stands with a group of lower-court cases which in recent years have indicated that the merger amendment of 1950 will have a more sympathetic reception in the courts than its predecessor of 1914. The development of this trend should soon indicate the effectiveness of the statute in serving the ambitions of Woodrow Wilson's first Congress, and in limiting habits of merger which

75. 353 U.S. at p. 630. Mr. Justice Brennan's reply appears at p. 607: "The fire that was kindled in 1917 continues to smolder. It burned briskly to forge the ties that bind the General Motors market to DuPont, and if it has quieted down, it remains hot, and, from past performance, is likely at any time to blaze and make the fusion complete."

76. Cases cited above, n. 31.

for seventy years have been regarded as normal and common-place in American business.

Do the antitrust laws, and the attitude they represent, have any effect on the economy? Are they more than a façade for monopoly, a ritual we perform to prove to ourselves that we are loyal to competition, although we live by monopoly?[77] If the laws have economic consequences, are those consequences constructive and worth seeking? Do the antitrust laws assist the markets of the American economy in the performance of their functions, especially as auxiliary weapons of stabilization policy?

The antitrust laws are a serious subject. They have not been a façade for monopoly. Despite notable weaknesses in certain areas of antitrust law doctrine, particularly those affecting the process of merger, the influence of the antitrust laws on the organization of American business has been important. The structure of industry has enormous historical momentum. The antitrust laws cannot accomplish miracles, but they can and do help to guide the trend in a more competitive direction.

The antitrust laws are to a considerable extent self-enforcing. As the courts clarify point after point, businessmen and their lawyers respond to a marked degree with their own decisions. Such a response would probably not occur except in the shadow of possible action by the government, or of private damage suits, which sometimes result in judgments of millions of dollars. It is too much to expect human beings to give up monopoly profits for the abstract pleasure of obeying a law. There must be some real possibility of enforcement before voluntary compliance can be expected.

The effect of the antitrust laws on business practice cannot be measured statistically, but it is nonetheless a reality.[78]

One might call attention in this context to the testimony of a business organization, the trade association of the American Machinery Industry, which remarked:

77. Thurman W. Arnold, *The Folklore of Capitalism*, New Haven, Yale University Press, 1937.

78. See Whitney's recent study, above, n. 5.

It has become fashionable in some quarters to disparage the influence of the antitrust laws in the United States, or even to write them off as completely ineffectual. In our judgment this is a grievous error, as the experience of Britain without such legislation strongly attests. It is true that the interpretation and enforcement of antitrust policy has been halting and inadequate. It is true that unfair application or administration of antitrust laws is possible. It is true also that many fish escape the net. Yet no one familiar with the climate of American business can fail to sense the pervasive influence of antitrust policy, which floats—to quote a phrase of the late Justice Holmes—like "a brooding omnipresence in the sky." Whatever its defects, it has helped to save American industry, by and large, from the gross and rampant restrictionism now afflicting Great Britain, certainly no mean achievement.[79]

American businessmen who have been in Europe since the war, on either private or public business, have uniformly come away with a renewed appreciation of the antitrust laws. Their reaction is significant evidence of the part which these laws play in the complex cultural phenomenon of American business drive.

I do not of course mean to imply that the antitrust laws have been enforced to their maximum or optimum extent, or that they have been fully successful even where they have been enforced. The record is spotty, as very schoolboy knows. The courts and the Congress have gone through various states of opinion on these matters, and the enforcement agencies have had different philosophies, enthusiasms, and appropriations. But if we compare the organization of the economy in 1890 or 1900 with the economy today, the contribution which the antitrust laws have made, for all our shortcomings in interpretation and enforcement, stands out sharply. In general, we no longer have great industries domi-

79. W. F. Yelverton and George Terborgh, *Technological Stagnation in Great Britain* (Washington, D.C., Machinery and Allied Products Institute, 1948), p. 65.

nated by single large firms, as was often the case then; nor isolated local markets dominated by local monopolists. There is probably more competition in wholesale and resale trade than in 1900. Alternatives to the consumer, whether families or business firms, have increased. The progress of science and technology, the decline in transportation costs, and the development of new methods of production, transportation, and distribution have been both the result and the cause of competition. In this process the antitrust laws have provided not only a favoring climate but a positive influence in preventing the use of many available methods of restriction.

The purposes of the Sherman Act have not been fully realized in our economic life. Its history is one of futility and half-measures, of gallant attempts, occasional victories, frequent retreats, of false starts and missed opportunities. Above all, it is a history marked by the absence of any planned and systematic effort to gain the basic strategic ends of the statute. Cases are brought piecemeal, in response to the pressure of complaints or the political winds.

To guide the evolution of industry and commerce in a more competitive direction is one of the significant tasks of American government. It cannot be done without the support of the courts. But it cannot be done by the courts alone. Our chances of materially increasing the degree of competition in the economy at large depend on the ability of the Department of Justice and the Federal Trade Commission to conceive and carry out imaginative programs of enforcement. Commodities, concentrations of power, and market practices should be selected for litigation in order of their priority, on the basis of a dynamic analysis of the way in which the economy actually works. We can expect worth-while results from our investment in the antitrust laws only if they are directed against targets of general importance to the economy as a whole.

Even if the application of the antitrust laws were planned systematically to carry out the implications of their history, would they provide a suitable economic policy for the organization of unregulated markets? How much competition do we want to see prevailing in industrial markets, assuming that we follow fiscal and wage policies which permit us even to contemplate the luxury of unregulated freedom in business affairs?

The recent Report of the Attorney General's Committee to Study the Antitrust Laws recapitulated the economic justification for an antitrust program in these terms:

> Generally speaking, economists support competition for four series of reasons, which are of coordinate importance: (1) because the actual level of prices in competitive markets should in the short run more accurately reflect the influence of demand and of cost, and thus in the long run help guide the flow of capital and other resources toward the most productive possible uses; (2) because the goad of competition provides powerful and pervasive incentives for product innovations and product development and for long-run cost-reduction, both through improved technology and improved management; these forces make themselves felt in the constant process of product variation, and through the pressures implicit in the fact that competitive conditions offer an open opportunity to new entrants in a particular industry; (3) because competitive conditions in business should lead to an equitable diffusion of the resulting real income among consumers and factors of production; and (4) a view held with somewhat less unanimity than the others, because the more flexible prices of competitive markets should make it easier and cheaper for the economy to adjust to industrial fluctuations, and for the Federal Reserve System and the Government to carry through effective contracyclical programs of stabilization, primarily utilizing methods of monetary and fiscal policy.[80]

The antitrust laws seek these goals not only for their own sake but as a means of accomplishing important social and political objectives. They aim to keep economic opportunity open to all comers. They work in the direction of preventing the kind of concentrated economic power that could stultify

80. Above, n. 60, at pp. 317–18.

and destroy political democracy. In this way they reduce the risk that large groups might lose faith in the fairness and efficacy of the business system. They help keep the emphasis in the economy on enterprise rather than on ownership and profit. With this orientation they make a significant contribution to the viability of the business system as one of the bases for our social and political life.

These familiar opinions are the economic and social premises of the antitrust law, and much of the rest of our law regarding unregulated markets. Tenable as they are, they should be re-examined. The evidence now available generally supports them, but that evidence is often sketchy, and not infrequently inadequate. We should know much more than we do about the functioning of the economy before we ratify these policies again, as an integral part of the system of law for directing an economy of stabilized full employment, with its recurring tendencies toward inflation.

There is neither time nor space here for more than a few comments on the law of regulated industries and of labor.[81]

I regard the law of regulated industries as one of the most urgent fields for research and reform in the whole of our law dealing with economic affairs. The present role of the state and federal regulatory agencies controlling railroads, utilities, and the transportation and communications industries raises fundamental questions both of substance and of procedure. The statutes which they seek to enforce are usually out of date, often confused, ill-drawn, and needlessly complex. Many of their rules echo forgotten battles, and guard against dangers which no longer exist. They comprise vast codes, understood only by a jealous priesthood which protects these swamps and thickets from all prying eyes. In the main, the agencies follow routines established for the control of local gas companies and street railways. The relevance of

81. These concluding observations at the end of a long lecture were necessarily sketchy at the time they were offered. To have developed them systematically would have required a radical change in the plan of the book. However desirable such a change might have been, it was altogether beyond the reach of my schedule, despite its great appeal to me. I have therefore not ventured to enlarge on these comments, or to document them.

the model is not immediately apparent, in dealing with progressive and expanding industries like air transport or trucking.

The control of price and production in the agricultural and extractive industries is another facet of the problem, equally thorny and equally rewarding in its promise of high returns for bold thought. Often employing syndicalist techniques of industrial self-government, these programs play a mysterious role, little understood by the public at large. How many citizens, I wonder, know that the cost to the federal government of its agricultural programs doubled between 1954 and 1958? Agriculture will probably absorb about 18 per cent of all federal expenditures in 1958 outside the realm of national security—as much as veterans' payments, and almost 70 per cent as much as payments of interest. The programs of agricultural price support were advanced as devices to smooth the adjustment of agricultural prices and production to changes in demand. They have been defended as procedures that can encourage production in time of need by giving farmers assurance of the price their crops will bring. During the last few years, for all the speeches of the Secretary of Agriculture, the rise in the cost of agricultural subsidies has begun to approach the point of scandal. Far from adjusting prices gradually to changes in demand, support programs have aimed heroically high. The price supports they announce to farmers in advance of the planting season bring in far more than can be sold at such prices. Surpluses accumulate in a granary which expands far more rapidly than the normal rate of growth of the economy. Some of the surplus has been well used to provide food cheaply, or as gifts, to India, Poland, and other countries. The rest is stored, at vast expense— Homeric revenge for the principles of market analysis.

The contradictions of the agricultural price-support program are apparent. At the same time, unsubsidized agricultural industries have done well in a full-employment economy. Their success sharply raises the question whether cartelization is needed, or can perform a useful function, in part of the agricultural sector, if we can assume reasonable success for programs of general stabilization. The inexorable movement of workers from agriculture to more productive and rewarding jobs in industry goes on at its steady pace—the very foundation of the industrial revolution in all countries. Science and capital raise the productivity of better farms at a rate that would have astonished Ricardo. It would be cheap and sensible to facilitate these processes by encouraging the establishment of industry in agricultural areas, rather than continuing to pay vast subsidies to farmers who don't need them, in order to be able to pay small subsidies to farmers who in most cases should be working in factories or stores. Industrialization in agricultural areas is the key to recent progress in the Southeastern states, and in Texas and Louisiana. It is the only approach to the problem which permits one to look forward to a constructive liquidation of support and subsidy programs.

The basic theme in the reform of these complex charters should be to release the competitive potential of the regulated industries as fully as circumstances permit. It could hardly be assumed, for example, that the railroads would be worse off than they are now if they were given more freedom in price policy and more chance to use their undoubted cost advantages in long hauls of freight. This approach would be even more promising if trucking were altogether released from the strait-jacket of economic control, imposed during the Depression as a restrictive measure to protect the railroads.

There are some areas of control in the economy where more competition is hardly even the beginning of an answer. There are a limited number of airwave frequencies, for example, and they have to be allocated by government. But could not some progress be made by selling these valuable franchises to the highest qualified bidder, rather than corrupting the administrative process, as we now do, in unseemly, behind-the-scenes maneuvering to obtain political support for one candidate rather than another?

The state and federal controls of dealings on organized securities and commodity exchanges constitute another class of market regulations which merits attention. Control devices in this field are of special significance in programs to stabilize employment generally, by reason of their impact on forward prices, speculation, and views of the future. These control methods developed both out of the medieval law of auctions and organized markets and out of modern attempts to deal with fraud. For the most part, they establish rules for the conduct of open and competitive markets. Questions are sometimes raised as to their adequacy in preventing manipulation, or the breadth of their commodity base. Recent legislation provides administrative weapons to curb what may be regarded as "excessive" speculation, although the term is undefined, save perhaps in terms of the rapidity of price movements. Thus the Secretary of Agriculture can suspend trading for a time on commodity exchanges, in the interest of allowing passions to cool. And the Securities and Exchange Commission has a variety of powers, both of investigation and of action, which have thus far been little used.

In the field of labor law, I believe the broad outlines of the present law are generally sound, with one exception. The time has clearly come to require trade unions to disclose their financial condition, as is done in Great Britain and other countries, and to recognize that union officers are fiduciaries in every aspect of their conduct of office. To this end, union officials should be within reach of the law as firmly as the officers of banks or business corporations. The proper investment of union funds, and especially of welfare funds, is a problem of magnitude that should be regulated by special legislation, recognizing the economic functions of these specialized trusts. Legislation of this kind would be greatly to the advantage of responsible unionism. There can be no excuse for leaving union finances the only significant pool of money in the country beyond the reach of public policy.

It is often contended that the antitrust laws should be amended to apply to the unions. This proposal represents a misunderstanding of the problem. The antitrust laws now apply to any activities in which unions join with employers in trying to fix the price of the goods or services the employers sell, or in comparable violations of the antitrust laws in the product market. But to apply the antitrust laws to the collective bargaining process would abolish it. The purpose of collective bargaining is to allow workers to combine, and to assert a considerable degree of monopoly power, by strike or otherwise, in influencing their own wages and working conditions. That policy is justified as an act of law designed to redress the unequal bargaining position of the individual worker and his employer. It was a sound policy, rooted in a long and bitter history, when it was adopted. And it is sound policy still.

The protection of society against the excessive use of labor's power over wages must be sought in another direction. Collective bargaining, as was contended earlier, should be a tolerable procedure for wage-making if fiscal and monetary policy strike a balance between the flow of goods and of funds; if the law improves the organization of the labor market, to assure a fuller and more efficient use of labor; and if antitrust policy can remove the taint of monopoly from the level of business profits.

It does not follow, however, that the law can do nothing to improve the procedures through which the labor market makes wage policy. Collective bargaining is essential for many reasons, social as well as economic. But it need not and probably will not remain forever in its present form. If excess demand is generated and permitted to persist for a considerable period, industry-wide bargaining is likely to yield smaller wage rises than firm-by-firm or plant-by-plant collective bargaining. On the other hand, in periods of reasonable balance between aggregate spending and full-employment output at stable prices, more flexible bargaining procedures should make the labor market a more effective pricing mechanism. Under such circumstances, policy might usefully seek wage bargains of considerable variety, resulting in wage schedules which reflected differentials in the productivity of labor in different sectors of the economy and different sections of the country. Such a pattern of wage rates, supplemented by government procedures for financing the transfer and retraining of workers, could help shift resources to their most productive possible use, and to offset labor shortages promptly.

If productivity is the norm of wage policy, it follows that cost-of-living factors should have no role in wage-making.

Indeed, linking wages to the cost of living would prevent wages from serving any effective market function at all; such a rule in wage-making would keep real wages constant through all stages of industrial fluctuation. There are times, however, when real wages need to be reduced in the interest of full employment. And real wages should rise gradually over time, as a consequence of improved productivity.

A Review of Recent Experience

THUS far, this book has sought a synthesis of ideas. Its concern has been to define the goals for legal action in controlling the economy. Part IV will attempt to give these concepts some empirical content and to explore the problem of their empirical verification. Its method will be that of case study, in reviewing some of the highlights of recent experience during industrial fluctuations in peacetime.

The emphasis here will be on the relationship of the several procedures for public action to each other. Most particularly, we shall try to stress the ways in which the markets of the economy have responded to changes in fiscal and monetary policy, and equally, the ways in which the market responses of the economy have influenced its fiscal and monetary programs, and the course of fluctuations in income, production, and employment.

These observations do not pretend to be a history of industrial fluctuations since 1929. Rather, they propose to assay the functioning of legal institutions for the control of the economy. Their concern is to help clarify, if possible, the lines of thought and study we should pursue in the interest of discovering both the purposes of the law in its government of the economy, and the means best calculated to satisfy those purposes.

If we start with 1929, recent experience is divided into several distinct periods. There was an intense and cumulative deflation, from 1929 to 1933, during which the gross national product was reduced some 30 per cent in volume to a low point of less than $60 billion a year. The fall in value was even greater, as prices were reduced more than output. A period of stagnation and slow recovery followed, between 1933 and 1935. A further fall in national income was arrested, and a gradual rise began. Then came a period of quite rapid recovery, ending in the acute and instructive recession of 1937–38. Beginning in the spring of 1938, there was a second period of brisk recovery, which merged into the war *boom. From 1940 to 1945 the level of national income in money roughly doubled, and physical output increased about one-third. Between the war and 1956 or early 1957, with an interesting pause in 1948–49, the inflationary, expansionist movement proceeded rapidly, accelerated but not caused by the financial shock of the Korean War. In 1953–54 there was another recession, somewhat similar to that of 1948–49. This dip was followed by a sharp rise, lasting until late 1956, when the economy slowed down. It remained stable for some months, and then, during the summer of 1957, it slipped into the recession we experienced till the summer of 1958, after which another turning point was passed.*

In the field of market structure, many changes took place. During the early thirties labor unions were gravely weakened, as the pressure for wage reduction degenerated into a war of all against all. The early policy of the Roosevelt Administration, from 1933 to 1935, was to encourage the mobilization both of labor into trade unions and of business into trade associations and equivalent combinations, with considerable monopoly power over price. The NRA was declared unconstitutional in 1935, in its application to business. But it had a temporary effect, and for many industries a significant long-term effect, in the development of patterns of association not easily broken by the Supreme Court's decision. While the economy never returned to the pattern of monolithic one-firm industries popular at the turn of the century, the twenties, and the NRA period, did strengthen private control procedures of small groups of leading firms in a number of industries. For labor, of course, the stimulus to union organization, especially that which developed after the Supreme Court upheld the National Labor Relations Act in 1937, has incalculably changed the structure of the American economy. With the end of NRA in 1935 the Roosevelt Administration turned to the antitrust laws and began vigorously to explore the possibility of applying them to some of the major areas of monopoly power in the field of business and labor organization.[1] That effort has now continued, with little interruption, for more than twenty years. It has led to

1. See above pp. 280 ff.

a variety of important decisions on the part of Congress, the courts, and the administrative agencies. The antitrust element in American public law has grown dramatically. In fact, it has been transformed as a factor in business policy. At the same time, and closely linked to its development, large-scale business has pursued price policies of cautious moderation, especially during the early years of the postwar period. The extent of such policies is still obscure and should be carefully explored. If policies of private price restraint are found to be significant, they could result in far-reaching distortions in the flow of capital. It may be generally true, and it certainly was true at intervals during this period, that small business made more money on its capital than big business. During this period also, price movements in part of the agricultural sector of the economy have been governed by national and in part by international control procedures. The influence of these controls extends to all phases of land use for agriculture and forestry, and beyond.

12. From the Crash to the War

THE GREAT DEPRESSION started with the Great Crash of the stock market in 1929. In my judgment the Depression was caused largely by that crash, and the boom which preceded it. Both boom and crash had a crushing impact on the world's fragile monetary system and on American financial institutions. And neither American nor any other authorities did anything sensible or forceful to offset their consequences. Nothing in the pattern of events before the crash made a depression inevitable, or even very likely.

The stock market boom and crash of the twenties was a phenomenon more in the realm of social psychology than of economics. It ranks with the tulip mania, the Florida land craze, the South Sea Bubble and other manifestations of man's occasional flights into the irrational. When the dawn came, much had to be undone before the inflation of values could be cured. By and large, the government and the banks allowed this process of liquidation to go on undisturbed. It became a vicious and unnecessary catastrophe of mass deflation.[1]

Counter action began seriously only in 1932 and 1933, with the first beginnings of conscious reflation, and of steps to strengthen banks and other financial institutions.

However, the sudden increase in the effectiveness of mo-

1. Thomas Wilson, *Fluctuations in Income & Employment*, 3d ed. London, Pitman & Sons, 1949; Lionel Robbins, *The Great Depression*, London, Macmillan, 1934; Bertil Ohlin, *The Course and Phases of the World Economic Depression*, League of Nations, Secretariat, Economic Relations Section, 1931; Joseph A. Schumpeter, *Business Cycles* (New York and London, McGraw-Hill, 1939), Vol. 2; Lauchlin Currie, *The Supply and Control of Money in the United States*, Cambridge, Harvard University Press, 1934; J. Kenneth Galbraith, *The Great Crash, 1929*, Boston, Houghton, Mifflin, 1955; Solomon Fabricant, *Manufacturing Output, 1929–1937*, NBER, Occasional Papers, 1 (1940).

nopoly controls under the NRA, between 1934 and 1935, seems clearly to have slowed up the recovery in employment and output, by raising prices faster than the increase in aggregate demand. The recovery movement was based on government deficits, spent in part through a public works program. While actual cash deficits during the thirties were small and irregular, taking state and federal action together, their occasional spurts did stimulate the economy somewhat, if not nearly enough. And the combination of recovery forces led to some increase in private spending. A considerable share of the increase in money income was absorbed by price increases, at a time when capacity was not fully used and business spending for plant and equipment was therefore still low.[2]

The government used many procedures to frustrate the expansion of employment in response to rising aggregate demand. Code authorities raised prices directly. They restricted production, and attacked price discriminations, which at least lowered average prices. Campaigns were begun against sales below cost, loss leaders, and other forms of price competition. Plans of price-reporting were set up and carried out, all in the interest of raising prices as rapidly as possible. In many instances, policy sought to restrict the purchase of new equipment, and actually to reduce output. The cotton industry lost export markets as the dollar price

2. Wilson, *Fluctuations in Income & Employment;* Brown et al., *The Economics of the Recovery Program,* New York and London, Whittlesey House, McGraw-Hill, 1934; C. F. Roos, *NRA Economic Planning,* Bloomington, Ind., Principia Press, 1937; L. S. Lyon and others, *The National Recovery Administration,* Washington, D.C., Brookings Institution, 1935; Edwin G. Nourse, Joseph S. Davis, and John D. Black, *Three Years of the Agricultural Adjustment Administration,* Washington, D.C., Brookings Institution, 1937; A. C. Pigou, *Economics in Practice* (London, Macmillan, 1935), chap. 6; S. N. Whitney, *Trade Associations and Industrial Control,* New York, Central Book Company, 1934; E. V. Rostow, "Bituminous Coal and the Public Interest," *Yale Law Journal,* 50 (1941), 543, and W. H. Hamilton, "Coal and the Economy—a Demurrer," ibid., 593, with E. V. Rostow, "Joinder in Demurrer," ibid., 613; Waldo E. Fisher and Charles M. James, *Minimum Price Fixing in the Bituminous Coal Industry,* Princeton, Princeton University Press, 1955; T. W. Schultz, *Agriculture in an Unstable Economy,* London, McGraw-Hill, 1945; Geoffrey S. Shepherd, *Agricultural Price Policy,* 2d ed. Ames, Iowa, Iowa State College Press, 1947.

of cotton was forced up, and the cotton textile industry gave ground to rayon and other synthetic fibers. Minimum prices for bituminous coal accelerated the shift to crude oil and led the coal industry to demand comparable restrictions on oil prices. In many industries, sharp price rises were accompanied by less than proportional increases in output. The recovery movement gained accelerated momentum with the end of NRA in 1935.

The recession of 1937 offers a complex and significant opportunity to study the connections between market organization and the course of industrial fluctuations. By 1937, contemporary ideas about trade-cycle policy had begun to replace the naive views of General Johnson and his supporters.

The recession of 1937 was extremely severe and precipitate. The drop in production and employment, especially in the capital goods sector of the economy, was more rapid than that which followed the market crash of 1929. From 1936 to 1937 national income fell about 8 per cent and wholesale prices by 9 per cent; manufacturing employment dropped about 13 per cent, the index of manufacturing production about 24 per cent, business investment for plant and equipment by more than one-third, and all private domestic investment by almost one-half. Annual figures conceal the magnitude of the movement, for a considerable recovery took place during the second half of 1938, and in many parts of the economy the depression did not begin until the summer and fall of 1937.

The recession had far-reaching international consequences, but its origin seems entirely domestic.

Events followed this pattern. The year 1936 was one of rising production and employment. In 1935 the Supreme Court had freed the economy from the restrictive effects of the NRA. The government was operating at a substantial deficit, to which business was increasingly responsive. Total purchasing power was increased faster than output. Profits were pushed up, attracting more and more unemployed resources into production. Profits were still low, but were above the worst depression levels, and were increasing. Business investment for equipment was going up rapidly. As capacity was approached in different industries, new plants were begun in significant volume. It was a period of considerable optimism and of buoyant speculation. The elections in the fall of 1936 were President Roosevelt's greatest victory, and for a short period thereafter even his most implacable enemies were disposed to make peace. At the end of the year a veterans' bonus was paid out, giving an extra increase to the deficit, and dividends were forced in large volume by a special tax on undistributed profits. There were still 7 million unemployed, but people were confident that they would soon be absorbed by industry.

During 1936 the Treasury and banking authorities became concerned about the dangers of inflation. The banking system held an enormous amount of gold, in part representing the political flight of funds from Europe, and as a result of government financial operations the banks held reserves beyond their legal requirements. What the financial authorities feared was that if the recovery movement continued, it could become an uncontrolled inflation, since the commercial banks, by reason of their reserve position, were beyond the reach of normal restrictive action on the part of the Federal Reserve. In 1936, therefore, the Reserve Board decided to increase reserve requirements, in a series of three steps which would begin in that year and continue through the spring of 1937. The central bankers thought that in this way they would bring the commercial banks into a position where the Federal Reserve could keep any further expansions of bank credit under its control by open-market and discount operations. At the same time, a considerable volume of gold was removed from the monetary base and "sterilized." The ground for this action was that the presence of the gold in the United States was due to political rather than to economic forces. It was thought for this reason that the gold should not be allowed to have its normal effect on bank loans and prices. It was emphasized that neither the Treasury nor the Federal Reserve Board wished to tighten money rates, nor to limit the recovery movement. Their action was dominated by a fear of inflation beyond the point of full employment at some later point in time. They were convinced that booms cause slumps, and that the way to avoid slumps was to avoid booms. They were preparing for a rainy day. Their action helped the rainy day come, and sooner than they thought.

At the beginning of 1937, the government deficit dropped rapidly, and the economy was suddenly deprived of that support, at a time when the volume of private investment was still low and private incentives to invest conspicuously weak. In part, the change in fiscal policy was an accident. The soldiers' bonus of 1936 was finished, and on January 1, 1937, new social security taxes went into effect, removing a noticeable fraction of consumers' purchasing power, without compensating returns to the income stream. In part, however, the decision was deliberate. The Secretary of the Treasury thought the recovery had gone far enough to survive without government support, and the government acted abruptly on that hypothesis.

The economy hesitated under the shock. Certain leading indices, notably those of forward construction contracts, paused in January 1937. Profits dropped slightly. The damage could easily have been repaired, but it was made worse.

The second round of increases in reserve requirements went into effect on March 1, 1937. Although the Federal Reserve had carefully calculated that excess reserves would be large enough to meet the change, its calculations proved to be wrong. A considerable number of banks had to sell government securities in order to meet the new requirement. The market for government bonds weakened, at a time when the normal recovery shift from bonds to stocks had introduced an element of weakness in any event. Corporate bonds, and then stocks, fell also, and the flow of new security issues was interrupted. Short- and long-term interest rates rose. The Federal Reserve System stepped in to stabilize the market, but rather weakly. The spirit of the stock market never recovered.

Two other events during the winter and spring contributed to a basic change in atmosphere, and in economic circumstances. President Roosevelt launched his assault against the Supreme Court, ending the era of conciliation and good feeling which was introduced by his election in November. The country was passionately divided and deeply troubled. Many deplored as unwise and unnecessary the Court's action in striking down social legislation on constitutional grounds. But public instinct was loyal to the Court as a political institution. And President Roosevelt's attack on it impressed many, even among his followers, as repulsive and autocratic.

In April 1937, perhaps in response to President Roosevelt's campaign, the Supreme Court surprised the country by declaring the National Labor Relations Act to be constitutional and of wide scope in industry. Immediately after the decision, aggressive organizing drives were intensified, especially those of the newly formed Congress of Industrial Organizations. Sit-down strikes were imported from France, and we experienced several months of severe labor conflict.

When the smoke cleared away, the basic industries of the United States, notably the automobile industry and the steel industry, had recognized trade unions as agencies for collective bargaining. A new and far more orderly era in American labor relations had begun, based on law rather than on unrestrained violence. But wage rates had risen almost 25 per cent—under the circumstances an inevitable counterpart of labor victory on the fundamental issue of union recognition.

The combination of factors was too much for the recovery movement. The government's budget was still in balance. The securities markets were disorganized, and business opinion depressed. The level of investment outlay was low, profits were low, and the rate of increase of national income had fallen off. The motives for private investment could not withstand a 25 per cent increase in wage costs. The wage increases had a deflationary effect, and the government did not come forward with a dose of inflation sufficient to offset them. Investment outlays fell abruptly. The national income began to drop, and in the early fall the stock market collapsed, bringing home the nature of events to a bewildered public.

After six months or more of waiting for conditions to improve by themselves, the government began to use its fiscal and monetary powers in the spring of 1938. Reserve requirements were reduced, gold was desterilized, and public works programs were announced and begun. An effective housing subsidy was introduced, using a government guarantee of private investment, rather than direct expenditure. The economy began to respond to the stimulus of higher profits as rapidly as it had collapsed the year before.

In retrospect, it is difficult to see why fiscal authorities were so worried by the specter of inflation at a time when there were 7,000,000 men unemployed, and it is equally difficult to find an explanation for the extraordinarily abrupt change in budget policy which took place. Part of the trouble arose from faulty analysis, part from poor timing, the rest from a variety of circumstances totally unforeseen at the time when restrictive action was undertaken. On the other hand, it proved comparatively easy and cheap to reverse the downward trend after a short interval of depression. And it should be emphasized that the recovery movement of 1938 and 1939 owed little or nothing to European military expenditures, which did not affect the American economy until late in 1939, or even 1940.

The experience of 1937 was an important factor in our postwar monetary policy. Until comparatively recent years, the Federal Reserve System has been fearful of launching restrictive action which might precipitate a depression. The central bankers had received a vivid lesson in the fact that although banking action may not by itself overcome a severe depression, it can do a good deal toward restricting and even reversing a recovery movement.[3]

3. Kenneth D. Roose, *The Economics of Recession and Revival: An Interpretation of 1937-38*, New Haven, Yale University Press, 1954; Douglas A. Hayes, *Business Confidence and Business Activity: A Case Study of the Recession of 1937*, Ann Arbor, University of Michigan Press, 1951; Melvin D. Brockie, "Theories of the 1937-38 Crisis and Depression," *Economic Journal, 60* (1950), 292-310; Norman J. Silberling, *The Dynamics of Business*, New York, McGraw-Hill, 1943; Donald M. Marvin and G. M. Williams, *Design for Recovery*, New York and London, Harper, 1939; Sumner H. Slichter, "The Downturn of 1937," *Review of Economics and Statistics, 20* (1938), 97-110; C. O. Hardy, "An Appraisal of the Factors ('Natural' and

'Artificial') Which Stopped Short the Recovery Development in the United States," *American Economic Review*, Supp. Pt. II, *29* (1939), 170–82; John Bauer, *National Welfare and Business Stability*, New York and London, Harper, 1940; Alvin H. Hansen, *Full Recovery or Stagnation?* New York, Norton, 1938; Kenneth D. Roose, "The Recession of 1937–38," *Journal of Political Economy*, *56* (1948), 239–48; Broadus Mitchell, *Depression Decade*, New York, Rinehart, 1947; Arthur Smithies, "The American Economy in the Thirties," *American Economic Review*, Supp., *36* (1946), 11–27; E. Cary Brown, "Fiscal Policy in the Thirties: A Reappraisal," *American Economic Review*, *46* (1956), 857–79; Alexander Sachs, "The Financial Dynamics of the Recovery since 1933 and Latest Constriction Phase in Capital Flow," in *Corporate Finance and Taxation*, Financial Management Series, 53 (New York, American Management Association, 1938), p. 13.

13. The Postwar Years

As a consequence of the methods used to finance the war, we emerged into the postwar world with a tremendously inflated supply of liquid funds—cash, bank deposits, and government bonds—in the hands of both corporations and individuals. At prewar rates of turnover, the money supply was then capable of supporting a national income of $500 billion a year, while the gross national product at the end of the war was in the neighborhood of $200 billion. The impact of this flood of money on the American economy followed the general pattern which prevailed in Europe. The American economy had not been disorganized by the war, so that the response of American production to the pressure of funds was proportionately greater than was European production. Nonetheless, the supply of funds was excessive in all categories and was spent rapidly. As a result, the flow of money income was increased faster than any possible increase in the flow of goods, at a time when resources were quite fully employed. The wartime system of controls began to crumble rapidly, even where it was not enthusiastically dismantled. There was upward pressure on prices and profits, and cumulative strain. Wages, which had risen faster than prices during the war, now fell behind. Prices increased more than money wage rates and weekly earnings between 1946 and 1948.[1]

1. Frederick C. Mills, "Prices in a War Economy," NBER, Occasional Papers, 12 (1943); Charles R. Whittlesey, "The Effect of War on Currency and Deposits," NBER, Occasional Papers, 11 (1943), and "The Banking System and War Finance," NBER, Occasional Papers, 8 (1943); R. A. Gordon, "Investment Opportunities in the United States before and after World War II," in Erik Lundberg, ed., *The Business Cycle in the Post-war World*, London, Macmillan, New York, St. Martin's Press, 1955; Simon Kuznets, *National*

During 1947 and 1948, with notable political courage, President Truman fought hard to prevent tax cuts, in the interest of using the government surplus as a factor reducing the flow of available funds, or at least preventing it from rising as far as it might otherwise have done. In this policy he was successful until the spring of 1948, when Congress passed tax reduction legislation over his veto. The effect of that change, coupled with a change in economic conditions, reversed the position of the federal budget in the economy in 1949. From the point of view of cash transactions, a federal surplus of $5.7 billion in 1947 and one of $8.0 in 1948 was altered to a small deficit. In 1948 a very large surplus in the first quarter was followed by moderate surpluses in the second and third and a small deficit in the final quarter. In 1949, after a surplus in the first quarter, half the size of the 1948 first-quarter surplus, there was a second quarter deficit of $2.5 billion, until that time the largest deficit in any quarter since the war. There is a wide variation in this pattern from quarter to quarter, due to our erratic system of tax collections, but the remaining quarters of 1949 recorded a moderate deficit in this series, amounting to $1.3 billion for the year.

In 1948, however, despite the large governmental surplus, the flow of income was rapidly expanded by private deficit financing. Business spending for plant, capital equipment, and inventory was at extraordinarily high levels. Residential construction, consumer purchases of cars, refrigerators, and other durable goods, and state and local government spending for public works were made in massive amounts. The total of these expenditures was far above the level of personal savings and of undistributed corporate profits. Therefore business was adding more to the flow of income as investment spending than had been withdrawn from it as savings. The total level of spending outstripped the physical

Product in Wartime, New York, NBER, 1945; A. J. Brown, *The Great Inflation, 1939-1951*, London and New York, Oxford University Press, 1955; Lester V. Chandler, *Inflation in the United States, 1940-1948*, New York, Harper, 1951; Seymour E. Harris, *Inflation and the American Economy*, New York and London, McGraw-Hill, 1945.

capacity of the economy, at previous prices. It was impossible to build all the roads and houses, machine tools, and deep-freeze units that people were trying to buy at the same time. The result was that the economy was spending more than it earned, and trying to buy more than could be produced. This "deficit" or "inflationary gap"—the excess of all spendings over the previous volume of income—was financed in two ways: by an increase in bank loans of $7 billion between 1947 and 1948, and of $4.4 billion between 1948 and 1949, which provided business with new money to spend on equipment and inventory; and by an increasingly rapid turnover of the huge volume of money and near-money which the war had left in the hands of corporations and individuals.

During 1948, however, several healthy restrictive forces developed to limit the pressure of inflationary spending. Federal, state, and local governments collected far more taxes than they spent. The rate of such withdrawals from circulation rose rapidly during the first six months of 1948. In that period the comparable 1947 cash surplus was almost doubled, and the economy was subjected to the pressure of a pervasive braking influence.

But this vigorous fiscal policy of surplus to beat back inflation was being frustrated by the banking system. Far from being in harmony with fiscal policy, the Federal Reserve System, at the urgent request of the Treasury, was being forced, violently against its will, to expand member bank reserves.

Led by Marriner Eccles, the System campaigned for banking restraints on the expansion of money income. In speeches and statements before Congress, the chairman of the Board of Governors of the Federal Reserve System urged a series of measures to curb the banks' power to make loans. The Federal Reserve System, he contended, had become "an engine of inflation," because it was committed to stabilize the yield on government securities.

The pressures of wartime finance and the great volume of government debt outstanding had led to the adoption of a policy which took control over credit policy away from the Board of Governors of the Federal Reserve System and put it into the hands of the public. Since the beginning of the war, the Federal Reserve banks had been committed to purchase government securities offered them by the banks or the public at a price which kept yields on certain long-term Treasury bonds near 2½ per cent. The Treasury—deeply concerned, like all treasuries, to sell its issues as cheaply as possible—was adamant in fighting for a continuance of the policy. The Treasury economists steadfastly argued that a slight rise in interest rates could not discourage borrowers during an inflation. When borrowers anticipate rapid price increases, small changes in the price of money will not hold them back. Meanwhile, customers at the desks of bank vice-presidents clamored for more and more loans with which to finance their expansions of plant, their holdings of inventories and securities, and their purchases of equipment. The banks increased their loans. And they obtained reserves which made it legally possible for them to grant the loans by selling their government securities. In form, they sold to the market. In fact, however, they sold their bonds in large part to the Reserve Banks, which supported the market. It was good business for the banks to replace their government bonds, earning 2½ per cent or less, with business loans, earning 4, 5, or 6 per cent. But for the economy this shift in bank assets spelled inflation.

The policy of requiring the Reserve System to support the government bond market was not felt primarily in the level of interest rates. The Treasury economists were beating the wrong horse. The support policy fed inflation because it required the Reserve banks to increase commercial bank reserves as fast as the banks and the banks' customers wanted new loans. In 1948, the support policy required the Reserve banks to undertake what were in effect inflationary "open market" purchases, during a period of runaway boom. Reserve bank holdings of government securities rose by $1.4 billion during 1948, when by all the rules of central banking they should have been reduced several billions through systematic and deliberate sales.

In the course of prolonged Congressional hearings it became clear that the forces favoring Federal Reserve support for the level of interest rates on government bonds were too strong to be overcome in 1948. Most of the insurance companies and banks were on the Treasury's side. They were afraid of the possible drop in the capital value of the government securities they held if the market were left free to find its own level. The Federal Reserve was likewise refused its second proposal, for special emergency reserves which would have drastically reduced the availability of new bank credit. Instead, Congress passed a bill authorizing the Reserve System to increase reserve requirements above the previous maximum levels. While reserve requirements were increased above the previous maximum in September 1948, the emergency powers given in August 1948 were not fully used. By May 1949 downward tendencies were in evidence, and the Federal Reserve System reduced reserve requirements and took other measures to ease credit.

While the intense controversy about reserve requirements, the bond-support policy, and the proposal for special reserves was going on, during the spring and summer of 1948, the Federal Reserve System took other steps to limit the capacity of the banks to make loans. It used its powers under the Securities Exchange Act to raise margin requirements. Federal Reserve control over the extension of installment credit and similar credits to consumers, which was instituted in 1941 under the President's emergency powers, had been terminated on November 1, 1947. No statute specifically authorized it, and therefore the practice was given up as the wartime emergency passed. The statute of August 1948, however, restored the Federal Reserve Board's power to regulate the amount and duration of consumer credit, at least until June 30, 1949. Regulation was promptly reinstituted, specifying minimum down payments and maximum periods of repayment for many forms of consumer purchases. This action particularly restricted the sale of cars, refrigerators, and other durable goods.

While the conflict over banking policy grew in intensity during 1948, restrictive forces developed in strength. Hourly wage rates continued to rise, not so rapidly as in 1947 but with considerable momentum nonetheless. At the end of 1948 wages had risen 7 per cent in manufacturing, more than 7 per cent in the building trades, 5 per cent in bituminous coal mining, and lesser amounts in most other industries. It will be recalled that no studies of productivity find the average rate of increase to be much greater than 2 per cent per year. This figure crudely but significantly defines the possibility for increasing money wage rates without either unemployment or inflation. Taken in connection with the steady rise in prices, especially of building materials, wage increases began to cut sharply into investment plans. While construction activity remained high and even increased, the indices of orders placed for future building and for the delivery in the future of heavy industrial equipment began to fall as early as June 1948.

As we saw earlier,[2] paradoxes developed particularly at this time in certain markets where prices are established by a single large company or by a group of big companies acting in parallel ways to avoid price competition. Several of the administered prices of private monopoly rose less than the prices of goods sold under competitive conditions. Taking into account differences in cost schedules and demand conditions in different industries, this policy meant, in all probability, that these companies were not maximizing their short-run revenues. Steel, aluminum, and automobiles were probably all cases in point. The fear of possible antitrust litigation weighed with some. The effect of high profits or high prices on labor contracts was seriously considered by many. After all, whatever its form, no modern labor contract is really immune from escalation. Public opinion in a more general sense influenced others. Finally a few independent-minded men believed that prosperity would soon vanish again, making it wise to hold back on price rises so as to minimize the scale of the ultimate price fall.

Whatever its motivations, this policy of privately imposed price stability did not play a constructive role in the process of ending the inflation. Low prices meant that price could not ration supply, so that it was common to find "gray" mar-

2. Above, pp. 235–41.

kets, where newly purchased goods were resold at a premium. The low prices of some goods meant that others had to absorb the full price impact of inflationary spending. Prices and profits therefore rose more violently in some sectors of the economy than in others. This disproportion in profits affected the flow of new capital. The sustained policy of low prices in some situations of private monopoly power made the entry of new firms singularly discouraging. While the relatively low price policy followed in some big business markets did not help to arrest the inflationary movement, it introduced distortions in the price structure of long-range significance.

One important form of investment spending fell abruptly in 1948: the net export surplus. In 1947 foreign economic transactions added $8.9 billion to the money income of people in the United States, without any corresponding additions to the flow of goods they could purchase. In 1948 this strongly inflationary element fell to $1.9 billion. European countries, helped by the Marshall Plan, were gaining rapidly in economic strength. Their own production was recovering and their exports were rising. They were successfully limiting their dollar purchases and expanding their sales abroad, even in the United States.

Toward the middle of 1948 the restrictive forces in combination began to arrest the inflationary movement. The high government surplus and the drop in the net export surplus slowed the rise in incomes. Higher wage and raw material costs and banking restrictions on the flow of funds, backed by the threat of more to come, weakened the conviction of business that profits would rise indefinitely. The rise in consumer credit was halted. Forward contracts for heavy investment activities fell slightly. Actual expenditures for private nonresidential construction reached a peak in September 1948, and for utility and farm construction in August.

Inventory spending, the largest and most volatile component of private investment spending, reacted abruptly as 1949 began. After rising $12 billion in 1945 and 1946, and $8 billion from 1946 to 1947, the total of inventories in manufacturing and trade rose $6 billion from 1947 to 1948, and fell $5 billion between 1948 and 1949. Instead of adding to the volume of demand, inventories were liquidated on a large scale. Measured in another way, the change in the value of all business inventories was considered to have risen $5.5 billion in 1948, and to have fallen $3.7 billion in 1949. The disinvestment in inventories meant that the supply of goods available for purchase was substantially increased, out of inventories, without anyone earning incomes currently for work done in producing the goods. It increased the available supply of goods without increasing the level of money incomes.

The first part of 1949 showed signs of sharp reaction. As spending fell, the pressure on capacity was reduced and the profit outlook deteriorated. Private investment for equipment and construction was slightly below 1948 levels in the second quarter of 1949 and substantially below them in the third quarter. On the other hand, construction, which had reached a peak in August 1948, began to rally early in 1949. Public construction increased by 15 per cent, and private residential building recovered strongly, under the impetus of easier credit terms and public housing legislation. State and local governments all over the country were busy building schools, hospitals, roads, and other community facilities, to make up the immense backlog in public construction accumulated during the poverty-stricken years of the depression, and the years of shortage during and immediately after the war. Federal expenditures also increased, in the categories of defense and international aid and in construction programs for resource conservation, highways, and other purposes.

The impact of all these changes in spending on the national income was unmistakable. The level of national income, which had risen 12 per cent between 1947 and 1948, fell 1.3 per cent between 1948 and 1949, the level at the end of 1949 being 3 per cent below the level at the beginning. While consumption remained high and even increased, in all categories, the drop in the total flow of spending was caused by three primary forces: the government surplus, the severe decline in inventory purchases, and the drop in the export surplus.

However, the federal budget became a positive weapon of recovery toward the middle of 1949, just as the collapse of the inventory boom and other restrictive factors began to depress the level of national income, and then of profits and private investment in plant and equipment. The economy received the stimulus of a sharp change in fiscal policy before the doubts of early 1949 could become the cumulative decline of a serious depression. The government not only stopped reducing purchasing power; it positively added new money to the flow of income.

The economy was in a strong position to respond to such a pressure. Profit levels were still relatively high, although they fell sharply in 1949. But the incentives favoring long-term programs of basic expansion in the utilities, railroads, and other heavy industries of the country were not vulnerable to minor variations in profit. The likelihood of large expenditures for delayed public works, together with the persistent private demand for homes and automobiles, helped to prevent pessimism from gaining much headway. Both banking and fiscal policy reacted with speed and energy to enlarge the flow of money and thus to restore a profitable level of demand for the products of private business before much damage had been done.

If this analysis of what happened in 1948–49 is correct, the tale has more than a dash of irony. For the tax cut of 1948, which led to the crucial deficit of 1949, was accomplished by many congressmen who most deeply disapproved of government "planning," and yearned wistfully for the day when—as they thought—the economy would equilibrate itself without conscious direction. It was opposed by virtually all the economists of the country. The Administration, proclaiming its optimistic faith in the capacity of government to stabilize the economy, was certain that the signals for 1949 still called for a prudent surplus, like those of 1947 and 1948. Although he faced an uphill fight in the election of 1948, President Truman vetoed a popular tax cut, convinced that more inflation was a national danger. The flow of private spending changed suddenly, as it always can in a dynamic capitalist economy, dependent on the decisions of thousands of businessmen. The greatest change took place in spending for inventory, the form of private investment most sensitive to changes in atmosphere. If the government had planned its fiscal policy with full knowledge of what was to come, it could not have arranged things better.

Some observers believe that it would have been healthier to have allowed the depression in 1949 to go further, so that prices would have been more drastically reduced, and full employment restored later, at a somewhat lower and less difficult price level. Two elements of the situation made this doubtful counsel.

In the first place, the state of world politics makes American domestic prosperity one of the cardinal objects of American foreign policy. The dip of 1949, at its worst (in January and February 1950), reduced civilian employment only 3.7 per cent below the 1948 average, and raised unemployment from 3.4 per cent to 7.6 per cent, taking into account the increased size of the labor force. But it had a disastrous impact on the economy of the Western world. American imports fell off from the fall of 1948 to the late autumn of 1949. Exports dropped even more severely during 1949, as foreign countries first strove to reduce their dollar purchases and then, after the devaluations of September 1949, began to cut under American exports in price. The international consequences of an American depression have become increasingly severe during the last thirty years. In the insecure Western economy of the afterwar period the first international obligation of the United States is to stay a little —but not too much—on the expansionist side. Boom conditions in the United States, so long as they do not become strong enough to drive raw material prices to uncomfortable levels, guarantee the rest of the free world a high volume of American imports, and favorable conditions for competing elsewhere with high-priced American exports.

Secondly, the structure of the economy makes it more difficult than ever before to restore full employment by reducing wages and prices. Such an adjustment still seems somehow more orthodox to us, and "sounder," than a recovery which accomplishes the same result by governmental action. There would be no special virtue in such a feat, even if it could be accomplished. Even the most flexible of competitive economies never succeeded very well, once a depression had begun, in regaining full employment at reduced price levels. The feat has become almost impossible in the United States, with its wide zones of monopoly pricing, both in the labor market and in markets for goods and services. A long-term lowering of the price level can be sought only through gradual reductions in cost based on improvements in technique. Given the strength of trade unions in the economy, and of monopolistic price controls administered either by business or government, we shall be lucky in the long run if we keep high levels of employment at stable or at worst slowly rising price levels. In 1949–50, in fact, the process of market adjustment did accomplish more price reduction than emerged in 1953–54 or in 1957–58. Prices had risen faster than wages between 1946 and 1948, giving the economy some capacity to meet falls in demand through price declines.[3] Farm prices dropped nearly 20 per cent, and industrial prices showed a distinct fall. Between August 1948 and December 1949, the wholesale price index fell 8 per cent, while average weekly earnings rose 1.8 per cent. Between May 1946 and August 1948, however, the wholesale price index had risen 47.3 per cent, while average weekly earnings had gone up 29.5 per cent.

Taking these two factors into account, the promptness of the deficit in 1949—and its relatively small size—seem in retrospect to represent the wisest course the government could have followed. Most indices of business activity began to turn up in the fall of 1949. The panicky liquidation of inventories ceased, and they started to rise again, though not precipitately, in the spring of 1950. The total of construction increased steadily after a low point in April 1949, although this low point was above the average level of construction in 1948. By May 1950 the total of private construction was over 20 per cent above the average for 1948, and the total of all construction up 25 per cent. Business expenditure for new plant and equipment naturally lagged behind, but

3. See p. 330.

this form of spending, after holding up at levels slightly below those of 1948 during most of 1949, rose sharply in the second quarter of 1950. And the higher level of incomes yielded higher tax revenues and quickly balanced the budget.[4]

By mid-1950, before the Korean War broke out, the American economy had completed an impressive recovery. To a considerable extent, the various sectors and regions of the economy had oriented themselves to the new scale of wages and prices which emerged from the impact of wartime and postwar policies on the economy. "Reconversion" was about over and had proved not too costly. The recovery seemed potentially stable and durable. It was dependent neither on large-scale inventory speculation as to a future rise of prices nor on extraordinary exports for the purpose of restoring the damages of war. The American export surplus was dropping, as imports rose and exports fell off. By June 1950 it had almost disappeared. Civilian employment in June 1950 was 3.7 per cent above the average level in 1948, and unemployment had fallen 2.4 per cent in four months. National income had risen about 7 per cent from its low point in the last quarter of 1949. It had been driven upward by an increase of 50 per cent in private domestic investment expenditures, led by increases of $2.8 billion in spending for farm equipment and construction; of almost $3 billion in the annual rate of residential construction; and by a net increase of $3.4 billion in the value of inventories, for the second quarter of 1950, compared to a net decline at the annual rate of $5.7 billion in the last quarter of 1949.

The recession of 1949 was brief but important. With reasonable expectations of foresight and luck, it is probably about as severe a depression as we shall ever have again,

4. Benjamin Caplan, "A Case Study: The 1948–1949 Recession," *Policies to Combat Depression*, New York, NBER, 1956; Daniel Hamberg, "The Recession of 1948–49 in the United States," *Economic Journal, 62* (1952), 1–14; E. C. Bratt and J. P. Ondrechen, "1948–49 Recession Re-examined," *Economic Journal, 63* (1953), 98–104; Daniel Hamberg, "1948–49 Recession Re-examined: A Rejoinder," *Economic Journal, 63* (1953), 104–10; C. A. Blyth, "The 1948–49 American Recession," *Economic Journal, 64* (1954), 486–510; Rendigs Fels, "Theoretical Significance of the 1949 Recession," *American Economic Review*, Supp., *45* (1955), 358–66.

within 10 per cent or so, although all future depressions may not be so short. The economy reacted with extraordinary vitality and resilience to large-scale changes in the direction of spending. What was crucial about economic experience in 1949 and early 1950 was that government fiscal and banking policy intervened promptly to offset and counterbalance a genuine deflationary tendency. And that limited and remote intervention, climaxed by the second-quarter government deficit, was effective in restoring high levels of employment. The recovery which took place before the fighting began in Korea is one of the first and most significant victories for the policy of compensatory government action to smooth and minimize the inevitable fluctuations of a free economy.

What happened in the eight months after June 1950 constitutes an illuminating episode in the history of governmental efforts to control the economy. A rapid and far-reaching inflation took place—the most violent inflation we have ever experienced, except for the rise in prices which followed the liquidation of the OPA in 1946. It was not caused by government military spending nor by a governmental deficit.[5] Throughout the entire period, the government operated at an increasing cash surplus, in relation to the flow of income. Its cause was a rush of buying by consumers and by business firms. They purchased cars and deep-freeze units, new machinery and additional inventory, because they were certain that announced programs of government military spending would sooner or later create shortages.

The burst of private buying which began in June 1950 was concentrated at first on durable goods, both for consumers and producers, and on the construction of residential housing and business buildings. The volume of buying was

5. M. Cohen, "Post-war Consumption Functions," *Review of Economics and Statistics,* 34 (1952), 18–33; Bert G. Hickman, "The Korean War and United States Economic Activity, 1950–1952," NBER, Occasional Papers, 49 (1955); Bert G. Hickman, "Postwar Cyclical Experience and Economic Stability," *American Economic Review, 48* (1948), 117–34.

so heavy that inventories were reduced for some time. At the same time the net foreign position of the economy worked against inflation as the volume of imports spurted. On balance, during the first nine months after K-Day, international transactions added more goods than money to the American market and therefore served, with the government surplus, to dampen the inflationary movement. Government purchases of goods and services rose slowly—from the annual rate of $20.9 billion for the federal government in June 1950 to a rate of $21.2 billion in September, $27.3 billion in December, $31.9 in March 1951, and $38.5 in June 1951. At the same time, however, the sharp increase in income payments immediately increased government tax receipts, especially of income taxes withheld and anticipated, and social security taxes. The result was that the government operated at an increasingly large cash surplus, withdrawing far more purchasing power from circulation in tax collections than it added as payments for purchases of goods or services, or as transfers of interest on the public debt, veterans' or pensioners' remittances, and the like.

The volume of private spending, however, far overbalanced the total of private savings, the government surplus, and the net deficit on international account. The private sectors of the economy spent more than they had previously earned. And private deficit financing was on a large enough scale to offset both private and public saving. This excess of private spending was financed by bank loans and by an increasingly rapid turnover of existing stocks of money. Bank loans rose nearly $10 billion, or 22 per cent, between June 1950 and March 1951. In order to make these loans, commercial banks sold nearly $8 billion in government securities, of which $5 billion were ultimately purchased by the Reserve banks.

The unwanted inflation after K-Day finally broke the back of the compulsory bond-support program. Without Reserve bank bond purchases, the inflationary movement would soon have run out of fuel. After a violent Washington quarrel, characterized by competing leaks to the press, contradictory accounts of what had happened at the same meeting, and other edifying details, the Treasury and the Federal Reserve System announced their agreement, early in March of 1951. The System was released of the obligation to buy bonds in order to maintain a given level of interest rates, although it agreed to use its resources to preserve "orderly" conditions in the market for government securities. The Treasury offered to convert certain 2½ per cent issues into nonmarketable securities earning 2¾ per cent, and the offer was largely accepted by the investing public. Thus the Treasury immobilized a considerable volume of securities, which insurance companies and savings banks had been selling to finance housing and business expansion.

The end of the support program was the signal for a series of sharp drops on the securities markets. New issues of securities bore somewhat higher yields, and the process of expanding bank loans came to a temporary halt. The Federal Reserve System stopped inflating bank reserves, and the economy began to feel the pinch of tighter money conditions. At the same time, the banks organized a voluntary program of credit restraint under the provisions of the Defense Production Act, which may possibly have helped somewhat to limit the growth of bank loans. This restrictive pressure was heightened by the mortgage and consumer credit regulations issued by the Federal Reserve Board. Housing starts fell sharply, and so did the sales of some consumers' durable goods.

Business opinion changed. Many were uncertain as to how high prices would ultimately be allowed to go. The heavy tax payments in the first quarter of 1951 resulted in a cash surplus of $6.8 billion, the largest in history, and severely reduced purchasing power. The frenetic accumulation of business inventories became a burden. Spending for inventory fell from the peak annual rate of $16.3 billion in the second quarter of 1951 to $8.9 billion in the third quarter, $5.8 in the forth, and almost zero during the first half of 1952. Inventory accumulation did not become significant again until the end of 1952, when it was being built up at the rate of less than $4 billion a year. The occasional price wars which broke out in a few cities after the Supreme

Court weakened "Fair Trade" laws in the spring were a symptom of business caution, especially in the field of inventories. They were more spectacular than important, although they did symbolize the position of the economy as the defense program slowly gathered momentum.

A lull ensued for several months, and prices even dropped slightly. But the Defense Department kept on making contracts. Gradually it began to receive deliveries, and to pay for them. In 1950, national security expenditures were $18.5 billion; in 1951, $37.3; in 1952, $48.8. The whole economy moved forward in sympathy. By the end of 1952, private investment had recovered pretty well. Spending for producers' durable goods was higher than in 1951, inventory purchases much lower, and construction slightly, but only slightly, below the peak of 1951. Consumption expenditures rose steadily in each quarter. The total volume of spending therefore increased in a rather peaceful rhythm. Federal security spending reached its peak in 1953, and fell off gradually thereafter, from a high of $51.5 billion in 1953 to a low of $41.3 billion in 1955. The mid-1958 rate was somewhat above $45 billion a year and rising, after a severe cutback in the last half of 1957.

The recovery continued irregularly throughout 1951 and 1952. The rate of growth of production slowed down appreciably in 1952 but rose again rapidly toward the end of the year, led by increases in private rather than governmental spending. Prices were stable, unemployment lower than at any time since World War II. While scattered portents of inflation appeared here and there, particularly in areas of the economy affected by the defense program, they were balanced by declining prices elsewhere. The price of imported raw materials, particularly, dropped significantly as the world economy recovered from the first shock of the post-Korean inflation. The resources of the economy were being utilized at close to full capacity. There were intermittent shortages of labor, leading to bursts of wage increases. At the same time, increases in output per man-hour slowed down, as the economy began to reach zones of rising mar-

ginal cost at close to capacity output. Increases in output
could be accomplished only by paying overtime, by hiring
relatively inefficient labor, or by using plant beyond the
point of minimum cost per unit of output. Turnover rates
rose. Average weekly earnings in manufacturing industry
increased 11 per cent between 1951 and June 1953, while
the wholesale price index fell 4.5 per cent.

In 1953 a conjuncture of factors disturbed this process of
relatively stable employment and growth. Government
spending for defense purposes continued to rise. The relation of all governmental units to the flow of cash payments
shifted from a position of slight surplus in 1951 to a deficit
of $3.1 billion in 1952. Private consumption expenditures
moved forward strongly, and so did nonresidential construction. Despite the ominous rise in wage rates, forecasters
were divided—and their division was altogether reasonable
—as to whether the elements making for more inflation were
stronger or weaker than those typical of the culminating
phases of a long boom, when costs normally outstrip prices
and put the future into peril.

At this moment the new Administration took several steps
in the field of monetary policy and debt management which
helped to precipitate a recession. Then, when it was reasonably clear that a recession had begun, it moved promptly and
effectively to reverse the trend, so that the recession of
1953–54 turned out to be only slightly more costly, in terms
of output foregone, than the recession of 1948–49.

The Federal Reserve Board began to lean against further
credit expansion late in 1952 and early in 1953. It took steps
to free the money market by restricting its interferences to
the range of short-term Treasury issues. Interest rates rose.
Early in 1953 the discount rate was raised, for the first time
since 1950. Bond prices weakened steadily during the last
half of 1952, rapidly during the first six months of 1953.
The stock market followed early in 1953.

The Administration feared that its symbolic abolition of
the last direct controls surviving from the post-Korean inflation might release new inflationary drives. It therefore
pushed credit restraint somewhat more vigorously, as it

turned out, than the situation required. Its highly desirable step toward refunding the national debt into longer-term securities failed. The policy of credit restraint and higher interest rates began to seem almost a doctrine. Investment opinion drew some adverse inferences, and the securities markets reacted sharply.

Both the Federal Reserve System and the Administration counterattacked early and with force. The Reserve banks bought government securities in May and June and reduced reserve requirements in July. Reserve bank holdings of government securities rose $1.1 billion between April 1953 and June 1954. The rediscount rate was reduced in stages from 2 per cent to 1.5 per cent during 1954. And a second reduction in reserve requirements put the banks into a strong position to make loans. The first result of the increase in member bank reserves was an increase in their holdings of government securities. This development helped ease monetary and credit conditions further and paved the way for large increases in bank borrowing during 1955 and 1956, when the banks sold governments and increased their loans. The terms of mortgage financing were liberalized, and housing spurted ahead. Savings rates fell, as consumption was maintained.

Fiscal policy was well coordinated with monetary policy in taking swift and deliberate contracyclical action. The Secretary of the Treasury announced as early as September 1953 that the Administration would favor allowing statutory reductions to occur both in the excess profits tax and in the income tax. The Administration favored, and the Congress approved, a series of tax changes which, on net, reduced projected revenue $6 billion a year. The federal cash deficit was $6.2 billion for the calendar year 1953 and $1.1 billion for the calendar year 1954. In addition, the government reviewed its procurement programs, and its several programs affecting private spending, in the interest of speeding up the rate at which it spent its own appropriations, and encouraged others to do likewise.

The response of the economy was remarkable. The recession was confined largely though not entirely to investment in inventories. The net change in business inventories shifted

from \$10.4 billion in 1951 to \$3.6 billion in 1952, and during
1953 from positive figures during the first three quarters of
the year—at annual rates of \$2.8 billion, \$5.4 billion and
\$2.0 billion—to a negative rate of \$4.2 billion in the last
quarter. Disinvestment in inventory continued at about the
annual rate of \$4 billion until the fourth quarter of 1954,
when it slowed up. In 1955 it became a strongly positive
factor again. Sales of producers' durable equipment rose to a
peak in the third quarter of 1953, then fell about 13 per
cent to the fourth quarter of 1954. Construction, however,
actually increased, save in farming. The net drop in gross
private domestic investment between 1953 and 1954 was
therefore \$5.3 billion, of which \$5.1 billion consisted of the
change in spending for inventory.

The recovery began about a year after the downturn, and
by late 1954 began to be visible. The number of unemployed
persons was 1.6 million in 1953, and 3.2 million in 1954; it
fell to 2.6 million in 1955, and to 2.5 million in 1956.[6]

The period of recovery that lasted until mid-1957 has
been called a capital goods boom, and also a boom in the
service trades. Government claims on output dropped and
then rose again to the 1954 level, in constant prices. But
there was a strongly positive, if rather mixed, movement in
most forms of private spending. Net foreign investment rose
in 1956 to \$1.9 billion, and in 1957 to \$3.3 billion. Construction rose in 1955 but fell back both in 1956 and in 1957.
Sales of producers' durable equipment nevertheless increased
steadily in 1955 and particularly in 1956. The rate of spending for inventory reached a moderate high which was sustained for about a year, between the second quarter of 1955
and the first quarter of 1956. Thereafter, spending for inventory dropped gradually during 1956 and sharply during

6. Bert G. Hickman, "The Contraction of 1953–1954," *Review of Economics
and Statistics*, 40 (1958), 36; Kenneth D. Roose, "Business Fluctuations in the
United States since 1951: Selected Developments," *American Economic Re-
view*, Supp., 45 (1955), 367–74; T. Balogh, "Some Theoretical Implications of
International Aspects of the United States Recession 1953/54," *Economic
Journal*, 65 (1955), 641–53; Arthur F. Burns, *Prosperity without Inflation*
(New York, Fordham University Press, 1957), chaps. 1–2.

1957, showing the negative figures of disinvestment during the last quarter. The algebraic sum of these rising and falling movements was an increase in spending. As a result, all forms of consumption expenditure went up. Between 1954 and 1957, in constant prices, gross private investment increased 17 per cent and consumption about 12 per cent, with consumers' expenditures for durable goods increasing slightly more than those for services or nondurables.

This increase in the volume of spending was financed in large part by a renewed increase in bank loans, despite Federal Reserve concern about inflation, and its relatively cautious and restrictive policy. Commercial bank loans increased $11.6 billion in 1955, $7.6 billion in 1956, and $3.7 billion in 1957. In order to be able to make these loans, the banks reduced their holdings of government securities $7.4 billion in 1955, $3.0 billion in 1956, and $0.3 billion in 1957. Persistent efforts at credit restraint induced a small decrease in the money supply despite the increase in loans.

The result of these changes was that in constant dollars the gross national product, which fell 1.6 per cent between 1953 and 1954, rose 8.1 per cent in the following year; 2.7 per cent between 1955 and 1956, and 1.2 per cent between 1956 and 1957. In current dollars, however, the picture was different. Price increases were substantial after the beginning of 1956. In current dollars, the fall in the gross national product between 1953 and 1954 was about ½ of 1 per cent; the rise between 1954 and 1955 was 9.4 per cent, as compared with 8.1 per cent in constant dollars. Between 1955 and 1956 the increase in current dollars was 5.4 per cent, that in constant dollars only 2.7 per cent. And between 1956 and 1957, while real output rose only 1.2 per cent, spendings for it went up 5 per cent.

The actual fall in output began during the summer of 1957, led by a fall in spending for inventories. Ominous signs had appeared earlier. While business spending for durable goods had remained reasonably stable, dropping slowly from a high point in the first quarter of 1957, new orders for durable goods fell 19.3 per cent between July 1957 and

January 1, 1958. During the same period residential construction contracts fell 4.5 per cent and commercial building contracts 11 per cent.

Why did the crucial indices of forward business investment begin to slide in the summer of 1957, spreading a sense of uncertainty about the future which was soon translated into a rapid change in inventory policy?

One reason was the steady tide of wage increases and price increases, which spread relentlessly from the leading to the lagging sectors of the economy, eroding profit prospects and weakening motives for investment as it flowed. In a mobile society, where people migrate on a considerable scale in search of work, the various parts of the economy are more closely linked than ever before. Sooner or later, wage increases in a highly productive sector pull wages elsewhere up, as employers discover they must pay more to keep their staff on hand. In the industries manufacturing durable goods, the hourly wage rate, which is only a partial index of labor costs, rose 9 per cent between 1950 and 1951, during the opening phases of the Korean War, 6 per cent during each of the next two years, 3 per cent between 1953 and 1954—a period of recession—and between 4 and 5 per cent a year in the following three years. Similarly, the wholesale price index and the consumer's price index crept up, despite the weakness of agricultural prices, 2 or 3 per cent between 1956 and 1957.

In part these rises are the normal signals of the end of a boom, as strong demand bids hard for available resources. In part they are the consequence of delayed adjustments, spreading throughout the economy, as wages and prices which had lagged behind the procession are forced to adjust, or fall out of the race. To an undetermined extent, rises in the various price indices are illusory, since the goods and services included in the indices change both in quality and in quantity from year to year. It is not hard to explain the principle that wages and other prices are set by the productivity of resources in alternative employments to any one associated with a private university, a school system, or the government. Such institutions have to keep increasing their wage payments in order to hold their staffs, even during the opening stages of a recession. Many great industries, which had been operating at prices that failed to maximize their short-period profits, raised prices cautiously, taking advantage of every favorable occasion to do so. The utilities, the professions, and other areas of slow-moving price habits, began to achieve the relative price changes which other areas of the economy had reached years before. For some areas, the character of costs and the impact of shortages made for especially acute price changes. The price of medical care, for example, rose more than any other price paid by consumers during the postwar period.[7]

There seem to be no fundamental differences among the problems presented by the economy at each of the three downward turning points of the postwar period—1948, 1953, and 1957. The combination of circumstances that defined the downward turning point was different on each occasion. But the differences are not striking. And there is no evidence that gross distortions have developed, beyond the reach of any but the most painful and prolonged adjustments. On the other hand, the three boom periods were considerably different, at least in the amount of real growth they achieved before reaching a period of congestion. In this vital respect, the recession of 1957 really began in 1956.

The dominant economic force in the period between the end of the war and 1948 was the legacy of liquid funds bequeathed to the economy by the Second World War. The Korean War and its aftermath were conspicuous features of the period between 1950 and 1953 or 1954. And the high rate of government expenditure associated with the Cold War has weighed heavily on the economy since 1948 or 1949. Beyond these pressures, although responding to them as well as to other influences, the structure of the economy continues to change. Chemicals, plastics, light metals, elec-

7. Federal Reserve Board, "The 1957-58 Recession in World Trade," *Federal Reserve Bulletin*, 44 (1958) 1153-60; idem, "Money and Credit in 1958," *Federal Reserve Bulletin*, 45 (1959), 103-9; Bert G. Hickman, "Postwar Cyclical Experience and Economic Stability," *American Economic Review*, 48 (1958), 117.

tronics, and other industries became the industries of unusually rapid growth and unusually high and profitable capital needs. Such industries become the shock troops of progress, succeeding to the role the railroads and the automobile industry once fulfilled in the process of capital accumulation. The orientation of market policy changed, in twelve years of boom. And wage-making moved to the center of the stage.

Still, the factors of similarity seem far greater than those of dissimilarity in this period.

Looking back at the three booms which ground to a halt in 1948, 1953, and 1956 or 1957, could better forecasting, the better timing of action or wiser policies have avoided recession and sustained high levels of employment indefinitely and without serious price rises?

In considering this question, let us return to the boom of 1955–57 as a situation less directly affected by the turbulent backwash of wartime finance than those which ended in 1948 and 1953.

Some have found the cause of the depression of 1957 in the unusually high rate of private capital formation during 1955 and part of 1956. Manufacturing capacity, they claim, rose faster than the actual demand for manufactured goods—faster, too, than any rate of increase in demand that could have been financed without inflation; or at least faster than any rate of increase that could have been financed under the prevailing restrictive policies of the Federal Reserve Board.

From the middle of 1956 or thereabouts there was a period virtually without growth. Between 1956 and 1957, consumption rose almost 3 per cent, in real terms, but capital formation rose imperceptibly, then began to fall. Net foreign domestic investment increased, and government purchases of goods and services increased slightly, while the government operated at a cash surplus of $5.5 billion in 1956 and one of $1.3 billion in 1957. Meanwhile, manufacturing capacity increased as earlier investment projects were finished and their output became available. In the absence of an increase in aggregate spending, private capital formation was bound to be less than that required to sustain a long term growth rate of 3 or 4 per cent. Unused capacity is necessarily a poor background for private investment spending.

It is certainly possible that the rate of private investment in 1955 and 1956 was unusually high, perhaps "too" high to be long sustained in one sense or another of that phrase. No such case has been proved, but it is not an inconceivable situation. It would be remarkable if there were not pauses in some areas, after a season of abundance. Spectacular as the skyline of New York now is, with its glass and aluminum buildings sprouting everywhere like mushrooms, the economic welfare of the country would not suffer if they gave way for a while to schools, hospitals, and better residential housing. There is no doubt that in 1956, as at other times, changing technology and the changing composition of all demands on the economy were causing changes in the direction of investment expenditure. But there was no general shortage of investment opportunities, at close to the prevailing level of interest rates, costs, and price prospects, and no evidence that changes in the composition of capital, and in real capital needs, made full employment impossible at a slightly higher level of total expenditure.

It seems more reasonable to find the cause of the downturn in 1956 and 1957 in the failure to achieve a rate of aggregate spending which could have come much closer to using the potential output of the economy. The substantial federal cash surplus was one aspect of the situation; the Federal Reserve's fear of inflation was another. The failure of the gross national product in constant prices to rise at least 3 per cent a year is in itself a dangerous signal. That fact depresses investment prospects, insofar as the demand for investment goods is keyed to and derived from the growth rate of the economy. On the other hand, I can find no significantly large areas of overcapacity in the economy, in 1957 and 1958—that is, no areas of capacity that would have been redundant for long at full employment, and that represent a considerable competitive or noncompetitive "overshooting of the mark" in the process of capital formation.

The comparative stagnation of investment in 1956 and its fall in 1957 do not seem in retrospect to represent much more than the tapering off of investment in 1948 or 1953. Rising costs and interest rates, changing the horizon of the future, affected first inventories and construction, then producers' durable equipment, and finally consumers' durable goods. The Federal Reserve was slow to start, and hesitant. The government fought hard to prevent recourse to the weapon of tax cuts, which had proved so effective in 1949 and 1954.

I find it hard to believe that a program of monetary ease in 1956 and one of fiscal and monetary action combined in early 1957 would not have revived the boom without greatly changing the problem of price levels. The restrictive monetary policy of 1955, however necessary then, was pressed a bit too hard and too long. It affected interest rates, the balance of optimism in the economy, and the level of investment spending.

Experience since the war provides ample evidence of the capacity of the economy to respond quickly and flexibly to very large changes in the volume and direction of spending. It provides equally convincing evidence of its capacity to sustain the use of large volumes of private and public capital. I can see no reason why the economy would have been less responsive in 1957 than in 1946 or 1950 or 1954 to the stimulus of enlarged spending, even if the pattern of spending showed a different distribution than that of 1956.

The argument against this view is that a revival in 1956 of the boom of 1955 could not have been accomplished without inflation of the money supply and of prices. Such an inflation, the argument continues, could only have made the ultimate crash worse.

Walking a tightrope is not easy. But the increased output and rising productivity associated with high levels of spending for producers' durable equipment should not be ignored. We cannot readily accept the view that the economy should be kept stagnant by the drug of excessively high interest rates in order to avoid the risk of inflation later on. As Chapter 10 urged, policies to stimulate high growth rates are crucial, both in themselves and as forces that might minimize the risk that full employment would result in socially intolerable increases in prices. For one of the chief morals of the postwar period is that neither policies of stagnation, as in 1956–57, nor those of periodic unemployment can do much in themselves to arrest the process by which a great dose of inflation works itself out slowly through the market mechanism.

It follows that programs to encourage growth are central to the problem of full employment without inflation. They are not only desirable but indispensable, if we are to avoid having to choose, in Robertson's phrase, between totalitarianism and chaos.

This is not to deny the reality of the "cost-creep," nor the importance of policies which would confine the movement of money wage rates to the zone of productivity change. Several calculations suggest that in 1953, and in 1956–57, real average hourly earnings rose faster than increases in output per man hour, making unemployment inevitable until the prior ratio was restored. These calculations, however, oversimplify the problem of policy in one sense and conceal it in another. First, average hourly earnings are a slippery and unreliable guide to actual wage bargains. Secondly, "real wages" are calculated by weighing together the movement of money wages and consumers' prices. They do not rise if prices and money wages increase together. But the social problem of inflation can be quite as bad if prices and wages go up together, as if they rise for a time at different speeds. It was suggested earlier that the pull of excess demand has been the decisive factor initiating the long waves of postwar wage adjustment—far more important than the maximum exploitation of labor's monoply power. There has been some exploitation of labor's bargaining power, in all probability. But the degree of that exploitation thus far demonstrated hardly justifies the conclusion that recovery was impossible in 1956 and 1957, without a substantial cut in real wages.[8]

On the whole, I cannot suppose that a prompt deficit in 1957 or 1958 would not have produced very much the same pattern of reaction achieved in 1949–50 and in 1953–54. I

8. See above, pp. 241–48.

trust that no reader of this book will misunderstand that sentence to imply that a prompt deficit in 1957 or 1958 would have been a sufficient policy for a government confronting the problems of those years. But none of the other programs the situation required would have been advanced by a recession; and all should have been easier to achieve under circumstances of full employment.

It is a matter of high concern that full employment be secured reasonably soon. There is strength in every successive invocation of the policy contemplated by the Employment Act. By using these powers successfully, as was done in 1949 and 1953, to offset inevitable variations in the level of private and public spending, the government can help build the conviction that we have indeed exorcised the risk of another prolonged depression such as that of the thirties. It is of importance to the nation that this fear be killed, both at home and abroad. At home the fear of a general depression is a factor of needless instability in investment. The pace of investment is unstable enough, in the nature of things, not to be complicated by such extraneous contingencies. Abroad, the specter of a great depression is a basic theme in the reputation of the United States, a favorite argument of the opponents of capitalism. It is an important element in the debate of East and West now proceeding wherever men gather in Europe, Asia, and Africa—a debate which is helping to determine the international status of the United States and its potential for effective international action.

Beyond all these considerations, however, we owe it to ourselves not to have recessions. Unless we propose to act on the bleak view that suffering is good for the character, we can reap no advantage from a prolonged depression. There is suffering enough in human life to provide salvation for our characters, without adding unemployment to the list. On the contrary, our policy should be not only to restore full employment but to increase the growth rate of the economy, if we are to conquer poverty at home and provide the government with the wherewithal of its diplomacy.

In the long run, perhaps the hardest of all the problems presented by the pursuit of these linked goals—high em-

ployment, high rates of growth, and tolerable price stability
—will turn out to be not the relationship of fiscal and monetary policy to wages and prices but the control of the money
markets. How can fiscal and monetary policy be used to
achieve a schedule of interest rates slightly tipped in favor
of investment, in order to offset the influence of pressures
adverse to investment which have so far arisen at intervals
since the war from the performance of labor and commodity
markets in a full employment economy? Can central banking, or central banking and fiscal policy together, exert such
influences when they are desirable without at the same time
releasing new reserves to the banking system, or otherwise
permitting too much new money to be created? Policies to
stimulate growth may be so successful as to permit us, at
intervals at least, the luxury of a free market for money. But
I doubt whether so Utopian a goal is a possibility. No such
policy has been known, at any rate, for a century or more.
We may begin to see strange experiments tried—budget deficits accompanied by central banking restriction, or open-
market purchasing joined with rising reserve requirements.
These are not altogether paradoxical approaches to the problem which policy faces in harnessing the unruly horses of
Thrift, Productivity, and Speculation (or Liquidity Preference) to the task of maintaining a socially sufficient volume
of investment expenditure.

Where We Are Now

Where We Are Now

14. The Goals of Legal Action in Controlling the Economy

IT HAS BEEN a major theme of this book that the law should seek more, much more, than full employment in the formation and execution of its plans for governing the economy. The success or failure of efforts to control business in the name of public policy should be determined in the end by more comprehensive criteria, indeed in large part by noneconomic criteria. By way of conclusion, Part V will return to that line of inquiry about the making of economic policy through the institutions of law, as part of the general process of law-making.

Henry Carter Adams urged over the years that political economy be studied as "a branch of general jurisprudence." [1] There is much to be gained from such a view of the multiple relations between law and economics.

In considering the connections of the two fields, I shall not take my lead either from John R. Commons or from Marx. Commons contended that law and economics are so closely linked as almost to deny economics any separate existence. And to Marx the law was no more than a formalized projection of the facts of economic life. In his view the law has no substantive content but merely states relationships determined by material conditions—that is to say, by the techniques of production and by the resulting distribution of power in the economy. The problem is both simpler and more complicated.

1. Joseph Dorfman, ed., *Relation of the State to Industrial Action, and Economics and Jurisprudence* (New York, Columbia University Press, 1954), p. 15.

The sociologists might say that the relationships between economics and law are those of "two-way interchange," at the level of both events and ideas. As sociologists' phrases go, this one is not too oppressive. Economics is one of the most advanced of the social sciences, with a well-developed tradition of theory and a literature of applied studies. Like other social sciences, it has much to tell the lawyer about his tasks. It provides the law with essential knowledge about the workings of the economy which the law seeks to control and to which it must respond. The economics of welfare offers the law certain norms for policy—those of productivity for wages, and of cost and demand for price. The concept of competitive equilibrium is the clearest definition of efficiency in the use of resources so far devised. Economics at large gives the law an indispensable analysis of causal relations, and a means for discriminating among possible approaches to policy. It permits, or it should permit, an identification of the efforts worth making, and of those which are too costly, or not worth the trouble. Economics can thus contribute to the law essential parts of the material of policy.

But the law is also an independent universe, formed by its own central ideas. If economics proposes, the law must dispose. The ends of the economist become policy only through the means provided by the law. And the aims of the economist must themselves be viewed in a wider perspective than economics purports to offer. In the making of policy, the conclusions of the economist are transformed by their exposure to the law, as the procedure through which society expresses and seeks to fulfill its ideal of justice.

Thus law responds to economic forces, and to the prevailing state of knowledge or of ignorance about them. And equally, it is one of the influences shaping the state and structure of the economy. The law has causes and effects. It is not an artifact, a mere register of history, but a positive instrument for realizing certain social and human goals. If it is true to itself, it should define its goals in terms which transcend the limits of economics, and draw their strength from a wider range of aspirations. For example, the economist's analysis of situations of monopoly is of the utmost value in helping to determine whether an antitrust law is needed, and in clarifying its development. But economic monopoly alone is not a sufficient criterion for invoking the sanctions of law, which must also satisfy specifically legal standards of personal guilt or personal responsibility before its penalties or remedies are applied.

We may distinguish two phases of the process by which law seeks to use its knowledge of economics, as it responds to other aspects of social experience, in the advancement of its own purposes. The first is to improve the actual positive law, the law in fact, with the object of bringing it into closer conformity with the existing ideal of law, the highest standard for law which the culture has so far produced. In the name of this principle, to take an instance, we strive to eliminate racial discrimination in our schools, a condition which exists, although it has already been declared illegal.

The second, and deeper part of the task of law is to use its powers in ways which gradually improve the culture's ideal of law itself. This sentence presents a delicate issue in definition. From what source do we distill a better concept of justice through law than that which the culture has thus far produced? And how do we know it is better than the existing norm? The problem is easily solved by those who can accept a natural law of supernatural origin. For the less fortunate, the question involves a real dilemma, if they are to avoid merely personal and idiosyncratic standards of subjective preference. Yet the words have a shared core of meaning. The history of civilization as a whole, as distinguished from the history of any one of its cultures, offers an ethical code of some power. It embodies the most valued elements of the religions and philosophical tradition. It constitutes a scale of values, including an ideal for law, which will be accepted in a given culture as an aspiration beyond the present stage of its development.

In terms of such a target, we may view the ethics of the law as an evolving force, which should permit the law not only to keep pace with the ethics of society but strongly to influence its course. For the law regularly confronts society

with ethical problems, previously ignored or only dimly
seen, and declares itself in favor of a given ethical solution.
A good example of this kind of action by law is the decision
of the Supreme Court in the school segregation cases, altering an accepted practice in the name of the evolving standards of law. Or, to take another example, in one decade in
the United States, the prevailing code of law, reflecting the
experience of prolonged depression, and an advance in accepted ideas of social justice, declared the principle that men
should be protected by the state against the risks of old age
and unemployment.

For a culture like our own, the criteria which can be invoked to guide both phases of the process of development in
law are general but not hopelessly obscure, at least in the
context of particular situations. They are the ideals of equality, responsibility, and justice, in the relation of man to man,
and in the relation of men to the state. These standards may
be expressed, for our society, as the ideal of human freedom
—to achieve and perfect the freedom of man within a just
society, and to permit and encourage his personal development as a mature, civilized, and responsible being. In our
culture, freedom implies a society of consent, organized politically to satisfy the rule that the people as a whole are the
source of sovereign authority. These concepts dominate the
ideal for law which exists today, and that which we are
creating for tomorrow, in part by what we do today. Both
views of the goal for legal action show continuity and
change. They derive from the whole history of our civilization, including the history of our law. And they grow
slowly with it, expressing themselves through the procedures
for self-reform which the law provides.

When I say that the supreme goal of law is the assurance
of personal liberty for the individual, within a just and free
society, I do not mean to imply too much. It is or should be
true, in a society which aspires to freedom, that man is an
end in himself and not a means, and that his freedom, as my
colleague Charles Black has said recently, "is, in justice, the
portion of man. . . . Freedom, no matter how much it has

done for us or may promise to do, is chiefly to be loved for itself alone." [2]

But that Kantian proposition cannot be accepted without an important qualification. In an organized society men have duties as well as rights. As Holmes said, rebelling at Kant's thesis, "If we want conscripts, we march them up to the front with bayonets in their rear to die for a cause in which perhaps they do not believe." [3] Both themes are relevant— the individual and the state; freedom and responsibility; liberty and order; personal freedom, and socially imposed limitations on freedom; the vagaries of personal choice, and the coercion of collective decision, asserted in accordance with the established and appropriate modes of law.

It follows that it is never enough to say that the purpose of our legal arrangements is to assure full play for individual initiative in the economic sphere, however attractively this thought echoes in our inner ear. Nor will it do to beg the question by saying that our goal is a maximum of freedom for the individual, within a framework of general laws established by state action. We should seek more precision than that, if it can be attained.

For it has never been accurate to describe the spirit of our law as the embodiment of individualism in its most extreme form.

André Siegfried has said somewhere that travel necessarily involves movement in time as well as space, and that a traveler in America still breathes the stimulating air of the eighteenth century. There is truth in the observation. We are loyal to Jefferson, who defined the object of society as the promotion of man's "life, liberty, and pursuit of happiness." Individualism in this sense is surely a major theme in the symphony of American life. But the premise of political democracy had its consequences from the beginning. Our individualism never was the simple faith of the eighteenth- and nineteenth-century English reformers, who swept away

2. Charles L. Black, Jr., "Practice of Forbearance," *New Republic* (Dec. 30, 1957), pp. 17–18.

3. O. W. Holmes, *Collected Legal Papers* (New York, Harcourt, Brace, and Howe, 1920), p. 304.

the remnants of feudalism and mercantilism with the ringing doctrine that the best interests of the individual were also and necessarily the best interests of society as a whole.

Americans have not been reluctant to legislate what was conceived to be the advantage of the majority, or of the people as a whole, at the expense of individualism. The development of all branches of our law, public and private, shows a resolute willingness to establish limitations on personal discretion in the name of public policy. Neither our judges nor our legislators have hesitated to declare criteria of the public interest in the exercise of freedom of contract, and in that work they radically extended the common law. The callous maxim *caveat emptor* was substantially modified, both by judicial decision and by later legislation, such as the Pure Food and Drug laws, the securities legislation of the states and of the nation, and the act establishing the Federal Trade Commission. Statutes have sought, with varying effect, to redress the inequality of bargaining strength between the parties to many classes of contracts—those of insurance and labor, for example, those dealing with the carriage of goods and passengers, and many others.

The line between private and public action is blurred, and always has been blurred, in American law. It is hard to imagine any business decision, from the planting of a wheat crop to the building of a house or a steel mill, which does not at some point confront the assertion of a public policy declared by law. We have even ventured—much too far in my opinion—to establish legal rules which impinge upon men's freedom to hold and express unpopular opinions.

It was, of course, long orthodox in this country, and indeed it still is, to proclaim the view of Carlyle that the ideal state should be "anarchy plus the constable," that government, in Spencer's phrase, "is begotten of aggression and by aggression." It is a familiar part of the nominal creed that all state action is to be regarded dubiously, as a necessary evil at best, and kept to an irreducible minimum.

In fact, our law has proceeded on no such premise. As Adams pointed out, the American tradition seventy years ago differed from both the laissez-faire of the older English rule and the state-dominated approach of German law.

"Neither governmental activity nor private enterprise," he wrote, "exists by sufferance. There is no presumption against either the one or the other in itself considered, for both are essential to the development of a highly organized society, and the purpose of constructive thought should be to maintain them in harmonious relations." [4] The protection of infant industries, the promotion of a merchant marine, the grant of lands and franchises to stimulate private investment and the settlement of the West—these are obvious illustrations from our earlier history of a principle which from the beginning rejected the dogma of laissez-faire as a working rule of American law.

If we are not anarchists in our political philosophy, we are, however, surely committed pluralists. All our political and economic arrangements show a most sensitive concern to avoid overwhelming concentrations of authority. The powers of government are separated, according to the rules of Locke and Montesquieu, in every microcosm of our government. Religious and educational establishments are afforded autonomy. Political activities are fragmented among thousands of governmental bodies—states, municipalities, school and sewage districts, bridge authorities, and bodies corporate created by interstate agreement. We believe in states' rights, in competition, in reserved powers. And property is owned, and economic decisions are initiated, by men, corporations, and trade unions, deriving their primary authority from the laws of the forty-eight states as well as from those of the nation.

Despite this healthy interest in the problem of power, we have always managed to establish the institutions for which there has been a felt need in providing an effective control of the economy. The Interstate Commerce Act, the Granger laws, and the Sherman Act were the product of one generation. The same impulses led later to the income tax, the Federal Reserve System, and the burst of legislation accomplished during the New Deal.

It is against the background of this history that we should judge the purposes and the prospective impact of the law we

4. Above (n. 1), at p. 87.

are in process of creating for the direction of economic affairs. In Chapter 2 it was called a system of law. That system has three principal elements—the law governing fiscal and monetary policy; that regulating the markets for products and services; and the labor law. These three pre-existing bodies of law, it was suggested, are being drawn together into a new field of magnetic force by the influence of the Employment Act of 1946, which is giving them new dimensions, a new orientation, and a new momentum.

Most of the law we have been examining does not exist in the familiar form of judicial opinions, or opinions of administrative tribunals. But it is law nonetheless. It represents the application and elaboration of the general prescriptions declared in the Employment Act. These criteria are beginning to take on meaning, as they are used in a variety of decisions made by executive officers and administrative bodies, by the Federal Reserve Board and by Congress. Thus the legislation develops, trade cycle by trade cycle, as the proliferation of a policy, modified as it clashes with other policies but at work as a living force in the growth of the law.

In this perspective the first question to be considered is whether the system of law we are establishing for the management of the economy is consistent with one of the most fundamental aims of our jurisprudence—that of preventing a concentration of authority so formidable as to imperil the economic and social basis of freedom. I should answer the question with a categorical "yes." Governmental programs to regulate the relationship between the flow of funds and the flow of goods in a market economy do not require any change in the prevailing pattern of power distribution. For this reason our law of economic regulation, in its emerging form, is entirely compatible with American political tradition, so far as concerns the preliminary issue of power. There is no imperative in the theory of such policies which would require programs for sustaining high levels of employment to become engines of collectivism. On the contrary, if well conducted they should fortify, and not weaken, the health, vigor, and autonomy of the free institutions of business and labor. Thus they should minimize the risk of Socialism, Fascism, or other forms of collectivist domination by the state.

If the analysis of Part III is correct, the control of over-all fluctuations in the level of demand is an inescapable duty of government. For the performance of this function there is no choice between state action and private action. The only choice is that between state action and no action at all. The federal government is the only institution of society capable of acting against a trend in the direction either of inflation or of depression, which as it develops would necessarily dominate the process of private decision-making. Such trends are bound to appear, from time to time, in an economy of private decisions, unless they are offset by compensating action of the state. Assuring all the institutions of business and labor a fair and favoring field for their competitive efforts is an altogether proper function of government. The ascription of this duty to the state would hardly have shocked the classical economists, or even the Manchester School. It involves no more than the duty of the state once advanced by Bentham—that the Board of Trade should continually revise its regulations to meet "the effect produced on the money prices of commodities . . . by variations in the relative aggregate quantity of money of various sorts, as compared with the aggregate quantity of commodities destined for sale." [5]

The problem, however, is not a static one. Programs of fiscal and monetary action to sustain full-employment levels of demand do not now, and need not in the future, require a radical enlargement of the direct administrative powers of government within the markets of the economy. But it will not be easy to avoid this risk, and the pattern of society would be different if such a development took place.

For one should distinguish a system of government control over the economy which depends primarily upon fiscal and monetary policy, and the responsive functioning of free and regulated markets, from those methods of planning which universally require direct controls, like price-fixing,

5. Quoted in Lionel Robbins, *The Theory of Economic Policy in English Classical Political Economy* (London, Macmillan, 1953), pp. 42–43.

rationing, licensing, the establishment of production quotas and wage rates, and government allocation of funds or materials. Such procedures do not represent planning, but attempt to mitigate the effects of a failure of planning. The need for such action arises only from a defeat for planning in its fundamental task of achieving equilibrium between aggregate demand, on the one hand, and the full employment output of the economy on the other. When aggregate demand outstrips full employment supply long enough, and prices rise enough, a pressure develops to institute direct controls over wages and prices.

As was pointed out earlier, administrative control of price is far easier to enforce in a regime of monopoly than in one of competition. Under NRA, OPA, and OPS—if those once familiar initials stir any echoes—it was equally apparent that harassed administrators had far more success in the concentrated industries than in those industries where they had to deal with vast numbers of elusive, evasive, and recalcitrant small businessmen. We could expect the Sherman Act and the tradition of free trade unions to be among the first victims of prolonged inflation, in fact if not in form.

If the twin purposes of the Employment Act, full employment and free competitive enterprise, are both to be fulfilled, the aim of policy, in concrete terms, should be the achievement of full employment without perpetual inflation. For continued inflation is economically so unstable and socially so threatening that it would probably lead to the development of centralized controls over wages and prices, and also, in all probability, over investments, the use of materials, and so on. The imposition of detailed administrative regulations of this kind would establish a form of government for the economy which could repress the consequences of monetary inflation for a time, as we saw during the war. In the long run, however, such institutions would transform the psychological atmosphere and the political power structure of society. Full employment accomplished by maintaining an adequate level of monetary demand for the potential output of a market economy is a policy entirely compatible with the future of political and social freedom, and should contribute positively toward an improved realization of its values and promises. Full employment maintained by the forced draft of excessive demand would, on the contrary, put the markets of the economy under such erratic and cumulative pressure as to make even "the muddle and distortions and bureaucracy" [6] of centralized control comparatively attractive after a time. There is an "absolutely decisive" difference between the two forms of planning, in Rehn's phrase. This choice has many ramifications, whose deliberate consideration should be part of the process through which we make policy.

A second corollary of this analysis is worth stressing again. The policy of American government before the dilemma of cumulative inflation under conditions of full employment has been entirely too restrictive. The control of the flow of money, through Federal Reserve action, debt management policies, and the shift of Treasury funds is certainly an indispensable part of any program designed to achieve an appropriate balance between over-all demand and full-employment supply. But the emphasis of policy should equally be to enlarge output; this part of the problem has been almost completely neglected. As Part III contends, much can and should be done by imaginative governmental action to eliminate waste, to enlarge the effective labor force, and to improve the efficiency with which it is employed.

There are reasons of convenience in administration, too, which favor a policy of avoiding inflation and its long-run consequences. One of the scarcest resources in any society is the supply of trained men. And one of the slowest of all known processes is the process of reaching a governmental decision. Even in time of war a government can have only limited numbers of adequate personnel at its disposal, as against the pull of industry, business, and the professions. And it can only make a limited number of decisions every year. Parliaments, government departments, and the writers and readers of memoranda can do no more. It is important, therefore, that the energies of government in the field of

6. Rehn, "The Problem of Stability," in Ralph Turvey, ed., *Wages Policy under Full Employment* (London, Hodge, 1952), p. 35.

planning be confined to the tasks which matter. They should not be wasted on a variety of attempts which have little or nothing to do with the essential problems of employment and economic welfare. It is singularly easy to waste resources in this type of enterprise, for the failure of the attempt is not often visible for some time after it has been made, and may be a matter of doubt even then.

There is another aspect of the problem of planning, which should also help persuade us to restrict governmental control methods to those which are most crucial and which influence the economy as a whole, and to minimize both the number of such interventions and their discriminatory or particular character. As Lundberg has recently remarked:

> The problem is to find such forms for our economic system that we do not become heavily dependent on having a small number of very outstanding people—politicians, administrators and economic experts—at the top and that we do not count on what first-class leaders could possibly accomplish when they are themselves at their very best and when conditions are the most favourable imaginable. . . . The system should, in other words, be such that bad politicians, bad administrators, bad economists and bad businessmen, all of whom are among us, have the least possible chance of doing harm. An economy based largely on a highly decentralized market economy with a fairly freely functioning price system meets these requirements to a greater extent than any other system. General economic policy sets no such unreasonably large claims on the management of the Central Bank and the Ministry of Finance, *if* these institutions refrain from assuming unnecessary tasks which involve strongly discriminative interventions and the accompanying scope for power. The economic welfare of private individuals, and the success and progress of economic activity in all sectors of the economy will not be directly dependent on administrative measures so long as the prime rule of economic policy is that it should grope forward by means

of methods which are as general as possible. All this should mean, in my view, that economic controls and specific interventions should be used for purposes of stabilizing general economic development only in the last resort in difficult crises of the type discussed earlier, but that their use should not be reckoned with all the time. Among the advantages of the highly decentralized market economy is the fact that it does not allow too much room for the exercise of private and public monopolistic power and arbitrary administrative decisions in economic life. Competition should always offer so many alternatives to the consumers that the risk of abuse of power remains small. The anonymity of the market, the automatic workings of the price system and the driving force of competition are means of achieving not only a rational use of productive resources and rapid economic progress but also a minute subdivision of economic decisions and a decentralization of power such as we wish to have in a true democracy.[7]

There are other objections to achieving full employment at the cost of a sustained and significant rise of prices, apart from its tendency to generate wasteful, cumbersome, and dangerous administrative controls over markets.

The first is an objection of fairness in social policy. As has been bluntly evident since the war, the burden of inflation falls unequally on different groups within society. Wages and profits advance together, at the expense of the rest of the community. The pensioners, school teachers, bond holders, and others who live on fixed incomes are impoverished. The pre-existing pattern of incentives and rewards is changed by accident, and without even the excuse of social justification. Some callings are gravely weakened. Young men leave the army or the teaching profession. Not enough candidates apply for the civil services. Such a process, if long continued, generates resentment of considerable magnitude. The principle that wages tend toward the level of

7. Erik Lundberg, *Business Cycles and Economic Policy* (Cambridge, Harvard University Press, 1957), pp. 336-37.

marginal productivity in alternative employments has a degree of revenge in the end. The wage of a school teacher or a domestic servant is set after a time as the amount required to prevent him or her from shifting to a factory or a commercial establishment. Cumulative waves of adjustment and readjustment occur throughout the economy, as each sector struggles to keep up with the trend.

But the direction of change during inflation certainly favors those who earn profits and wages. Between 1929 and 1957, rental income and net interest each increased about 100 per cent, while wages rose just over 400 per cent, corporate profits 400 per cent, and the income of unincorporated enterprises about 235 per cent. Adjustments of this order in the relative rewards of groups within the population can be both expensive and socially damaging. There can be no justification for action of the state which accomplishes such widespread and unequal discriminations among its citizens. When price changes were regarded, like the weather, as the result of uncontrollable natural phenomena, there was no one to blame for them. The character of the problem is altogether different today.

We have finally recognized the responsibility of government to control industrial fluctuations, primarily through fiscal and monetary action. It is certainly a sound axiom that the discretion of government officers in exercising that power should be guided and controlled by explicit rules of policy, which, as rules of law, could permit the coherent development of their programs. The achievement of coherence in the exercise of these powers should facilitate the effective functioning of markets in response to stabilizing monetary and fiscal action. As was suggested earlier, the criterion of stable prices is the most workable of possible legislative limitations on the discretion of government in carrying out the policies of the Employment Act. Such a target for long-range policy would permit the economy the advantage of some inflationary pressure, as productivity improved, to compensate for the chronic upward tendency of costs and prices in a full-employment economy. But it would restrict the availability of that attractive lubricant and serve to dampen the ardent optimism of those businessmen who have gambled in recent years on enough inflation to validate any cost commitments they might make.

An acceptance of price stability over the long run as an essential goal of full employment policy is most desirable also from the point of view of the international relations of our economy and of our country. We have enjoyed exceptional freedom since the early thirties to pursue inflationary policies at home without regard to their international consequences. In part, that freedom derived from factors of accident, particularly the presence of capital seeking political refuge in the United States. High levels of employment in the United States tend to favor the development of the economies of other countries, by maintaining our demand for imports and by making American exports relatively expensive. We have received a double reward for the pleasures of the great boom. But the economy of the Western world is moving beyond the stage of postwar reconstruction, and seeking a more stable basis for its international economic life. An object of our policy should be to encourage the largest possible flow of long-term private investments, as an indispensable condition of world economic development, unless the United States government is willing to become the world's chief banker for the indefinite future. Exchange stability is not by any means the only condition to be satisfied before an international economy can be rebuilt on the basis of short- and long-term capital movements. International and national laws must also be developed to reconcile the legitimate interests of investors with those of borrowing countries, and particularly with those of the less industrialized countries. But a reasonably stable dollar could be a useful foundation for the gradual construction of a world monetary system which could permit the Western world to enjoy the advantages of international private lending on a substantial scale.

These are, then, a few of the more general issues which now seem conspicuous on the agenda of a program to provide an appropriate legal basis for a stabilized economy whose principal social goals are economic freedom and political liberty. As Henry Simons said twenty years ago, it will take "years of careful planning and wise legislation" to achieve what he called "a liberal system adapted to modern conditions." [8] And he observed that such a system might well be even more complex than that of authoritarian collectivism.

For all its difficulties, however, we have come far enough in the quest to be sure that the goals we seek are not beyond the hope of reason. Both the theory of our system of law for governing the economy and the experience we have had in trying to use it support the conclusion that capitalist democracy is and should continue to be a conspicuous economic success. Many mistakes were made in the eventful years since 1929. But much can be learned from what has been done and what was not done. The New Deal failed to achieve full employment: it failed, that is to say, in terms of its own high values, despite its accomplishments in the realm of social welfare. But its pioneering trials and errors paved the way for later successes.

Now the benign processes of American politics have ratified the basic work of Presidents Roosevelt and Truman in this area. Their fundamental contributions to our political economy have been accepted, and put beyond the range of partisan controversy. The Eisenhower administration did not seek to repeal the principal economic and social legislation of the thirties and forties, but acknowledged their permanence and employed them with varying degrees of skill.

Working with native stone, we have formed the principal institutions we need to achieve the economic and social goals of American democracy. The American economy does not depend on military expenditures to maintain full employment. It has long since demonstrated its capacity for adaptation to quick and drastic changes in the volume of particular forms of spending. And American law is developing the ideas and mechanisms which should permit the government and the economy together to meet the challenges of the years ahead. That the tasks are difficult merely adds interest to a labor which can be tackled with confidence in its outcome.

8. Henry C. Simons, *Economic Policy for a Free Society* (Chicago, University of Chicago Press, 1948), pp. 160–61.

15. Is Freedom Interesting Enough?

LET US ASSUME, for the moment, that the economic goals defined in these pages can be achieved—high levels of employment and growth, and considerable price stability. Would the regime we could then envision be a sufficient goal for policy? Is a full-employment, free-market, competitive society the highest aspiration our culture can produce? Does the acceptance of such a goal condemn us to a hopeless commercialism in values? Would it foster brutality, fraud, self-seeking, and like vices, which Veblen and other critics of American society have always found in such profusion among the manifestations of our life?

The socialist critics of our civilization would say that questions of this order merely confirm what they have always thought about a society based on the selfish premise of individualism. The economic progress of capitalist communities seems on the surface to produce more unhappiness rather than less. Art, music, and literature become cold, melancholy and remote. Our writers glory in the misery of man's fate, and find little to cheer them in the prospect of ever more prosperous suburban living. Tragedy has not ceased to be the dominant preoccupation of creative minds.

This issue is a classic theme in the debate between Socialism and Liberty.

Socialism is one of the popular and appealing faiths through which modern man has sought to escape from the loneliness, the responsibility, and the burden of self-judgment which come with the maturity of human freedom. Those who believe in what Croce once called the Religion of Liberty must admit that it is an austere faith, not nearly so consoling nor so comfortable as many of its rivals. Modern man has often been unable to find an answer to the isolation of his life through love or family or creative work. Frequently, he is incapable of the absorbing religious faith of other centuries. Sometimes, therefore, he has looked for relief from the burden of freedom to the brotherhood of man. As a Socialist he has dreamed of a world of idealism and fraternal cooperation, where there could be no cruelty. There selfishness would disappear, and with it rivalry, crime, and prostitution, for these are all considered by the Socialists to be the inevitable products of capitalism and its class struggle. Values and human relations would be purged of commercial influences; cynicism and self-seeking would vanish; and life would become a Utopian round of plain living and high thought, of folk-dancing, grave pleasures, and idyllic peace.

In this sense Socialism is one in the long list of rituals through which man has sought to transform himself into his hope of virtue. Perhaps such faiths play a useful part in the war between good and evil. It is certainly to the glory of man that he dreams such dreams, which become a vital force in his striving for advance. Unhappily, however, the socialist panacea has been no more effective than its predecessors. The difficulty, alas, is not capitalism. Serpents have been found in the most cooperative gardens. Work is just as tedious in a nationalized factory as in one privately owned. Crime doesn't disappear with full employment, nor even with Socialism. Egos are as tiresome in Paradise as elsewhere, and it is as common there as in less perfect places to confront Pride, Envy, Sloth, Intemperance, Avarice, Ire, and Lust. Capitalism, the Polish story goes, is the exploitation of man by man, while under Socialism it's just the other way around.

As Keynes once remarked, the quest for wealth offers a comparatively harmless outlet for human proclivities which might otherwise find dangerous expression "in cruelty, the reckless pursuit of personal power and authority, and other forms of self-aggrandisement. It is better that a man should tyrannise over his bank balance than over his fellow citizens . . ." [1]

1. *The General Theory of Employment, Interest and Money* (New York, Harcourt, Brace, 1936), p. 374.

There is another series of questions sometimes posed about the consequences of a full-employment policy to men, and to the social order. Will the security of full employment deaden initiative and weaken men's ambition to excel? Could we expect what Weber called the Protestant ethic of hard work and high standards to vanish in a climate which requires less and less struggle to assure at least the simpler forms of survival? Will our citizens become less self-reliant and more passive? Or would life in the welfare state, as some of the angry young British novelists suggest, become so tame, so devoid of risk and challenge, as to offer nothing better than "pure Novocain for the soul."

We cannot claim that our legal machinery for guiding the economy is so simple or so smooth and self-adjusting as to make life boring. The happy Utopian point Keynes described twenty-seven years ago is further away than he thought—the time, as he said, "when the Economic Problem will take the back seat where it belongs, and . . . the arena of the heart and head will be occupied, or re-occupied, by our real problems—the problems of life and of human relations, of creation and behaviour and religion." [2] No doubt it would be delightful if we were freed of the sentence of Genesis and could live like lotus-eaters, without the tensions of competition, or the vulgarity of money as a standard of judgment and of success in our lives. But Keynes sighed too soon for an end of thorns and thistles. Neither automation nor nuclear energy, important as they are, will much accelerate the pace at which an ever-increasing world population actually succeeds in increasing its standards of living.

If we reread the reformers of seventy or eighty years ago, we find that most of their objections to the injustices of American society have been met, in whole or in large part. Welfare legislation and legislation against fraud and deception have accomplished much. A social security system is developing. It still has tasks to accomplish, notably in the provision of medical and legal care for the poor, but it has made progress. Monopoly is a problem, but I should say a less serious problem than in 1900. By and large, repression and brutality have disappeared as serious factors in the con-

2. *Essays in Persuasion* (New York, Harcourt, Brace, 1932), p. vii.

duct of labor relations. Social, educational, and economic
opportunities are more widely available than ever before.
The administration of justice is far from exemplary, but it
has made visible progress.

Some economic and social problems have been solved—
notably that of avoiding prolonged depressions—but others
loom up, as hard as any that were faced in the past. Our
educational system is weak, uneven in quality, and, as a
whole, unworthy. Great efforts of reform are needed before
it can offer our people what they are entitled to demand.
There are social problems of intense difficulty to resolve—
the achievement of racial equality, the linked mysteries of
crime and family patterns, the improved organization of
medical care. The future of the cities presents a major challenge, involving not only the conservation of huge capital
funds but the sociological basis of community and political
life as well. It will take sustained thought and sustained effort to create an effective world economy that can replace
the one which expired in 1914. The threat of devastating war
is as real as it was in 1913 or 1938, despite the horror of
twentieth-century experience. And, more important than the
rest, we face the question of perpetuating the motives and
values which produce the socially indispensable virtue of
responsible citizenship. Unless the people of Western societies care enough about public affairs and exert themselves
enough in their conduct, we may discover that apathy has
led to weakness, and weakness to a vacuum of authority.
When social institutions fail in this way, as they did in Russia in 1917, a passing gang finds it easy to seize power and
end the relevance of inquiries into the nature and adequacy
of freedom.

All in all, the task of survival in our society is not likely
soon to test the hypothesis that freedom from anxiety and
tension would reduce man to a vegetable status. Our characters are not likely soon to be subjected to the insidious
threat of excess leisure.

On the contrary, the challenges which are emerging in
many areas of social study and of social action should provide
ample work for many years. Many of these problems were

obscured in the past by the overriding crisis of the depression, manifestly the first of our problems to be solved. We do not lack the opportunity to satisfy those human impulses for adventure and struggle, and for voluntary and cooperative association with our fellows, which William James and Bertrand Russell have often assured us must be given innocent and, if possible, productive outlets in our working lives. Russell recalled the anthropologists' sad story of the Papuan head hunters, who were deprived of their favorite sport by white authority and lost all zest for life and interest in it. "Civilized Man everywhere is, to some degree, in the position of the Papuan victims of virtue," Russell says, in that society permits few, if any, adequate ways to express "the instincts we inherit from long generations of savages." [3] No one who has tried to fight a redevelopment program through the labyrinth of decisional authority in a city, or helped build a new institution of business or of public service, would complain of frustration on this front. Nor would complaint come from those who have tried to contemplate the causes and cures for juvenile delinquency, crime generally, racial conflict, and some of the other social problems now on our minds. In a society of increasingly open opportunity, the ordinary citizen continues to find life an effort, often a struggle, as he strives to advance in social status and to match in achievement the various aspirations he has absorbed. The tasks of daily life offer both students and men of action a rich, not to say exhausting, prospect for vigorous self-expression, as an effective psychological equivalent for the bitterness of the older struggle for existence or the fatal attractions of war.

It is true that politics have not yet caught up with the swift pace of change in the life of society itself. On the stage of politics the actors, by and large, are mouthing old lines. Very few have yet begun to translate the emerging issues into the poetry of effective political emotion. That will happen, in due course, for politicians throughout the country are grappling with some of the newer problems, and seeking to interest the voters in them. In any event, dullness in politics

3. Bertrand Russell, *Authority and the Individual* (New York, Simon and Schuster, 1949), p. 21.

is not a serious social desease. The country has survived long periods of dullness in the past, without material harm. Political excitement is probably not even necessary to the accomplishment of further reforms, although reform movements have historically had to generate a good deal of steam before they could overcome the massive inertia and conservatism of public opinion. The degree of consensus which the last generation has accomplished about the basic duties of government is quite remarkable. It might well permit a good deal of improvement in the functioning of our legal institutions without the help of a new Bryan or a new Roosevelt, who could electrify the country, but disturb it too.

We groan about conformity, about the dominance of the mediocre and the vulgarity of a mass culture. Our schools are poor, and much that passes for higher education is a sham. We speculate whether the necessity for collective action will reduce us all to the anonymity of membership in a mass. It has become a cliché to identify the complexity of modern forms of social organization—the national state, the great corporations and trade unions, the whole of our procedure for living in large groups—as a totalitarian force which must in the end transform man into a cog, and require freedom itself to submit to implacable authority.

All this nay-saying is sound, and indeed necessary. The dangers are real. But the nay-saying is only part of the process of decision that will shape the future. It measures the force of our aspiration for freedom, individuality, and excellence. And it gives us reasonable ground for hope that out of the cross-currents of the moment, our educational system and our social life generally will continue to progress, stage by uneven stage, toward a level of richness, maturity, and freedom that was enjoyed a century ago only by the happy and self-conscious few.

The vulgarity, the inadequacy, and the superficiality of much of our mass civilization is a formidable fact, which I should be the last to minimize. But this I view as froth on the surface of a more hopeful movement. All the graduates of all our colleges and universities may not be ready for cultivated conversation in the drawing rooms of Paris and

Oxford, Boston, San Francisco, and Ann Arbor. But that is hardly the point. More men and women are being well educated today, in proportion to our population, than was the case a hundred years ago, or fifty years ago. That fact alone reflects a change for the better in motivation and ambition. Many of the new students may come to college for the wrong reasons, and some go away untouched or disillusioned. But many more do not. Colleges which were academies in 1900 now offer and require demanding programs of genuinely intellectual instruction; and others, which were colleges then, provide instruction at the university level. The hunger of our people for more rewarding fare is a reality constantly manifest. A television program on comparative literature, shown at seven in the morning, clears every bookstore in New York of its stock of Stendahl, Conrad, or Henry James by noon of the day of the lecture. The style of furniture and home decoration, of clothing, and of the other domestic arts has certainly advanced in taste and sophistication for the mass of the people, and even for the rich. Football is still popular at our colleges, but so are books, symphonies, and museums. We observe with concern that the younger generation has abandoned the necktie. But we must admit also that students read Greek tragedy, collect records, and write ever longer and more learned papers.

No, the forces making for a leveling down are strong, but the forces making for a leveling up are stronger. The quest for education alone is a portent upon which we can rely, if we have energy enough to meet the demand.

A little historical perspective may provide a useful corrective for the gloom of those who see us all transformed into gray-flanneled Organization Men, the hopeless Babbitts of a new age. Who can doubt that the modern farmer or factory worker has a richer life and more opportunity for personal growth than his counterpart of a hundred years ago? Some of the proceeds of full employment are spent on whiskey, sports, and recreation, without doubt. What is so very wrong with that, after all? But some, too, are invested in museums and orchestras, travel and education, books and the creative arts. If one compares the life of our cities and towns and universities now with their atmosphere even twenty-five years ago, it seems indisputable that these twelve or thirteen years of boom have been invigorating and creative, not stultifying. The diversity and curiosity of the people is a vindication of full employment, not a reproach to it.

It is perverse puritanism to think that the social advances of the last hundred years will destroy our souls. Hard work may be, and probably is a Good Thing for man. But is it reasonable to believe that man needs the crushing pressure of poverty and depression, of fear and humiliation, of hunger and loneliness, in order to assure his virtue? The realization of social goals which men have regarded for centuries as desirable can hardly be considered the root of all modern evil.

It is fair to say that many aspects of modern life do threaten the security of man, and his sense of identity. We live in an age that is witnessing new heights of social justice and new depths of social degredation. This has been the century of Wilson and Roosevelt and Lloyd George, of Churchhill and Leon Blum—but it is also the century of Hitler and Lenin, Khrushchev and Mussolini and Stalin. No one can be sure that we can avoid another war, or the development of a government that will, in fact, severely limit personal freedom.

Yet the spirit of man fights back. And that spirit may well win out. Totalitarianism need not be the wave of the future, by 1984 or any other date. If we succumb to regimes which order our lives and thoughts in these bleak ways, our fate will be recorded in history as suicide, not as the tragic consequence of inexorable forces. Neither the programs we need to achieve economic stabilization and growth nor the necessities of our international position require us to abandon a philosophy that puts the liberation and the self-development of the individual as the first of our social goals.

Index

THE YALE PAPERBOUNDS

YALE WESTERN AMERICANA PAPERBOUNDS